D1245832

Opening the Government of Canada

COMMUNICATION
STRATEGY
AND POLITICS

Communication, Strategy, and Politics

THIERRY GIASSON AND ALEX MARLAND, SERIES EDITORS

Communication, Strategy, and Politics is a groundbreaking new series from UBC Press that examines elite decision making and political communication in today's hyper-mediated and highly competitive environment. Publications in this series look at the intricate relations among marketing strategy, the media, and political actors and explain how they affect Canadian democracy. They also investigate such interconnected themes as strategic communication, mediatization, opinion research, electioneering, political management, public policy, and e-politics in a Canadian context and in comparison to other countries. Designed as a coherent and consolidated space for diffusion of research about Canadian political communication, the series promotes an interdisciplinary, multi-method, and theoretically pluralistic approach.

Other volumes in the series are

Political Marketing in Canada, edited by Alex Marland, Thierry Giasson, and Jennifer Lees-Marshment
Political Communication in Canada: Meet the Press and Tweet the Rest, edited by Alex Marland, Thierry Giasson, and Tamara A. Small
Framed: Media and the Coverage of Race in Canadian Politics, by Erin Tolley
Brand Command: Canadian Politics and Democracy in the Age of Message Control, by Alex Marland
Permanent Campaigning in Canada, edited by Alex Marland, Thierry Giasson, and Anna Lennox Esselment
Breaking News? Politics, Journalism, and Infotainment on Quebec Television, by Frédérick Bastien
Political Elites in Canada: Power and Influence in Instantaneous Times, edited by Alex Marland, Thierry Giasson, and Andrea Lawlor

See also

Canadian Election Analysis 2015: Communication, Strategy, and Democracy, edited by Alex Marland and Thierry Giasson. Open access compilation available at http://www.ubcpress.ca/canadianelectionanalysis2015.

Opening the Government of Canada

The Federal Bureaucracy in the
Digital Age

Amanda Clarke

UBCPress · Vancouver · Toronto

28 27 26 25 24 23 22 21 20 19   5 4 3 2 1

Printed in Canada on FSC-certified ancient-forest-free paper (100% post-consumer recycled) that is processed chlorine- and acid-free.

Library and Archives Canada Cataloguing in Publication

Clarke, Amanda, author
    Opening the government of Canada : the federal bureaucracy in the digital age / Amanda Clarke.

(Communication, strategy, and politics)
Includes bibliographical references and index.
Issued in print and electronic formats.
ISBN 978-0-7748-3692-0 (hardcover). – ISBN 978-0-7748-3693-7 (softcover)
ISBN 978-0-77483-694-4 (PDF). – ISBN 978-0-7748-3695-1 (EPUB)
ISBN 978-0-7748-3696-8 (Kindle)

    1. Internet in public administration – Canada. 2. Information technology – Political aspects – Canada. 3. Information society – Political aspects – Canada. 4. Bureaucracy – Canada. 5. Canada – Politics and government – 21st century. I. Title. II. Series: Communication, strategy, and politics

| JL86.A8C63 2019 | 351.0285'4678 | C2018-904916-2 |
| | | C2018-904917-0 |

Canadä

UBC Press gratefully acknowledges the financial support for our publishing program of the Government of Canada (through the Canada Book Fund), the Canada Council for the Arts, and the British Columbia Arts Council.

This book has been published with the help of a grant from the Canadian Federation for the Humanities and Social Sciences, through the Awards to Scholarly Publications Program, using funds provided by the Social Sciences and Humanities Research Council of Canada.

Printed and bound in Canada by Friesens

Set in Minion and Scala by Apex CoVantage, LLC
Copy editor: Dallas Harrison
Proofreader: Lauren Cross
Indexer: Noeline Bridge
Cover designer: David Drummond

UBC Press
The University of British Columbia
2029 West Mall
Vancouver, BC V6T 1Z2
www.ubcpress.ca

For Ben

Contents

List of Tables   viii

Preface   ix

Acknowledgments   xii

Abbreviations   xv

1   Opening Government in the Digital Age   3

2   Canada's Closed Government   38

3   #Fail: Adopting Social Media in the Government
    of Canada   70

4   Stephen Harper's Open(ish) Government Initiative   97

5   Internal Openings in the Federal Bureaucracy   130

6   The Digital Skills Gap in the Federal Bureaucracy   153

7   The Future of Digital Government   182

Appendix: Interview Index   232

Notes   235

References   247

Index   273

Tables

3.1 Government of Canada tweets categorized by content 80

3.2 Government of Canada tweets categorized by type 81

3.3 Government of Canada retweets and user mentions
categorized by user referenced 82

3.4 Types of websites linked to in Government of Canada tweets 83

4.1 Internet access across Government of Canada departments,
June 2015 104

6.1 Traditional approaches to government IT versus digital era
government IT 157

Preface

Elected in October 2015, Justin Trudeau took the reins of the public service just as the writing for this book was coming to a close. The Trudeau government entered office with ambitious plans to renew the federal bureaucracy for the digital age, promising an open relationship with the media, an appetite for policy innovation, and a desire to restore the so-called golden age of the public service. In Chapter 7, I assess some of the early initiatives introduced by the Liberal government following their electoral win, but a number of other developments have arisen since the time of writing. These developments deserve a mention.

The Canadian Digital Service (CDS), housed in the Treasury Board Secretariat, was officially launched in July 2017 after being announced in the March 2017 budget. CDS is working to bring about a more agile, innovative, and user-centred approach to service delivery in the federal government, and has recruited a fleet of new digital talent to the ranks of the public service to do so. Those leading CDS, and its observers assessing its progress, will find insight in Chapter 6's discussion of the digital talent needs of today's governments. In this chapter I assess the benefits and potential shortcomings that digital government units such as CDS and its predecessors in Australia, Ontario, the UK, and the US have brought to light.

Alongside the creation of CDS, the appointment of Alex Benay as Chief Information Officer (CIO) has changed the tone of federal IT management. Benay is instituting a number of reforms recommended in this book, advocating for open-source technologies, the release of federal data, and the adoption of agile design methodologies. An active and outspoken voice on social media, Benay is often dubbed a "disruptor" (KPMG 2017; Pilieci 2017). His work as CIO provides an opportunity to investigate how a more tech sector-inspired style of leadership contends with the legacy systems – both technical and cultural – at play in federal departments.

Also under the Liberals, the government has partnered with Code for Canada to bring private sector tech talent into the public service on time-limited bases. In 2017, Canada took a leadership role in the international Open Government Partnership as its lead government co-chair. Alongside a series of other promising renewal initiatives introduced by the Liberals (detailed in Chapter 7), these actions suggest that the Trudeau government has made progress in its efforts to update the public service for the digital age.

At the same time, the Trudeau government has in certain other respects fallen short of its initial ambitions on public service renewal. The government has been heavily criticized by the Access to Information Commissioner for obstructing the release of information, a record that undermines Trudeau's broader promises of open government and his pledge to restore trust in the institution of the public service (News Media Canada 2017; Office of the Information Commissioner of Canada 2017). While partially a problem inherited from the Harper government, the Phoenix pay-system disaster has nonetheless rolled on and intensified under the Liberals, racking up millions of dollars in costs and disillusioning hundreds of thousands of public servants, and the broader citizenry, as they question the government's handling of this large IT project.

The pay-system failure inspired a scathing critique by Auditor General Michael Ferguson in June 2018, in which he blamed the project's mismanagement on a "broken government culture" (Auditor General of Canada 2018). Testifying before a parliamentary committee, Clerk of the Privy Council Michael Wernick took issue with the Auditor General's comments, calling them "sweeping generalizations" offered without robust empirical evidence to back them up (Canada 2018). Whatever the merits of the clerk's critique of the Auditor General's comments, the cultural problems Ferguson identified are nonetheless well-documented in a long list of academic and practitioner assessments on the health of the public service (many of these assessments offered by Wernick's predecessors in the Clerk's office, see Charette 2015; Himelfarb 2005; Lynch 2007; Pitfield 1976). These assessments criticize the federal bureaucracy for its closed government traditions: hoarding information and resources, failing to collaborate sufficiently across departments and with non-government actors, favouring the status quo at the cost of innovation, and defaulting to excessive hierarchy and top-down auditing in lieu of generating an open culture of learning and experimentation.

Justin Trudeau inherited this institution – dubbed a "bit of a fixer upper" by Wernick himself (May 2016b) – and its ingrained closed government traditions. However earnest Trudeau's commitment to public service renewal has been, political leadership alone has not thus far proven potent enough to upend the deeply rooted and complex legacies that stand in the way of an open, digital-ready public service. In the pages that follow, I diagnose these legacies and the ways in which they manifest today. I underscore how Canada's closed government traditions constrain the public service's capacity to experiment with new technologies, to attract and leverage talent, to adopt innovative policy solutions, and to collaborate productively across departments and with citizens and non-governmental organizations. At the same time, I depart from dominant perspectives on digital government offered thus far by considering the accountability and effectiveness breaches that can arise when governments dispense wholesale with established structures and practices born of their closed government traditions. In certain instances, these potential breaches justify a more restrained, calculated opening of the Canadian federal public service than is advocated in mainstream writing on digital government, with its enthusiasm for all things "disruptive."

The project of opening the federal public service remains a pressing challenge facing Justin Trudeau's Liberal government. This challenge will continue to present itself to whichever government succeeds in the 2019 general election. By diagnosing the various dimensions of this challenge, and suggesting the ways in which they can be overcome, this book aims to strengthen ongoing efforts to build a more effective and accountable federal public service, a longstanding project that endures and gains new urgency in the digital age.

Acknowledgments

This book would not have been possible without the individuals who generously offered their time and insight as interviewees. I am grateful to them for their candor and eagerness to support this project.

I would also like to extend my sincere gratitude to the institutions that funded this research: the Social Sciences and Humanities Research Council of Canada (SSHRC), the Oxford University Press Clarendon Fund, Carleton University's Faculty of Public Affairs, and the Pierre Elliott Trudeau Foundation.

I benefitted immensely from the advice and insights of colleagues at the Oxford Internet Institute (OII). In particular, I owe a debt of gratitude to Helen Margetts, whose expertise and critical eye were instrumental in conceptualizing this book. I am also grateful to Victoria Nash and Tony Bovaird; their enthusiasm and thoughtful feedback continue to fuel my interest and thinking on the subjects explored in these pages.

Building on work completed at the OII, the arguments I present here were refined through conversation with Canadian and international colleagues at a series of events on public sector renewal that I attended in the past few years. These include a colloquium on Westminster governance hosted by Margaret Biggs at Queen's University in 2014, meetings informing a 2016 Mowat Centre report on civil service reform (led by Mark Jarvis), and conferences convened through a SSHRC-funded Digital Governance Research Network.

To Alex Himelfarb, I owe thanks for a conversation shared in the Edmonton airport in 2012, in which his perspectives on digital government provided me with both a confidence boost and renewed curiosity. I am grateful as well for thought-provoking discussions on public sector renewal that I have shared in the past few years with Jonathan Craft, Mark Jarvis, Luc Juillet, Evert Lindquist, and Justin Longo. Erin Tolley is an indispensable source of wisdom on writing and methods, and I count myself lucky to have had access to her brain and friendship throughout the course of producing this book.

At UBC Press, Emily Andrew generously shared advice and enthusiasm at the genesis of this project, editorial support that continued with Randy Schmidt, Megan Brand, and Nadine Pedersen. The book's text was enriched by the able copy editing of Dallas Harrison, and the helpful suggestions of three anonymous reviewers. As editors of UBC Press' Communications, Strategy, and Politics series, Thierry Giasson and Alex Marland were valuable shepherds through the production process. I am thankful for their feedback on early proposals and the encouraging words they shared as the book developed.

Alex Marland is owed a second thank you for the academic mentorship he has provided me over the years. Alex was in the audience at the Canadian Political Science Association when I first presented sections of this work in 2012. He offered detailed feedback on my research, encouraging me to think ambitiously about its broader scholarly and practical implications. Alex continues to serve as a source of sage advice, sharing his time to discuss writing and research whenever a question arises. This book draws on the significant contributions Alex made to the field in *Brand Command*, and I hope that my work will be of use to him as he continues his research into the intersections of communications and politics.

This book was written throughout my first years as a professor with Carleton University's School of Public Policy and Administration (SPPA). I'm grateful to my colleagues for providing a supportive and stimulating intellectual environment, one in which I am never short of the eager ears and critical counterpoints that are essential in the writing process. I am particularly grateful to Susan Phillips, whose teaching and research inspired me to pursue an academic career in the first place, and to Les Pal, who offered helpful advice when this project first took form. In addition to these colleagues, I am grateful to Andy Kim, Christine Smith, and Stevie-Ray Talbot, SPPA graduate students whose superb work as Research Assistants informs Chapter 3. Lastly, I owe a debt of gratitude to the SPPA students I have had the pleasure to teach since joining the department. They have allowed me to use our classroom as a testing ground for the ideas in this book, and have kept me on my toes with their fresh perspectives. Many of these students are now working in the federal government. Their bright minds and dedication to public service ensure a promising future for the Government of Canada.

Writing is supposed to be a solitary act, but this project was always more of a team sport than it was a single-player event. I am surrounded by a loving and immeasurably supportive family of aunts, uncles, in-laws, siblings, and parents, each of whom has contributed to the pages of this book in important ways – providing childcare, reviewing chapters, debating ideas, sharing news articles, and offering comic relief. My daughter Leah arrived in the world toward the close of this project and played her part in bringing this book to fruition by providing motivation and many smiles as I neared the finish line. Finally, to Ben I owe endless gratitude. He encouraged me to take on this research in the first place and has provided invaluable suggestions, perspective, respite, and unwavering excitement about this work since. This book is dedicated to him.

Abbreviations

AANDC	Aboriginal Affairs and Northern Development Canada
API	application programming interface
ATIP	Access to Information and Privacy
CCCO	Canada's Communication Community Office
CIO	chief information officer
CIOB	Chief Information Officer Branch
CODE	Canadian Open Data Experience
CRA	Canada Revenue Agency
DEG	Digital Era Governance
DFAIT	Department of Foreign Affairs and International Trade
DFATD	Department of Foreign Affairs, Trade, and Development
DFO	Department of Fisheries and Oceans
DGU	digital government unit
DM	deputy minister
DMCPI	Deputy Minister Committee on Policy Innovation
DND	Department of National Defence
DTA	Digital Transformation Agency
DTO	Digital Transformation Office
ESDC	Employment and Social Development Canada
FAA	Federal Accountability Act
GDS	Government Digital Service
GSS	General Social Survey
HRSDC	Human Resources and Skills Development Canada
ICTs	information and communications technologies
IM	information management
IP	Internet Protocol
IT	information technology

NPM	New Public Management
NRCan	Natural Resources Canada
OGP	Open Government Partnership
PCO	Privy Council Office
PHAC	Public Health Agency of Canada
PIFs	Presidential Innovation Fellows
PMO	Prime Minister's Office
POR	public opinion research
PPA	Progressive-Era Public Administration
SME	small and medium-sized enterprise
TBS	Treasury Board of Canada Secretariat
USDS	United States Digital Service

Opening the Government of Canada

1
Opening Government
in the Digital Age

Wikipedia, the world's first user-generated encyclopedia, is now the fifth most popular website globally (Alexa 2018). Its English language version receives roughly 250 million page views daily (Wikimedia Statistics 2018). The business model of the online commerce giant Amazon rests on the collection, analysis, and publication of the roughly 35 million product reviews that its 6.6 million users have contributed to the site (Leskovec 2013). The alternatively titled "sharing" or "gig" economy – which allows individuals to monetize their labour, household items, parking spaces, cars, and homes – also relies on web-based, crowdsourced user reviews of the items being shared and of those doing the sharing, thus producing peer-to-peer networks of "collaborative consumption" that disrupt established industries by seamlessly linking market demand and supply through low-cost online information exchange (Botsman and Rogers 2010).

Iceland crowdsourced a first draft of its new constitution on the web, political parties have used interactive websites for vote delegation (Meyer 2012), and legislative committees have employed Twitter as a platform for involving citizens in their deliberations.[1] Social movements have turned to online social networking platforms as low-cost, real-time means of recruiting followers, advocating to decision makers, and coordinating protests, thus capitalizing on new logics of collective action enabled by networked information communication technologies (Margetts et al. 2016). These technologies underpinned the Arab Spring and Occupy Wall Street protests inspired by economic crises in Greece, Iceland, Portugal, and Spain, and the #blacklivesmatter movement. In Canada, the web has also provided a low-cost platform for citizen protest and advocacy, as witnessed in the Indigenous rights Idle No More movement, the Maple Spring student protests in Quebec, and a 2011 e-petition on Internet governance that received over 400,000 signatures, leading to direct regulatory change and amounting to the largest political campaign in Canadian history (OpenMedia, n.d.). Acknowledging the impressive forms of technology-enabled collective action that emerged in the late 2000s and that have continued since, *Time*'s 2011 "Person of the Year" was "The Protester."

Five years earlier, in 2006, *Time* recognized the contributions of Internet users to crowdsourced websites and their participation in online social networks (Grossman 2006) by proclaiming the "Person of the Year" as "You," published on the issue's cover with the tagline "Yes, you. You control the Information Age. Welcome to your world!" Since the issue's release in 2006, online social networks have grown immensely. Daily, roughly 500 million tweets are issued (Aslam 2018). In 2016, Facebook reported 1.13 billion active daily users, with just over 1 billion of these users accessing the platform on mobile devices (Facebook Newsroom 2016). Although data on Canadian Internet use are sorely lacking compared with data collected in other jurisdictions, the data available suggest that Canadians are prolific users of the Internet and social media specifically.[2] Eighty-four percent of Canadian Internet users have a Facebook account, 46 percent have a LinkedIn account, and 42 percent have Twitter accounts (Gruzd, Jacobson, Mai, and Dubois 2018).[3] Reuters Institute for the Study of Journalism reports that 76 percent of Canadians receive their news via the web (Newman et al. 2017).

As participation in commercial social media platforms has proliferated, so has participation in online networks of common interest, fuelling phenomena such as "mommy bloggers," whose parenting forums can attract more than 50,000 visitors per day and blend discussions of toddlers' temper tantrums with substantive debate and advocacy on policy issues (Lopez 2009). And, as digital technologies – especially the smartphones that 76 percent of Canadians carry around in their pockets (Catalyst 2016) – have come to punctuate almost every action that an individual takes throughout the day, massive amounts of data are produced, informing on-the-fly data-driven adjustments to service interactions, product designs, and communication strategies.

Much of this data is generated through our interactions with the platforms of a small number of private technology firms – Amazon, Google, Facebook, and Twitter. In turn, these tech firms now wield incredible power in our societies, a contemporary reality that underscores just how quaint and naive was *Time*'s 2006 proclamation on the power of the individual, who evidently does not "control the information age," as promised. Instead, rather than the digital age ushering in a democratization of information control, largely unaccountable private tech firms serve as today's information gatekeepers, shaping what we know through their opaque algorithms and capitalizing on the traces of data left behind as citizens live their lives through these digital platforms (mapping the journey to work, searching for information on a health problem, commenting on a political candidate's profile page, and so on). As they wield their information capital, these firms have come under fire. They are lambasted as hosts of "fake news" that informed the 2016 US presidential election and the UK Brexit referendum, as producers of algorithms that reinforce ideological preferences and digital echo chambers, as merchants of advertising that can be micro-targeted along racist lines, and as irresponsible stewards of the personal data their users share with them (Howard 2016; Maheshwari and Stevenson 2017; Owen and Greenspon 2017). In light of these developments, governments, traditionally viewed as comparatively powerful information actors – that is, as organizations relatively well placed to collect and distribute information across a population (Hood 1983; Hood and Margetts 2007) – find themselves scrambling to develop policy responses to regulate private tech firms' newfound information capital, while ultimately remaining dependent on these firms to communicate with the digital citizens whom they serve.

Alongside these shifts in the distribution of information capital, the digital age has introduced notable shifts in organizational management philosophies. The proliferation of new data sources, and our capacity to make in-the-moment, data-driven tweaks to products and services, have raised "agile" methodologies to prominence, supplanting traditional "waterfall" models of service and product design and delivery: that is, long-term, largely internal development cycles in which the experiences of end users are considered only once services and products are largely complete (Clarke 2017; Rasmusson, n.d.). The rise of "prosumers" (consumers of products/services who are also their producers, such as Wikipedia editors), the shift to iterative, agile design cycles, and the potential of big data–driven decision making call organizations to collect and act on data describing the behaviours of their "users" (clients, service users, audiences), and to build a range of new skills into their inventories, including data science and user-centred design (Bason 2010). Thus, organizations considered the success stories of the digital age aggressively recruit workers with these skills into their ranks and prioritize work processes and incentives that drive a culture of continual innovation, drawing on the insights of individuals across a range of functions and throughout the organizational hierarchy. In this way, the digital age not only demands that organizations produce a range of new digital products and services but also disrupts the management orthodoxy that has traditionally informed the design and delivery of those products and services.

Meanwhile, in Ottawa, a federal public servant has just received the ninth approval required to tweet a link to a press release. She publishes the tweet, but her colleagues do not know it; Twitter is blocked on departmental computers outside the communications office.

The digital age has profoundly disrupted all aspects of human society, altering how we shop, date, work, travel, and produce and consume culture. Particularly relevant to government, the digital age has also transformed how individual citizens access information, use services, and engage with the political issues of the day and how organizations form and subsequently manage their work. Yet, evident in the anecdote of the federal public servant awaiting her ninth tweet approval, the bureaucracies comprising today's governments have proven to be impressively steadfast in their ability to evade the disruptive impacts that digital technologies have had in other sectors and in the daily lives of citizens.

What might be the "disruptive impacts" of digital technologies on the public service? This question has inspired a series of normative digital government theories that have cropped up as of the mid-2000s and that provide the point of departure for this study of Canada's federal bureaucracy and its encounter with the digital age. These theories of digital government are best explained by considering what they oppose: the closed government traditions that to this day shape daily life in our public sector institutions.

Theories of Digital Government: An Attack on Closed Government

Beginning in the late nineteenth century, Max Weber's theory of bureaucracy and the model of Progressive-Era Public Administration (PPA) that followed it in the late nineteenth and early twentieth centuries organized the public service into distinct silos and hierarchies. These structures limited the scope for information and people to move fluidly across the bureaucracy and instituted rigid, standardized, top-down processes that produced circumscribed, low-trust, closed relationships among bureaucrats. These early theories of state management equally narrowed the interfaces by which those outside the bureaucracy engaged with those within it, producing a low-trust, closed government-citizen relationship (Dunleavy and Hood 1994). In the Westminster system in particular, the government-citizen relationship was limited – in fact, at a philosophical level, rendered properly nonexistent – through the conventions of public servant anonymity and hierarchical ministerial accountability structures (Kernaghan 2010). These conventions cast the elected minister as accountable to citizens via the executive and Parliament and public servants as servants of the Crown, not of the citizenry.

To be sure, the silos and hierarchies of Weber, PPA, and the Westminster system were pursued not as ends in themselves but as instruments that would ensure coordinated, efficient, equitable, and accountable governance. Following this logic and in the name of these principles, early formulations of the modern state prioritized closed government by design. This closing operated at two levels, limiting or denying the open flow of information and collaboration among bureaucrats operating in different siloed units and at different levels of the hierarchy within government and also limiting or denying contact between bureaucrats and citizens outside government.

In contrast, dominant theories of digital government argue that the tenets and practices of closed government are incompatible with the demands of governing in the digital age and that, instead, resilient digital era governments must be open by default (Lathrop and Ruma 2010; Margetts and Dunleavy 2013; Noveck 2009, 2015; O'Reilly 2011). Here it is important to distinguish between the interpretation of open government adopted in the digital government literature of the mid-2000s on and the more narrow interpretation of open government as it was originally conceived when introduced in the 1950s. At this earlier period, open government referred primarily to transparency and accountability achieved via freedom of information regimes (Clarke and Francoli 2014; Yu and Robinson 2012). In this classic view, open government presumes that citizens and the state exist in a low-trust, adversarial relationship, with the public acting as auditor and scrutineer of government decisions and finances.

This classic interpretation of open government lives on, evident in Canada, for instance, in the use of Access to Information and Privacy (ATIP) requests by journalists, lobbyists, researchers, and individual citizens to scrutinize government action and expose corruption. However, with the rise of networked digital technologies as defining features of the digital age from the mid-2000s on, a new body of literature and practice has expanded the concept of open government beyond its original narrow, and more adversarial, emphasis on information disclosure and citizen scrutiny. In this case, theories of digital government, and government programs that draw on them, are premised on the idea that open government demands not only disclosure of information but also more significant transformations to the machinery and culture of government and to the government-citizen relationship. Specifically, digital era open government advocates that the rigidly siloed and hierarchical organizational structures inherited from government's late-nineteenth-century and early-twentieth-century roots be dissolved. In this argument, resilient digital era open governments efficiently and fluidly organize information and people around problems and tasks, not entrenched organizational structures, and defy strictly hierarchical approaches to decision making and authority, favouring instead flatter structures amenable to whole of government systems thinking, bottom-up innovation, iterative and rapid experimentation and learning, and the mass participation of citizens in governing (Bason 2010; Christiansen 2015).

Theories of digital era open government thus replace Weber, PPA, and Westminster narratives of the state with models of social production and organization that have developed alongside the Internet, as reflected in theories of "cognitive surplus" (Shirky 2009, 2010), the democratization of innovation (von Hippel 2005), peer-production (Benkler 2006) "wikinomics" (Tapscott and Williams 2006), and platform thinking (O'Reilly 2011; Raymond 1999). Each of these theories explores how the Internet and related information and communications technologies (ICTs) reduce the costs of information exchange and co-production among large groups of distributed individuals. Applied to government, these theories have spawned a new language of public management that brings concepts from the tech sector into theories of government, as in Government 2.0 – a riff on Web 2.0 – and Open Source Governance, based on the open-source development model that allows anyone to build on, tweak, or repurpose a product, most famously in open-source software, as in that which underpins the Linux operating system and the web browser Mozilla Firefox.

In applying these concepts to the public sector, authors advancing theories of digital government have been particularly preoccupied with opening the government-citizen relationship, thus creating space for the public to feed into the work of the public service. Technology entrepreneur and writer Tim O'Reilly, credited with creation of the term "Web 2.0," calls for "government as a platform," which he describes as "a system that allows people inside and outside government to innovate," with government acting "as a service provider enabling its user community" (2011, 15). As with other theorists of digital government, O'Reilly relies primarily on private sector examples to elaborate his model, using the example of the Apple iPhone as a platform that enables users to produce apps in lieu of Apple taking on this task alone, thus greatly augmenting the value and utility of the device. O'Reilly is particularly inspired by the Linux operating system and other open-source success stories, and he uses these examples to argue that governments should abandon the tradition of developing policies and services behind closed doors, releasing them for outside feedback only once they are finished products. Instead, he argues that, operating as platforms, governments should work openly through agile methodologies that allow for continuous feedback and iterative modifications of policies and services based on the experiences of their "users" and for outsiders to tweak and develop these "products" alongside, or in lieu of, governments.

Similarly, Beth Noveck, former deputy chief technology officer for the Obama administration, head of New York University's GovLab, and another key voice animating dominant digital government theories, advocates for a new model of public management inspired by wikis. She dubs this model "Wiki Government," in which the "closed model of decision making" (2009, 25) that has traditionally defined government bureaucracy is replaced with open and collaborative processes that enable distributed groups of self-selecting citizens to deliver services and inform policies previously managed exclusively by government.

Along the same lines, when describing the second wave of their Digital Era Governance (DEG) model, Helen Margetts and Patrick Dunleavy (2013, 4, 16) describe Facebook groups, multiauthored blogs, and peer-produced goods such as Wikipedia as "alternative organizational forms and 'ways of producing'" that might set the stage for "open book government" as citizens participate in service delivery and policy development via the web. More prominently than other theories of digital government, the DEG model (Dunleavy et al., 2006; Margetts and Dunleavy 2013; Dunleavy and Margetts 2015) also emphasizes the *internal opening* of government – the dissolution of silos among various actors across the bureaucracy. These internal openings are described as a "recentralization" of government, a trend that Dunleavy and Margetts posit as a defining feature of Digital Era Governance and contrast with the "agencification" of government (i.e., the proliferation of decentralized agencies) that New Public Management ushered in, in particular jurisdictions, in the 1980s and 1990s (especially the United Kingdom – a primary point of reference for British scholars Dunleavy and Margetts in their theory of DEG).

One particular digital era policy instrument enjoys relative prominence in theories of digital government: open data, the release of raw, machine-readable, public sector data sets with accompanying licences that allow for reuse of the data to a range of ends, notably to empower citizens to feed into the work of government (e.g., by developing mobile and web applications that support government services or by using the data in external policy analyses). In other cases, advocates of open data argue that they will enable public servants to make better use of data internally, across the silos of government (Lathrop and Ruma 2010; Noveck 2009; Robinson et al. 2008). In Canada, open government advocate David Eaves has been a central voice on digital government in general, and on open data specifically, using his blog to espouse its potential to disrupt closed government. As he wrote in 2011:

The challenge of the old order and the institutions it fostered is that its organizing principle is built around the management (control) of processes, it's been about the application of the industrial production model to government services. This means it can only move so fast, and because of its strong control orientation, can only allow for so much creativity (and adaption [*sic*]). Open data is about putting the free flow of information at the heart of government – both internally and externally – with the goal of increasing government's metabolism and decentralizing societies' capacity to respond to problems. (Eaves 2011b)

Alongside open data, theories of digital era open government also promote the uptake of new digital policy instruments that, to varying extents, call on the public service to ensure that its operations are more open and responsive to those outside its walls, including crowdsourcing (Grabosky 2013; Lodge and Wegrich 2015), "hackathons" (time-limited events in which web developers produce web or mobile applications that address a social challenge, often using government data), digital citizen engagement (e.g., online deliberative dialogue, real-time collaborative policy development, e-petitions, mobile and web user reviews) (Coleman and Moss 2011; Longo and Kelley 2016; McNutt and Carey 2008; Peters and Abud 2009), A/B testing (controlled experiments that allow government to redesign services based on users' experiences with them), and big data generated from administrative processes and citizens' interactions with the web and related technologies (Clarke and Margetts 2014; Reimsbach-Kounatze 2015).

In sum, whether by challenging the silos and hierarchies that have long underpinned a closed bureaucrat-bureaucrat relationship, or by calling for the uptake of new agile and open policy making and service delivery approaches, the dominant theories of digital government offered to date argue that closed government is entirely incompatible with the demands of governing in the digital age. Authors argue this point with a sense of urgency, warning that governments that do not adapt to a world defined by decentralized production models, rapid and networked information flows, and iterative, user-driven design processes at best miss out on significant opportunities to improve policy making and service delivery and at worst become ever more out of touch with the societies that they serve, propelling existing crises of confidence in the state. This sense of urgency raises two questions that are at the heart of current debates on digital era government and that drive the research and analysis that form this book.

The first of these questions asks simply, in practical terms, are today's bureaucracies capable of adopting the model of open government that has emerged as the preferred paradigm of digital era public administration? The second question asks, at a normative level, is it even desirable for governments to adopt the model of open government for which mainstream digital government theories advocate so urgently? Or, put bluntly, do these theories pass the "smell test" for accountable governance, thus serving as a reliable and comprehensive roadmap for public administrators navigating the digital age? Next, I survey the responses that have been offered to each of these questions thus far before outlining how this book builds on, and challenges, this thinking.

The Resilience of Closed Government in the Digital Age

To date, the bulk of the empirical research dedicated to digital government has focused on answering the first question: are today's bureaucracies capable of implementing the model of digital era open government advocated in theories of digital government? In response to this question, authors have overwhelmingly responded with a no. In practice, governments have not abandoned the deeply entrenched structures, policy and legislative constraints, and cultural attitudes born of their closed government origins despite the emergence of technologies and related social phenomena that in theory can upend these traditions. For example, preliminary empirical research on government's uptake of digital era policy instruments from the early 2010s on finds that bureaucrats struggle to use social media for more networked, interactive exchanges with the public; suffer from a dearth of coherent and joined-up information management across silos, thus limiting the scope to capitalize on open data and big data; and continue to default to "behind closed doors" command and control approaches despite the availability of technologies that could usher in unprecedented forms of agile, iterative, and participatory policy making and service delivery (Clarke and Francoli 2017; Clarke and Margetts 2014; Craft 2013; Longley and Zimmerman 2011; McNutt 2014; Mergel and Desouza 2013; Noveck 2015; Small 2012). New technologies and commitments to open data, digital citizen engagement, and networked service delivery in most cases have simply been bolted on to existing cultures, legislative and corporate policy regimes, policy styles, and organizational structures tailored to closed government, lacking an accompanying effort to meaningfully confront and amend these legacies. Thus, returning to the public servant invoked at the start of this chapter, in practice bureaucrats are still waiting for the proverbial tweet approval, operating in governments that are as siloed, hierarchical, and closed as those of decades past.

These findings fall in line with earlier research on the first wave of "electronic" or "e-government" (as digital government was dubbed at the time) in the 1990s and early 2000s, in which governments took up websites, computing systems, and early online service delivery mechanisms as part of the "Web 1.0" phase of digital government.[4] This earlier research found that when public sector bureaucracies integrate information technologies into their operations, existing organizational characteristics, administrative cultures, and established activities are more often reinforced than they are reversed (Danziger et al. 1982; Fountain 2001; Norris and Reddick 2013). These findings sobered enthusiasm for early e-government programs; academics and elected officials dazzled by the Internet's potential had been quick to presume that ICTs would transform government for the better and, importantly, predicted the same types of "opening" of policy and service delivery that Digital Era Governance, Wiki Government, and government as a platform have advocated as of the mid-2000s. In this first wave of e-government enthusiasm, authors and political leaders dwelled almost fanatically on "the 'new' and the 'modern' as a way of fulfilling dreams and escaping nightmares" (Margetts 2010, 39), presuming that ICTs would lead to more effective, more democratic, and less costly government. "Computers were supposed to cut paperwork and costs, reduce crime, and give managers and policymakers better information" (Starr 2010, 2) thus transforming government for the better, an expectation not met in practice.

For example, in their review of local-level e-government studies, Donald Norris and Christopher Reddick (2013, 167, 165) explain that "we do not cite empirical works that validate claims made in cyber-optimist writings because, after an extensive review of the e-government literature, we have not been able to find any" and that "e-government has developed incrementally and has not been transformative, as many early writers envisioned." This conclusion is shared by a broad range of authors who have highlighted the overblown expectations that shaped early predictions on and prescriptions for the role of digital technologies in government, leading to books with titles such as *ICTs, Citizens, and Governance: After the Hype!* (Meijer, Boersma, and Wagenaar 2009) and a consensus that, though "ICT is put forward as an instrument which can be used to achieve different goals of modernization ... for instance a shift towards self-government, market-governance and self-regulation and an empowerment of citizens ... the potential of ICT in order to achieve institutional innovation has not been fully acknowledged" (Meijer and Thaens 2010, 114).

Recalling that, "in each phase [of e-government], early enthusiasms have run up against stubborn and uncomfortable limits" (Starr 2010, 5), digital government skeptics have been quick to remind us that governments are not "born digital," emerging in the digital age as a *tabula rasa* as in the technology organizations on whose experiences today's digital government theories draw (Apple, Facebook, Linux, Wikipedia). Rather, these skeptics caution, governments bring to the digital age the legacies of closed government to which they have traditionally defaulted, in many cases despite deliberate efforts to dispense with them. Thus, these critics argue, bureaucrats will struggle to integrate open, networked technologies and approaches into the "home system" of silos and hierarchies deeply entrenched in the public sector (Roberts 2011, 684), and argue that "as organizational forms are increasingly catalysed toward complex networks and computer mediated communication, the traditional hierarchies associated with twentieth-century bureaucracy and the institutional arrangements embedded therein ... may truncate the implementation of networked technologies as parochial attitudes in the public service resist transformation" (McNutt and Carey 2008, 12).

Given these findings, some digital government enthusiasts have already begun to temper their theories to account for the layering effects that ensure that digital efforts to open the bureaucracy remain constrained by Weber's grip on contemporary public sector institutions. For instance, in two subsequent updates to their DEG model (originally described in 2005), Dunleavy and Margetts (2013; 2015) adopt a more cautious tone in describing the impact of the digital age on the public sector, noting that their vision of a recentral-ized, joined-up, open-book government has not proven a *fait accompli*. Instead, Digital Era Governance has been marked in the first instance by the austerity measures of the 2010s and, more fundamentally, by the enduring legacies of Weber and PPA in the machinery of government, policy design processes, and service delivery models. Likewise, reflecting on her work advancing Obama's open government initiative in her role as deputy chief technology officer, the first few pages of Noveck's 2015 follow-up to *Wiki Government* candidly depict the institutional inertia and bureaucratic insular-ity that can ensure that digital era open government remains as difficult to achieve as – and in certain ways even more difficult than – its pre–digital era variants. Notably, Noveck reaches this sobering conclusion even in a context where there was significant top-down political support for digital era open government reforms; former US President Barack Obama had campaigned on a promise of open government and committed to it in a formal directive on his first day in office (Orszag 2009).

Now, it is at this stage in the history of digital government research that the seasoned public administration scholar is likely to intervene with the remark "well, that was predictable." The history of public administration from the 1980s on in many ways is a story of governments and their observers attempting, but typically failing, to open the closed governments that Weber, PPA, and in certain jurisdictions (as in Canada) the Westminster system have produced. Advocates of silos and hierarchies are a rare breed (Olsen 2006), and horizontal, joined-up government has long been a pursued but unachieved objective of public service reformers (Bakvis and Juillet 2004; Lindquist 2012; Peters 1998). Public administration scholars, including those in Canada, regularly criticize the excessive red tape, oversight, and risk aversion that theories of digital era open government challenge (Jarvis 2016; Phillips and Levasseur 2004; Savoie 2003). Canadian practitioners, too, get in on the game; annual reports from the Clerk of the Privy Council and previous reform initiatives dating back decades perennially decry the culture of risk aversion, information control, excessive hierarchy, and silos of the public service (Cha-rette 2015; Himelfarb 2005; Lynch 2007; Pitfield 1976). And, where govern-ments meet citizens, dominant reform movements from the 1980s on have equally attempted to open up the work of government to outside participation, albeit as part of varied ideological projects and with differing framings of the citizen's role in governance.

For instance, the 1980s and 1990s saw New Public Management (NPM) open service delivery up to a range of nongovernmental service providers, if only through the low-trust mechanisms of contracting and outsourcing (Barnes, Newman, and Sullivan 2007; Hood 1995; Phillips and Levasseur 2004). Alongside these providers, individual citizens were also promised a new but limited role in the processes of governing under NPM. Versus being treated merely as passive end users of government services, they were framed as consumers and clients who, armed with government-provided information on the quality of services (e.g., league tables ranking school and hospital performance), could "vote with their feet," selecting among providers of services as the "invisible hand" rationalizing the market (Needham 2003; Pierre 1995).

Following NPM, and referenced with various prefixes in the literature ("shared," "new public," "collaborative") (Bixler 2014; Jones, Hesterly, and Borgatti 1997; Rhodes 1997; Salamon and Elliott 2002; Torfing 2005), network governance has surfaced as a second dominant alternative to closed government in the field of public administration. Network governance picks up and extends NPM's emphasis on service externalization – the act of transferring all or part of government activities to those outside the bureaucracy (Alford and O'Flynn 2012) – in particular emphasizing how third sector organizations, groups of citizens, and individual citizens can support government services as partners in their delivery. Network governance equally acknowledges the benefits of achieving broad consensus on policies with stakeholders and that an increasingly educated and engaged citizenry can meaningfully inform government policy work. Finally, network governance acknowledges the deficiencies of siloed and overly hierarchical operations within the public service itself, instead advocating system-based, horizontal government that breaks down silos across policy areas, functions, and individual departments and subunits of governments.

Theories of digital government follow on the heels of these predecessors, adding a digital lens to certain NPM tenets (e.g., releasing data on government performance to empower service users and drive better outcomes, and encouraging an ecosystem of nongovernmental service providers) and, more prominently, bringing the tenets of network governance into the digital age by emphasizing service externalization alongside citizen engagement in policy and the benefits of an open bureaucrat-bureaucrat relationship. Like today's theories of digital government, though, whereas both NPM and network governance have endeavoured to upend Weberian and PPA legacies, each has been met on implementation with significant challenges and resistance from the bureaucracy, which has proven to be steadfast in its ability to reinforce silos, hierarchies, and closed models of service and policy development. This reflects a larger body of research and theory in the field of public administration that highlights how policy regimes, path-dependent trajectories, and entrenched organizational/institutional characteristics can constrain the scope for change in the public sector, producing resilient status quo defaults in government (Aucoin 1990; Freeman 1985; Hall 1993; Howlett 2003; Howlett and Ramesh 2003; Streeck 1995).[5]

In other words, though the categories of Weberian bureaucracy/PPA, NPM, and network governance are discussed as distinct from each other in the literature, each contends with the shadow of its predecessor, in particular with the silos and hierarchies of Weber and PPA living on as enduring structures of government despite over forty years of public management orthodoxy calling for their upheaval. When it comes to reforming the public service, one never truly gets a "do-over," and thus previous reform efforts have not served as reset buttons by which the entrenched worldviews, practices, and corporate policy and legislative constraints of the past are easily and comprehensively upended.

Why was this research apparently absent from early theories of digital government, lacking as they initially did sufficient appreciation for the stickiness of institutional legacies that mark all public administration reforms and ensure that Weberian bureaucracy has stood the test of time – and would likely do the same in the face of networked digital technologies? To answer this question, it is instructive to consider the *source* of mainstream theories of digital government.

With few exceptions, these theories and related research emerge from scholars operating outside the traditional field of public administration. This reflects the long-standing marginalization of IT in mainstream public administration research and theory, a trend alive and well today (Margetts 1999; Meijer 2007). For example, a 2013 analysis of the top fifteen ranked public administration journals indicated that only 89 articles of the roughly 3,600 articles published by these journals from 2007 to 2013 even mentioned phenomena related to the digital age, let alone offering substantive discussions of this theme. At a basic level, by ignoring the digital age, the field of public administration proves to be out of touch with and oblivious of the empirical world that it claims to speak to, leading to anomalies such as the fact that, while over 250 million Europeans were members of Facebook in 2013 (Internet

World Stats 2013), according to the pages of the *Journal of European Social Policy* Facebook did not even exist at that time; the word had not been mentioned once in its pages as of 2013.[6] Even more consequentially, though, because public administration scholars have ignored the proliferation of digital technologies in society, insights from the field have not sufficiently informed theories on the digital age and its likely impact on government. In turn, at a descriptive level, theories of digital era open government have proven to be thin and largely unhelpful in practical terms, lacking an appreciation for the sticky institutional legacies that decades of mainstream public administration research illuminate and that any seasoned public administration scholar would rightfully predict would accompany efforts to dissolve silos and hierarchies and integrate citizens into the processes of governing in the digital age. Most fundamentally, however, the costs of public administration scholars' absence from discussions on digital era government have been felt at the normative level: that is, in determining not the *possibility* of achieving digital era open government as currently envisioned in the literature but the *desirability* of doing so.

Digital Era Open Government: Risky Business?

Although evidence suggests that governments struggle to achieve the model of digital era open government so urgently called for in the literature, one might ask: is this a problem? Is this preferred paradigm of digital era public administration even a worthy pursuit, providing a sound roadmap to good governance in the digital age? With few notable exceptions (often focused on critiquing open data and hackathon/app contests in particular; see Biddle 2014; Clarke and Margetts 2014; Johnson and Robinson 2014; Kitchin 2013; Longo 2011; Morozov 2014; Porway 2013), this question is never posed explicitly in research on digital government. Theories of digital era open government have mostly escaped normative scrutiny, taken for granted as accurate prognoses of the preferred path for digital era public administration. Thus, discussions on digital government begin from the premise that, to be resilient in the digital age, governments must abandon siloed and hierarchical approaches to their work, release data and information, and experiment with agile, iterative, and networked models of policy and service delivery – and quickly, for the pace of change in the digital age demands rapid adaptation and fundamental upheavals of closed government traditions. And when, as noted, research finds that governments are incapable of reversing these traditions, authors lament the risks of government sclerosis, critiquing bureaucrats' resistance to change, their reliance on traditional policy and service instruments, and their default to ineffective siloed and hierarchical models of organization.

Among practitioners, the normative theory of digital era open government espoused in the literature has equally gained favour as the preferred paradigm of contemporary public administration. It is now rare, if not impossible, to find a public sector renewal agenda that does not place agile design, open data, big data, digital by default service delivery, innovation, experimentation, and open government reforms at the centre of its strategies for bolstering policy capacity and, more generally, for public sector modernization.[7] The words *digital* and *open* are now sprinkled throughout governance best practices as produced by organizations such as the Organization for Economic Cooperation and Development and the United Nations.[8] Some seventy countries have signed the Open Government Partnership created in 2011, and in 2013 the G8 countries signed into effect an Open Data Charter. Far from fringe commentators, theorists of digital era open government speak the *lingua franca* of what has now become the mainstream public management discourse among practitioners the world over.

In some cases, governments have invoked digital government theorists' language and ideas directly. The research that supported the DEG model of Dunleavy and Margetts heavily informed parliamentary scrutiny of government IT management in the United Kingdom, which subsequently fed into the creation of the Government Digital Service, an organization that now has near whole of government jurisdiction over all digital services (and that, in essence, manages the government-citizen interface in the United Kingdom). More overtly, the Government Digital Service and its equivalent in Australia, as well as Canada's recently appointed Chief Information Officer (CIO) Alex Benay, regularly cite O'Reilly's "government as a platform" as their guiding public management philosophy (Benay 2017; Bracken 2012, 2015a; Digital Transformation Agency 2015).

As noted above, Noveck led the open government initiative that Obama signed into being on his first day in office and that arguably defined the core of his administration's public management reform agenda. In Canada, David Eaves directly informed the City of Vancouver's open data initiative and, at the federal level, the open data strategies of the Treasury Board Secretariat (TBS), even joining Stockwell Day (then the president of the TBS) at the press conference announcing the initiative. And O'Reilly (2011), Shirky (2009, 2010), and Tapscott and Williams (2006), all technology writers informing dominant theories of digital government, are directly cited by Canadian federal public servants when discussing the rationale for a series of under-the-radar open government initiatives introduced within the bureaucracy as of 2008. Most recently, the Liberal government of Prime Minister Justin Trudeau elected in 2015 has turned to the language and promises of mainstream digital government theories, enthusiastically naming open policy making, open data, data-driven decision making, user engagement on digital services, and experimentation as key features of its governing agenda (Prime Minister's Office 2015a).

Evidently, the tech sector–inspired theories of public administration that have emerged of late offer governments – both political leaders and administrators – an enticing account of the deficiencies of classically siloed and hierarchical approaches to state management and an equally convincing case in favour of digital era open government approaches, instruments, and values. However, by stepping outside the orthodoxy of digital government theories, and again invoking the public administration research missing from this discussion thus far, we have reasons to be more critical of the normative assertion that a wholesale upheaval of Weber, PPA, and core Westminster traditions is an uncomplicated and cost-free solution to the challenges of governing in the digital age. In fact, a traditional public administration lens illuminates a series of practical and ethical conditions ensuring that silos and hierarchies might well live on in today's government not simply because of the bureaucracy's lethargy and unmitigated resistance to change but for entirely legitimate reasons.

For instance, though it has long been fashionable to critique silos and hierarchies as passé and ineffective models of organization, these structures have traditionally played and continue to play important roles in securing coordinated and accountable government. The top-down management of bureaucrats and the parcelling of particular tasks to siloed actors allow for clean lines of accountability within government, rendering it possible to identify and hold to account particular actors responsible for particular tasks (Jarvis 2014a) while facilitating centralized, whole of government management of large-scale government organizations that, absent a central coordination mechanism with top-down authority, might otherwise work at cross-purposes. Joined-up, horizontal, and open (internal) government – that which sees bureaucrats across silos coordinating their activities as one unit – rests in part on centralized, hierarchical centres of control across the machinery of government. This was particularly true for early e-government programs, a phase in which the Canadian government emerged as a leader specifically because it instituted centrally coordinated control over its websites and online services as opposed to fostering a pluralistic, bottom-up ecosystem of web products (Borins 2007; Roy 2006). Yet theories of digital era open government are silent on the accountability and coordination gaps that can arise when the silos and hierarchies that they critique are dissolved and thus deny their adherents theoretical or practical insights into the new or adapted accountability and coordination mechanisms that could safely usher in the open government models that they propose.

Forays into pluralistic online government-citizen interaction and open policy making raise a raft of potential equity and accountability dilemmas insufficiently accounted for in the dominant theories of digital era open government offered to date. How can we ensure that autonomously governed interactions between government bureaucrats and citizens online are equitable – that is, accessible to all citizens – regardless of official language or citizen ability? The siloed allocation of the "voice" of government to particular actors in the bureaucracy, and the top-down management of these interactions through corporate policies and approvals, have traditionally alleviated the risks of inequity that a decentralized model of government-citizen interaction can invite. Yet the rapid, informal, and personalized forms of communication facilitated by digital technologies are entirely at odds with siloed, hierarchical models of government-citizen interaction, demanding new frameworks of flexible oversight, training, and self-governance that would see public servants empowered to engage with stakeholders, service users, and everyday Canadians online. In practice, what would such a system look like? Existing theories of digital era open government offer little concrete insight that could help us to answer this question.

In Westminster systems such as that in Canada, decentralized, open communication between public servants and the public raises particularly acute concerns given that it can conflict with the traditional public service bargain, which relies on public servant anonymity as a guarantor of public service neutrality and ministerial accountability (Grube 2013; Savoie 2003; Tait 1996). Although this tradition has eroded over the years, in particular among those in the higher ranks of the public service, such as when deputy ministers are called to account in the public forum of parliamentary committees, the model of fluid, decentralized government-citizen interaction that theories of digital era open government call for would effectively thrust a whole range of new players across the bureaucracy and at lower ranks of the hierarchy into potentially politically contentious public policy debates. This raises crucial but unanswered questions about the training and values and ethics guidelines required to accommodate this expanded government-citizen relationship and to resolve the complex accountability dilemmas that will arise when formerly anonymous public servants engage online with citizens and stakeholders and are held to account for unpopular or failed policy initiatives properly attached to the ministerial master whom they serve. However, instead of addressing these dilemmas head-on, theories of digital government attempt to depoliticize the inherently political context in which public servants operate, naively framing the citizens and stakeholders with which digital era open governments engage as mere "users" of government services or dispassionate, neutral collaborators with whom public officials can interact in strictly benevolent and responsive ways.

This ill-advised act of depoliticization equally ensures that theories of digital era open government do not sufficiently account for the unintended retreat to closed government that their reforms might inspire. This critique draws on research on earlier, analogue era open government (focused on access to government information), which finds that, when the processes of governing are opened to public view, public servants who fear public scrutiny from media, opposition parties, and critical stakeholder and citizen groups can render government more opaque, for instance by refusing to document decisions in written forms that can be accessed by outsiders (see Legault 2015b). Others observe that, as the activities of the state are opened to external view, public servants become overly risk averse, resisting untested, innovative approaches to policies or services as a rule because of the potential for public-facing failure that they invite (Clarke 2016b; Jarvis 2016). As damaging as they can be to citizen trust and government effectiveness, these impulses are a rational response to a competitive culture of permanent campaigning that sees ministers wishing to avoid politically costly public exposé and thus demanding "error-free government" from their public servants (Marland 2016; Marland, Giasson, and Esselment 2017; Savoie 2003, 2013).

Extending this argument, in a rare acknowledgment of the role of digital technologies in contemporary governance by public administration scholars, some authors have argued that the digital age actually exacerbates the risk that efforts to open government to external actors will lead to opaque public administration (Clarke and Francoli 2017). This argument posits that, in exposing the operations of the public sector to greater scrutiny, the digital age's 24/7 media cycle of which social media are a part propels an existing trend toward information hoarding and risk aversion (Marland 2016; Savoie 2003, 2013). In other cases, government's uptake of social media is included in blanket criticisms of the communications function in government. Far from supporting a more collaborative, open, responsive model of governance, authors argue that, when governments adopt social media to engage with the public, they inevitably politicize public servants by compelling them to abandon their duties to neutrality through public promotions of the government of the day (see Aucoin 2012). To be sure, these arguments are not based on systematic, holistic, empirical analyses of the actual impact that the digital age has had on the public service or of how the public service uses social media in practice (an empirical gap that this study fills). Nonetheless, these criticisms of social media, and of open government more generally, compel theorists of digital era open government to confront questions about the competitive environment of permanent campaigning in which their reforms would unfold. They must also account for historical patterns suggesting that the adoption of technologies and practices intended to open government might at best be undermined by existing political pressures to avoid public scrutiny and at worst render the public service even less amenable to public engagement and potentially failure-ridden digital era innovations.

Adding another dimension on which the normative bases of digital era open government can be challenged, crowdsourcing and digital service externalization (e.g., achieved through open data and hackathons) raise questions about government's capacity to ensure that services are coordinated, that data generated from nongovernmental actors' service interactions with citizens are fed back into policy processes, and that players in a decentralized ecosystem of service providers satisfy the higher accountability standards that government's high-stakes suite of services and public good considerations necessitate. And, with so much of the literature emphasizing the benefits of leveraging outsiders' digital expertise, for instance through hackathons and open data app contests, the digital era open government literature says little about the need to build in-house digital talent within government. A baseline of that talent is necessary lest the public service render itself entirely dependent on outside firms for technology solutions and a vulnerable blind shopper in procuring such services and policy advice (Clarke 2017). Again, eschewing a discussion of these risks, dominant theories of digital government offered to date have instead tended to presume that governments can only become more efficient, effective, and responsive to citizens' needs by dispensing with their control of public services, an assertion that existing research on failed service externalization would quickly caution against (Alford and O'Flynn 2012; Phillips 2006; Williams, Kang, and Johnson 2015).

Beyond these specific potential risks of digital era open government, one might argue at a larger level that any theory that calls for urgent and rapid public administration reform warrants at least some skepticism given the high stakes of government failings and, in particular, the costs that certain governments have borne historically by moving too quickly to adopt new and fashionable public management reforms. The prime example here is New Public Management, whose earliest and fastest adherents suffered immense setbacks to policy capacity, service failures, and significant cost overruns (Dunleavy et al. 2006; Hood 1995). Canada is typically framed as the cautious reformer, hesitant to move too quickly or too drastically in any direction of reform (Brock 2000; Halligan 2004), an approach that helped the government to avoid the failings of NPM as other early adopters offered cautionary tales of its deficiencies. Taken to an extreme, a strictly conservative approach to public administration might argue that government systems are designed to resist change, to safeguard against drastic transformations, facilitating instead cautious incremental evolution that protects against the societal costs that can arise when untested approaches to governing are adopted rapidly and without an appreciation for their unintended or unpredictable consequences. In this view, the fact that the public service has managed to avoid disruption in the face of digital technologies upending other sectors might prove to be a virtue, not a weakness. In other words, whereas mainstream digital government advocates decry "parochial attitudes in the public service" that "resist transformation" (McNutt and Carey 2008, 12), a traditional public administration perspective might praise this parochialism and resistance as safeguards of the core values of neutral public administration, equitable treatment of citizens, and vertical accountability for decision making, ensuring that these principles of democratic governance remain constant as the context in which governments operate undergoes rapid and unpredictable changes. Reflecting this view, Obama, under whom significant investments were made in open government and digital service initiatives, nonetheless publicly criticized the idea that the challenges facing the public sector can be easily solved if only governments would quickly adopt the open, agile, and user-centric methods of today's tech sector success stories. As Obama commented in 2016,

government will never run the way Silicon Valley runs because, by definition, democracy is messy ... If all I was doing was making a widget or producing an app, and I didn't have to worry about whether poor people could afford the widget, or I didn't have to worry about whether the app had some unintended consequences – setting aside my Syria and Yemen portfolio – then I think those suggestions are terrific ... But the reason I say this is sometimes we get, I think, in the scientific community, the tech community, the entrepreneurial community, the sense of we just have to blow up the system, or create this parallel society and culture because government is inherently wrecked. No, it's not inherently wrecked; it's just government has to care for, for example, veterans who come home. That's not on your balance sheet, that's on our collective balance sheet, because we have a sacred duty to take care of those veterans. And that's hard and it's messy, and we're building up legacy systems that we can't just blow up. (quoted in Etherington 2016)

Following this line of thinking, and applying a traditional public administration lens to the orthodoxy of widely accepted theories of digital era open government, a crucial normative debate thus emerges. Do our dominant theories of digital era open government provide a sufficiently robust roadmap for good governance in the digital age? And, if their prescription of rapid, tech sector–inspired "transformation" is not the answer, then what model of public administration should guide governments as they navigate the demands of governing in the digital age? It is in this debate that this book intervenes and from which its central arguments emerge.

Central Arguments of This Book

In this book, I argue that Canada's current model of closed government does not offer an effective, sustainable, or democratically robust paradigm of public administration suited for the digital age. In arguing this point, I follow mainstream theories of digital era open government proposed thus far; to secure its resilience and democratic legitimacy, the federal public service must become more open internally (challenging strict silos and excessive hierarchy and generating a culture amenable to innovation) and more open externally (engaging with citizens, releasing data and information, and opening service delivery processes to external participation). These openings are necessary for four central reasons, each reflecting specific risks that closed government raises in the digital age. These are the "stakes of the game," the reasons why scholars, elected officials, public servants, and citizens alike need to put digital era open government on the agenda as a core priority of public service – and broader democratic – renewal in Canada.

First, closed government perpetuates a lethargic metabolic rate of change in the public service, ensuring that government lacks the internal and external networking capacity, tolerance for iterative learning and innovation, and skill sets essential to keep pace with a rapidly changing external environment. Acknowledging this cost of the status quo, I reject the time-honoured Canadian tradition of conservative, lagged, incremental public management reform, arguing that, whatever its historical virtues, this tradition now raises more clearly identifiable risks than it does discernible benefits.

Second, and in part emerging from the first risk, closed government ushers in policy, program, and operational failures whose costs are felt by citizens, administrators, and elected officials alike. These failures emerge as the bureaucracy is shielded from new data sources, expertise, and production models; restricts opportunities for internal and external collaboration; facilitates an awkward and ineffective uptake of new digital policy instruments (or limits their adoption altogether); and inspires a status quo default anathema to innovation.

Third, I document the human resource costs of closed government, illustrating how siloed and overly hierarchical management models, limited access to technology, and barriers to innovation hinder the recruitment and retention of emerging top talent while ensuring that the existing skills and enthusiasm of public servants are not leveraged.

Fourth, and most crucially, I argue that governments that continue to operate as closed institutions – awkwardly integrating networked technologies into corporate processes and cultures at odds with them, and suffering from the inevitable policy, program, and service failures that this invites – exacerbate existing crises of confidence in the state, suggesting to citizens that government is out of touch, ineffective, irrelevant, and democratically illegitimate. Acknowledging these four costs, I reject a conservative public administration perspective that prioritizes the status quo as the safest path to good governance and instead align with theorists who advocate digital era open government reforms.

Some might take issue with my assertion that digital era public administration demands a transformation from closed government to open government. It is useful to address such critiques up front. First, some will argue that openness is not necessarily a requirement of effective digital era government, noting that certain countries, such as China and Singapore, match superb digital services with questionable records on government account-ability, transparency, and human rights while doing little if anything to meaningfully engage the public or to challenge command and control models of public management.[9] This is true; however, when we move beyond the narrow question of the quality of a country's digital services, and consider the broader range of functions and activities that underpins legitimate demo-cratic governance, the sustainability of closed government as a model of digital era public administration is more difficult to defend, in particular in jurisdic-tions, such as Canada, that benefit from strong civil societies and transparent elections and that are thus held to comparatively robust democratic checks and balances.

In this context, facing wicked policy problems that demand collabora-tion across silos and sectors, limited fiscal resources, growing citizen expectations for responsiveness and innovation, and dwindling levels of citizen trust in the state, closed governments – however impressive they might be at providing stellar digital services – cannot meet the requirements of robust and effective democratic governance, casting doubt on their long-term political viability. Arguably, we saw this scenario play out in the Can-adian context when the 2015 federal election saw the Conservative government of Prime Minister Stephen Harper ousted in part because of its perceived adherence to strict command and control, opaque public management. Meanwhile, the Liberal Party was rewarded on the back of a platform emphasizing collaboration, data-driven decision making, and restoration of a high-trust government-citizen relationship (all tenets of digital era open government).

Second, some will argue that one of the most impressive examples of digital government activity to date is entirely incompatible with the tenets of open government, whether defined classically or by its digital era variant. Here I am referring to large-scale monitoring of citizens' online activities via secretive government surveillance programs – in which Canada, as a member of the Five Eyes Intelligence consortium, is implicated – as uncovered by US National Security Agency whistleblower Edward Snowden. To be sure, though I advocate for digital era open government, my arguments in the empirical chapters that follow equally acknowledge that many closed government activities will endure or even be intensified in the digital age. In some cases, they will undermine the uptake of digital era open government reforms; in others, they will exist in paradoxical tension with them. The normative call for digital era open government does not erase a descriptive reality that sees closed government endure (however precariously as a long-term strategy for governing).

Third, in confronting potential critiques of my argument in this book up front, I want to underscore that I do not adopt the analogue and more limited view of open government with its primary emphasis on access to information regimes, nor do I advocate an extreme view of open government that would see all government activity open for public access; there are important reasons to create space for private and frank discussions to unfold in government. But more to the point, focusing on digital era open government, I am not primarily preoccupied with freedom of information legislation and reform or engaging in debates on where the line between open and closed should be drawn when dealing with issues such as cabinet confidence exemptions. If you are seeking an extensive exploration of Canada's Access to Information regime, this is not the book to consult.

Here I adopt the broader interpretation of open government that has emerged in the digital age and focuses on challenging siloed and hierarchical work models within the public service and fostering new models of public engagement and co-production and a culture of public service amenable to risk taking, failure, iterative learning, and innovation. These issues intersect in important ways with the ATIP regime, but it is only a small player in the broader analysis and empirical focus of this study. Instead, I look to the larger issue undermining the robustness of both historical and digital era open government reforms (including ATIP): a political culture of permanent campaigning that rewards closed government.

Today's combative political culture rationalizes strict information control, a fear of public-facing failure, and excessive top-down oversight and risk-averse management in government, exacerbating the challenge of instituting a more open, collaborative culture in the federal public service and in many instances undercutting public servants' willingness and ability to experiment with innovative digital tools and approaches that divert from the status quo. I underscore in this study that, though political leadership is not a sufficient condition for digital era open government, it is a necessary condition. Serving as Canada's first digital era prime minister, Harper provided a particularly powerful depiction of the barriers that permanent campaigning, and more specifically a political leadership captured by it, pose to digital era open government; despite having the initial ambition to bring in new standards of government accountability, Harper enacted a public management philosophy anathema to open government from 2006 on, a historical reality undeniably to blame in part for the bureaucracy's lagged embrace of digital era open government from 2006 to 2015. Conservative public administration scholars have responded to this permanent campaigning culture and the information-hoarding public service that it cultivates with unrealistic calls for a return to the so-called golden age of the public service, one not burdened with onerous demands for transparency and public engagement. Their solution to the closed government effects of open government reforms is essentially to stop asking for open government or at least to lament the growth of transparency demands imposed on government.[10] Charting a different course in this study, I acknowledge that calls for open government cannot be wished away (we cannot travel back to the public service of the 1950s and 1960s), that these calls *should not* be wished away (since they pave the path to improved governance), but that these calls will fail without concomitant reforms to a political culture that, at present, seriously undermines the bureaucracy's willingness and ability to meet not only the demands of the ATIP regime but also the broader and essential demands of digital era open government. Is this proposed solution ambitious? Yes. Is it nonetheless the only effective means of resolving this challenge? Absolutely.

In this book, I uncover, alongside permanent campaigning effects, other conditions that ensure that today's bureaucracies not only continue to undertake activities that clearly align with closed government (as in secretive online surveillance of citizens) but that also ensure they are ill-equipped to implement digital era open government reforms even when they intend to and however urgent this imperative might be.

The findings reveal that a dearth of digital expertise within the ranks of the public service represents a direct but so far underappreciated barrier to the digital government reforms espoused in the literature. This barrier reflects an emerging preoccupation with digital skills acquisition in government human resource strategies and in part drives a global trend that sees government recruiting tech talent to new elite digital units within the state.

In addition, illustrating that the Canadian experience falls in line with larger global trends documented in recent empirical digital government research, I find that, in the federal bureaucracy, closed government is reinforced in large part by current interpretations and manifestations of Weberian bureaucratic structures (silos and hierarchies) and PPA's framing of the government-citizen relationship as properly circumscribed. And, picking up on important earlier contributions from Brown (2013), Roy (2008), and Kernaghan (2014a, 2014b), who have brought an appreciation for the peculiarities of the Westminster system to current theories on digital government, I illustrate the mismatch between open government reforms as currently conceived and conventions of ministerial accountability, public servant anonymity, and the traditional public service bargain. But it is here – in exploring the constraints imposed by current manifestations of Weberian, PPA, and Westminster norms – that my argument departs from mainstream thinking on digital era open government thus far.

Rather than arguing that entrenched legacies of closed government should simply be upended, I delve in this study into the dilemmas and trade-offs that a wholesale and rapid upheaval of these traditions would initiate. In doing so, I argue that Canada's current model of closed government is ineffective and ripe for reform, but I advocate a more cautious, holistically designed "opening" than that envisioned by dominant theories of digital government. This opening demands that governments carefully account for the risks that accompany both status quo closed government approaches (lagged adaptation, policy failures, human resource challenges, and breaches of democratic legitimacy) and the costs that accompany departures from closed government, as documented in a rich tradition of public administration research on the unintended costs of public service reforms and given the enduring relevance of core principles of neutral, equitable, accountable public administration. In other words, in this book I support the *direction* of reform advocated in dominant theories of digital era government – from closed to open – but raise and respond to questions (so far ignored) on the means by which this reform should be pursued while respecting the dictates of democratic governance. In particular, recognizing that the literature to date emerges primarily from American scholars and those outside the field of traditional public administration, I add an appreciation for the enduring relevance of values and tenets of the Westminster system to current theories of digital era open government.

To be sure, while critiquing existing theories of digital era open government for their naive and superficial treatments – or their wholesale denials – of the effectiveness, equity, and accountability risks that their reforms might invite, I make it clear that in practice an overzealous adherence to closed government approaches currently raises greater risks for the Government of Canada, not moves toward open government. The traditionalist perspective, preoccupied as it is with the potential risks and costs of open government reforms, dominates the public service to its own detriment. This unquestioned traditionalism has partly fuelled excessive top-down oversight of operational questions, undermining responsiveness to citizens' needs and stifling bottom-up innovation. The status quo equally rationalizes siloed approaches to information management that mean that data are not always shared or effectively used across various units of government. It can also mean that the time lag between mainstream societal adoption of new technologies and even early experimentation with such technologies in government is depressingly vast. The pendulum between closed and open government has currently swung too far toward closed. However, acknowledging the enduring relevance of traditional principles of public administration as laid down by Weber, PPA, and the original Westminster formulation, I argue equally that a wholesale swing toward an open government that abandons these principles is not the solution.

In sum, though theories of digital era open government have been quick to dispense with the past and eager to adopt tech sector–inspired principles of governance, I offer a defence in this book of the enduring relevance and efficacy of Weberian, PPA, and Westminster principles in the digital age, albeit a defence that acknowledges the need to update how we bring these principles to life in the daily practices of government. At present, excessive reliance on silos and hierarchies, unmitigated risk aversion, and models of policy development and service delivery closed by default must be upended, but in doing so we need to balance reform with an appreciation for the principles of accountability, equitable treatment of citizens, and public service neutrality that historically have underpinned, and continue to underpin, robust democratic governance.[11]

How can these principles be made consistent with a more open government in the digital age? In which cases will these principles override the impetus for widely promoted digital government reforms? And how quickly and by which specific measures should this project of reform be implemented given the rapid pace of change and uncertainty characterizing the digital age? It is to these questions that the following chapters respond.

Research Design

My arguments in this book draw on five separate data sources compiled and analyzed from 2011 to 2016. The first of these data sources consisted of media reports covering the federal public service, the leadership styles of Prime Ministers Harper and (toward the close of the project) Trudeau, and the key initiatives and technologies relevant to digital government reforms in Canada at the time of the study (e.g., social media, open data, open government, GCTools, Blueprint 2020, and policy innovation). They were identified using Google Alerts, through manual monitoring of major national newspapers, and by following hashtags on Twitter that track activity within the federal public service, including "#w2p," "#goc," "#cpsr," "#GC2020," "#policyinnovation," and "#GCDigital."

These Twitter conversations also formed part of the second major data source from which the study drew: Government of Canada social media activity. Twitter conversations organized around these hashtags and a series of public servant–led unofficial blogs covering federal public management provided insight into public servants' perceptions of digital technologies and their implications for governing and provided information on the digital government initiatives that I explore here.[12] In most cases, this information was culled simply by following these hashtags and blogs as sources of data in their own right, but in other cases I worked with the community of public servants engaged in these networks to fact-check and crowdsource information.[13]

More formally, over a two-month period in 2012, I archived and analyzed all Government of Canada departments' activity on Twitter to categorize the content of tweets and to investigate the types of actors with whom government departments interact on the platform. More details on the methods used to collect and analyze these data are included in Chapter 3.

Government documents served as the third source of data informing the study. In this category, I include official government websites, publications, and reports as well as internal unpublished documents. I identified and collected public documents through automated Google Alerts, on the recommendation of interviewees, through systematic scans of government websites and document repositories, and through references to relevant documents within documents already collected. Several interviewees shared unpublished internal documents (e.g., "decks," departmental reports, and GCpedia pages[14]). I also systematically searched the Government of Canada's online repository listing already completed Access to Information requests, using terms relevant to the research (e.g., "social media," "policy innovation," "Blueprint 2020," "open data," and "open government") to guide the search. This proved to be a more efficient and expedient means of accessing relevant internal documentation and ensured that I did not issue new requests that duplicated those already completed.

The fourth source of data informing this study is composed of in-depth interviews conducted with thirty-one Canadian federal public servants and one external adviser to the federal government between 2012 and 2016 (see the Appendix for an anonymized list of interviewees).[15] In many cases, I conducted follow-up interviews and engaged in subsequent email exchanges to clarify points and follow up on initiatives that had advanced since the initial interviews.[16] To ensure that I accessed a broad range of perspectives within the government (as opposed to interviewing only like-minded individuals or those in particular functional areas), throughout recruitment I balanced snowballing with deliberate efforts to recruit interviewees from functional areas and levels in the hierarchy underrepresented in the sample. To be sure, in doing so, I did not attempt to generate a statistically representative sample; I selected interviewees because of their unique perspectives and knowledge, which meant in some cases that they were entirely unrepresentative of a broader grouping within government, as is the case for elite, key informant interviews (Van Audenhove 2007). In this process, interviewees were deliberately selected from the areas of communications and stakeholder engagement, policy analysis and program delivery, information management, and information technology to ensure that a broad range of functions relevant to digital government informed the study. I also interviewed officials across varying levels of authority – from co-op students to senior executives.

Most of the initiatives by which the federal government has integrated digital technologies into its work are led centrally, from within the Chief Information Officer Branch of the Treasury Board Secretariat. Accordingly, this unit is well represented in the sample of interviewees. I also draw a "view from the centre" through interviews with officials in the Privy Council Office (PCO), in particular those tasked with communications and consultations functions. Capturing the varied experience of line departments adapting to the digital age is necessarily more complicated given the variety of organizational cultures, service and policy remits, and management styles that exist across the federal government. It is not possible to provide an in-depth study of each department and each of its constituent program areas and functional operations in one study. So, in Chapter 3, I focus on the uptake of digital technologies in one department – Employment and Social Development Canada – selected for its large size and varied programs (providing the occasion to explore how the digital age supports horizontal collaboration among actors in large, differentiated bureaucracies) and given that the department manages the lion's share of the government's citizen-facing services. The interview sample thus includes a higher number of interviews with officials in this department than in other line departments. To provide a more varied departmental perspective, I include analyses of other line departments' experiences with digital technologies where they arose in interviews, social media analyses, and documentary reviews.

Most interviews were recorded and transcribed (one was not recorded because of technical difficulties, and in one case the interviewee did not agree to being recorded or quoted). Except for this interviewee, all agreed to be quoted anonymously in the study (save one who requested attribution). In a number of cases, interviewees engaged in the federal government's official digital government initiatives proved to be enthusiasts of open government and networked information sharing. They lived highly public lives as public servants – far from the ideal of anonymity described in the traditional Westminster bargain – and were therefore easy to identify and contact and eager to participate in the research study. Indeed, investigating digital government in the federal bureaucracy during the time period of this research (from 2011 to 2016) was a fascinating study in contrasts, with the Harper government regularly criticized for closing government to the public, as I enjoyed unprecedented access to public servants who openly and frankly discussed their work online.

Seven semi-structured, in-depth interviews conducted with officials in the UK government comprised the last source of data for this study. These interviews support analysis of the drivers of the federal government's open government initiative in Chapter 4 and, given the UK government's current role in shaping international digital capacity-building trends, the discussion of digital government units (DGUs) in Chapter 6.

I thematically studied media reports, social media data, government documents, and interview transcriptions. I developed themes both deductively (based on previous literature and the study's guiding theoretical propositions) and inductively as they arose on reviewing the data (Fereday and Muir-Cochrane 2006). The process was iterative and reflexive, relying on a "careful reading and re-reading of the data" (Rice and Ezzy 1999, 258), as individual data sets were analyzed in parallel in a complementary fashion. I revisited documents in light of findings generated in interviews, cross-checked interviewees' statements against those of other respondents, and recoded documents/transcriptions once new themes arose. Following good practice in qualitative case study research, I combined the data sets to triangulate individual findings, "continually checking, questioning, and theoretically interpreting the findings" (Kvale 1996, 241) to uncover biases, inaccuracies, and misrepresentations (both my own and within the data).

Structure of the Book

From Chapters 2 to 5, I follow a quasi-historical structure, moving from a discussion of the federal bureaucracy as it operated in the pre–digital age and tracking the various initiatives by which the bureaucracy encountered – in some cases clashed with – digital phenomena from the mid-2000s on. In Chapter 2, I detail Canada's particular brand of Weberian-Westminster closed government, laying a foundation for subsequent chapters by walking through the reforms and enduring constraints ensuring that silos and hierarchies continue to narrow both the bureaucrat-bureaucrat relationship and the relationship that links the federal government to citizens. In Chapter 3, I explore what happens when a closed government integrates social media into its operations. I detail the mismatch between the rapid, networked information exchanges that social media facilitate and the siloed, hierarchical approaches to government-citizen interaction at play in Weberian bureaucracies. I also present a series of coordination and accountability dilemmas that a pluralistic model of open government–citizen interaction raises and that are not easily answered with our existing theories of analogue era or digital era government alike.

Following on departments' efforts to take up social media, the federal bureaucracy next sought to adjust its operations for the digital age through an official open government initiative, launched in 2011. I analyze this initiative in Chapter 4. In an effort to bring together two disparate literatures addressing the digital age and its impact on government, I investigate the extent to which a political culture of permanent campaigning and the unique styles of individual political leaders shape the potential for digital era open government. In Canada in particular, one might argue that public servants faced what is possibly the least amenable political environment imaginable to engage in the kinds of open government that mainstream theories of digital government promote. The digital age emerged in the wake of the Human Resources Development Canada grants and contributions "boondoggle" and the Sponsorship Scandal, each of which introduced new command and control auditing and top-down oversight mechanisms that constrained the scope for collaboration with nongovernmental actors. These mechanisms also exacerbated an existing reporting burden and a bureaucratic fear of public failure at odds with innovation and experimentation in the public service.

Enter Stephen Harper, a prime minister under whom government communications were tightly controlled, and in some cases (notably in the Economic Action Plan) politicized to serve partisan ends, and under whom mainstream media were denied access to ministers and scientists' ability to speak publicly about their research was limited. Rather than encouraging open public debate on policy decisions, the Harper government twice prorogued Parliament to avoid a vote of nonconfidence and scrutiny of controversial government actions. The Harper government also withheld information on public expenditures, leading to regular criticism from Kevin Page, who occupied the position of parliamentary budget officer that Harper himself had created (Harris 2014; Marland 2016; Martin 2011; Page 2012). With Harper serving as Canada's first digital era prime minister, could we really have expected the public service to embrace a more open, collaborative style of public management in the early phases of social media, crowdsourcing, and the global open data movement? Situating Canada's official open government initiative in its broader political context, in Chapter 4 I argue that the open data, open dialogue, and open information commitments comprising this initiative produced at best an open(ish) government under Harper, at once spurred by a neoliberal interest in open data among Stockwell Day and Tony Clement (presidents of the Treasury Board under whom the open government initiative was instituted) but ultimately marred by a dearth of credible political leadership, the insularity of public servants, and an absence of appropriate skills and accountability and management frameworks to guide mass online public engagement.

In Chapter 5, I shift gears, exposing that the federal public service was not strictly confined in a closed government framework throughout the Harper years. Rather, federal public servants undertook a series of incremental and largely under-the-radar efforts to open the bureaucracy internally from the late 2000s on, challenging the silos and hierarchies that have long been decried as barriers to the effectiveness of government. I highlight an unknown narrative of public service renewal that unfolded under Harper's watch, but I also argue that these efforts were so small scale and incremental that their impact was necessarily minimal. I conclude the chapter by considering the limits of public servant–led management reforms, returning to consider the crucial role of political leadership in efforts to renew the public service for the digital age.

In the last two chapters, I turn from diagnosis to prescription. In Chapter 6, I address a barrier to digital government that has become a top concern of governments globally: the digital skills gap. The traditional toolkit of IT specialists and policy and program officers alike has not kept pace with the demands of the digital age. I evaluate the contracting, partnership, and recruitment strategies that could help to address this skills gap, focusing on the digital government units that have emerged as the option of choice for digital government reform globally.

Finally, in Chapter 7, I use the book's findings as a springboard to launch five recommendations to guide digital government reform in Canada, integrating into this analysis a discussion of changes instituted under the Liberal government elected in October 2015. In doing so, I provide one of the first scholarly evaluations of the Trudeau government's early record on public management reform. I evaluate how a change in leadership to one that overtly champions the benefits of open government will, as per the findings from this study, serve as a significant driver of digital government capacity building. I also flag the enduring administrative barriers and political dynamics ensuring that open government remains, as it always has, an incomplete project with no guarantee of success. In particular, in this final set of recommendations, I challenge political leaders, public service officials, and citizens alike, calling for a change in political culture that would ensure the imperative to become more open does not lead to the perverse outcome of ever more closed governments impervious to innovation, riddled by fear of public-facing failure, and driven by narrow, partisan media management strategies.

This book is inspired in part by the need to tell Canada's story of second-wave digital government, as has emerged from the mid-2000s on, a substantive, comprehensive account of which has not yet been provided or blended into larger international debates on digital era government.[17] Equally, I have endeavoured to combine the fresh perspective of unconventional theories of digital government inspired by the tech sector with the insights of traditional public administration scholarship. These literatures have developed as two solitudes, yet as I argue in this book each is strengthened by contending with the other.

Digital government theorists must better account for the potential risks of the open government reforms that they call for and the practices and principles that will mitigate these risks in practice. Mainstream public administration research offers this insight to theories of government as a platform, Digital Era Governance, and Wiki Government and to their enthusiasts within the halls of government institutions. For their part, public administration scholars have largely been asleep at the wheel, producing scholarship that ignores the digital technologies and related societal transformations with which governments and citizens are grappling, a blind spot that, should it persist, will cast doubt on the enduring relevance of the field. In this regard, theories of digital government proposed thus far should open public administration scholars' eyes to the pressures and opportunities that digital era governance raises. Finally, acknowledging the widespread uptake of digital era open government reforms across the globe, I aim to provide practical prescriptive insight that at once asserts the need to reform closed government traditions that have developed from late-nineteenth-century and early-twentieth-century theories of public administration while also respecting the core democratic values that these early theories rightfully branded on the modern welfare state.

The next chapter sets the foundation for this work, detailing how and why closed government has endured as a cornerstone of Canadian public administration despite decades of reforms that have attempted to upend this legacy.

2

Canada's Closed Government

My dear boy, it is a contradiction in terms: you can be open or you can have government.

– *Yes, Minister* (1980)

At the risk of falling into the cliché of citing *Yes, Minister* in a public administration text, I invoke this quotation from the first episode of the BBC series because it perfectly captures the reality that public sector bureaucracies have traditionally been closed not by accident but by design. In this scene, Sir Humphrey Appleby, a senior civil servant, offers this observation to his colleague while commenting on his new minister's early desire to institute open government reforms in his ministry. Although the episode focuses on the classic interpretation of open government as a vehicle of transparency and public accountability – with Appleby arguing the cynical view that staying in power demands opacity – his argument on the incongruence of governing and openness extends much further in practice. It is in fact at the heart of the foundation narratives on which Canada's Westminster bureaucracy is built.

Beginning in the late nineteenth century, Weber's theory of bureaucracy and the model of Progressive-Era Public Administration that followed in the early twentieth century dictated that the civil service be closed internally, with strict lines of authority and responsibility parcelling bureaucrats across mutually distinct vertical silos and horizontal lines in the hierarchy (Dunleavy and Hood 1994; Hood 2000). These traditions equally circumscribed the scope for bureaucrats to interface with those outside their walls, made manifest in the Westminster concept of bureaucratic anonymity (Grube 2013; Tait 1996) but also in PPA's concern over the inequity that can arise when public officials interact with the public outside standardized, tightly managed protocols.

Canada's public service has attempted to depart over the years from the closed government foundation on which the institution was built. But forays into horizontal government and efforts to engage with the public have met the stickiness of historical legacy, hindered by a concomitant strengthening of siloed and hierarchical structures and worldviews among public servants. The advent of permanent campaigning (Marland, Giasson, and Esselment 2017; Savoie 2013) in Canadian politics has further rationalized closed government in the federal civil service, limiting bureaucrats' willingness and ability to break from silos and hierarchies internally, to interact fluidly with citizens and organizations outside these silos and hierarchies, and to experiment with new service and policy approaches whose potential failings might invite public criticism. Yet more than simply proving to be a case of institutional sclerosis, or a breach of democratic responsiveness, in certain cases closed government endures in the Canadian public service for compelling pragmatic and ethical reasons.

In this chapter, I detail the legacies and constraints that have traditionally complicated and continue to complicate the transition from closed government to open government in the Government of Canada. And, recognizing that any effort to "transform" established procedures, worldviews, cultures, and structures – as theories of digital era open government intend to do – are best launched with an appreciation for why the objects of transformation were instituted in the first place, I outline the original and enduring rationales for closed government. In doing so, I set the stage for subsequent chapters. These chapters illustrate: first, how these barriers to open government persist in the face of networked digital technologies; second, why contemporary manifestations of closed government are incompatible with the demands of governing in the digital age; and, third, the complex dilemmas that must be confronted and resolved to upend these historical legacies while continuing to respect core principles of democratic governance.

The Closed Bureaucrat-Bureaucrat Relationship

The first closed relationship at the heart of closed government is the relationship, or more accurately relationships, linking bureaucrats operating within the public service. These are the relationships at play in the daily internal management and operations of the federal bureaucracy, including the relationship between superiors and their subordinates (e.g., between managers and their staff); between bureaucrats operating in different departments; between bureaucrats operating in different subunits of the same department;

and between bureaucrats operating in different functional areas (e.g., those in information technology versus those in program evaluation).

The closed bureaucrat-bureaucrat relationship developed in response to the foundational principles underpinning the organization and operations of the federal public service. These foundational principles are documented in the work of Max Weber (1994), the German sociologist whose theory of bureaucratic organization, originally based on observations of the Prussian army, informed the earliest formal theorization of public administration in the late nineteenth century and early twentieth century: Progressive-Era Public Administration (or "traditional" or "old" public administration as it is sometimes called) (Dunleavy and Hood 1994; Hood 2000).

Drawing on Weber's theory of bureaucracy, and following the same logic that inspired top-down, functionally specialized allocation of tasks and authority in the "scientific management" theories underpinning manufacturing at the turn of the century (Taylor 1967), PPA asserted that administrative efficiency and effectiveness are achieved through tightly managed internal workflows. This rigid management is achieved first by classifying individuals into mutually exclusive lines of operations defined by distinct functions; these are the "silos" (sometimes called "stovepipes") into which different departments, units, and functions in government are organized as nonoverlapping units with designated authority for specific tasks. The second mechanism through which PPA organized the work of the public sector is hierarchy, the principle by which the personal discretion of individual bureaucrats is ever more limited as one moves down the hierarchical chain of command, with superiors allocated greater discretion and authority than the subordinates reporting to them, and subordinates enjoying discretion and authority only to the extent that their superiors delegate it to them (Dunleavy and Hood 1994; Jarvis 2014a).

Importantly, the silos and hierarchies of government are not simply organizational structures pursued in the name of efficiency and effectiveness. Rather, these silos and hierarchies also serve as accountability mechanisms in bureaucratic organizations. With tasks siloed off to particular actors, it is possible to identify who is responsible for which tasks and accordingly to hold these individuals to account for failures in the execution of those tasks. And, with authority expanding as one moves up the chain of hierarchy in a given government organization, it is possible to identify superiors and make them accountable for the actions of their subordinates. As a corollary of this vertical accountability relationship, superiors possess "the legitimacy to hold to account – to scrutinize, pass judgment and levy sanctions or rewards – [that] derives from the direct authority a superior holds over subordinate actors" (Jarvis 2014a, 459). In Westminster systems of government, PPA's hierarchical accountability mechanism is embodied most clearly in the convention of ministerial accountability, whereby the minister, as the highest level of authority in his or her department, can be called to account for all activities taking place within the department.

The silos and hierarchies advocated by Weber and enshrined in PPA and the Westminster system have served as a cornerstone of the Canadian federal public service since its earliest years of development (Prince 2007; Savoie 2003, 2004). However, these silos and hierarchies – and the individuals occupying them – have evolved over time. In the post–Second World War era leading up to the 1970s, the silos and hierarchies comprising the federal bureaucracy were occupied by a comparatively small cadre of officials, with much of the public service housed in offices in the East Block of Parliament (Granatstein 1982; Savoie 2003), a far cry from the sprawling public service that we see today, with its 257,034 employees (Treasury Board Secretariat 2016a), looming office complexes in Gatineau and Ottawa, and its regional offices and Service Canada centres across the country.

The bureaucrats comprising the early public service were also far less diverse than those of today's federal government, not only in terms of demographics (composed as the public service was primarily of white men of similar educational pedigree), but also in terms of function. That is, in the early days of the federal public service, the tasks of government were comparatively one-note, focused on a narrow range of policy advisory and service delivery tasks, versus those of today, when the expansion of the welfare state, globalization, and the emergence of a more complex, diverse Canadian society have opened up a slew of new functional areas of responsibility for the federal government, both in terms of the policy issues addressed and in terms of the tasks required to address them. There are now officials responsible for communications, information technology, information management, access to information programs, language translation, stakeholder engagement, evaluation, and scientific research, to name but a few of the tasks that make up daily life in today's federal public service.

Reflecting on the smaller and simpler federal bureaucracy of days past, Donald Savoie (2003, 65) has characterized Canada's early public service as "a world akin to a small village, where everyone knew everyone else, recognized their own place in the general scheme, and knew how to get things done without a fuss." Although rightfully acknowledging that a return to the exclusive, monochromatic, and male-dominated public service inhabiting Savoie's "small village" is neither desirable nor feasible, scholars and practitioners nonetheless continue to pine for this "golden age" of the public service: that is, for a bureaucracy in which everyone (i.e., public servants and their ministers and staff) "recognize their own place" and "get things done without a fuss," to use Savoie's language (see Axworthy and Burch 2010; and Granatstein 1982). This desire – consistent in the classics of Canadian public administration – reflects the idea that the silos and hierarchies organizing work in the public service used to be fit for purpose but are now out of step with a large and heterogeneous bureaucracy. That is, though today these organizational structures endure, depicted in departmental "org charts" with their vertically arranged, functionally distinct lines of operations, the benefits of these structures – as means both of efficiently and effectively organizing government's work and of holding government to account – have waned as the public service has become larger and more complex in tandem with the larger and more complex set of public issues and functions with which the federal government is now tasked. The first set of attacks against these enduring structures of closed government in the federal public service targets the historical expansion and strengthening of silos.

Silos: A Barrier to Horizontality

Writing as early as 1976, two-time Clerk of the Privy Council and eventual Senator Michael Pitfield remarked that "we have not viewed government sufficiently as a total system" (19), an observation consistent across Canadian public administration scholarship and practitioner literature for decades. Observers complain that public servants lack peripheral vision, focusing only on the issues and tasks at play immediately before them, as opposed to adopting a horizontal, whole of government, or systems view within and across departments and functions. This siloed model produces duplication, allows policy or service gaps to arise, and undermines the potential for necessary collaboration and coordination across departments addressing increasingly cross-cutting policy issues and wicked problems, such as climate change and poverty reduction (Bakvis and Juillet 2004; Jarvis and Levasseur 2015; Peters 1998; Sproule-Jones 2000). A rumour popular in Ottawa today goes that access to information requests – instituted to allow outsiders to access government information – are initiated in some cases from within the bureaucracy itself, with public servants claiming that this formal procedure can be easier to navigate than the fractured channels of information sharing (and with-holding) within the public service. This is emblematic of a larger networking deficiency within the public service, inspiring concern about the costs that a deeply ingrained culture of silos imposes on today's federal government.

To be sure, the federal bureaucracy in certain cases has successfully fought against the trappings of siloed work models. For example, early forays into e-government in the late 1990s and mid-2000s showed that the bureaucracy was capable of adopting a more horizontal perspective in its work. Growing out of Government Online, which brought 130 services onto the web between 1999 and 2006, Service Canada earned the government global praise for its integration of multiple services, previously delivered by individual depart-ments, into one web portal. Importantly, the portal earned praise because it organized information according to citizens' service needs (a "citizen-centric" perspective) in lieu of organizing information according to the siloed depart-mental structures of government, structures that, though meaningful to federal public servants working in these silos, mean little to the average service user unacquainted with the opaque alphabet soup of acronym-labelled depart-ments, programs, and sections that comprise the secret language of federal bureaucrats and Ottawa insiders (Allen et al. 2001; Borins 2007). More recently, Shared Services Canada, introduced in 2011, adopted a horizontal perspective in rationalizing the IT services provided to forty-three depart-ments and agencies, producing common data centres, email services, and corporate services in lieu of departments managing these services individually (albeit while facing delays, cost overruns, and criticism from departments and the auditor general).

Herman Bakvis and Luc Juillet (2004) note that horizontality has long been a goal of Canadian public administration, evident in the mandates of central agencies such as the Treasury Board Secretariat and the Privy Council Office, and Public Services and Procurement Canada (formerly Public Works and Government Services Canada), each tasked with bridging the work of disparate departments through common corporate policies and guidelines and through central direction and infrastructure to coordinate implementa-tion of government policy. Deputy minister (DM) committees, which bring together DMs from across departments to discuss common issues, also sup-port horizontality across departmental silos. And, though its place in the governance of the federal bureaucracy has waned from the 1970s on (Savoie 1999) (with a promise of its return under Justin Trudeau's Liberal govern-ment), the convention of cabinet government is well accepted as an ideal (if at times unpursued) means of horizontally coordinating the independent work of ministries. Bakvis and Juillet (2004) also document four specific horizontal initiatives in which line departments were engaged from the 1990s to the mid-2000s: the Climate Change Secretariat, the Innovation Strategy, the Vancouver Agreement, and the Urban Aboriginal Strategy. Evidently, silos do not trump collaboration as a rule, and horizontal government is an achievable objective in certain cases.

Federal public servants themselves are clearly aware that, contradicting Weber's framing of the functional separation of tasks, siloed work models reduce government's effectiveness and efficiency more than they enable it. Nine separate task forces struck by the clerk of the Privy Council in 1995 affirmed the need for whole of government, horizontal approaches in the federal bureaucracy (Task Force on Horizontal Issues 1996). One of these taskforces was dedicated specifically to the subject, titled "The Task Force on Horizontal Issues," and called for senior management to bring a "'Team Government of Canada' perspective into daily decision-making and direction" in order to "help shift corporate culture" (35). The report offered specific suggestions for senior managers attempting to implement this shift, including the introduction of senior management meetings and departmental work plans focused on horizontal policy issues and the recommendation that senior management challenge policy staff to develop partnerships across departments.

However, despite a clear recognition that today's policy issues demand collaboration and coordination across the government, and despite the notable exceptions discussed here, the bureaucracy in general is ill-equipped and in some cases unwilling to support horizontal initiatives in practice (Jarvis 2016; Lindquist 2012). Public servants struggle to define common goals across silos and suffer a dearth of human resource capabilities favourable to collaboration. In addition, though central agencies such as the TBS and PCO are crucial enablers of horizontal initiatives, these agencies are not always sure how to provide the leadership, nor do they possess the skills and knowledge, that would allow them to play this role (Bakvis and Juillet 2004). As Guy Peters (1998, 1) has observed, horizontal government remains "the Administrative Holy Grail," a "perennial quest for the practitioners of government."

Finally, and most fundamentally, cross-silo collaboration remains a difficult endeavour given the accountability challenges that it raises. Although the core questions of accountability – who is accountable for what and to whom? – can become muddied when actors across different silos are asked to collaborate without a clearly defined horizontal, or shared, accountability framework, such frameworks can be made compatible with vertical hierarchical accountability structures in individual departments (Aucoin and Jarvis 2005; Jarvis and Levasseur 2015; Phillips and Howard 2012; Phillips and Levasseur 2004; Sproule-Jones 2000). However, in practice, accountability in the comfort zones of vertical silos is standard fare, and public servants tend to continue to view themselves as accountable within the hierarchical structures of their departments before they perceive their accountability to cross-departmental initiatives; observing this trend in the government of Saskatchewan, Ken Rasmussen (1999, 342) observes that "departmental loyalties" endure. And, lest we forget, defined vertical ministerial accountability is partnered with defined vertical ministerial attribution. In a context of silos, a minister must own departmental failures, but she also gets to own departmental success. Given this, horizontality can be resisted because it means that an individual minister and her loyal public servants have to share the announcements, the praise, and the political capital that they would otherwise enjoy in whole. Here Weber's legacy, embodied in ministers' and public servants' default identification with their own functionally distinct silos of operations, shines through. Absent an appreciation for "corporate," "enterprise," or "whole of government" accountability and success, the initiation and implementation of horizontal initiatives suffer.

So, whereas in the "small village" that constituted the early public service collaboration across portfolios was a case of scheduling a lunch among a small group of like-minded, acquainted officials – the example that Savoie (2003) himself uses in describing this small village life – rendering silos a less obstructive barrier to coordination, today's large, varied, and deeply siloed bureaucracy defies coordination and even basic information sharing.[1] Just as a bird can love a fish but find no place to live (Stein 1964, 131), so too actors who attempt to collaborate across silos have traditionally lacked a common home. On which closed intranet will their common documents live? To which manager will they report? More fundamentally, how will these bureaucrats even know that the others exist, addressing a complementary policy issue that could provide a possible opportunity for collaboration? There is no lunch table large enough to house and coordinate cross-silo collaboration in today's federal bureaucracy. Thus, lacking the experience and capacity required to institute horizontal coordination mechanisms and concomitant accountability frameworks, silos have persisted in large part because the business of government must roll on, and silos currently provide the default (if suboptimal) structure most readily available to organize this work.

Adding to concerns about the closed relationships that silos introduce to the federal public service, observers and practitioners also take aim at hierarchy, the Weberian legacy that can render the vertical superior-subordinate relationships of the bureaucracy closed.

Hierarchy: A Barrier to Decision-Implementation Coherence and Innovation

Despair over the hierarchical relationships linking superiors and subordinates is a long-standing theme in Canadian public administration. Indeed, three key historical reform initiatives of the federal government – the Glassco Commission of 1960, Public Service 2000 in 1990, and La Relève in 1995 – as well as the government's latest reform proposal, Blueprint 2020 (introduced in 2011), all contend that the health of the public service hinges largely on the health of the relationships linking superiors and subordinates and specifically in enabling more empowering, trusting, and open relationships between management and staff. However, despite historical and ongoing efforts to engender such a relationship, the hierarchical ties linking higher- and lower-ranked bureaucrats remain generally characterized by a top-down desire for control, a dearth of trust, and limited or ineffective communication. So, as with silos, despite efforts to improve these hierarchical relationships, they remain objects of attack in contemporary discussions on the federal public service. This attack is launched on two fronts – on hierarchy as a barrier to decision-implementation coherence and on hierarchy as a barrier to innovation.

In the first of these attacks, hierarchy as the organizational structure of choice in government is viewed as problematic today because, as government has become larger and more complex, the efficiency and effectiveness of hierarchical reporting mechanisms – upward information flows from subordinates to superiors and vice versa – have waned (Roy 2008; Savoie 2003). This issue, in a sense, is the same as that for the silos discussed above (since it reflects a dearth of opportunities for information sharing among bureaucrats), though it is distinct as a problem of hierarchy specifically insofar as the inability of lower-level staff to communicate effectively with higher-level staff, and vice versa, can create two problematic scenarios. First, there can be a gap between the superiors with the power to make decisions and the subordinates with the information that could strengthen those decisions. Second, there can be a gap between those with a "bird's-eye view" of the organization and those completing tasks and making decisions meant to implement this strategic view at lower levels.

This problem is particularly acute when decisions and their implementation relate to cross-cutting policy issues and different functions across the bureaucracy: that is, when issues and operations are horizontal. For example, how will a senior manager in Public Services and Procurement Canada become aware of the implications of a decision on IT procurement for a low-level policy analyst in a line department – say, Health Canada – reliant on a particular piece of software for her work? When a communications officer recognizes a growing demographic of users requesting information on a program of another department, how will he feed this information to the senior officials briefing a minister on the ongoing utility of that program? When hierarchical chains of information exchange meet strict silos, the efficiency and effectiveness gains that these organizational structures are meant to achieve are difficult to discern.

Predictably, the limitations of hierarchical information flows appear to be more prevalent as the space between superiors and subordinates widens. The 2014 Public Service Employee Survey found that employees have strong relationships with their immediate supervisors, with 75 percent noting in particular that their immediate supervisors effectively share information relevant to their work and 72 percent finding that their immediate supervisors provide useful feedback on work performance.[2] However, when we consider the relationship between these lower-level staff and senior managers, the picture is more dismal. Only 45 percent of employees thought that their senior managers make effective and timely decisions, and only 47 percent thought that essential information flows effectively from senior management to junior staff. Slightly better, but still low, only 58 percent of staff believed that they had access to senior management in their particular department or agency (Treasury Board Secretariat 2014a).[3]

With this final survey result, one might reasonably retort that by design, in a bureaucracy, junior staff are not supposed to have access to senior staff. That is, in an organizational structure geared to efficiency and effectiveness, senior officials should receive information through the filters of intermediate layers of authority, avoiding the information overload that can impede decision making. But there still remains a sense that, just as the bureaucracy has grown in complexity, so too have the hierarchical information flows and feedback mechanisms in the federal government, producing problematic knowledge gaps that limit both the quality of high-level decisions and the quality of low-level implementation. The filters through which this information flows have become clogged as the hierarchies of the bureaucracy have become more complex and reporting processes more dense (Savoie 2003). This problem has been exacerbated by the introduction of email and word processing software and the explosion of documentation that they produce, generating in turn mass frustration and significant time costs as documents move up and down chains of hierarchy, subject to layered and often incomprehensible tracked changes, version control issues, and processing delays.

The second and more commonly cited complaint against hierarchy targets its role in limiting public sector innovation (Borins 2002; Carstensen and Bason 2012; Jarvis 2016; Olsen 2006). Here public sector innovation is defined as per Bason (2010, 34), as "the process of creating new ideas and turning them into value for society." This definition acknowledges that "new ideas" in some cases are existing ideas applied in new ways to different contexts (versus always resulting from inventions created "from scratch") and that even failed innovations "create value for society" insofar as identifying optimal solutions demands experimenting with (and subsequently discarding) ideas that, when tested, prove to be suboptimal. This definition frames innovation as a process – as a verb – versus innovation exclusively as an output or end product – as a noun (Schultz Larsen 2015).[4]

Hierarchy is critiqued as a barrier to innovation in part because of the weak information flows that dense hierarchical reporting relationships foster; when new ideas for improving policies, services, or internal corporate processes are generated lower down the chain of command, it can be difficult for these ideas to make their way up the chain of command to those with the power to act on them. In addition to strengthening these information flows, another solution would see those lower down the chain encouraged and enabled to divert from the status quo in order to test novel approaches to policy development, service delivery, or internal process. This approach essentially calls for a more open, trusting relationship between superiors and subordinates, one that allows discretionary power to be distributed more fluidly throughout vertical accountability structures, versus most or all power residing at higher levels in the organization, and tightly regulated through draconian top-down rules and dictates.

In practice, we have not seen this fluid approach to discretionary power and a concomitant tolerance for diversions from the status quo in the federal bureaucracy. Instead, overly dense bureaucratic structures preserve stability and consistency and prioritize consistency of process through rigid rule compliance over quality of result (Borins 2002; Hood 2000; Mendelsohn 2015). In this context, the Canadian bureaucratic system tends to produce and reward risk-averse superiors, prone to micromanagement, as opposed to managers who encourage experimentation, embrace change and uncertainty, and exhibit trust in their staff to navigate diversions from status quo procedures (Savoie 2013).

This trend has been reinforced by the emergence of permanent campaigning tactics (Marland, Giasson, and Esselment 2017; Savoie 2013): that is, aggressive, adversarial, partisan electioneering outside the official election period. In this context, governments and political parties now face constant and more potent threats of politically costly public scrutiny and exposé, producing political leaders who demand "error-free government" from the public service (Himelfarb 2005; Jarvis 2016; Lynch 2007, 2008; Savoie 2013).

The current climate of governing is equally thick with top-down accountability regimes that impose onerous reporting burdens on managers, ensuring that repeated calls to "let managers manage" since Glassco have been deafened by an ever-growing web of rules and reporting requirements that stifle managers' ability to manage their staff with sufficient discretion and flexibility (Savoie 2013). Many of these new demands have resulted from the directives of central agencies, especially the Treasury Board Secretariat, the "bureaucracy's bureaucracy" and holder of the pen on corporate rules. Others emerge from the introduction of new legal requirements imposed on the public service (e.g., the Official Languages Act and the Access to Information and Privacy Act). The growth in the number of officers and agents of Parliament, beginning with the auditor general in 1878, has also created new oversight mechanisms and reporting requirements. The Gomery Commission's conclusion that the Sponsorship Scandal was the product of bureaucratic and not simply political failings spawned a new slate of "command and control" regulations applied to the public service – dubbed an "overkill" (Aucoin 2006, 20) – and eventually to the Federal Accountability Act (FAA), introduced by Stephen Harper's Conservative government in 2006. The passing of the FAA was followed by the creation of three new agents of Parliament to oversee the executive: the conflict of interest and ethics commissioner, the public sector integrity commissioner, and the commissioner of lobbying.

These dual pressures – political demands for error-free government and growth in rules and oversight – present challenges at all levels of the bureaucracy, but they pose particularly acute constraints on managers' willingness and ability to foster innovation among their staff. That is, for managers, the present culture of governing creates incentives dictating that "it is better to avoid sin than to ask for forgiveness" (Savoie 2013, 227). Staying the course is a safer bet than diverting from the status quo and failing, even if the status quo produces suboptimal outcomes. In turn, these risk-averse managers limit the scope for bottom-up innovation by modelling a risk-averse, status quo orientation to their staff. Subordinates parrot the behaviour of their superiors and, responding to the reward structures that risk-averse managers institute, become status quo oriented, focused more on adhering to established rules and processes than on identifying and acting on opportunities to improve policies, services, or corporate processes. Crucially, this rules-obsessed, risk-averse culture of accountability displaces measures that prioritize learning from successes and failures (Jarvis 2014b), the very model of accountability on which innovation hinges, given that this approach to accountability embraces reflective learning from failure as a stepping stone to the adoption of superior policy solutions and improved public services.

Public servants themselves express disdain for the rules and overly complex corporate oversight mechanisms that they face, as revealed in the 2014 Public Service Employee Survey. Twenty-one percent of employees responded that they "always/almost always" "feel that the quality of [their] work suffers because of too many approval stages," 25 percent thought that it "often" suffers, and 27 percent said that it "sometimes" suffers. Only 7 percent said that it "never" suffers from too many approval stages. On whether "overly complicated or unnecessary business processes" reduce the quality of their work, 18 percent reported that it "always/almost always" does, 24 percent that it "often" does, 31 percent reported "sometimes," and only 14 and 8 percent, respectively, responded "rarely" and "never/almost never" (Treasury Board Secretariat 2014a).

Commenting on the confluence of permanent campaigning and the proliferation of rules limiting the capacity for innovation among both managers and their staff, then Clerk of the Privy Council Kevin Lynch noted in 2008 that

> the reality is not one of poor attitudes but bad incentives. We have mired public servants in a complex, and often conflicting, web-of-rules that encourages inaction over taking responsible risks, and discourages innovation in favour of the status quo. This is amplified

by a "gotcha" mentality in the press and at times in Parliament, where error free government, not risk management by government, has become the benchmark for success or failure.

In sum, risk-averse and ever more complex hierarchical management structures produce an innovation vacuum in the public service, contributing to a public service often accused of embodying the pejorative stereotype of bureaucracy: sclerotic, outdated, and inefficient, focused on short-term issues, red tape, and process as opposed to the more uncertain, potentially failure-ridden pursuit of policy, service, and process innovations.

Thus far, I have explored the internal dynamics of closed government as reflected in a dearth of horizontal, systems-based governance across silos and in the attitudes and actions of superiors that little trust and encourage their subordinates to operate outside tightly managed processes. Having explored the closed bureaucrat-bureaucrat relationship, I next consider a second closed relationship underpinning Canada's closed government – that between public servants and citizens and organizations outside the silos and hierarchies of the bureaucracy.

The Closed Bureaucrat-Citizen Relationship

In the strictest and most conservative interpretation of the Westminster model of government, public servants do not share a direct relationship with members of the public. Rather, as servants of the Crown, public servants have indirect relationships at best with citizens, relationships that are mediated through their ministers, who as members of the executive accountable to Parliament are in turn immersed in relationships with the voters to whom Parliament is ultimately accountable. This structure of relationships is also reflected in the traditional Schafferian "bargain" linking ministers and the public service in the Canadian Westminster system, whereby public servants are properly anonymous, avoiding the gaze of the public eye (and thus the potential for praise or blame), while ministers, for their part, serve as the "faces" of their departments, with the potential to benefit or suffer, as the case may be, from this public profile (Hood and Lodge 2006; Savoie 2003; Tait 1996).

Digging yet deeper into the theoretical underpinnings of Canada's system of government as detailed in PPA, we equally find that the bureaucrat-citizen relationship has traditionally been marginalized not by neglect per se but often by design. Emerging in the midst of the Progressive Era of reforms under way in the United States in the early twentieth century, PPA sought to reduce government corruption that had resulted from the undue influence of outside actors on decision makers and the unchecked discretion of government officials in their dealings with these outsiders. The bureaucracy's strict silos and hierarchies were instituted in part to prevent these dealings. That is, with all decisions flowing top-down, tasks parcelled out to specific actors, and the discretion of individual bureaucrats limited, decisions would be formulaic and standardized (ensuring that citizens were treated equally and fairly), and individual citizens and bureaucrats would lack the scope to manipulate the machinery of government to their favour without such manipulation becoming evident from the diversion that it would represent from standard operating procedures (Cooper, Bryer, and Meek 2006; Hood 1995; Olsen 2006; Peters 2010). This reflects the guiding principles of hierarchical accountability structures: first, that defined hierarchies reduce uncertainty about actors accountable for specific actions in complex, multiactor systems (as in public sector bureaucracies); second, that hierarchical chains of command allow superiors to levy sanctions on subordinates should these subordinates abuse the power delegated to them by their superiors (Jarvis 2014a).

In this sense, PPA, as enshrined in early formulations of Canada's federal bureaucracy, was in fact premised on two low-trust relationships, the first evident in a lack of trust in bureaucrats to manage their interactions with the public accountably, the second evident in a lack of trust in citizens to interact with government in ways beneficial to the broader public. PPA framed the government-outsider relationship as one fraught with principal-agent dilemmas, with the agendas of both the self-interested individual citizen and the corruptible individual bureaucrat in competition with the agenda of the state (the pursuit of collective well-being). Accordingly, within this paradigm, government is cast as "an efficient and effective provider of goods, information, and services," achieved through strict adherence to rules and procedures that limit the scope for corruption and inequitable outcomes, "in an authoritative, regulatory relationship with citizens and voluntary groups" (Brainard and McNutt 2010, 838). In turn, citizens face limited opportunities to manipulate government to maximize individual benefit at the expense of the collective. In this view, rather than sharing a high-trust relationship, bureaucrats and citizens properly operate on separate tracks that intersect only in the case of tightly managed transactions.

Historical Openings of the Bureaucrat-Citizen Relationship

Over the years, a series of developments has ensured that the Canadian government has departed from these classical framings of the closed bureaucrat-citizen relationship. For example, public servant anonymity comes under threat as public servants are thrust into the public eye by Access to Information and Privacy requests, media coverage of the public service, senior officials' appearances before parliamentary committees, and in certain cases ministers' willingness to publicly name and blame public servants for their roles in program and policy failures (Grube 2013; Kernaghan 2010). The government itself deliberately facilitates the de-anonymization of public servants, in both small ways – Global Affairs Canada celebrates one of its past mandarins, O.D. Skelton, with a lecture series named for him – and large ways, as in the Government Electronic Directory Service, which details the names, institutional affiliations, and contact information of public servants.[5] Recently, this information was released as an open data set, rendering it easier than ever to identify and contact individual public servants in the federal bureaucracy.

We have also witnessed the growth of public service functions premised on the idea that public servants must interface with members of the public to implement government agendas effectively. Most obvious here is the communications function, which expanded during the First and Second World Wars as part of censorship and propaganda campaigns and now represents a significant area of operations for the federal government (Brown 2012; Kozolanka 2014; Marland 2016), with an ever-expanding class of officials dedicated to government advertising, press relations, and information services that invite the bureaucracy to communicate directly with citizens, for example through the distribution of public health warnings, the provision of consular services to Canadians abroad, and the distribution of information on programs and services.

In addition, New Public Management, though only cautiously and partially adopted in Canada, nonetheless infiltrated the framing of the bureaucrat-citizen relationship in the federal government. The preference in NPM for nongovernmental provision of public services, embodied in Canada in experimentation with alternative service delivery models (Ford and Zussman 1997), betrayed PPA's state-centric vision of public service provision, calling on government to engage outside firms, both corporate and nonprofit, to take on service delivery tasks formerly managed by the state alone. Typically, this has been achieved through grants and contributions and contract-based service externalization, but in the early to mid-2000s the Canadian government also attempted to build more collaborative partnerships with nongovernmental organizations engaged in alternative service delivery arrangements, and organizations of the nonprofit sector in particular, as part of the Voluntary Sector Initiative, which received $94.6 million in federal funding from 2000 to 2005. This resulted in framework agreements struck to promote more productive collaboration between government and organizations in the nonprofit sector. Most relevant in the case of collaboration in service delivery was the Accord between the Government of Canada and the Voluntary Sector, introduced in 2001 (Voluntary Sector Initiative 2014b). The accord included a Code of Good Practice for Funding, which prioritized government funding mechanisms and accountability regimes that "enhanced [the] ability for each sector to carry out its mandate" and "strengthened sustainable capacity of the voluntary sector organizations" (Joint Accord Table of the Voluntary Sector Initiative 2002a). In other words, the code emphasized government's responsibility to develop partnerships with third sector organizations to function effectively, as opposed to government being cast simply as the auditor holding the purse strings in a low-trust, principal-agent relationship.

More prominent and sustained than its efforts to build greater ties between government and external actors in the sphere of service delivery has been the Government of Canada's efforts to engage external actors in its policy development processes (Doern 1971; Lindquist 2006; Phillips and Jenson 1996; Phillips and Orsini 2002). Demands for participatory policy making in Canada formed part of a larger movement among both activists and scholars, who advocated from the 1960s on for pluralistic policy processes involving deliberation, dialogue, and shared government-citizen decision making (democracy between elections versus just at the polls), directly challenging the legitimacy of policy solutions derived solely from the rational-legal authority of the bureaucracy and elected officials (Arnstein 1969; Schindeler and Lanphier 1969). As former Clerk of the Privy Council and subsequent President of the Treasury Board Marcel Massé observed in 1993, this movement reflected the view that

> those who traditionally simply made decisions will have to spend much more of their time explaining situations, setting out the various options and trade-offs, and persuading those involved, before proposed solutions become acceptable. A good part of the present unpopularity of both politicians and public servants is due to

our insufficient adaptation to these new requirements of our jobs. (quoted in Savoie 2003, 107)

Alongside these democratic responsiveness arguments, citizen engagement has also been pursued for more pragmatic, instrumental reasons, following the "two heads are better than one" logic, whereby public servants acknowledge that they do not hold a monopoly on policy expertise, especially when facing an increasingly educated Canadian population with the capacity to provide useful input to improve policies. This pragmatism also sees federal public servants engage with stakeholders because of their recognition that policies benefit from stakeholder buy in, especially in cases in which these stakeholders are key to a policy's implementation.

Driven variously by democratic legitimacy arguments and pragmatism, the Government of Canada through the years has adopted a range of different instruments to support citizen participation in policy development.[6] Royal commissions in some cases have represented large-scale and elaborate efforts to open up the federal policy process to external actors. For example, the 1985 Royal Commission on the Economic Union and Development Prospects for Canada (the Macdonald Commission) consulted with twenty-seven communities over three months and, through open consultations and multistakeholder dialogues, engaged members of the Canadian public in discussions on their long-term vision for the country. All submissions were recorded electronically (amounting to 40,000 pages of transcripts) and then used in a deliberative dialogue. Similarly, the 2001–02 Royal Commission on the Future of Health Care in Canada (the Romanow Commission) consulted with tens of thousands of stakeholders, experts, and members of the general population. Ten different processes were employed, including open public hearings, expert roundtables, public dialogues, online consultation workbooks, televised forums, regional forums led by experts, and university campus policy dialogue sessions.

White papers, task forces, ministerial roundtables, public opinion research, and consultations are other commonly employed instruments of public engagement in Canada, having spawned a fleet of new functional areas of responsibility in the bureaucracy, including stakeholder engagement officers and consultation shops. Public consultation in some cases is an obligatory or recommended duty of ministers under legislation. For example, the Canadian government has a "duty to consult" when its decisions or actions might have adverse impacts on Aboriginal or treaty rights.[7] The 1985 Official Languages

Act was the first act to mention consultation as one of the minister's duties (though only on a voluntary basis). Although not an exhaustive list, the Canadian Environmental Assessment Act (1992), Saguenay–St. Lawrence Marine Park Act (1997), Canadian Environmental Protection Act (1999), Canadian National Parks Act (2000), Pest Control Act (2002), Nuclear Fuel Waste Act (2002), Yukon Environmental and Socio-Economic Assessment Act (2003) and Canadian Environmental Protection Act (2012) also recommend that ministers undertake public consultation exercises.

A series of initiatives in the 1990s and 2000s further institutionalized the role of public participation in federal policy development. The government developed official guidance advising that each department adopt principles for consultation, appoint senior officials and an advisory council to reinforce a consultative culture in the public service, make deputy ministers accountable for their departments' consultations, and introduce training to build public servants' consultation skills. The 1999 Social Union Framework Agreement made an explicit commitment to develop and offer "effective mechanisms for Canadians to participate in developing social priorities and reviewing outcomes" in government (Canadian Intergovernmental Conference Secretariat 1999). And the 2000–05 Voluntary Sector Initiative, discussed above in the context of service externalization, also "funded a number of projects designed to enhance policy dialogue" and sought to "strengthen the opportunities for input by voluntary organizations and to strengthen the voluntary sector's capacity to contribute to departmental policy dialogue" (Voluntary Sector Initiative 2014a). Alongside the Code of Good Practice on Funding, the Accord between the Government of Canada and the Voluntary Sector produced a Code of Good Practice on Policy Dialogue. As stated in the code, the document "confirms that the two sectors are committed to deepening their dialogue in order to create better public policies for the benefit of Canadians. The Code also affirms the importance of a respectful, transparent and inclusive policy dialogue that acknowledges the independence and interdependence of both sectors" (Joint Accord Table of the Voluntary Sector Initiative 2002b).

The federal government at various periods has also directly funded external organizations in order to facilitate their participation in federal policy processes. Most notably, from 1994 to 2009, the government commissioned the Canadian Policy Research Network to lead a series of deliberative dialogues with the public on a broad range of issues, including the future of health care, nuclear fuel, biotechnology, racial and ethnic tensions, and youth engagement.

Similarly, the government has provided direct funding to external groups so that they can offer insights to policy makers; these groups include the Canadian Council for International Cooperation (founded in 1968), the Canadian Environmental Network (founded in 1977), and the Institute for Research on Public Policy (founded in 1972). And the Policy Research Initiative – created as a government organization in 1996 by then Clerk of the Privy Council Jocelyn Bourgon – endeavoured to engage academics and research organizations in policy development, in some cases in concert with the federal Social Sciences and Humanities Research Council. Academics and researchers continue to feed insights into federal policy processes, for example through their research, commissioned reports, and participation in departmental talks. In addition, an ecosystem of think tanks, research institutes, consultants, lobbying associations, and polling firms has emerged, adding new outside voices to previously closed federal policy processes (Bakvis 2000; Prince 2007).

In sum, through initiatives that seek to "open up" the work of the federal government to external scrutiny (e.g., the ATIP regime and DM appearances before Parliament), the emergence and expansion of the communications function, forays into alternative service delivery arrangements, and a range of institutionalized policy engagement mechanisms, the Government of Canada has attempted to depart from early framings of the bureaucrat-citizen relationship as properly limited, tightly regulated, and based on a low-trust, principal-agent dynamic. Betraying both the preference for bureaucratic anonymity and limited bureaucratic-citizen interaction of the Westminster bargain and Progressive-Era Public Administration, the federal bureaucracy and Canadians are now thrust – by a variety of mechanisms and functions – into a direct relationship. In turn, the world of federal policy making is much more pluralistic than it was at its origin, leading Michael Prince (2007, 175) to observe that, though the public service policy advisory function was once conceived as resting on a bipartite, hierarchical relationship in which career officials "speak truth to power," with power held by ministers with decision-making authority, the populated field of policy work today is better captured as a horizontal process of "sharing truths with many actors." In this view, power is understood as being "more diffused, complex and nuanced inside and outside the state than a generation or more ago. Governments are not impotent, but certainly, they need to work with networks of governance to create new approaches and responses to the hard choices of economic, environmental and social issues found in the new context playing out in political communities" (177; see also Bakvis 2000).

However, despite recognition that the bureaucrat-citizen relationship should be bolstered by systematic efforts to involve the public in the work of the state, the government-citizen relationship remains in certain ways as low trust, tightly managed, and circumscribed as it was originally envisioned under the Westminster bargain and the PPA model that comprise the foundation narrative of the Canadian bureaucracy. As with the closed bureaucrat-bureaucrat relationship, we can also understand the closed government-citizen relationship by considering the enduring influence of silos and hierarchies on today's federal public service, an influence that has allowed only partial openings of the government-citizen relationship.

Siloed and Hierarchical Quasi-Openings of the Government-Citizen Relationship

At a basic level, we can label the government-citizen relationship as only quasi-open by considering that only particular actors within the bureaucracy are invited to take part in this relationship. That is, though much has been made of the erosion of anonymity (Grube 2013, 2015; Kernaghan 2010; Savoie 2003), in reality it has expired in earnest only for a particular group of bureaucrats whose elite status and unique functional areas of responsibility demand that they directly engage with the public. De-anonymization is siloed off to certain bureaucrats, not the entire bureaucracy. This includes senior officials such as clerks (e.g., in their public speeches) and deputy ministers (e.g., in their appearances before parliamentary committees) and the diplomatic corps, whose unique function as representatives of the government abroad have always allowed them a public personality that renders them distinct from the anonymized "bureaucracy proper." Government scientists participate in conferences and media interviews to disseminate their research findings (a practice allegedly constrained under the Harper government, inspiring debate and criticism; see Cappe 2016; and Levinson King 2015). The public servants working in communications and public affairs shops, including those dedicated to stakeholder relations and consultations, also adopt the government's public voice as part of their work. Indeed, the unique capacity to "speak" externally for the Government of Canada is reinforced by the emergence of the official designation of "spokesperson" (Treasury Board Secretariat 2006a) (a designation eventually eliminated in 2016). The historical existence of the concept of spokespersons indicates that most public servants traditionally have been limited in their capacity to network and engage with outsiders in their official capacities. Huge swaths of the bureaucracy remain isolated from those affected by their work – the targets of policy interventions, the users of services – and outsiders who might be able to contribute to this work. In particular, those in lower positions across all functions, or those in areas outside the program/policy and stakeholder engagement/consultation spheres (e.g., information management, IT, and human resources), are still presumed and expected to remain "faceless," out of the public eye, as per the original bargain.

The siloed infrastructures that have developed to facilitate bureaucrat-citizen interactions are coupled with the top-down management of these interactions, equally undermining the scope for bureaucrats and those outside their walls to interface. To be sure, these hierarchies undermine the scope for these interactions not as a rule but because of the dense, time-consuming process that they add to such interactions, embodied primarily in the series of top-down reporting and policy requirements to which bureaucrat-citizen interactions are subject and the concomitant stages of approval and centralized control that these requirements necessitate. For example, until it was revised in May 2016, the *Communications Policy of the Government of Canada* reflected the concerns and dictates of eighteen different pieces of legislation on government management (e.g., the Official Languages Act, Canadian Charter of Rights and Freedoms, and Privacy Act) and twenty-eight TBS policy instruments (e.g., the Common Look and Feel Standard, Federal Identity Program, Contracting Policy, and Procedures for Publishing). The revised version of the communications policy, the *Policy on Communications and Federal Identity,* is slightly less tangled in a web of rules but only comparatively so; it is to be interpreted alongside nine pieces of supporting legislation and nine other TBS policy instruments.

Similar centralized, top-down management structures have cropped up around public opinion research (POR), the official vehicle by which departments can systematically gather input from stakeholders, service users, and citizens, typically through surveys and focus groups and often focused on informing the communications strategies by which policies are implemented (versus determining the content of policy) (Page 2006). POR has been subject historically to the *Communications Policy of the Government of Canada* and all of its constituent legislation, guidelines, and policies as well as the TBS Procedures for Planning and Contracting Public Opinion Research; eight pieces of legislation and fifteen policies and directives were implicated in these procedures. The 2016 TBS policy suite reset claimed to have streamlined the rules governing POR as part of the 2016 *Policy on Communications and*

Federal Identity. The directive implementing this new policy did remove the requirement of ministerial approval that had been added to the POR process, but otherwise POR remains as process heavy as ever, featuring many layers of approval and requiring significant preplanning and coordination across communications branches and a series of actors in Public Services and Procurement Canada, the PCO, the Library of Parliament, and Library and Archives Canada.

Likewise, consultations are couched in a thick framework of top-down oversight. The TBS communications policies and guidelines must be respected, and the PCO Communications and Consultations Secretariat must approve all consultations. These consultations are then managed through stakeholder relations and communications branches in departments, each with its own internal procedures and approval processes. In this context, policy engagement is a significant undertaking, requiring substantial time and resources ensuring that it is necessarily episodic and tightly managed as opposed to occurring on a more regularized, flexible basis.

In addition to necessitating processes that limit the regularity and fluidity of bureaucrat-citizen engagement, the hierarchical management of this engagement limits its scope for robust, collaborative, and regularized interaction in a second way. In this case, hierarchy manifests not in internal government processes but as the structure through which government agents interface with outsiders.

When the limited number of bureaucrats empowered to interact with outsiders eventually work through the internal procedures that lead to these interactions, traditionally they tend to approach these interactions in a top-down manner as opposed to treating outside actors as teammates on a level playing field. In policy consultations, government "calls the shots," deciding which issues will be the subjects of consultation, how consultations will take place, and in some cases who will be invited to take part (Phillips and Jenson 1996; Phillips and Orsini 2002). For instance, as explained in interviews with stakeholder engagement officers, in the case of a stakeholder roundtable hosted by the minister, public servants in the department in question and in some cases the PCO will preapprove all subjects to be discussed. They will also vet and control all participants invited to the session, determine the time and place of the roundtable, and produce and disseminate information on the findings generated from it, typically through a "what they said" report drafted and edited by the department.

A similarly regimented and hierarchical process is at play in the Government of Canada's efforts to support greater collaboration with outsiders in service delivery. Despite explicit efforts in the Voluntary Sector Initiative, in particular in the Code of Good Practice on Funding, to support high-trust partnerships between the government and nonprofit organizations delivering services to the public, the government continues to frame its relationship with the sector in low-trust terms. Such terms are embodied in the principal-agent agreements by which the government allocates funding to external bodies delivering services in lieu of the bureaucracy (Aucoin and Jarvis 2005). As described by Phillips and Levasseur (2004, 452): "as a policy instrument, contracting necessarily gives government the controlling hand in its relationship with third parties because it sets the terms of contracts and the requirements for performance and has produced under NPM ... an explosion in accountability and auditing."

This "explosion in accountability and auditing" (Power 1994) was partly a product of the government's response to the media's overreaction to the 2000 soft audit of the Human Resources Development Canada Grants and Contributions program. Even though subsequent analyses of the unaccounted-for funding revealed it to be much less than the original billion dollars cited, the affair ramped up oversight and auditing functions in the government (Sutherland 2001). This audit explosion undermined efforts to produce horizontal partnerships with outside organizations via the voluntary sector accord, and in some cases it ensured that these external actors were hesitant to engage in government policy processes, fearing that in doing so they would expose themselves to greater scrutiny by public auditors (Phillips and Orsini 2002).

Why has the bureaucrat-citizen relationship remained as circumscribed and, on certain fronts, even more low trust and closed than it was framed in its late-nineteenth-century and early-twentieth-century founding theories? The reasons are part political, part pragmatic, and part ethical.

The Politics, Practicalities, and Ethics of Closed Government-Citizen Relations

At one level, we can explain the closed government-citizen relationship as a component of the culture of permanent campaigning that has emerged as a powerful force in Canadian politics in recent years and that is thought to have ramped up in particular under the leadership of Prime Minister Stephen Harper between 2006 and 2015 (Aucoin 2012; Marland 2016; Marland, Giasson, and Esselment 2017; Savoie 2013). By this argument, political leadership succumbs to the partisan impulse to tightly control the government-citizen interface, using silos to limit which bureaucrats can speak for the government and top-down management to ensure that, when these select bureaucrats do interface with the public (e.g., in official communications, via consultations, through POR), they promote themes and pieces of information in line with the political brand of the government of the day as part of the centralized control of court government (Savoie 1999). Extending the centralization thesis, Alex Marland (2016) argues that all aspects of Canadian public administration are now filtered through a centrally calibrated "branding lens." In this view, the government-citizen relationship is far from open, trusting, and collaborative; rather, it is one in which citizens are essentially customers to be marketed to or, as Susan Delacourt (2016a) has argued, voters to be bought through carefully microtargeted messages and policies.

Although generally viewed as a trend amplified under Harper, the consumerization of government communications is not a new phenomenon. Marland's and Delacourt's arguments build on an existing literature arguing that neoliberalism and the language and values of the market have punctuated our conceptions of citizenship since the NPM reforms of the 1980s and 1990s reframed citizens as self-interested consumers in the marketplace of public services (Aberbach and Christensen 2005; Dutil, Howard, and Langford 2010; Jung 2010; Needham 2003; Pierre 1995). Marland (2016) extends this argument even further back in history, arguing that Prime Minister Wilfrid Laurier used the Canadian Exhibition Commission in 1901 to centralize government communications, did not hold formal news conferences, tightly controlled his MPs' public speeches, and patronized newspapers favourable to the Liberal government. These were all careful efforts to craft government interactions with the public versus using these interactions to support a more informed, engaged citizenry, as per the ideal of open government. Along with mainstream treatments of digital technology in Canadian public administration, Marland argues that digital communication technologies have accelerated this careful stagecraft, such that in the digital age "it is inevitable that prime ministers will demand message consistency from their agents. In politics, the desire to control permeates all" (xv).

Public servants are among the agents from whom political leaders will demand message consistency, a point reflected in Peter Aucoin's theory of New Political Governance. Aucoin argued that "the communications function of government has become the black hole of public service impartiality," an effect of the new "economic marketplace of the media" (2012, 183, 181). This leads to a complete perversion of the government-citizen relationship as laid out by Weber, in the Westminster bargain, and in PPA. Rather than tightly controlling government-citizen interactions to limit the inequitable and/or partisan political allocation of public resources, governments directly use such interactions for partisan gain, leading to what Aucoin labelled "promiscuous partisanship" as public servants actively promote the government in public communications (see also Grube 2015). All of these trends – centralization, consumerization, and politicization – thin the government-citizen relationship into one that is at best a vehicle by which citizens undertake self-interested individual transactions and at worst a weapon of manipulation in a larger partisan political battle, developments that led former Clerk of the Privy Council Alex Himelfarb (2012) to conclude that Canadians are now offered a model of "bargain basement citizenship."

Adding to these dynamics, observers have remarked that – facing greater scrutiny from a 24/7 media environment, the proliferation of auditing bodies, and especially ATIP requests – public servants now face greater pressures to withhold information from the public than they do to support an informed citizenry, fearing the political costs that could accrue from releasing potentially damning information into the permanent campaign in which their political masters are competing (Aucoin 2012; Marland 2016; Marland, Giasson, and Esselment 2017; Savoie 2013). This is the argument that "efforts to open the government paradoxically lead to an ever more closed government." The fear of tarnishing the minister's public profile is colloquially captured in the "*Globe and Mail* Test," by which public servants seek to avoid any action – especially the recording and release of information – that might land their minister in hot water on the cover of a daily newspaper.

Information Commissioner Suzanne Legault (2015b) has been a particularly vocal critic of the culture of secrecy that marks the federal public service. At a basic level, this culture dilutes the reach and robustness of the ATIP system, ultimately limiting citizens' ability to scrutinize and participate in the work of the government on an even informational playing field. However, more fundamentally, this culture of secrecy speaks to a low-trust, antagonistic relationship between the public service and the public. It is difficult to argue that the public service and Canadians share a robust, collaborative relationship when bureaucrats actively withhold information from Canadians, fearing the scrutiny that they might invite by releasing it. In this sense, just as the viciously competitive communications culture of contemporary politics can reinforce a closed bureaucrat-bureaucrat relationship (in that case limiting superiors' willingness to trust in the discretion of subordinates or to divert from the status quo), so too permanent campaigning invites a closed bureaucrat-citizen relationship, driving bureaucratic secrecy.

But more than simply being a product of the political climate in which the public service operates, there are also pragmatic considerations ensuring that the bureaucrat-citizen relationship is at best quasi-open. Responsibility for communications and policy consultations is allocated to particular actors and managed by top-down, dense approval processes in part to ensure that these activities are coordinated and coherent across the government. This is one of the key objectives of bureaucracy – coordinating simultaneous activities in complex systems by allocating tasks to particular actors and adhering to systematic, replicable processes. Accordingly, through policies such as the Federal Identity Program and standard guidelines for the "look and feel" of websites, since the 1960s the government has endeavoured to rationalize and standardize its communications into whole of government strategies, branding, and imagery so that verified information from the Government of Canada is easily identifiable and to ensure that government communications do not work at cross-purposes.

In comparison, a decentralized model of government-citizen interactions – one that might see individual units variously shaping the information that they share, how they share it, and the language that they use – is not only more costly (with each department managing its own suite of communication materials) but can also, more importantly, create confusion among citizens and service users, a lack of coordination across and within departments, and thus inefficiency and possible policy and program failures. In other words, centralization is not exclusively an instrument of PMO-led court government or politicization. In certain instances, it is also a necessity of effective governing, a component of the systems-based horizontality that large bureaucracies are regularly criticized for failing to adopt.

In web-based communications specifically, this model of centralized coordination won early praise for Canada as an e-government leader from international consulting groups and the United Nations E-Government Rankings when its centralized web portal, Service Canada, was launched (Accenture 2005; United Nations and Department of Economic and Social Affairs 2014). As discussed above, Service Canada's logic asserts that, by ensuring that the government speaks with one voice, web-based communications adopt a citizen-centric view: that is, they reflect the perspectives of citizens who do not want to (or who cannot effectively) navigate multiple websites developed by each department and program, each with its own structure, language, and visual look and feel (Borins 2007; Roy 2006). Centralization in this case is thus driven by the pragmatic goal of ensuring that citizens can easily find information and services from the government, a logic underpinning the international trend of combining all government department websites into one master site, as in gov.uk, Ontario.ca, Australia.gov.au, govt.nz, and Canada .ca, introduced in 2013. In particular, one goal of these sites is to ensure that citizens receive accurate information on government services from reliable government sources – developing a consistent and easily recognizable look and feel for government communications is one way of doing so.

It is important to underscore this last point given research finding that citizens are not always equipped to verify the credibility of information sources or their authors on the web. For example, a 2012 study noted that young Americans unknowingly sought information on family planning from pro-life sites masquerading as neutral public health sources, incorrectly assuming that any site with a ".org" domain name could be considered "official" and "government issued" (Hargittai and Young 2012). One can imagine similar deception and misinformation online on recent controversial topics in which government has a stake, such as the safety of childhood vaccines. The risk of online misinformation masquerading as the accurate, official record recently caught the attention of the UK government. As they note on their website:

> If you type the names of some popular government services into search engines, some of your search results might be ads for sites that offer a service you could get for free (or for much less) on GOV. UK, the government's own website ... We know from users that it's sometimes hard to tell the difference between the adverts, that appear at the top of the search result pages, and the actual search results, which take you to the government service. (Government Digital Service, n.d.b.)

To address this risk, the government is working with the Advertising Standards Authority and the National Trading Standards Board to ensure that misleading ads are better regulated. The government has also launched an initiative inviting citizens to report misleading websites and web ads to Google. But the government's primary line of defence asks citizens to ensure that they are on a recognizable gov.uk website when they access information relevant to government services, and creating a standardized, centrally coordinated, and thereby easily recognizable government website is key to doing so. In a digital context where information is overwhelmingly abundant, the need for coherent, consistent, centralized government communications is ever greater.

We can also interpret much of the top-down, centralized process mediating government-citizen interactions as a response to the equity and accountability breaches that can arise when governments interface with citizens. For example, rules related to the preapproval and transparency of engagement initiatives seek to ensure that they are balanced and not directed to partisan ends (as in the use of POR to inform communication strategies that favour strictly partisan gains of the governing party). In the case of open consultations, top-down guidance and rules aim to ensure that the consultations are advertised in ways that do not exclude certain segments of the population. Likewise, contracts to manage external services ensure that funds allocated by the government to these services are used responsibly, limiting the scope for corruption and waste. In this sense, whatever their detrimental impact on partnership building, their goal is uncontroversially virtuous: ensuring that public funds are expended accountably.

Similarly, government communications and consultations that do not conform to guidelines on accessibility and official languages (ensuring that they accommodate the needs of those with disabilities and are available in both English and French) will exclude certain segments of the population, betraying the government's duty to treat citizens fairly and impartially, a requirement underscored by a 2012 judicial decision that any government website not accessible to the disabled would constitute discrimination under the Charter of Rights and Freedoms.[8]

Further, though much can be derided in the complex, many-layered approval processes, guidelines, and policies by which official government communications are crafted, it is precisely these processes, guidelines, and policies that safeguard against the politicization of properly nonpartisan public communications. For instance, the Conservative government led by Harper was criticized for abandoning standard colours, identifiers, and logos in its Economic Action Plan advertising, for switching the colour of government websites to blue (versus the Liberal-friendly but nonetheless official red), and for swapping the nonpartisan term "Government of Canada" for "Harper Government" in official communications. These diversions from the status quo were able to be identified as such only because the status quo for government communications was established in a suite of institutionalized, rigid processes, policies, and guidelines to which these communications have traditionally been subject.

Finally, lest we forget, much of the contemporary process and "red tape" surrounding government communications and public opinion research emerged from efforts to reduce the politicization of these functions. Government advertising contracts have long been a means of rewarding partisan-friendly marketing firms, most infamously uncovered in the Sponsorship Scandal. Although Jean Chrétien had introduced new rules to oversee communications, advertising, and POR as of 1994, exposure of the Sponsorship Scandal in the early 2000s led to a more robust system of procurement and oversight for these functions (Page 2006). Regardless of these efforts, the Gomery Inquiry found that the Sponsorship Scandal was partly the product of a dearth of internal checks, rules, and oversight for contracting in communications, advertising, and public opinion research (Gomery 2005). Thus, the inquiry's report turned to greater oversight, clearer rules, and systematic bureaucratic processes to limit future ethical breaches (Gomery 2006), and Harper's ensuing Federal Accountability Act (2006) instituted the new requirement that written reports on advertising and POR be shared with Library and Archives Canada within six months so that they could be made publicly available for scrutiny (Marland 2016, 231–32).

Falling in line with this longer history, the Trudeau government's 2015 commitment to add greater oversight to government advertising, like the efforts of his predecessors, has been framed as a move in step with democratic principles, an effort to guarantee nonpartisanship in the public service. Top-down processes and rules thus have traditionally played and continue to play important roles in safeguarding equitable and accountable government-citizen interactions and are not strictly the products of political centralization of power or bureaucratic inefficiency. In fact, these centralized rules can have the opposite intent and – if applied in the spirit of that intent – impact, a sentiment that has led J.P. Olsen (2006) to argue that in our rush to embrace a more networked, open model of governance we need to "rediscover bureaucracy" and its role in securing coordinated, predictable government processes and equitable treatment of citizens within democratic systems (see also Goodsell 2004; and Terry 2005).

Evident in these turns to oversight, process, and top-down rules, the Canadian federal public service clearly need not "rediscover bureaucracy"; it never forgot it and, rather, has doubled-down on its commitment to silos and hierarchies. Efforts to link the public service and external actors retain a guiding assumption of early bureaucratic theory – that significant breaches of accountability can arise whenever the government interfaces with the public and that, in turn, efforts to link the bureaucracy and outsiders should be managed through standardized rules and hierarchical processes. In this sense, though the Canadian government has departed over time from the strictly closed model of the bureaucrat-citizen relationship, public servants continue to interpret their relationship with the public through a Weberian-PPA lens. This leads to a hybrid model in which the relationship is opened – through public servants' communications with the public, in consultations, in public opinion research, in alternative service delivery arrangements – but this opening is tightly managed through hierarchical bureaucratic processes and by particular actors functionally designated to interface with the public. The government-citizen relationship is thus at best quasi-open, in some cases, for entirely legitimate reasons.

You Can Take the Government Out of the Early Twentieth Century ...

Despite operating in a context entirely different from that before Max Weber and the architects of Progressive-Era Public Administration at the turn of the twentieth century, today's federal bureaucracy has not only stayed the course but also, in many senses, increased its reliance on the silos and hierarchies originally developed at the early foundation of the Westminster state. Public servants work in an elaborate system of silos defined by department, unit, and function. Information and discretionary authority live in defined places along an ever more dense bureaucratic hierarchy. The vast majority of federal public servants are still expected to exist in anonymity, and interactions between the bureaucracy and outsiders are tightly managed and necessarily episodic given the elaborate top-down approvals and preplanning that they require. The federal bureaucracy's closed government tendencies are further reinforced by a contemporary political culture that rationalizes information control, dense oversight, and risk aversion anathema to innovation.

Yet silos and hierarchies have endured not strictly because the public service resists change or because of undue political pressures but partly because of their roles in securing coordinated, equitable, and accountable government. In other words, you can take the bureaucracy out of the early twentieth century, but you cannot so easily take the early twentieth century out of the bureaucracy – and in some cases *you shouldn't*.

Detailing how and why the Government of Canada has remained a closed institution internally, and in its dealings with outsiders, despite explicit efforts in some cases to engage in a more horizontal, systems-based, collaborative model of governance, in this chapter I have laid out the baseline – the raw materials, if you will – that the federal bureaucracy had to work with in adjusting to a digital age defined by networks, open information flows, iterative experimentation, and peer-to-peer production. At the same time, while I have revealed the current deficiencies of these structures, surveying critiques launched against them throughout the history of Canadian public administration, I have highlighted the original and enduring rationales that underpin silos and hierarchies as structures that coordinate activities across complex bureaucracies and that aim to secure accountable, equitable public administration. These enduring rationales point to the potential risks and dilemmas that a wholesale or reckless upheaval of these traditions might initiate. With this baseline in place, in the chapters that follow, I illustrate how historical complaints about closed government continue and are intensified in the face of networked digital technologies and the pressures of governing in a digital age while also fleshing out the particular managerial and accountability dilemmas that digital era open government nonetheless raises. I begin this analysis by responding to the question: What happens when a closed government gets a Twitter account?

3
#Fail: Adopting Social Media in
the Government of Canada

In 2007, a group of twenty-three federal departments commissioned public opinion research to investigate Canadians' opinions on the use of social media and Web 2.0 technologies by the Government of Canada. The Canadians consulted expressed high hopes, indicating that the use of these technologies

> represents an opportunity to transform the "face" of the Government of Canada, to make it appear more approachable, less remote, and more responsive to Canadians. Use of these applications was . seen to increase access, to make information and services more convenient, to increase transparency, and to enable the GC to better reach youth. Some even said government use of these types of applications would increase their confidence in the government. (Phoenix Strategy Perspectives 2008, ii–iii)

> Participants also expressed a sense of urgency when discussing the government's uptake of these technologies, for example arguing that, "if it does not adopt these types of applications, the GC risks being seen as more out-of-touch than it is already perceived to be" and that "government cannot ignore these applications precisely because they are becoming more prevalent" (Phoenix Strategy Perspectives 2008, iv, vii).

These high hopes for government social media use were echoed by then Clerk of the Privy Council Kevin Lynch, who stated in his 2007 report to the prime minister that public servants were indeed answering this call for a more open, accessible form of government-citizen interaction and information sharing in the digital age. Lynch explained that "the changes brought by the information revolution of the past 25 years, among other factors, have affected the business of government profoundly" and that the information revolution ... has dramatically enhanced public expectations for speedy decisions, for immediate responses from government, for transparency in government operations, and for public engagement in decision making. The information revolution has also eroded the value of secrecy and of what was once the unique knowledge held by government. Today, the Internet makes information readily accessible to billions of people around the world. Information is a tool for everyone, and that's a good thing.

However, despite Lynch's observation that the digital age had ushered in "profound changes" in "the business of government," when social media were first integrated into the operations of the federal government in the mid-2000s, the changes that they brought about were anything but profound, doing little to support the transparent and accessible government-citizen interactions and fluid information exchanges described in theories of digital era open government and cited by citizens in the 2007 public opinion research on social media.

Rather than using these new communication platforms to engage in a decentralized, fluid, and informal model of information sharing and dialogue with the public, the bureaucracy siloed responsibilities for social media to one functionally defined area – communications – and effectively marginalized these platforms as irrelevant to other activities in the daily management of the federal government, including policy development, program design, and service delivery. And since the bureaucracy was used to tightly managing government-citizen interactions through top-down policy requirements and strategic communication strategies, social media became yet another platform for the government to push its carefully crafted information to the public.

In this chapter I uncover the inertia that characterized the federal bureaucracy's initial efforts to adjust to the digital age, captured in its adoption of social media. Here I paint a picture of an organization desperately clinging to its siloed and hierarchical models of information exchange – both internally, among bureaucrats, and externally, with citizens – in the face of networked social technologies fundamentally at odds with these historically entrenched bureaucratic structures. Evading the disruption and transformation that have characterized the web's influence in other sectors, the federal bureaucracy proved to be a stubborn, unmovable institution in its initial efforts to adjust to the digital age, producing outcomes that were humorous at times in their absurdity but that, more consequentially, poignantly highlighted why

undertaking the difficult transition from closed government to open government is an essential yet dilemma-ridden component of resilient digital era
governance.

Social Media in a Silo

The Government of Canada's first official effort to adapt to the digital age
came as departments developed corporate accounts on the mainstream
social media platforms to which Canadian Internet users had flocked from
the mid-2000s on, especially Facebook, Twitter, and YouTube (Anonymous
Government of Canada Official 2012). As opposed to creating accounts
representing "real people" – that is, accounts that use human faces as profile
pictures and use real names as the usernames for the accounts – these
accounts used the same official corporate logos, identifiers, and names (e.g.,
Transport Canada) of all other departmental communications and were
managed by departmental communication officers who added social media
to their existing suites of communication tools (e.g., press releases,
Government of Canada websites, paper pamphlets, and television advertising). As the "home" of social media in departments, the communications
shop also served as the access point to social media for program officers
and policy analysts wishing to integrate social media communications into
their work. For example, communication officials would need to approve
and then manage any program-specific social media account, and, should
a program's communications plan call for a tweet advertising a new service,
for example, the request for such a tweet would be sent to communication
officials as part of the general communications plan attached to the
announcement.

In addition to managing what departments published on these social
media accounts, communication officers took on the task of collecting information from online social networks such as Twitter and Facebook to distribute
across their departments. Social media were integrated into the communications shop's existing media monitoring duties, typically achieved through
commercial social media monitoring tools such as Hootsuite and Radian6.
Using these tools, communication officials would identify information shared
on social media deemed to be relevant to the department, in the same way
that they scan daily print, radio, and television news sources for mentions of
the department, its policy portfolio, and its minister. These social media
updates would then typically be included in media roundups distributed
across the department.

In one example of such a roundup created in what was then Human Resources and Skills Development Canada (HRSDC)[1] and covering a one-week period in April 2012, the eight-page document included only brief references to social media amid its more dominant focus on reports in mainstream legacy media. These brief references would note things such as the emergence of a new Twitter account that critiqued a program in the department or provide commentary such as "the TFW [Temporary Foreign Workers] program peaked [sic] a huge interest on Twitter this week. The chatter was focused primarily on Minister Finley's announcement made in Alberta on April 25th" (Human Resources and Skills Development Canada 2012, 3). The document did not provide sophisticated or instructive analyses of the content or volume of such tweets, or of the relative influence of those tweeting about these subjects, raising a number of questions. What could a policy analyst, political adviser, or program officer draw from these social media updates? The analysis was rather rudimentary, falling far below the standards of sophisticated big data analytical techniques that are appropriate to large-scale social media data sets and that could provide instructive insights to those in the department (e.g., social network analysis, data visualization, and automated classification).[2]

Meanwhile, outside the communications shop, the rest of the bureaucracy was cut off from social media. An Internet firewall, with rare exceptions (e.g., what was then the Department of Foreign Affairs and International Trade), limited public servants outside the communications shop from accessing mainstream social media sites. This firewall essentially created a censored Internet environment within the federal bureaucracy, one that not only prevented public servants from directly publishing information on these platforms as official spokespersons for their departments (given that communication officers were granted control over this function) but also limited public servants from drawing insights from the social media platforms rapidly becoming central sites of information sharing and networking for stakeholders, other governments, international organizations, researchers, think tanks, nonprofit organizations, service users, and "everyday Canadians." Thus, while the clerk suggested that "the Internet makes information readily accessible to billions of people around the world" and that "information is a tool for everyone, and that's a good thing" (Lynch 2007), in practice information shared on social media was *not* framed as a tool for everyone in the public service, siloed as it was to the communications shop.

Social Networking in a Hierarchy

With departmental communication teams initially developing corporate social media accounts on an ad hoc basis, the federal bureaucracy next sought to integrate social media more officially into its operations through the creation of a dense hierarchical infrastructure of rules, policies, and guidelines. Thus, if the first impulse in the bureaucracy was to silo off responsibility for social media to particular actors, the second was tightly to govern this new access point to the bureaucracy by layering on the same top-down governance structures that have traditionally constrained the scope for networking between the government and those outside its walls.

This process began in earnest in April 2008 when the Chief Information Officer Branch (CIOB) of the TBS asked Canada's Communications Community Office (CCCO), a cross-departmental group focused on the communications function of the federal government, to provide input on the implications of social media use in the government. In response, the CCCO spent a year developing an internal document titled "Considerations for the Government of Canada's Use of Social Media to Communicate with and Engage the Public." The document offered basic descriptions of what it termed "Web 2.0 and collaborative technologies," case studies illustrating potential applications of such technologies to the government, policy considerations, and related recommendations, and it was the seed for an official TBS policy drafted throughout 2010 and 2011. Extensive internal consultations and revisions contributed to the final TBS policy, titled the Guideline for External Use of Web 2.0 (Treasury Board Secretariat 2011c), which moved through internal committee processes and final approval in the spring and summer of 2011 before finally being adopted and announced in November 2011 by then President of the Treasury Board Tony Clement. The entire process – from the CIOB's initial request for input on a policy to support uptake of social media in the federal government in April 2008 to an official policy supporting this uptake – lasted just over three and a half years.

The Guideline for External Use of Web 2.0 (the Guideline) stated that "Government of Canada departments are encouraged to use Web 2.0 tools and services as an efficient and effective additional channel to interact with the public" (Treasury Board Secretariat 2011c). The policy referred to social media's applications to consultation and its uses as "a collaborative tool." It also clarified that departmental accounts need not be managed solely as part of corporate communication strategies; rather, individual public servants could use social media in a professional capacity, outside the confines of official communication strategies. However, these potential applications were not delineated in any detail. Instead, following the existing framing of social media as a phenomenon relevant primarily to the communications function, the Guideline largely emphasized the applications of social media to official government communications and to tasks that rely on these communications, including recruitment and staffing, risk and emergency management, stakeholder outreach, and public education.

Having outlined how departments could employ social media as a new platform for communications, the Guideline described the policy considerations that departments had to take into account when integrating social media into their work. The policy thus became long and dense, totalling just over 12,000 words while detailing a dizzying list of existing legislative and policy frameworks deemed relevant to the government's uptake of social media.

They included

- the Standard on Web Accessibility (ensuring that initiatives involving third-party sites are compatible with screen readers for the visually impaired)
- the *Communications Policy of the Government of Canada* (directing that accounts and their content are congruent with government communication themes, messages, and advertising policies)
- the Federal Identity Program (using approved government identifiers and logos)
- information management frameworks (ensuring that content with business value can be identified and stored)
- *Policy on Official Languages* (stipulating that all site features are available in English and French, ensuring that significant exchanges in one language are translated into the other, and questioning the need to use third-party sites that cannot accommodate bilingualism)
- the Access to Information Act and the Privacy Act (preventing the release of personal information)
- procurement and contracting procedures (developing custom terms of service for third-party tools and services where needed)
- security protocols (developing strategies to prevent identity theft, viruses, or phishing scams).

Developed with the goal of encouraging public servants to engage in the rapid-paced, informal, and networked exchanges taking place on social media, but ultimately requiring three and a half years of development and resulting in a document drenched in an overwhelming list of policy considerations, top-down processes, and related risk management strategies, the Guideline was the subject of much criticism and ridicule upon its publication. Referring to the document as the "Guideline for Digital Oblivion," one blogger observed that "these new guidelines are so heavy that they handcuff the public service" and "aren't useful in communicating what social media is, how you should use it, or why. They're useful only in adding so much process that everyone's ass is covered in case it blows up" (Khan 2011). Echoing this sentiment, open government advocate David Eaves (2011b) argued that the process-heavy Guideline was about "control, not communication," and specifically complained that it listed "eleven different manuals you need to have at your desk when using social media for departmental purposes. That makes for a pretty constricted hole for information to get out through, and I suspect it pretty much kills most of the spontaneity, rapid response time and personal voice that makes social media effective."

Indeed, in emphasizing the risks and related policy considerations that accompany the use of social media by the public service, the Guideline did little to curb a trend already under way in departments, whereby communication officials were developing dense, hierarchical approval processes to manage their social media accounts. For example, the former HRSDC social media team created a "Tweet Approval Process," as they dubbed it, demanding that all 140-character tweets issued via the department's central Twitter accounts move through six stages before being published online. The process was organized as a workflow:

1   "Tasking" (the request for a tweet is sent to the relevant program's communication advisors)
2   "Drafting" (three tweets are drafted for an event, and Linguistic Services are recruited to help with translation)
3   "Consultation" (the tweets are sent to Media Services; Media Services in consultation with Program Communications will review tweets and "research previous messaging" and "determine strategic messaging and timing"; Media Services dispatches the tweet to Corporate Web to determine the "optimal audience reach. In consultation with Program Communications, Corporate Web will research and review #hashtag use, ensure

Twitter style guide is applied, request shortened URLs if possible." Then Corporate Web will send revised tweets to Media Services)

4   "Program Communications Approval" (Media Services sends the revised tweets to Program Communications, who then obtain approval at the director level)

5   "MO [Minister's Office] Approval" (Program communications advisors send the director-approved tweet to Media Services, who then seek approval from the Minister's Office)

6   "Distribution": "On the day of tweet, Media Services will post Tweets and coordinate with Media Relations, re. media advisory, news release, sound bite, etc. Media Services will send final approved copy to Program Comms."

(Human Resources and Skills Development Canada, n.d.)

When asked how long this process might take, one member of the communications team explained that, in an emergency, the process could be sped up, but generally it could take weeks to produce a single tweet. When asked how many people are involved in the approval process, another member of the team replied, "Don't laugh. Could be between five to nine people" (C3). And the approvals did not end there. Staff elaborated that they would sometimes seek approval for a retweet, in this case from the minister, which they undertook to ensure that they did not accidentally appear to be promoting an organization with a partisan agenda relevant to the department's mandate. This follows from the fact that the account was not managed by program or policy experts in the department who could more readily identify inappropriate retweets without needing to check in with superiors. Rather, it was managed by communication officials who could not possibly be intimately informed about the range of stakeholders with whom a department such as HRSDC, whose varied programs take Canadians from "womb to tomb," interacts.

As with the Guideline for External Use of Web 2.0, tweet approval processes such as that of HRSDC have provided fodder for journalists who frame the government's use of social media as just another example of bureaucratic inefficiency and waste, a humorous but depressing example of a paranoid, control-obsessed, and information-hoarding public service out of touch with the rapid, informal, and personalized forms of communication typically associated with social media and increasingly the norm in daily communication patterns of digital era citizens and organizations (Hannay 2013, 2016; Levesque 2013). As lamented by the Canadian Press (2014), in this case commenting on Industry Canada's whopping twelve-step tweet approval process, "pity the poor government tweet, nearly strangled in its cradle before limping into the Twitterverse."

While avoiding such colourful imagery when describing how tweets are managed in HRSDC, a senior official in the department's web communications team nonetheless frankly acknowledged that it is not by accident but by design that they avoid the informal, "on the fly," person-to-person exchanges that social media allow but that are virtually unattainable when all content must be processed through multiple stages of bureaucratic approval and polishing. As he explained, rather than viewing social media as a tool for rapid and informal information exchange and networking, the department uses these media as a means of drawing people back to the much more controlled Web 1.0 (i.e., static and noninteractive) world of the departmental website. Commenting on their social media accounts, he noted that "it's always linked back. There's one rule that we have regarding tweets. It's always got to link back to the website." He clarified that "for me social media [are] just a different way to push information. It's the same info" (C3). This point was reflected in a departmental report on social media noting that, far from representing a disruption to "communications as usual" in the department, "social media [are] really just another way of doing business" and "present no changes from [Web] 1.0" (Human Resources and Skills Development Canada 2010, 13).

Another HRSDC official echoed this assertion:

> Our approach is to situate our Web 1.0, our static websites, at the centre of our universe, you know, for our web presence. So any forays that we have, say our YouTube channels or our Facebook pages or our Twitter accounts, all are designed to direct people back to the authoritative, comprehensive, definitive information that resides on our websites. So everything that we do here is in support of this. (C1)

Analysis of one popular social media platform employed by federal departments – Twitter – reveals that the early approach of HRSDC to social media was not unique in the federal government.

Bureaucrats on Twitter

Using a custom script and the Twitter application programming interface (API), I archived all content published on official Government of Canada

Twitter accounts for a period of just over two months between late February and early May 2012.[3] This archive consisted of 6,114 tweets and included all original tweets, all retweets (i.e., tweets that share content from another user's account by republishing it on one's own account), and all mentions (i.e., references to or conversations with other users on Twitter, noted by the use of @ username in the tweet) published by departmental accounts.[4]

I then analyzed a simple random sample of Government of Canada tweets (n = 909) to categorize the content of tweets and the type of tweets (e.g., original tweets, retweets, and mentions) published by departments.[5] Where another user was retweeted or mentioned in a government tweet, I categorized the type of Twitter user retweeted or mentioned (e.g., government, individual citizen, academic institution). Where URLs were included in tweets, I noted the type of website to which the tweet linked (e.g., government, traditional media source such as the *Globe and Mail*, academic institution). I recruited three additional coders to analyze a sample of the 909 tweets that I coded in order to investigate if my classifications were sufficiently reliable using intercoder reliability tests.[6]

The first level of analysis applied to each tweet – content classification – responds to the question "what does the Government of Canada tweet about?" Here tweets were classified into three content categories. "Informational" tweets provide information, such as how to access a government service, or highlight a new program or policy. "Participatory" tweets attempt to engage other Twitter users in dialogue, policy consultation, or service design and delivery. Lastly, tweets categorized as "amicable ties" support amicable government-citizen relations through the use of friendly, informal language and tone. These tweets do not provide information, nor do they explicitly endeavour to engage other Twitter users in dialogue on policies or services; rather, they stand on their own as unique forms of government-citizen exchange on Twitter, and they represent a departure from the formal, authoritative language and tone typically used by governments and large organizations in official communications. An example of a tweet categorized as amicable ties is "@username Thank you for following us!"[7]

As indicated in Table 3.1, 7 percent of Government of Canada tweets fit into the amicable ties category, employing informal, friendly language but not providing substantive information or soliciting participation. Just under 3 percent of the tweets analyzed explicitly prompted citizens to contribute to policy development or service delivery, for example by directing users to a government consultation exercise (e.g., "Community meetings on the Halibut Experimental Recreational

TABLE 3.1

Government of Canada tweets categorized by content

Category	Tweets N	%
Informational	820	90.2
Amicable ties	64	7.0
Participatory	25	2.8
TOTAL	909	100.0

Fishery; See details at: http://ow.ly/a6BHk") or attempting to use Twitter as a platform to solicit such contributions (e.g., "Have you seen wolverine prints in the snow in #GlacierNP recently? Our biologists want to hear about it! http://ow.ly/9oGDY").[8]

The overwhelming majority of tweets (90.2 percent) fit into the informational category, offering information about services (e.g., "Are you a worker with low income? You may be entitled to the Working Income Tax Benefit. http://bit.ly/wE3uyM") or representing an informational service, as is the case for product recalls, such as the following issued from the Public Health Agency of Canada: "Health Hazard (C. botulinum) – salted and cured fish products: Recalling firm – Lotus Fine Foods. Distribution – ... http://bit.ly/IfMIFD." Reflecting the sentiment that "social media [are] just a different way to push information," to quote the HRSDC web communications manager cited earlier, these tweets represent one-way information pushes.[9]

To be sure, issuing participatory tweets that explicitly seek to engage other Twitter users in dialogue on policy or collaboration in service delivery is not the only way in which departments could use Twitter to exchange information and network more fluidly with the public than they have traditionally been able to using Web 1.0 or offline communication channels. For example, research in the field of computer-mediated communications suggests that, by retweeting other users' content, or by directly engaging with other users through user mentions, Twitter users can engage in a more personalized, interactive manner than is achieved by the simple, one-way information sharing accomplished via original tweets (boyd, Golder, and Lotan 2010; Honeycutt and Herring 2009). Applied to the Government of Canada, retweets and user mentions could usher in a more networked form of interaction than we have traditionally witnessed in the strategically designed, carefully controlled, one-way informational pushes issued by the federal government.

TABLE 3.2

Government of Canada tweets categorized by type

Type	N	%
Original tweets	476	52.4
User mentions	249	27.4
Retweets	184	20.2
TOTAL	909	100.0

As shown in Table 3.2, departments' tweets are split roughly in half, with 52 percent representing original tweets issued without a specific effort to engage with particular users and the remaining 48 percent representing tweets in which departments attempt to network with other users through user mentions or by retweeting content published by another user. This suggests that, even if departments largely use their Twitter accounts to publish informational tweets, as opposed to explicitly engaging outsiders in participatory policy dialogue and collaborative service delivery, they nonetheless attempt to engage in a more interactive, personalized style of communication via Twitter.[10]

However, this raises the important question of *whom* the government engages with through its user mentions and retweets. As depicted in Table 3.3, when government departments engage directly with other users through user mentions, or when they retweet content, most often they do so in reference to other government departments' Twitter accounts; 26.1 percent of all user mentions and retweets referenced other departments. After government bodies, individual users were the next most commonly engaged Twitter users, referenced in 24.2 percent of all government user mentions and retweets. Accounts representing civil society were directly engaged by government tweets in only 4.9 percent of cases, falling behind academic institutions, media, commercial users, non-Canadian government bodies, and Government of Canada ministers.

In interpreting these percentage values, one might suggest that, even though engagement with non–Government of Canada organizations is relatively low, and departments are most inclined to engage with other departments on Twitter (representing 26.1 percent of all their user mentions and retweets), the fact that 24.2 percent of all government tweets endeavour directly to engage with accounts of individual people does point to a more networked, interactive model of government-citizen interaction emerging

Table 3.3

Government of Canada retweets and user mentions categorized by user referenced

Type	N	%
Federal government	113	26.1
Individual user	105	24.2
Academic institution	40	9.2
Media	39	9.0
Commercial sector	34	7.9
Foreign government	27	6.2
Government of Canada minister or parliamentary secretary	23	5.3
Civil society	21	4.8
Canadian provincial/territorial government	12	2.8
Multiple users	12	2.8
Canadian municipal government	4	0.9
Nongovernmental research organization	2	0.5
Member of Parliament	1	0.2
TOTAL	433	100.0

on Twitter. However, this interpretation should be checked by considering the universe of possible Twitter accounts with which the government could interact on the platform. In 2012, when these data were collected, there were 145 million Twitter users.[11] Of these users, only 139 were Government of Canada Twitter accounts, indicating that, as a total proportion of all departmental user mentions and retweets, other government departments are grossly overrepresented. In short, yes, the Government of Canada does use user mentions and retweets to engage in a more networked, interactive model of information exchange on this platform; however, when it does so, it is most inclined to network and interact with its own departments' content (e.g., retweeting another department's tweet about a new program offering), supporting a type of departmental echo chamber – a conversation among themselves – on the network.[12]

Finally, we can evaluate the extent to which government departments use Twitter to engage in a more networked form of information sharing and interaction (versus simply using the platform to push government information) by analyzing the weblinks included in Government of Canada tweets.[13] That is, we can ask "do departments use Twitter as a means of rerouting people to their own static, government-controlled websites (as the HRSDC manager quoted earlier suggested)? Or do they use the platform to link to

TABLE 3.4

Types of websites linked to in Government of Canada tweets

Type	N	%
Federal government	565	74.3
Media	72	9.5
Commercial sector	52	6.8
Individual	23	3.0
Non-Canadian government	19	2.5
Civil society	15	2.0
Academic institution	7	0.9
Other Canadian government (e.g., provincial, territorial, or municipal)	4	0.5
Nongovernmental research organization	3	0.4
TOTAL	760	100.0

nondepartmental websites that provide information not controlled by the government but that supports government policies or services, representing a more networked, open model of information provision?"

As Table 3.4 indicates, of the 760 tweets that included weblinks, 74.3 percent linked back to Government of Canada websites. As with its re-tweets and user mentions, the federal government was much more inclined to connect with its own carefully managed web content on Twitter than it was with content generated by those outside its institutional walls. Combined with a strict reliance on tweet approval processes and a preference for informational tweets that push government-crafted information out, versus attempting to draw information in through dialogue and collaboration, departmental use of Twitter was emblematic of the broader approach taken by the Government of Canada in its earliest efforts to account for the proliferation of networked social web technologies in the mid-2000s. Social media were framed as tools to be tightly controlled by a defined set of actors (communication officers) and governed through defined top-down approvals, centralized government policies, and in support of existing government-crafted communications, strategies, and products.[14]

Why did the federal bureaucracy default to siloed and hierarchical control of social media in its earliest stages of adapting to the digital age? I turn to this question in the next sections.

The Stephen Harper Effect?

In explaining the Government of Canada's siloed and hierarchical management of social media in the early stages, many might be inclined to look to the prime minister at the helm of the bureaucracy at the time, Stephen Harper. By this argument, those responsible for integrating social media into the work of the bureaucracy faced particularly potent barriers to using these platforms for open, fluid engagement given that they operated under a prime minister who – through various mechanisms – was infamous for a governing style that rested on centralized information control, as detailed in a series of academic and popular books on the Harper government published throughout the 2010s (Delacourt 2016a; Harris 2014; Marland 2016; Martin 2011; Wells 2013).

None of the officials interviewed or the documents reviewed indicated that draconian TBS guidelines or departmental policies on social media use were the products of directives from the PMO or ministers' offices; in fact, one interviewee who had helped to craft the TBS social media guidelines laughed at the idea that political staff or ministers cared about the minute details of an internal TBS policy developed by bureaucrats for bureaucrats (I9). And, when asked directly whether the bureaucracy's approach to social media was a symptom of Harper's approach to communications and public engagement, interviewees typically explained that it would be hard to determine whether a different leadership style would have fostered a more open approach to social media given that platforms such as Facebook and Twitter entered the scene under Harper; no previous government had governed in the digital age.[15]

Interviewees were more telling regarding the influence of Harper's governance style on the management of social media when they discussed a barrier to open government in the federal bureaucracy that both predated and was intensified under Harper: risk-averse management as a response to permanent campaigning. Operating under political leadership deeply immersed in a culture of permanent campaigning, and whose own political communications style prioritized centralization and control, managers in the bureaucracy already prone to adopt risk-averse models of government-citizen interaction (a trend well established before Harper entered the PMO) faced acute pressures to avoid a more decentralized, open, fluid approach to social media. Responding to this impetus among Harper-era executives, officials in the TBS responsible for crafting the Guideline on social media use explained that they were conscious it might attract criticism for its length, formality, and emphasis on policy considerations. However, they underscored that it had been written that way deliberately to assuage the concerns and "speak the language" of risk-averse managers who needed to see in detail how the potential risks of social media – a new and untested government activity with the potential for "viral" information flows to embarrass the department – could be mitigated by well-established policy guidelines and internal procedures. Tony Clement, himself a prolific tweeter and president of the TBS under whom the Guideline was introduced, acknowledged that, without these rules, risk-averse public servants paranoid about crossing an "invisible line" toward "offside" behaviour would simply avoid social media altogether (quoted in Marland 2016, 283). This view was shared by a former public servant, an early trailblazer in encouraging departmental use of social media to engage with the public:

> They [the federal government] have a guideline in the use of social media that ... is really disturbing because it reads like it was written by lawyers for lawyers, because it's like twenty-four pages long, and the motivation behind it was there was two years' worth of internal discussion and dialogue and debate about the guidelines. And the motivation I think was to create guidelines that gave deputy ministers and chief executives of organizations within the government the framework within which they could make risk-based decisions about how they behave online. And it was meant to be a positive step because the framework hadn't existed before, so it was – "Okay, here you go, here are your obligations, here are the potential risks, and remember you have the leeway within th[is] range of policies to take decisions appropriate to the risk you want to assume." A lot of people that are engaged online would really rather see very permissive and very flexible frameworks that simply identify the landmines and then leave everything else open to interpretations. What the Treasury Board people told me were those guidelines were meant to be empowering for executives, but, when you read them with a history of interacting with stakeholders who traditionally are reluctant to engage on Government 2.0 initiatives, there's also a lot of space there for them to say "I am not willing to take on this risk." So the guidelines there ostensibly create the framework, but they also create the mechanism through which people can hang their hats on, not willing to assume the risk, and that's the challenge I see across the implementation. (A1)

One official conducting a review of the TBS policy suite comprising these rules and processes remarked that in practice, when it comes to digital technologies such as social media, there is a "cover-your-ass culture" in which officials are more comfortable assuming that a set of existing TBS policies applies to a new TBS instrument, such as the Guideline, leading to "scope/mission creep on all the [TBS] instruments." As he argued, this "speaks directly to the cultural obsession with IT security, privacy, [and] communications" in senior management (P8). This underlying culture of risk-averse management was not confronted and reformed when social media were added to the toolkit of the public service in the mid-2000s. In fact, tools such as Twitter entered the scene when permanent campaigning is thought to have reached unprecedented heights under Harper's leadership (Aucoin 2012; Marland 2016; Marland, Giasson, and Esselment 2017; Savoie 2013). So the same "cultural obsession" with tight, policy-laden use of technology and communication tools naturally marked the bureaucracy's approach to social media, as it did all other communication platforms.

Recognizing that social media were simply bolted on to this existing culture, we should not be surprised that a 140-character tweet in some cases can be assessed by nine people – including senior directors and the minister – or pass through twelve stages of approval before it is released amid the roughly 350,000 tweets published every minute (Aslam 2018). Put differently, absent an ill-guided indulgence in technological determinism, there is no reason to believe that the same managers responding to a political climate rewarding "error-free government" (Himelfarb 2005; Jarvis 2016; Lynch 2007, 2008; Savoie 2013) and a communications culture steeped in fast-paced, antagonistic exposé would adopt social media in any other way than through tight centralized controls, achieved through the well-entrenched mechanisms of functional separation and hierarchical governance. The alternative – opening the floodgates and allowing any public servant to speak autonomously for the department on these open, networked platforms – would represent a nightmare for both the political leaders competing in a permanent campaigning culture marked by strategic communication battles and the managers responding to these leaders.

However, when explaining why social media were initially integrated into siloed and hierarchical models of information exchange anathema to open networking, the partisan impulse toward centralization of communications (amplified under Harper), and the bureaucracy's response to this dynamic of contemporary political culture, is only part of the story. That is, when asked to explain why social media were managed as they were, interviewees (as with the documentary evidence analyzed) more commonly pointed to conditions that limit open government-citizen interaction that far predate the Harper government and are not related to the pressures of a permanent campaigning culture. These conditions are those that have long limited the scope for an open, decentralized federal bureaucracy.

The Virtues of Communications Centralization

In integrating social media into their work, bureaucrats defaulted to the long-standing trend in the public service of both functionally defining and separating tasks into isolated, nonoverlapping silos and of identifying particular actors within the bureaucracy to serve as the designated voices for departments. This system ensures that the bulk of the bureaucracy remains anonymous and disconnected from the citizenry, as per the traditional Westminster bargain and the model of Progressive-Era Public Administration animating early theories of the bureaucratic state. The same informational gatekeeping function that has seen communication officials and other designated spokespersons serve as the filters through which department-outsider relations are managed was replicated, not reformed, in the face of social media.

In some sense, this outcome was entirely predictable. The bureaucratic mind defaults to siloed and hierarchical control of information and communication, and there is little reason to believe that the advent of social media would necessarily upend this "closed by default" instinct among bureaucrats. However, more than simply being the product of unthinking instinct, there are also entirely legitimate reasons to treat social media as the bureaucracy did.

One reason is the *pragmatic* impulse driving communications centralization in the bureaucracy. Best practice in government communications cautions against a decentralized model that would see departments variously defining the languages, fonts, colours, logos, and messages used in their communications. When explaining why departments had allocated responsibility for social media to communications shops alone, as opposed to allowing a more decentralized model of social media communications, respondents in line departments, the TBS, and the PCO directly invoked the logic of centralization accepted as best practice for government communications, especially those online, and for which the government has historically been praised (see Accenture 2005; Borins 2007; Roy 2006; and United Nations and Department of Economic and Social Affairs 2014). As one communications manager explained, "you're trying to rationalize it to one place to go, no wrong door ... We don't want to be spread out all over the place. We can't afford it, it's not good for business, it's not good for Canadians" (C8).

Building on this sentiment, an official in the PCO's Communications and Consultations Secretariat explained that in 2012 they decided to implement a PCO review requirement for all social media accounts in order to reduce the potential for departments to create accounts without thinking about whole of government and whole of department communication strategies already under way, to avoid wasteful and confusing duplication of accounts, and to ensure that standard identifiers and logos were used to allow government accounts to be recognized as such by Canadians (S2). Further, recognizing that communications shops are already expert at handling the relatively onerous and complex corporate requirements, strategies, and procedures applied to communications, the PCO official explained that it made sense to have these actors manage social media as another channel through which departments interact with the public. In this sense, we can explain the bureaucracy's decision to centralize control over social media in one particular group of actors as a move in step with a longer pattern in the government-citizen relationship. The points from which the government "speaks" have become ever more rationalized and limited with a view to ensuring coordinated, efficient, and effective service delivery and information provision. Although social media can usher in a more informal, decentralized model of information sharing in other contexts, in the federal public service such a model would defy the centralization logic now accepted as orthodox best practice within the sprawling bureaucracy of the government, in which the potential for a costly, ineffective, and uncoordinated "wild west" of communications to emerge is high.

Finally, we can explain the bureaucracy's reliance on siloed and hierarchical management of social media by considering the unique accountability requirements and related policies and processes at play in all government-citizen interactions. Although we might reasonably criticize managers averse to *any* diversion from the status quo (including the use of social media) for fear of the risks that such diversions raise, and though we might equally offer legitimate criticisms of ineffective or excessive "mission creep" among TBS policies, some consideration of risk, and some adherence to certain policies and processes, are necessary to ensure that departments use social media accountably. These risks and the policies and processes in place to reduce them reflect a core premise of the PPA model: whenever the public service comes in contact with outsiders, accountability breaches can arise should these contacts usher in the inequitable treatment of certain citizens and organizations.

Reflecting these concerns, regardless of the time lags and bulky processes that rule adherence can necessitate, rules cannot be simply whisked away in the name of embracing innovative opportunities for government-citizen interaction in the digital age. For instance, interviewees explained that exchanges on social media must take place on platforms that do not exclude those with disabilities, a preoccupation of the Standard on Web Accessibility (Treasury Board Secretariat 2011b), which mandates that any social media platform used is compatible with a screen reader for the visually impaired (recall that the former HRSDC was successfully sued under a Charter challenge for not complying with this requirement in its web communications). Equally, as per the Official Languages Act, the Government of Canada must ensure that it can accommodate both official languages on any platform that it uses, requiring that all single-language content be translated or produced initially in both English and French. The bilingualism and accessibility for those with disability requirements also demand that in certain cases custom terms of service be drafted with social media companies (one of the tasks that the PCO review provides for departments). Where such terms of service cannot be accommodated, these requirements can ultimately render certain social media sites ineligible for government use, despite their popularity outside the government.

Departments must also ensure that social media posts do not employ language or use symbols and colours that favour particular political parties over others, a betrayal of the principle of nonpartisan public service. Thus, the Guideline invoked the *Values and Ethics Code for the Public Sector* (Treasury Board Secretariat 2011d) and the Federal Identity Program (Treasury Board Secretariat 2003), each of which provides standards that limit the scope for public sector communications to become politicized. Restrictions will also come into play where a site does not allow the Government of Canada to adhere to legislative requirements for protecting the personal information of citizens or where viruses and phishing scams pose risks to the integrity of government computing systems.

It was in considering these legitimate policy and legislative requirements that the Guideline and departmental social media processes became as dense as they did, garnering the criticism that they "handcuff" (Khan 2011) the public service and limit the scope for open, networked engagement. Yet those offering these criticisms could not comfortably or convincingly argue that the Government of Canada should throw these considerations aside, encouraging use of social media that betrays the rules calling for communications that are nonpartisan, accessible in both official languages and to those with disabilities, and do not pose security risks.

Thus, though centralized and department-specific policies governing the creation, management, and use of social media might limit the scope for interactive, on-the-fly, and informal exchanges, resulting instead in time lags as content is verified, translated, and approved, it is not strictly the case that these policies intend to limit the scope for less regulated, more spontaneous exchanges. Reflecting this point, lower-level communication officials in particular consistently explained that they wished they could be more interactive in their use of these tools, but they were often unsure how they could engage more fluidly with outsiders on social media given accountability concerns and the related rules and processes in place to address them.

So, facing a political climate with little tolerance for communications slip-ups, an orthodox model of communications that reinforces the pragmatic value of reducing and centrally coordinating the government's "voices," and onerous policies guarding against equity and accountability breaches, when the public service first integrated social media into its work, it did so in what was possibly the least compatible organizational context imaginable for the brand of open, networked, and on-the-fly information exchange associated with social media. Both by design and by default, and driven by political, pragmatic, and ethical factors, the Government of Canada has traditionally proven to be a closed institution. At its first encounter with the digital age, embodied in the adoption of social media, the bureaucracy revealed its instinctive impulse to preserve this well-entrenched closed model of organizing internal work and of interacting with outsiders.

Yet, in highlighting the incompatibility of the federal government's traditionally closed work model with the social media technologies emerging as defining features of the digital age, evident in the apparent absurdity of twelve-step tweet approval processes, and government communicators' inability to engage in fluid interactions on these networks, we can see that this earliest encounter with social media equally set the stage for the public service to question the long-term sustainability – and importantly the risks – of closed government enduring in the digital age.

The Cracking Foundations of Closed Government
Reflecting on the advent of crowdsourcing, wikis, and other platforms for web-based collaboration, one federal government executive remarked that

the "old model of the contained policy process doesn't work anymore" and that this model needs to be adjusted in light of new public servants who have a worldview fundamentally different from that of the traditional, anonymous, under-the-radar Westminster public servant:

> I think of policy personas, like the people I have come across, like the people who have been doing the job for twenty-five years and know everything about the policy and the history and the consultative processes, and they could tell you who the stakeholders are and what their positions are. And then you have the policy generalists who aren't that deep on a specific policy but are wider ranging across a number. And then you have new policy analysts who aren't necessarily experts on a policy, but what they have done is gotten an MPA [Master of Public Administration], they've been on Twitter since they were in, you know, Grade 12, or they've been online. They also have a sense of urgency about their career, and they have a need to be recognized and validated outside of their own little branch or office, so they want their life and their professional work to be externally focused. So they're presenting a fundamental challenge to the policy process, simply by being that type of person. (A1)

Echoing this sentiment, and commenting on the practice of siloing off government-citizen interactions to the communications shop, as opposed to allowing a more decentralized, autonomously governed model of social media use that might see individual public servants engaging publicly about their files on social media, one policy analyst remarked that

> the natural answer is just let comms handle it, and I disagree because in a world where comms is the only point of contact to anything it means that you can never have a discussion about anything. So we have to change the perception that the only role for outside is one point of contact. We [public servants] have access, we have growing access, to what's happening outside. (P1)

This observation accurately describes the experience of the communication officials who managed the HRSDC Twitter account. The inability of these lower-level public servants to retweet in the moment, without first seeking approval, was a direct reflection of their comparatively shallow understanding of the department's varied stakeholders. Equally, the requirement that social media content be filtered through communication officers renders substantive online dialogue on departmental policies and programs impossible. In most cases, these officers need to check in with subject matter experts in the department to respond appropriately to a question or comment offered by the public on a social media platform. Given the closed bureaucrat-bureaucrat relationship, and the decision-implementation incoherence that it can introduce, it is unlikely that this intrabureaucratic dialogue can move quickly enough to support a real-time bureaucrat-citizen exchange online. As observed by one federal public servant, the

> government could try to ask general, light questions about broad thoughts on policy or services via social media, such that such in-depth knowledge is not needed, but it'll inevitably get to a complicated request or question. Then the only response available is "That's interesting, we'll consider that and get back to you" and suddenly the people engaging are reminded that they're not talking to the people responsible, and it breaks the spell ... People talk to people, not organizations, and it's impossible to have a conversation that hypothetically could include everything that an organization "knows." The departmental level is too *big* for conversation. (Aitken 2015)

An alternative model might see individual public servants managing their own personal accounts or official, subject-specific government accounts in lieu of, or as a complement to, depersonalized departmental accounts. In this approach, public servants would enjoy more direct and tailored access to social media platforms, improving the inefficient, ineffective, current model that casts the communications shop as the gatekeeper of these networks. At one level, this model would allow public servants to directly monitor and collect information relevant to their work, improving on the scant exposure to social media data that they receive in media roundups, such as the media roundup from HRSDC mentioned already. This decentralized model would also allow the public service to use social media more effectively as a platform for real-time, rapid information exchange and dialogue with the public. This is precisely the case in the quotation from Kent Aitken above, taken from the blog *Canadian Public Sector Renewal*.[16] This is a personal blog, not sanctioned by the government, authored by federal public servants – self-dubbed "virtuous schemers" (Charney 2008) – who, since the mid-2000s, have been breaking from the traditional mould of the anonymous public servant by openly discussing public management reform on this blog and as part of a group of federal public servants engaging on Twitter via the hashtags "#w2p," "#cpsr," "#gcdigital," and "#policyinnovation" (Clarke 2014c).[17] Other senior officials have also developed professional social media presences, such as Andrew Treusch in his capacity as commissioner of the Canada Revenue Agency.[18] Yet these individuals hardly fall into the category of the mainstream public servant, for whom speaking publicly for the department or about his or her work online would raise a raft of questions and dilemmas. Although senior officials have long had their anonymity stripped from them as they have been called to speak publicly on the work of the public service, the average public servant still enjoys relative anonymity. A professional social media presence could entirely undermine this anonymity, raising questions about the training required for these newfound public spokespersons, the implications that this proliferation of government voices would have for the consistency and accountability of government information sharing, and perceived and actual public servant neutrality (Aitken 2015; Grube 2013, 2015).

The issue of neutrality is particularly salient given Aucoin's (2012) observation that, in rendering public servants spokespersons for their departments, properly neutral officials can be compelled to promote the government of the day through acts of promiscuous partisanship. Even officials who resist this trap can still be drawn into politically contentious dialogue online and called to personal account for government failings properly associated with and addressed by the accountable minister. And, given the near impossibility of delinking one's personal online presence from one's professional online presence, public servants engaging on social media might find their neutrality quickly questioned given the digital footprints of partisan activity that follow them online. For instance, it only takes a quick search on Google to match LinkedIn, Twitter, and Facebook accounts, and any website that mentions an individual's name, and in doing so to learn a great deal about public servants today, including the petitions that they have signed, the political leaders whom they have "followed" or "liked," or the policy issues that they have supported and critiqued. This rich, networked, public information covering virtually all public servants – not just those in senior positions, such as deputy ministers and the clerk – signals yet another departure from the concept of public servant anonymity, casting further doubt on the enduring practicality of this tenet of the original Westminster bargain as currently conceived. Citing public tweets and blogs, this study itself "outs" several lower-ranked public servants who in days gone by would not have been named in publications on Canadian public administration but who today are easily identifiable using a simple Google search or following the right Twitter hashtags.

Pointing to these new realities, an HRSDC report on social media stated that "the public servant who uses Social Media finds themselves in a shifting paradigm of communications" and that "many of the current and planned uses of Social Media present a shift, and sometimes even a fracture, to the assumptions which underlie the current controls on GC information dissemination" (Human Resources and Skills Development Canada 2010, 22). Siloed and hierarchical management of social media in the communications shop was favoured as one immediate means of attempting to remedy (or perhaps more accurately ignore) these fractures, but this "remedy" ultimately proved to be fraught. In turn, the bureaucracy's early management of social media illuminates the risks that accrue when closed government endures in the digital age.

First, as complex as upending siloed and hierarchical controls of the government-citizen interface is given the long legacy of public service anonymity and information control shaping contemporary thinking in the bureaucracy, without doing so the public service runs the risk of seriously undermining its effectiveness. For example, this risk arises when policy analysts cannot access timely and sufficiently analyzed social media data relevant to their work or when opportunities for timely information provision in emergencies are hindered because of lagged communication processes. Siloed and hierarchical models of social media use equally pose human resource costs, potentially alienating digital era public servants entering an institution out of touch with the digital world with which they are familiar. Working in the public service is "like entering a time warp," offered one young, highly critical public servant interviewed (P8).

At a more fundamental level, a closed government model of social media adoption risks a loss of credibility among a digital citizenry, as is the case in the harsh criticism that tweet approval processes and government social media guidelines have received (Eaves 2011c; Hannay 2013, 2016; Khan 2011; Levesque 2013). One official pushed this point further, arguing that the government's impulse to treat social media as a relatively inconsequential medium that should be used to replicate traditional models of tightly managed communications missed the more fundamental implications of the digital age for democratic governance, calling into question the legitimacy of a government that cannot engage meaningfully with citizens online:

> The whole social open media stuff, like, all of these, kind of, forays into new areas, is primarily driven by communications professionals, whose job, whose bread and butter, is to get out the message ... But no one is looking at how communication technology is fundamentally reordering citizens' ability to organize, what that means for government, and how government needs to respond nimbly when those organizations occur. Like, when that organization kind of happens. So, I don't know, Idle No More. Hugely amplified by social media. Was there any response in the space on behalf of government that wasn't tweeting a press release about it? (P8)

It is instructive to consider this interviewee's reflection in light of the 2007 public opinion research with which this chapter began. As noted initially, respondents explained that "government use of these types of applications [social media] would increase their confidence in the government" and that, "if it does not adopt these types of applications, the GC risks being seen as more out-of-touch than it is already perceived to be" (Phoenix Strategy Perspectives 2008, ii–iii, iv). Defaulting to elaborate, top-down approval processes and siloed, one-way, unresponsive control of social media communications did little to meet citizens' expectations in the early years of government social media use.

In sum, the bureaucracy's initial effort to adopt social media revealed three things. First, this effort uncovered the bureaucratic impulse to default to its entrenched closed model of government in the face of networked digital technologies. Second, this experience uncovered why the status quo model of closed government is incompatible with the technologies and communication patterns of the digital age, risking a loss of effectiveness, trust, and perceived democratic legitimacy among citizens while clashing with the expectations of a new corps of public servants socialized in a digital world at odds with closed government. And third, this encounter uncovered the practical questions and dilemmas that must be addressed to facilitate a shift to an open culture of governance suited to the digital age while still respecting the core tenets of the Westminster system, such as public service neutrality and ministerial accountability. Who should speak for the government? How can an organization structured on strict hierarchies, with little tolerance for public-facing failure, facilitate innovative experimentation with new technologies that thrust the public service into the public eye? How can a more open, networked model of information exchange be introduced to an organization operating in strict silos? How can the government remain relevant in an age of decentralized, informal, and frequent organization-to-outside interactions while still presenting coherent, consistent, and equitable access to information and services? If a greater number of public servants are empowered to speak for the government in networked online environments, then do established rules on political neutrality and assumptions about anonymity need to be updated? If so, then how? What training, skill sets, and internal networks will these deanonymized, digital public servants need to provide accurate, consistent, and values- and ethics-compliant information online? Is open government-citizen interaction possible in a context of permanent campaigning that rationalizes a partisan impetus to control government communications? Or, simply put, how can one open up an institution that – given its historical legacies and contemporary pragmatic and political realities – is designed to be closed?

The public service's first encounters with the digital age – captured in its uptake of social media – invoked new and exacerbated existing critiques of the ineffectiveness of closed government, critiques that take on new force in an age defined by rapid, informal, and decentralized information exchange. At the same time, the early bureaucratic response to social media indicates that the solution is not a simple flick of the switch from closed government to open government. Rather, the solution demands that the public service grapple with complex dilemmas of coordination and accountability and overcome the pressures of a political culture that rationalizes, rather than combats, tightly siloed, hierarchical models of government-citizen interaction.

Building on these findings, in the next chapter I explore the first phases of the federal open government initiative, the second central response of the Government of Canada to the advent of the digital age. At least in name and stated intent, this initiative sought to respond to the cracking foundation of closed government as initially exposed in the bureaucracy's encounters with social media. In practice, however, rather than responding to the questions that social media raised, the open government initiative further refined our understanding of the political and administrative realities that preserve closed government despite its incongruence with the demands of governing in the digital age.

4
Stephen Harper's Open(ish) Government Initiative

The Government of Canada's official and most overt effort to open the bureaucracy in the earliest years of adjusting to the digital age came in the form of an open government initiative, introduced in March 2011 by then President of the Treasury Board Secretariat Stockwell Day (Treasury Board Secretariat 2011a, 2013c). The commitment to open government came just prior to the Government of Canada's decision in September 2011 to sign the international Open Government Partnership (OGP), an organization promoting public sector transparency, accountability, and citizen engagement, which counted seventy member governments as of 2016.[1] Housed in the Chief Information Officer Branch of the TBS, the initiative was organized around three themes: open data (the release of machine-readable government data for reuse), open information (improving how information is shared with the public, as per traditional, analogue era definitions of open government), and open dialogue (improving how the bureaucracy engages citizens in policy making, drawing on new digital tools). After first announcing the initiative in 2011, and following requirements of the OGP, the Government of Canada released two Open Government Action Plans in 2012 and 2014 (with a third produced in 2016, as discussed in Chapter 7), and in 2014 it produced the Open Government Directive, which among other commitments pledged the government to be "open by default" (Treasury Board Secretariat 2014b).

At least rhetorically, these commitments to share data and information and to develop a more ambitious, digitized model of citizen engagement could have addressed head-on the logistical and cultural barriers, and the dilemmas of coordination, equity, and accountability, that have long limited the capacity of the federal bureaucracy to open itself to the public. In practice, though, beyond some advances on open data, Stephen Harper's open government initiative did little to tackle the closed by default tendencies of

Westminster bureaucracies born of Progressive-Era Public Administration, nor did the initiative provide a vehicle to address the dilemmas that digital era open government raises. This was partly a function of the political context in which the initiative emerged, with Harper's leadership more overtly modelling to the bureaucracy the tenets of closed government than it did the goals of transparency and public engagement. But Harper's leadership only partially explains why the initiative can be classified at best as having ushered in open(ish) government in the federal bureaucracy. As with the government's early forays into social media, the first phases of the open government initiative should be measured by the lessons that they offer about the political, logistical, and cultural challenges that must be faced in order to open the bureaucracy and in turn to update the federal public service for the digital age.

Open ~~Government~~ Data

Although the open government commitments were organized around three themes, promising open data, open information and open dialogue, in practice the bulk of activity centred on open data alone, so much so that at one point the website for the initiative intermittently swapped URLs between data.gc.ca and open.canada.ca. Open data entails the release of government data sets in formats and under a licensing regime that allow for their easy reuse and manipulation by outsiders, as opposed to formats such as PDFs, which render the data sets effectively useless without further and sometimes Herculean efforts. For example, imagine trying to add a column of thousands of numerical data entries in a PDF versus the same data set being released in a format that allows you to open it directly in a program such as Excel, in which functions such as addition can be automated and the data can be put to a range of different uses and combined with other data that is also available in an open, and thus interoperable, format. Such ease of manipulation and reuse is the essential difference between open data releases and data releases in general.

Interest in open data in the Government of Canada actually predated the open government initiative. Natural Resources Canada (NRCan) had long been developing common data standards with outside partners for its geospatial data and shared data sets with a liberal licensing policy via the GeoConnections, GeoGratis.ca, and GeoBase.ca programs. Outside the federal government, in 2007 a group of activists, academics, lawyers, librarians, and citizens formed Citizens for Open Access to Civic Information and Data, and a related website and mailing list (civicaccess.ca), advocating for open government data across Canada (Lauriault and McGuire 2008). After helping the mayor of Vancouver launch an open data initiative in 2008, David Eaves began advocating that the federal government release its data by creating a mock government website – datadotgc.ca – that pulled together federal data sets already available on the web. At the same time, a group of officials in Environment Canada met with Eaves in Ottawa to discuss his plans and committed to introducing their own open data pilot project, which the department subsequently shut down. Eaves launched datadotgc.ca in 2009; as he explained in a 2012 interview, it was introduced to demonstrate to the federal government that it had been releasing data online already, albeit not always in open, reusable formats or in one central space, a point that he made when presenting the site to federal chief information officers after its launch.

Outside pressure for open data mounted with the 2010 consultation on the digital economy, which pointed to widespread interest in the release of government data among participants (Industry Canada 2010). Following this consultation and in collaboration with Eaves, in 2010 Stockwell Day, then TBS president, introduced a whole of government commitment to open data. This commitment was captured in a five-point plan developed by the TBS CIO and made concrete in the introduction of an open data portal in 2011 – data.gc.ca – which, following the lead of data portals in the United Kingdom and United States, would serve as a "one-stop shop" for all government data releases (Treasury Board Secretariat 2011a). The portal was coupled with an open data licence heavily criticized initially. It included clauses removed within hours of its initial launch, such as one that limited users' ability to use the data in any way that "may bring disrepute to or prejudice the reputation of Canada" (Eaves 2011a). Another iteration of the licence, named the Open Government Licence, was released in 2013 and has been adopted in Alberta, British Columbia, and Ontario.[2]

At the time of writing, the open data portal housed 120,887 data sets, in some cases bringing together data already available to the public but not yet centralized in an integrated portal or released in open, reusable formats. The effort required to release these data should not be discounted; this was not a simple case of flicking the switch from closed to open on a master government database. Rather, the open data initiative exposed uncoordinated and in some cases insufficient information management practices in the Government of Canada.[3] Initial work on open data revealed that data sets were incomplete, contained errors, and lacked appropriate metadata (data about data to ensure that others can search and interpret data sets). In some cases departments were not entirely sure what data they actually owned and could release. Complicating these efforts, creating common standards for data across departments and making data interjurisdictional given Canada's federated system demanded time-consuming consultations and coordination, led by the open government team in the CIOB of the TBS (Clarke and Francoli 2017).

After moving through the time-consuming processes leading to their release, how have these data been used? Given that there is no systematic way for academics, nonprofits, businesses, and journalists to report on their use of the data sets, and that to date no systematic study has been undertaken to track the use of federal open data (though as of 2016 there was a GovLab study under way to track businesses' use of these data), it is difficult to draw robust conclusions about uptake and use of federal open data sets.[4] There is also little robust evidence to support conclusions about use of the data by the government itself, though those managing the open data initiative revealed that they had heard anecdotally that federal public servants were using the data, finding that the portal provided access to data that they otherwise would not have known existed or had trouble accessing across the bureaucracy (a testament again to the closed bureaucrat-bureaucrat relationship and a digital era variant of the anecdote of the public servant–initiated ATIP request mentioned in Chapter 2). This presumption is supported by research in other jurisdictions finding that governments themselves often use open data portals originally developed to support the public's uptake of government data sets, as in the Government of British Columbia, in which, in the first month of the open data portal's launch, 25 percent of those accessing the site did so from BC government Internet Protocol (IP) addresses (Longo 2016).

Easier to track are web and mobile apps that run on the data. Some of them are catalogued on the website https://open.canada.ca/en/apps, such as "Don't Eat the Meat," which, drawing on the Recalls and Safety Alerts data set from Health Canada, publishes food recall information on Facebook, Twitter, and a website. In other cases, departments directly engage outsiders to work with the data in support of departmental priorities. Environment Canada used government open data, and data collected from citizens, as part of a citizen science initiative focusing on the health of the Ottawa River system. Citizenship and Immigration Canada worked with Ajah, a company headed by Michael Lenczner, a leading Canadian open data advocate, to support analysis of its grants and contributions data. Ajah has also compiled disparate government open data sets to create a set of tools to support nonprofits seeking funding from the federal government.[5]

Although not directly connected to the open data initiative per se, under an initiative named the Web Experience Toolkit, the Government of Canada released all of the code underpinning its websites onto GitHub, a collaborative code-sharing site.[6] In other instances, open data sets are not used to support public services or policy development; rather, they form a sort of informational service, as in the data set detailing fuel consumption ratings of vehicles that can be used to inform consumers' purchasing decisions. Finally, some uses of the data are more playful than practical, as in the use of federal geospatial data to create a 1:1 scale model of the region of Niagara for the video game Minecraft, though even this application has potential social benefits, with the creators of the model explaining that it could be used in the classroom to explore the geography of the region.[7]

To stimulate further use of these data sets, in February 2014 and 2015 the Government of Canada hosted two forty-eight-hour hackathons, dubbed the Canadian Open Data Experience (CODE). CODE 2014 involved 900 developers, students, and "open data enthusiasts" (Government of Canada 2014c), and CODE 2015 attracted 1,300 participants (Government of Canada 2015a). Working with federal data sets, as well as other sources of open data, participants in these hackathons were invited to produce apps and websites in competition for cash prizes. One of the 2015 winners included a team that produced proliteracy.ca, a website that uses government data to provide advice to those attending postsecondary education by cross-referencing university programs to tuition and rent costs in Canadian cities and providing tailored advice on student grants and loans.[8] Another of the top apps at CODE 2015, the Farm Canada app, allows farmers to explore historical agricultural data and commodity prices to inform their decision making.

Having stimulated an ecosystem of actors directing government data to a range of ends but notably, in certain cases, to support policy objectives and government services, the open data initiative thus marked a departure from the historical default within Westminster bureaucracies, whereby the work of the public service and the work of those outside its walls are kept properly distinct. Following on previous disruptions to this tradition, including consultations and uptake of alternative service delivery arrangements, open data represented a digital era opening of the federal government and a concomitant digital era departure from classical framings of the bureaucrat-outsider relationship as properly circumscribed. Turning to the other two planks of the open government initiative (dialogue and information), however, we find less evidence of a digital era opening of the government during the first two Open Government Action Plans produced under the Harper government.

Under the rubric of open dialogue, the government pledged to promote "Web 2.0 and similar tools, such as crowdsourcing, to engage Canadians in a discussion on government policies and priorities" (Treasury Board Secretariat 2012b). Specifically, the TBS explained, when first introduced in 2011, the open dialogue program committed the federal government to four core tasks. First, the government would develop common guidelines on the use of social media and Web 2.0 tools by departments. This objective was met through the Guideline for External Use of Web 2.0. As discussed in Chapter 3, the Guideline was criticized for imposing a complex and stifling mix of policy requirements on departments' social media use, and did little to discourage multiple-step approval processes and tightly managed social media communications at odds with the goals of open dialogue.

Second, under its open dialogue commitments, the government launched internal and external consultations on best practices for consultation, collaborated with the Canada School of Public Service to develop training for the use of social media, and cited the work of a Social Media Community of Practice that had formed in the government (composed primarily of communications professionals). But this series of vague activities appears to have produced few concrete outputs, and these activities did not change the trend whereby social media were primarily framed as tools relevant to official government communications (Government of Canada 2015b).

The TBS attempted to support more expansive use of social media with a new policy in 2013 – the *Policy on Acceptable Network and Device Use* – which stated that departments could open up access to social media sites across the bureaucracy, as opposed to putting these sites behind departmental firewalls. The policy stated that "authorized individuals" – defined broadly in the policy as effectively anyone in the federal government authorized to access the Internet – should have "open access to the Internet including Government of Canada and external Web 2.0 tools and services" (Treasury Board Secretariat 2013b).[9]

In practice, however, this directive did not lead to whole of government access to social media and other collaborative web platforms, with CIOs in departments continuing to block access in certain cases, typically citing concerns about cybersecurity or bandwidth capacity as justification. On this point, one interviewee noted that employees were warned that, when watching the 2012 Olympics over lunch, they should do so in groups because too many devices streaming online video would overly tax the department's system, compromising core functionality required to deliver programs (P8).

The varied landscape of Internet access across the bureaucracy was explored in a 2015 experiment of the Deputy Minister Committee on Policy Innovation. Select committee members from across the government attempted to access a list of predetermined websites and services from behind the firewalls of various departments. The committee included social media sites but also tested access to commonly used document-sharing services (e.g., Google Drive, Dropbox, Prezi, SlideShare) and Google Chrome, a browser required to access certain websites incompatible with the standard Internet Explorer browser installed on government computers. The experiment's findings are reflected in Table 4.1, adapted from the original table created by the committee. In interpreting these findings, it is important to note that it is possible that a site could have been accessed by other individuals in the department, even if the individual on the committee involved in the experiment did not have access to it. For instance, it is likely that communications officials in all departments would have had access to the social media sites tested since they publish on them for their departments. Moreover, it is also important to note that in certain cases, access was not blocked by an Internet firewall, but that the site was effectively blocked nonetheless, because attempts to access it timed out due to the department's weak Internet connection, because the site demanded that the user have permission to download software or files from the web, or because the site did not operate on Internet Explorer, and other browsers, such as Google Chrome, were not installed on the desktop computer used. Finally, though in some cases the website or platform could be accessed, its full functionality could not always be used. For instance, officials in the TBS can access Google Drive but are not permitted to upload files to it or to edit documents on it.

The experiment revealed that, though the *Policy on Acceptable Network and Device Use* had the stated goal of facilitating "open access to the Internet including Government of Canada and external Web 2.0 tools and services," in practice the policy did not achieve this objective, a testament to the gap between official TBS policies and the reality of departments implementing these policies (Treasury Board Secretariat 2013b). For the open dialogue commitment specifically, this censored Internet access did little to support whole of government uptake of the web as a new means of engaging with outsiders in policy development. For instance, in departments in which

TABLE 4.1

Internet access across Government of Canada departments, June 2015

	Google Drive	Dropbox	Survey Monkey	Skype	Prezi	SlideShare	Twitter	YouTube	Hootsuite	Google Chrome
Canadian Heritage	X	X		X		X				
PCO										
Industry Canada										
NRCan					X					
DND	X	X	X	X	X	X		X	X	X
DFO										
Health Canada				X						
Shared Services Canada										
Veterans Affairs				X						
Public Safety	X			X			X	X		X
TBS		X			X	X				X
Finance Canada				X		X				X
ESDC	X	X	X	X	X	X			X	X
DFATD				X						
CRA	X	X	X	X	X	X	X	X	X	X
AANDC	X			X	X			X	X	
Environment Canada	X	X		X						X

NOTE: Cells marked with an "X" indicate that the site, platform, or tool could not be accessed from within the relevant department.

SOURCE: Adapted from Deputy Minister Committee on Policy Innovation (2015b).

mainstream social media sites remained blocked, program officers, policy advisers, and managers would be prevented from engaging in any dialogue with stakeholders and the public on these platforms, never mind simply being able to see what information these individuals shared on these platforms.

At a 2016 Public Policy Forum meeting hosted under Chatham House Rule, one federal government official retorted that in practice the blocked access raises no problem since officials can access these sites on their personal smartphones or tablets. However, this "solution" does raise a few problems. Employees should not have to use their personal devices and self-financed data plans for work-related activities, and it is impractical and inefficient to access certain sites and tools on a phone or tablet versus a computer. At a more fundamental level, while remaining blocked on official devices, employees would find little evidence to support the idea that their employer views these public online platforms as legitimate and sanctioned tools to support open dialogue in the bureaucracy.

One can also imagine that the inability to access tools such as Dropbox and Google Drive on work devices would impede collaborative policy development that rests on outsiders being able easily to produce and share files with those in the government. For instance, though the goal admittedly is not "collaboration," one lawyer informed me that facing the government in legal challenges can be incredibly frustrating in instances where departmental employees cannot use Dropbox to access large documents, illustrating the practical impediment that uneven Internet access would pose to substantive engagement with outsiders online even as the open dialogue initiative unfolded and promised to facilitate this engagement.[10] This impediment was evident in an online dialogue with student advisers that Employment and Social Development Canada (ESDC) attempted to undertake in 2014. Seeking a genuinely deliberative, interactive forum, the department selected Google+ to host the dialogue. The decision was vetoed by IT because it was perceived to present a security risk, which led the team to use an inferior, department-approved platform that, in the end, did not permit participants to submit their feedback via the web. Paper copies of submissions were typed and entered into the "forum" by ESDC officials instead.

In addition to its focus on social media, the open dialogue initiative pledged a commitment to develop an online platform to enable regulators to engage better with Canadians and businesses on changes to the regulatory environment and on service standards. In practice, the open regulation initiative merely asked that regulators post information on regulatory changes and service standards online, not that they engage those affected by the regulations. As highlighted in an independent 2013 audit of Canada's first Open Government Action Plan, though thirty-two regulators had posted information online as a result of the initiative, "it was not clear to stakeholders how open dialogue [was] achieved" by a website that supported only a one-way flow of information (Francoli 2014, 10).

Third, under the open dialogue initiative, the federal government pledged to update Consulting with Canadians (a website that compiles web links to all consultations under way across the government) and to develop "a new Web 2.0 citizen engagement platform that federal organizations can use to conduct public consultations" (Government of Canada 2014b). Consulting with Canadians was indeed updated as part of the government's web renewal strategy in 2014, though the site remained the same in terms of core functionality and purpose: that is, as a clearinghouse to list ongoing government consultations. The "new Web 2.0 platform" was never created, in part stalled by the onerous corporate policy requirements that the platform would have to satisfy (e.g., respecting rules on bilingualism and accessibility and upholding the security of private data). Eventually, instead of creating an in-house platform or procuring a government-wide platform, the TBS instituted a standing offer by which departments could use the services of preapproved firms to support any foray into online citizen engagement.

Fourth, the open dialogue commitment pledged the federal government to pilot crowdsourcing as a means of involving the public "in developing ideas and solutions for greater online dialogue and engagement on public policy initiatives" (Government of Canada 2014b). This commitment was nominally fulfilled through a Twitter townhall led in December 2011 by Tony Clement, then the TBS President. Notable as the first time a federal minister used social media to consult with the public, Clement's townhall centered on the subject of open government itself. The townhall lasted ninety minutes and generated approximately 550 tweets from participants (Treasury Board Secretariat 2012a). Building on the Twitter townhall, Clement hosted a series of Google Hangouts in 2013 to support the open government initiative. But while these exercises technically fulfilled the commitment to experiment with crowdsourcing, they were criticized for emphasizing open data alone, not online dialogue and ATIP reform, and, in the case of the Google Hangouts, for targeting primarily male web developers as opposed to a more representative sample of stakeholders (Francoli 2016b).

Unlike with the open dialogue plank, the government did take some notable strides forward on the third theme of the open government initiative: open information. In 2013, for instance, the TBS launched InfoBase, a searchable online database that allows users to explore budgetary information.[11] The federal government introduced an Open Contracting Data Standards pilot in November 2014, allowing users to search for information related to procurement across twenty departments. And in June 2015 the government implemented the Extractive Sector Transparency Measures Act, legislation that mandates reporting on payments related to the commercial development of oil, gas, and mineral reserves.

But on other fronts progress on the open information plank was more questionable. For instance, as a complement to the canada.ca site, which provides a "one-stop shop" for all government services (versus substantive policy content and historical documents), the government committed itself in its first action plan to introducing an information repository they dubbed a "Virtual Library" (Government of Canada 2012). It was to be a gateway to all federal publications, a site that would be of particular appeal to journalists, researchers, lobbyists, and civil society, and a means of ensuring that, in its efforts to create a streamlined, service-focused website in canada.ca, the government would not deny the public access to substantive information on government activities. The government claimed that it fulfilled this commitment not through a dedicated virtual library but by including all former and current departmental documents on the open information section of the open.canada.ca site. Nonetheless, access-to-information advocates have expressed skepticism and confusion about the precise digital archiving strategy employed on the site, questioning in particular whether certain documents would be lost as departments migrated from departmental sites to the centralized, service-focused canada.ca site (Francoli 2016a).

A more damning critique of the open information plank emerges when we consider its weak commitments on the cornerstone of information disclosure in the federal government: the Access to Information Act. To be sure, the open information plank made some advances on this file. For instance, information on completed ATIP requests was made available as an open data set, and the government introduced a website that allows users to search for and request previously released ATIP submissions. This was half a solution to making the files of all previously released ATIP requests simply available for download online. Although storing all previously prepared ATIP requests on a website for download is the most logical and direct way to ensure previously requested documents are widely available (versus those documents being sent only to their original requesters), government lawyers determined that any previously released ATIP documents had to be available in both official languages if they were stored for download online. The cost of translating all previous and future ATIP requests was deemed too prohibitive to justify making the files available for download, illustrating again how equity considerations can limit the government's capacity to open itself to the public.

In addition, Library and Archives Canada instituted a block review process to open access to 4 million pages of documents previously classified, and ATIP was expanded to include ten additional federal institutions. The TBS developed new ATIP training modules for public servants and expanded online ATIP request options. The federal government began developing GCDocs, a system to improve record keeping that in turn would make it easier to respond expediently and fulsomely to ATIP requests (Francoli 2016a).

However, despite these improvements, the Access to Information Act was not substantively revised as a component of either the 2012 or the 2014 Open Government Action Plan. Information Commissioner Suzanne Legault had repeatedly called for the act to be modernized. In a report to Parliament, Legault offered eighty-five recommendations for improving the act and argued that

> persistent calls to reform the Act have been made ever since its adoption. In the 30-plus year history of the Office of the Information Commissioner of Canada, my predecessors and I have documented multiple challenges and deficiencies with the Act. The Act is applied to encourage a culture of delay. The Act is applied to deny disclosure. It acts as a shield against transparency. The interests of the government trump the interests of the public. (Legault 2015b)

Thus, at a basic level, failing to update the act substantively seriously undermined the credibility of the open information commitments. For this reason, in an independent review of Canada's progress on its second Open Government Action Plan, completed for the Open Government Partnership, Carleton University professor Mary Francoli (2016a, 62) reported that

> this commitment [open information] was largely identified as the most disappointing of all of the commitments in the action plan by virtually all civil society interviewees and by many government interviewees as well. Most of the milestones are hold overs from

the first action plan. The ATIP modernization plan only focuses on technical improvements and does not deal with the fundamental problems facing the access regime in Canada that were spelled out in detail in the first IRM [independent reporting mechanism] report; namely, the antiquated nature of Canadian access to information legislation. Problems around access to information include: the timely fulfilment of requests, overly broad exceptions in the grounds to refuse access, limitations in the scope of public bodies not covered by the Access to Information Act, and high fees.

Finally, in addition to ignoring calls to modernize the Access to Information Act, the open information plank – and ultimately the broader open government initiative itself – were undermined because they did not address the culture of secrecy and information control at play in the bureaucracy, a culture that limits the efficacy of the act in its on-the-ground implementation (Legault 2015b). We see this culture of secrecy in the bureaucratic impulse to avoid the release of damning information that might land their minister or department in trouble in the public eye. This impulse has bolstered an oral culture and – paradoxically coinciding with the release of Open Government Action Plans in the 2010s – the emergence of a BlackBerry Messenger culture; messages sent between BlackBerry smartphones are not stored indefinitely, rendering them a popular route for public servants to communicate without leaving an "ATIP-able" trail (Bronskill 2016; Office of the Information Commissioner of Canada 2013). This culture of secrecy attests to the ongoing tension between traditional framings of open government – focused on access to information and premised on an adversarial, low-trust relationship between the government and outside scrutineers – and the digital variant of the term, which presumes a high-trust, collaborative government-citizen relationship.

Rather than addressing this culture of secrecy and related tension head-on, the first Open Government Action Plan denied its existence, proclaiming that "Canada's long standing culture of transparency and accountability has allowed us to propose commitments for our Action Plan that build on a solid foundation already in place" (Government of Canada 2012). By the time the 2014 plan was released, the government had changed its tune to one more in step with general perceptions of the bureaucracy's impulse to withhold information from the public. The plan noted that open government "represents a fundamental change in government culture that requires government-wide direction" (Government of Canada 2014b). Yet, beyond this statement, the plan and the subsequent self-assessment reporting on progress made toward its implementation offered no additional reference to this "fundamental change"; the documents were bereft of elaborations defining this change and equally lacked discussions of concrete, substantive measures to confront and upend this culture within the bureaucracy. In turn, in her 2014–15 annual report, Legault (2015a) concluded that "the government still does not see the necessity of adopting an integrated vision to ensure a successful open government initiative and a real change of culture toward openness."

What might this "integrated vision" include? Beyond concrete directives to mandate improved information disclosure – such as the duty to document important decisions, a recommendation that Legault (2015b) put forth – any such vision would need to address head-on the roles that political climate and leadership play in driving this culture of secrecy. This argument flows logically from the fact that the bureaucracy's impulse to withhold information is an inevitable response to the contemporary context of governing, in which public disclosure of mistakes and gaffes provides fodder for a vicious cycle of political attacks, 24/7 "gotcha journalism," and a high likelihood that not only the minister but also individual public servants will have their names dragged through the media for public scrutiny. Without confronting and attempting to reform this political culture, any effort to encourage a more open, engaging public service would continue to face significant barriers.

Thus, except in the area of open data, a file on which the bureaucracy made comparatively impressive progress with its first two action plans, the open government initiative did little to drive the bureaucracy's willingness and ability to disclose information to the public or to adopt a more ambitious model of government-citizen engagement. Ultimately, the initiative fell short by evading one of the thorniest barriers to open government: the bureaucratic culture of secrecy that inevitably follows from a competitive political climate that incentivizes information control and limited government-citizen dialogue. This discussion on the role of political culture points to the first explanation for Canada's paltry progress on the open information and dialogue planks and the comparatively more impressive advances on open data under Harper's open(ish) government initiative.

Stephen Harper: The Elephant in the Room of the Open Government Initiative

Beyond official OGP commitments, the Open Government Action Plans, and speeches from President of the Treasury Board Secretariat Tony Clement

(Clement 2011, 2012), Canadians and bureaucrats alike witnessed a starkly more opaque style of governance emerging at the federal level when the open government initiative was implemented. Having "muzzled scientists" (Manasan 2015; Turner 2013), prorogued Parliament to avoid a vote of non-confidence in 2008 and debate on Afghan detainees in 2009 (Aucoin, Turnbull, and Jarvis 2011), limited the media's access to ministers and politicized government communications on key files such as the Economic Action Plan (Blanchfield and Bronskill 2010; Cheadle and Ditchburn 2011; Jeffrey 2011; Marland 2016; Martin 2011), Stephen Harper himself revealed a distinct lack of commitment to the type of open, engaging political and bureaucratic culture that aligns with a concomitant "open by default" mentality in the public service. Although interviewees did not cite Harper's leadership style as a direct determinant of their approach to departmental use of social media, they frequently pointed to Harper when explaining why the open government initiative fell short. These interviewees suggested that his preference for closed government served as an awkward "elephant in the room" of federal open government, seriously undermining the credibility of the initiative as the government produced action plans, released data, hosted hackathons, and touted the benefits of transparency and dialogue. Specifically, concurrent moves toward a more closed government under Harper rendered it difficult for bureaucrats to believe that they were legitimately being encouraged to openly share information and engage with the public. As an official in the PCO who had worked on the open dialogue commitments explained, there was a general sense in the public service that the open government initiative "was a bit rich" given the broader emphasis on information control that permeated life in the bureaucracy under Harper's watch (S5).

The dissonance between the open government initiative and Harper's public management style was equally acknowledged by those outside the bureaucracy. As David Eaves remarked, "I know a lot of people find it laughable when they hear that Canada has an open government strategy, because they say 'How does that match with the fact that ministers don't give interviews to journalists?'" (A2). In completing her independent evaluation of the open government commitments for the Open Government Partnership, Mary Francoli noted that some of the experts on open data, access to information, and citizen engagement that she contacted were extremely angry at even being asked to comment on the government's progress on the open government commitments, slamming the phone in protest at what they perceived to be the absurdity of the very question (Government of Canada 2016b).

The legitimacy of Harper's open government initiative was further eroded by its small budget. The precise amount of funding allocated to the initiative under Harper is hard to discern, but it appears that it was about $1 million annually, based on the Liberals' 2016 promise to "double" the existing budget for open government.[12] The only funding explicitly allocated to open government in Harper era budgets during the first two action plans was Budget 2014's reallocation of an existing $3 million over three years dedicated to the Federal Economic Development Agency for Southern Ontario to support a public-private-backed Open Data Institute in Waterloo, not the broader open government agenda (Government of Canada 2014a). One interviewee explained that the CIOB leading the open government initiative was "begging, borrowing, and stealing" (S5), finding funding for full-time employees in other budgetary envelopes across departments and the TBS in order to deliver on open government commitments. Departmental interviewees regularly referred to open government as "corner of the desk" work (several used that phrase – P1, I1, C7), and departments were given no new resources to support the identification, cleaning, and publication of data on the open data portal or to adopt digital media for citizen engagement. Compounding this challenge, the open government initiative coincided with cuts to the federal workforce under the Deficit Reduction Action Plan. One information manager noted, "how can I ask my colleagues to look for their data to release when their team has just been cut back, but they have the same amount of work?" (I1). The paucity of funds for open government did little to bolster the credibility of the commitments in the eyes of public servants. This echoed the reaction of bureaucrats to PS2000, in which countervailing trends – in that case deep cuts instituted by the Liberals through Program Review – undermined the credibility of a reform initiative that rhetorically committed to strengthen the capacity of the bureaucracy (Lindquist 2006).

In addition to undermining the credibility of the initiative among bureaucrats, the political leadership under which the open government initiative was introduced helps to explain why the open data portion was the only one that made any real progress across the first two action plans. Given the international enthusiasm for open government, as captured in the OGP, an organization that had attracted the membership of Canada's peer countries and was at the time led by its closest ally, the United States, the government faced geopolitical and normative pressure to "get on board" with this latest "must-have" public management agenda. An external adviser on open government remarked that the Government of Canada, and specifically Tony Clement, also showed an interest in open government in part because it was a chance to be in "the cool group with the cool guys" (A1), in particular the United States and United Kingdom, active in the Open Government Partnership as two of its eight founding member countries.[13]

Given criticisms of Harper's record of transparency and citizen engagement, the government was in an admittedly awkward position to sign on to the OGP and deliver on the action plans that the initiative mandated be produced and monitored every two years. At one level, open data represented a relatively straightforward means of making progress on open government and joining this international movement despite broader turns toward closed government underway in the federal bureaucracy. The release of data sets does not also involve the more onerous task of battling a culture of secrecy and information control within the bureaucracy – a culture that the Harper government was not only ill situated to tackle credibly but also fuelled directly. For example, though robust operation of the ATIP system demands at a basic level that political leaders avoid encouraging a culture of secrecy through their own tactics of information control, the need for this brand of political leadership is less relevant in the case of raw data releases. These data sets must be downloaded, interpreted, and analyzed by those with the time and ability to do so. Given this, open data sets are less obviously potent seeds for external criticism versus, say, emails or internal reports and presentation decks released in response to specific requests from journalists, lobbyists, and researchers using the ATIP system. In turn, bureaucrats operating in the permanent campaign are less likely to fear the negative consequences of open data releases than they are a fulsome release of information in response to an ATIP request.

Thus, serving as a comparatively easier win on the open government file, the open data initiative was prized in part by the government as a means of making progress on its OGP commitments while serving as a counterweight to criticism of its otherwise opaque style of governance and turn from data-driven decision making, captured most clearly in the cancellation of the long-form census, as instituted by Clement in 2010 in his role as Minister of Industry. As Eaves observed in a 2012 interview, "so I will be honest too, with the census data, sadly I suspect it helps that the minister who killed the long-form census can get a win on the census by making it free – don't underestimate the politics of that" (A2). The branding opportunities offered by open data were not lost on the bureaucracy itself. A senior executive in the Chief Information Officer Branch explained that,

> from an open data perspective, we kind of, we are watching what the US w[as] doing ... So we thought, "Wow, what they are doing is exciting," and one of my directors came to me and said, "You know, we should be doing something in open data. The US is getting press here, and you know we should [as well]." (I3)

Similarly, an information manager explained at the time of the interview that his department actually had 600 data sets ready to be added to the open data portal but that the TBS was waiting until the government had a critical mass of new data sets since, "from a communication perspective, they would like to have a splash in announcing the additions to the portal" (I5). Thus, the open data initiative was advanced partly because of its branding potential and the access that it granted to the international open government craze (captured in the OGP). But the initiative was also favoured because it held particular ideological appeal to the Conservative government.

For Day and Clement, the two presidents of the TBS under whom the open data initiative began, open data was politically palatable given the potential connections among the release of government data, a leaner state, and a more self-reliant citizenry. Invoking the neoliberalism of New Public Management, this view posits that open data can enable citizens *qua* consumers to become more informed about their individual decisions and therefore less reliant on the state for protection; can enable citizens *qua* auditors to scrutinize the public service effectively and keep government spending in check; and, aligning with private sector approaches to state management, can fuel nongovernmental service provision in lieu of direct state provision (Bates 2012; Johnson and Robinson 2014; Longo 2011). Reflecting on his work advising Day on the early open data pilot launched in 2011, Eaves noted that the potential symmetries between open data and a less interventionist, more transparent federal state were highly appealing to Day given his Reform Party roots (A2). Similarly, while speaking on an open data panel hosted by the Manning Institute in 2012, Clement explained that "the dream of conservatives is that eventually through crowdsourcing ... governments can step back." He continued that, "when all the information is available, why does government need to make decisions? That's the holy grail for us as freedom lovers, who believe government should be limited" (quoted in Levitz 2013). This perspective seeped into the bureaucracy as well, with a senior executive in the CIOB remarking "so we need to put as much data out there [as possible] so that researchers, entrepreneurs, and anybody else who has the bright ideas can do it, but this government's view is that the government is not supposed to get bigger. It's supposed to enable the other sectors, which I support completely" (I3).

Finally, the open data initiative proved to be politically palatable given its potential as a driver of economic growth. Recall that the initiative was given a boost after the digital economy consultation revealed an appetite for government data among industry, a fact that Clement often highlighted when espousing the benefits of open data for Canadian entrepreneurs. In 2011, he announced that, "the more data we can get out there, the more applications can be thought of by brilliant people, entrepreneurs" (quoted in Thompson 2011). Elsewhere Clement stated that "our Government wants to make it as easy as possible for Canadian entrepreneurs and innovators to turn government data into user-friendly applications" (quoted in Treasury Board Secretariat 2012b) and that the open data initiative "is about making government data more easily and freely available, so that it can be leveraged by citizen-entrepreneurs to help bring about increased benefits in services to citizens and help spur innovation in the private sector" (Clement 2012). Although driving economic growth and spurring innovation are generally uncontroversial policy objectives that span the ideological spectrum, invoking them to justify open data nonetheless points to a tidy connection between the open data portion of the open government initiative and the Conservatives' traditional identification with the private sector and economic development, a fact that rendered open data naturally attractive to the government.

This follows on trends in other jurisdictions, where the unique styles and experiences of political leaders inform the particularities of their digital public management agendas. Take, for instance, Barack Obama, whose election in 2008 as president of the United States drew on the innovative use of social media and grassroots online engagement. It was not surprising that on his first day in office Obama signed a Memorandum on Transparency and Open Government in which he committed to "establish a system of transparency, public participation, and collaboration" (Obama 2009). Nor was it surprising that he followed the memo with initiatives such as Challenge.gov, a crowd-sourcing platform introduced in 2010, and We the People, an e-petitions site created in 2011. Similarly, the open government initiative of the United Kingdom, which, like Canada's, has focused on open data, was marked by the unique personalities and experiences of the political leaders under whom it was first instituted. In interviews, a number of UK public servants explained that open data became the focus of their open government initiative after Prime Minister Gordon Brown spoke with Sir Tim Berners-Lee, inventor of the World Wide Web, whom Brown had invited to Chequers Court when celebrating recipients of the Order of Merit. As one former senior adviser on digital initiatives in the UK Cabinet Office explained,

> Berners-Lee was sitting next to the prime minister. Gordon Brown himself is a very geeky communicator, and he enjoys talking in high theory ... They got on very well. I know someone else who was at that dinner, and they said it was obvious that they were only inter-ested in talking to each other. [Brown] said to Berners-Lee, "What can we do more to make the Internet leap forward in Britain?" And Berners-Lee said, "Open up your data." And that was a pivotal moment ... That was a really pivotal moment because then the mes-sage came back from Downing Street: "Right. Prime Minister wants to open his data up." (O2)

Following this prime ministerial direction, the newly created post of director of digital engagement focused on the task of developing a repository for government data – https://data.gov.uk – launched in January 2010, leaving aside the post's originally more expansive focus on engaging citizens in policy making through digital media.[14] As in the case of Day's and Clement's framing of open data as a vehicle of smaller government and economic growth, in digital government the unique personalities and experiences of political lead-ers matter.

On one level, then, it appears that Canada's open(ish) government initia-tive can be explained as the inevitable outcome of political leadership with little commitment or credible claim to transparent information provision and robust government-citizen dialogue but with greater interest in releasing open data for the ideologically and geopolitically appealing branding opportunities and economic gains that they provide. Acknowledging the politics of Harper's open government initiative does take us a long way in understanding why the federal government's OGP commitments did little to substantively improve the bureaucracy's capacity to engage openly with those outside its walls beyond some advances on the open data file. But to end the analysis here would offer only an incomplete picture of the conditions that produced an open(ish) government at best across the course of the first Canadian Open Government Action Plans introduced under Harper between 2011 and 2015. Instead, a more holistic appraisal emerges by again considering the closed government bureaucratic mindset entrenched in the federal bureaucracy well before Harper entered the scene.

Closed by Default Information Management in the Federal Government

The open data strategy revealed that the Government of Canada had not been operating as a data-driven organization, but instead had a patched-together and in some cases ad hoc approach to information management (IM). But more than simply uncovering a dearth of quality data management within the public service, the IM mess uncovered by the open data initiative highlighted that the bureaucracy had not generally been thinking about data as something that could be used by anyone other than their original creators. That is, poor IM is not only a *driver* of closed government, serving as a barrier to data releases, but also a *symptom* of closed government, since it attests to the reality that the bureaucracy had largely produced and managed data without ever imagining that they could or should be shared and repurposed to different ends by other units in the government or by those outside its walls. After all, if data are "single use," produced and applied within particular units or by individual actors in the government, then they can be managed in idiosyncratic ways, with data producers and users showing little regard for storing the data in ways that make them interoperable across a range of systems or with organizational schemes and metadata that would allow another individual to make sense of the data.

This siloed view of data was evident in a frequent refrain in interviews. Public servants both in line departments and in the CIOB leading the open data initiative would explain that open data was comparatively more difficult to capitalize on in the federal government because the government does not provide many front-line services. So federal data, they argued, would be less useful to outsiders than data releases from governments that more regularly interact with citizens in daily service transactions. The following quotation from a senior official in the CIOB captures this argument:

Well, there are a number of reasons, you know, we are more cautious and more conservative in our approach than the UK or the US. First of all, versus the UK, it's because of our national structures.

So the UK delivers health care and delivers services through the federal civil service right down to citizens a lot more than we do. So the Canadian federal government does not interface directly with citizens on many items. We interface with citizens obviously on taxation, and we interface with citizens on employment insurance, immigration, or passports, but we don't engage with citizens on a regular basis through health care, and so we don't have as much direct contact. So the nature of our data is different. In Canada, the cities have an awful lot of data that directly, if you will, impact citizens, and then the provinces have education and health and social welfare that directly impact citizens. So we could only go so far and fast on the federal agenda by nature of what our jurisdictions are and the kind of data that we have. (I3)

This narrow perspective ignores the many potential applications of federal data to research, policy advocacy, economic development, innovation, and social and economic well-being, and oddly it denies the federal government's role in the cited areas of education (e.g., by supporting postsecondary education and training) and public health. Yet interviewees – even those intimately involved in advancing the open data initiative – exhibited an absolute lack of imagination, data literacy, and awareness in framing their data as something that would likely be of little interest to anyone but those within the government. In turn, this perspective attests to another symptom and driver of the closed government mentality: bureaucratic arrogance. Interviewees who expressed the view that applications of federal data are limited implied that they can anticipate all potential applications of their data. This perspective is emblematic of the closed government mindset, which little appreciates the different skills and knowledge that outsiders bring to the work of governing.

This arrogance was evident again among interviewees who explained that public servants hesitated to release their data for fear that others would misinterpret them. Indeed, in some cases, the idiosyncratic nature of the data sets' management, and the poor quality of the data, could lead to misinterpretation among outside users. For this reason, webpages hosting each data set on the portal have a comments section, which could be used by government officials to discuss the specific data set with its users, thus forming relationships that might foster more productive applications of government data by nongovernmental actors and improvements to government data going forward. However, defaulting to a closed government mentality, interviewees did not instinctively invoke the relationship-building opportunities that open data should instigate, instead explaining somewhat condescendingly that outsiders using the data could create more problems than they solved or expressing fear that the government would be culpable if harm was caused by errors in the data or their misinterpretation. When asked to explain the benefits of open data for his department, one senior executive explained that

> often – and we find this too with written questions and letters that people send in or whatever – what they ask for we're not always certain if they really know what they mean, because people use different terminologies. And so part of our thing is really getting out to them the information that they need, not what they ask for, which is a little bit different, and it's also to what extent ... I mean, sometimes we proactively disclose things like hospitality expenses. Well, we do it, but do the public really need to know? Probably not, but it's their right to know, so we put it out. Do they really understand it? I don't know. I don't know what they do with the information, but they seem to be happier. Somebody's happy ... That's the other problem we have with a lot of the data. People want certain data, we give it to them, and then they add it with other data, and you can't do it. This is this fiscal year, that's calendar year. You get all sorts of crazy things going on. So again it's really easy for an academic – I'm not picking on you – or the public to say the government should be more open. We can be, but be careful what you ask for, because you may get information and then make false assumptions from the information. (S3)

In contrast, it is not surprising that federal geospatial data were released for public use earlier than other types of data in the federal government and that these data were generally of higher quality; the geospatial data communities within and outside the government have a tradition of sharing, combining, and repurposing data. Federal holders of geospatial data cultivated strong data management traditions early on and equally strong relations with their stakeholders in managing their data holdings (Lenihan 2015). In other words, their existing open government mindset enabled their open data initiatives.

Thus, more than simply revealing how weak IM traditions can slow progress on open data, the open data initiative exposed a more fundamental challenge to open government in the federal government: bureaucrats' shallow awareness of, and appreciation for, the benefits that might accrue when those outside their organization contribute to their work, specifically when that engagement rests on shared access to data resources. In this sense, the government's siloed approach to data pointed to the enduring lack of joined-up, systems thinking in the public service and directly illustrated why this type of thinking is required for the uptake of digital era policy instruments, in this case open data. Following a similar pattern, the government's efforts to implement the open dialogue initiative revealed at first a shallow digital data literacy among bureaucrats but more significantly how enduring closed government traditions can limit the bureaucracy's capacity to adjust to the opportunities and demands of the digital age.

Digitizing Consultations

The open dialogue initiative had the stated goal of improving how the bureaucracy engages outsiders in discussions on policy through the use of new digital tools, especially social media. As already explored above, the federal government made little progress in achieving this objective. This was predictable given that the initiative in certain ways was bound to fail by design, victim to barriers to fluid government-citizen interaction online and burdened by a series of unique complications that arise when the public service endeavours to consult Canadians via the web.

First, the name of the initiative, with its emphasis on "dialogue," indicates that it was designed not to usher in a revamped approach to consultation in the Government of Canada but to produce, essentially, a digitized model of the traditional talk-based consultations that are old hat in the federal public service. For instance, the basic design and desired outputs of Tony Clement's Twitter townhall were no different from those at play in a traditional ministerial roundtable. The ministry set the overarching theme of the dialogue, the minister was prepped by his staff and arrived ready to discuss issues with stakeholders, and stakeholders, for their part, arrived ready to discuss the issues, pose questions, and find out what the minister had to say in response.

The only difference between this talk-based model of consultation as manifested on social media and its in-person variant is the medium hosting it. The technological affordances of an open social media platform such as Twitter enable a consultation to scale such that it engages many more participants and supports much more dialogue, and that the dialogue itself moves at a more rapid pace than in-person or static, asynchronous online forums.

As one former government executive – a pioneer in encouraging social media use in departments – put it, "you take your consultative process, you move it online, and then it scales really hugely, and then you have a problem dealing with the scale" (A1).

What is the "problem" with this scale? In talk-based engagement, there is reason to question whether the marginal benefits of each additional participant's contributions outweigh the marginal costs that accrue when these contributions are analyzed. That is, as with offline consultations, when a consultation "scales really hugely" online, someone still needs to make sense of these contributions, which in the case of an online engagement in the federal public service means that someone has to engage in the time-consuming effort of reading and analyzing large numbers of comments and then producing a "what they said" report for the department to publish on its website and consider in decision making.

The large number of data produced in online consultations would be more manageable by applying techniques such as automated content analysis, natural language processing, social network analysis, and data visualization or by abandoning the conversational model of traditional consultations altogether, opting instead to monitor conversations already taking place on social networks or to capture big data trails tracking Canadians' interactions on these platforms, sometimes called "social listening" (e.g., archiving all references to a policy issue on Twitter as a means of taking the "pulse" of the population on the issue). Yet, the skills required to work with large sets of web data and to engage in sophisticated social listening are not in the toolkit of conventional public servants (especially those undertaking mainstream policy and program work), absent as these skills are from the traditional social science backgrounds that these public servants bring to the job. The first two Open Government Action Plans did not include any discussion of the need to fill this digital data skills gap in the public service, instead naively presuming that the traditional, talk-based model of consultation would simply be improved by scaling it up on the web.

The digitized model of consultation that open dialogue prized was equally impractical given that it presumes a degree of control and capacity for pre-planning that online environments typically do not permit and that, in turn, can ensure that the government comes across as awkward and nonresponsive when engaging citizens on the web. As one interviewee explained,

the model in Ottawa has always tended to be "I'm doing policy development; I want to hear what the public has to say." And then they'll set up a series of five townhalls across the country, and then they will give me a report which then I can integrate into my policy development process. That's still a very regimented and hierarchical process. (P2)

Given the open, networked, and rapid many-to-many exchanges that social media support, interviewees explained that this regimented and hierarchical approach cannot be sustained online. The Twitter townhall conducted by Clement in 2011 is an illustrative case. The ninety-minute townhall took three practice runs, demanded the development of forty preapproved tweets, and involved at least six staff, including a ghostwriter, a moderator, two policy experts, and two communications staff, along with the minister himself. As described by one official, "they were working feverishly" (S2), responding to a flurry of queries and comments submitted by participants during the townhall. An official who provided support explained that, though he found it remarkable to be able to communicate directly with citizens for the first time in his public service career (albeit under the handle of the TBS Twitter account), he concluded that the event could never become a mainstream practice.[15] The time and resources required to square a Twitter townhall with existing, top-down, controlled models of consultation rendered these online exercises unfeasible outside one-time, special exceptions (as in Clement's townhall). Reflecting on this challenge, an official in the PCO's Communications and Consultations Secretariat explained that the government was interested in developing its own online engagement platform partly to regain the control lost when it attempted to engage Canadians in third-party online forums:

I think there's a bit of a feeling that at least if they can come back into our sandbox then, you know, the conversation can ... help us more because it'll be more structured, right? They'll answer our questions, they'll go through our tools. But to just do it openly in a third-party platform, it's a little bit harder to structure that conversation. So, to go out into Facebook and to post a question, it's a little harder to get structured feedback ... It's a lot easier to manage if it's centralized and if it's structured and if you can ask them a series of questions as opposed to, you know, often in social media it just becomes, it snowballs, into something else, or it goes tangential, and the conversation is no longer focused on where you want it to be. (S2)

Beyond official open dialogue commitments, certain departments have attempted to engage with the public online in ways that do not merely digitize the traditional model of consultations and that, at least initially, were intended to usher in a less hierarchical and tightly managed model of citizen engagement. For example, acknowledging that meaningful, "in the moment," online conversation requires opening access to the "departmental voice" to policy and program experts (as opposed to limiting it to communication professionals, senior officials, or the minister), ESDC experimented with an innovative citizen engagement model with its Online Skills Forum. Launched in 2014, it consisted of a twelve-month online dialogue between stakeholders and ESDC officials on skills development and labour market issues. Rather than managing the forum exclusively, ESDC invited the industry association, Canadian Manufacturers and Exporters, to moderate the discussion and produce monthly reports for the department on key themes.

As described by the department, the initiative aimed to improve on "traditional consultation models," which are constrained by: "One-way conversations; pre-defined topics and questions; Rigid Design; Limited participants." Accordingly, the Online Skills Forum was intended to support "multi-party dialogue," "reflexive discussion modules to allow more productive conversations," and "results that have an impact on policy/program cycle" (Employment and Social Development Canada 2013). Most notably, the initiative called on program officers, not communication officials, to speak for the government in the forum.

However, though the language used to describe the forum suggested that the department was endeavouring to engage in a more fluid, personalized form of engagement online, we might question the extent to which the program officers involved were equipped to do so. The "Guidelines and Protocols" for the Online Skills Forum were drenched in the language of risk mitigation, noting that public servants would be limited to "probing questions," "clarifying facts," and "acknowledging valuable input" (Employment and Social Development Canada 2013). Director general–level approval was required for all "lead off posts" (those that start a conversational thread) or when clarifying the department's position, correcting errors in understanding, and responding to an evaluation of ESDC policies and programs. Preapproved communication lines were to be prepared to ensure that contributions from public servants were vetted in advance. As one ESDC official remarked,

The approval process/risk aversion of government make it that all responses will be in the form of official talking points, which are of little interest to stakeholders. So basically the tool gets it half right. The department can get valuable information from stakeholders, but stakeholders can't get good info from us. It is not a two-way street. So here is a hypothetical example:

ESDC TO STAKEHOLDERS VIA ONLINE TOOL: "Canada ranks below the OECD average in terms of employer-sponsored training. What are the barriers to training that affect your firm?"
BUSINESS 1: "I'm a small business. Cost is the biggest barrier to me."
BUSINESS 2: "I worry that if I train someone they will move on to a bigger firm."
BUSINESS 3: "Our firm is so busy that we don't have the time to dedicate to training."
BUSINESS 4: "Hey, Government of Canada, when is the Canada Job Grant going active, and what are the eligibility criteria? What is the evidence that this program will work?"
ESDC: "Economic Action Plan 2014 introduced the Canada Job Grant. The job grant is a collaboration between the Government of Canada, provinces, and employers to ensure that Canadians receive the training they need to succeed in the labour market."
Next question! (Anonymous Government of Canada official 2014)

A similar approach was adopted in the former HRSDC with a pilot on Corrective Blogging. Initiated by changes to the Canada Student Loans Program in the 2008 budget, Corrective Blogging called on officials to engage with nongovernmental blogs and forums on which misinformation regarding individuals' eligibility for the loans was being shared. Officials would draft responses clarifying the policy changes and publish them as comments to the blog/forum, identifying themselves as HRSDC officials. This followed a policy of inject, correct, and direct: that is, inject yourself into nongovernmental sites, correct misinformation, and direct people back to the department's website (Noeftle and Cloete 2010). Two-way interactions were explicitly rejected – the strategy noted that officials were permitted to "provide factual information to *correct* any misleading or inaccurate messages posted by others about the program," but "the blogger should not engage in nor encourage a policy debate" (emphasis in original) (Corporate Web 2010, 5).

In both cases – the Online Skills Forum and Corrective Blogging – we see clear evidence of the public service's instinct to limit the personality and autonomy of bureaucrats when they are invited to tread uncharted territory as the decentralized "voice" of the department online. The tight management of these exercises speaks to the unease that a traditionally anonymous fleet of bureaucrats – and the managers fearing the politically contentious and potentially damaging "dialogues" that they might be drawn into – face when they are asked to engage the public in an online environment that they cannot easily control.

To be sure, again reflecting the original rationale for siloed and hierarchical control of government consultations, a decentralized, ad hoc model of online citizen consultation is not risk free, raising the potential for public servant politicization, misrepresentation of government policy, incoherence across consultations, or inequity. That said, the outcome, a hybrid of hierarchical and depersonalized online engagement, ultimately reinforces perceptions of the public service as nonresponsive and produces ineffective uptake of what were intended to be innovative public engagement exercises, undermining the original intent of the open dialogue initiative.

One finds an entirely more relaxed approach to online engagement among foreign service officers in the federal government. As part of "digital diplomacy" initiatives, officials interviewed in the former Department of Foreign Affairs, Trade and Development explained that they felt entirely empowered to speak for their department online, engaging outsiders in both official, planned and informal, ad hoc communications and consultative exercises. Adopting the decentralized model of individual public servant–managed social media as discussed in Chapter 3, these officials explained how they used Twitter, Facebook, and foreign social media sites, such as Weibo (the Chinese equivalent of Twitter), to interact with Canadians, foreign citizens, stakeholders, and other governments, in some cases using the platforms to undertake substantive foreign policy work, to build networks with stakeholders, and to engage on controversial policy issues, not simply to share information as part of relatively banal, tightly managed communication strategies.

In one case, a foreign service officer with the Canadian Embassy in Beijing explained that one of its Weibo posts advertising the ambassador's new hybrid electric car (a modest sedan) sparked a discussion on Chinese officials' habit of acquiring expensive cars on the public dime, as well as on broader accountability issues in the Chinese state. The post was intended as a light-hearted, innocuous message; however, as explained by one Canadian official, "a dialogue that would normally be very difficult to initiate in China turned into just a fluke. That said, that wasn't our intent at all ... We just simply were showing the ambassador with his new hybrid car … But then it became a pretty healthy dialogue on government transparency" (P4).

Similar sentiments on public servants' use of social media for online dialogue were shared in interviews with foreign service officers in the United Kingdom. Providing a powerful illustration of the role that traditional conceptions of the bureaucrat-outsider relationship play in defining digital era framings of this relationship, these diplomats explained that, unlike Weber's purposely impersonal bureaucrat or Westminster's anonymous public servant (Grube 2013; Kernaghan 2010), British diplomats had always been empowered to engage in highly personalized, autonomously governed interactions with outsiders as they network, collect information, and consult with domestic and foreign governments, businesses, third sector organizations, and citizens, captured in the stereotype of the networking diplomat at a cocktail party. As described by officials in the United Kingdom's Foreign and Commonwealth Office, diplomats are "presumed competent," a term that developed to reflect the autonomy they have historically been granted to speak on behalf of their government when overseas and without practical means of seeking approval before doing so. British diplomats directly referred to the concept of presumed competence to justify their use of popular social media channels to consult, engage, and collect information online autonomously, without necessarily needing to check in with superiors or official communication strategies, as captured in the following exchange from a 2012 interview with a former Foreign and Commonwealth Office official:

INTERVIEWEE: In the Foreign Office, there is this phrase which I hope other people have mentioned to you, which we use when thinking about digital diplomacy, which is "presumed competency," which we borrow … So it is a, kind of the origin of it is diplomats, being before telefax even, before when it took quite an effort to talk to people in London, diplomats and ambassadors had to be trusted to speak on behalf of the government without checking back. They were trusted to act rather than to always check back with the political masters. So we applied that to the work and to actually the presumption of competence of our staff, and they can speak on behalf of the office.

INTERVIEWER: Is there something about diplomats that makes it easier for them to take on that role as spokesperson than, say, the people who work on health policy?

INTERVIEWEE: Yes, absolutely. So it is the mission of the foreign officer to engage and to influence and to change behaviour, so everybody in the

Foreign Office or just about – not everybody – a lot of people in the Foreign Office regard themselves as a professional communicator. So ... in a policy-making department like the Department of Health, that isn't how people regard themselves, [even though] there are still massive opportunities to do engagement online [in the department]. (O3)

As noted by this UK official, the bureaucrat proper (e.g., officials in the Department of Health) have never been presumed competent to engage outsiders autonomously on behalf of their departments, a tradition as true in Canada as in the United Kingdom, evident in the siloed, hierarchical, tight controls over departments' social media accounts and in the approvals, pre-developed messages, and deliberate instructions to avoid engaging in self-directed dialogue in ESDC's Online Skills Forum and Corrective Blogging exercises. So, as with departments' efforts to integrate social media into their existing communication models, the federal government's attempts to develop a program of open dialogue online again exposed how the closed government practices of Progressive-Era Public Administration and Weberian bureaucracy continue to punctuate our approach to government-citizen relations in the digital age. Policy consultations in the government are traditionally managed through hierarchies (requiring approvals), functionally separated (managed by designated spokespersons, such as the minister or communication profes-sionals), and "purposely impersonal" (conducted through formal processes emphasizing official government positions and voices, not at the discretion of individual public servants). Efforts to deviate from this model, whether through Clement's Twitter townhall or through other experiments in online dialogue, were hampered by the bureaucracy's instinctive impulse to revert to these traditions, producing awkward online hybrids that blend attempts at interactivity with formal, top-down rigidity. Reflecting this tension, one official explained that the Government of Canada was slow to develop a robust open dialogue strategy because "you have a very bureaucratic world trying to get their head around online engagement," which has proven to be "a hard nut to crack" (S5).

Yet the analysis presented here suggests that, ultimately, the public service did not earnestly attempt to crack this nut despite stated commitments to open dialogue. At a basic level, the initiative did not include efforts to recruit or train staff in the technical skills required to handle and interpret large-scale online engagement. More fundamentally, the government did not couple a more ambitious model of digital citizen engagement with concrete or thoughtful guidance on the dilemmas of anonymity, political neutrality, coordination, and equity that a more pluralistic model of online public engagement invites. Any effort to launch a more ambitious vision of social media–based open dialogue that evades these tricky but essential questions is necessarily shallow and ineffective.

The Federal Government in the Digital Age: Asleep at the Wheel?

From 2011 to 2015, the TBS' open government program was the official flagship initiative by which the federal public service claimed to be adapting to the digital age. With the exception of progress on open data, the open government initiative produced little except further evidence that Canada's model of bureaucracy inherited from the late nineteenth century and early twentieth century was alive and well and at odds with the demands of the digital age. Even the star of this initiative – open data – was marred by the legacy of closed government; the open data initiative revealed that the public service had largely been treating data production and use as a navel-gazing activity, showing little appreciation for how others within the bureaucracy, or those outside the government's walls, could use government data to support policy development and service delivery. Mirroring departments' uptake of social media, the open dialogue initiative highlighted that, though the instruments of anonymity, centralization, and top-down management of government-citizen interaction have traditionally been valued for their role in securing equitable, coherent, and neutral government-citizen interactions, these approaches are difficult to sustain – yet not so easily dispensed with – in an age of rapid, networked, personalized digital media. Finally, the open information initiative underscored how a culture of secrecy can continue alongside digital openings of the bureaucracy, creating paradoxical outcomes, such as deliberate efforts to thwart ATIP requests through instant messaging alongside unprecedented releases of raw government data.

Perhaps most importantly, as with the federal government's early uptake of social media, Canada's open(ish) government initiative revealed the crucial influence that political leadership had in shaping the early responses of the public service to the digital age. The closed by default tendencies of the public service are built on a deep foundation of administrative practices and worldviews, but they are also reinforced by a contemporary political culture that incentivizes risk aversion and information control. Stephen Harper, an active player in this culture (its leading icon, some have argued) could not credibly provide leadership to open the federal bureaucracy, ensuring that the public service undertook few substantive, external-facing efforts to adapt meaningfully to the digital age under his watch.

Thus, despite its stated intent, the open government initiative did little to confront and resolve the dilemmas that digital era open government raises. This was primarily a "bolt-on solution," layering new requirements and ambitions to open the bureaucracy onto a closed government base while failing to grapple with the practical managerial questions, accountability issues, and cultural barriers that open government raises and that are not easily or simply solved by mandating the release of data, creating action plans, and promising to digitize citizen engagement – especially amid a political culture that continued to favour closed government.

To the bystander, a bureaucracy using multiple step tweet-approval processes, struggling to find and release its data, and hiding information through instant messages would appear to be "asleep at the wheel," not only evading but also resisting disruption and change as other sectors and individual citizens experience unprecedented waves of transformation in the digital age. Yet these official, external-facing efforts tell only part of the story. Alongside them, a series of sometimes fringe and largely under-the-radar public servant–led efforts *did* work to address some of the complex barriers to digital era open government in Canada, notably the bureaucracy's entrenched culture of information control, reliance on silos, strict adherence to hierarchy, and risk aversion. I turn to these initiatives in the next chapter.

5
Internal Openings in the Federal Bureaucracy

From the mid-2000s to 2015, the federal bureaucracy attempted to build a more open government internally, breaking down the silos and hierarchies that have long limited the flow of information, skills, and people across the bureaucracy and that can limit the scope for innovative uptake of new policy instruments, work processes, and service delivery models. GCTools instituted the first government-wide social networking platforms. Blueprint 2020 represented an unprecedented cross-government, grassroots renewal agenda, and, supported by a deputy minister committee and several labs and hubs, the public service piloted and built capacity for digital policy innovation. Distinguishing these efforts from departmental uptake of social media and official open government commitments, these public servant–led initiatives did not naively view digital era adaptation as a simple case of layering new digital tools and approaches onto the bureaucracy's existing closed government worldviews and structures. Instead, these initiatives framed the digital age as a game changer facing governments, one that both exposed the need for and could enable an open, horizontal, and innovative culture of governance. In contrast to what we have seen in previous chapters, this was not simply an analogue government "playing digital."

Yet, despite having the right intentions and addressing head-on the culture of risk aversion, information control, and siloed, overly hierarchical management at odds with digital era open government, these initiatives ultimately fell short in meaningfully shifting the culture of the federal public service toward one more suitable for the digital age. In this chapter I detail what these initiatives *did* manage to accomplish – feats that in some cases were notable and should not be entirely discounted. In particular, initiatives focused on policy innovation highlighted the barriers to digital era open government and generated a focused, executive-level discussion on the need to overcome these barriers. But I also reveal that, despite these advances, internal efforts to shift the culture of the bureaucracy were ultimately small scale, affecting only a portion of the federal public service, and producing at best ephemeral diversions from status quo closed government approaches. I conclude the chapter by discussing the limits of public servant–led reforms, arguing that these initiatives once again illustrate how any effort to update the federal public service for the digital age will be hamstrung if coupled with a political culture, and concomitant political leadership, that rationalize closed government.

GCTools

The first public servant–led initiative that attempted to challenge the closed culture of the federal bureaucracy came in the form of GCTools, a set of internal social media platforms developed by a small unit in the Chief Information Officer Branch of the Treasury Board Secretariat. The CIOB's first GCTool – GCpedia – was launched by then Chief Information Officer Ken Cochrane in October 2008 at the Government Technology Exhibition and Conference. GCpedia is an internal, cross-government wiki developed using the same software as Wikipedia (mimicking its "look and feel").[1] Following on a successful wiki first introduced in NRCan, GCpedia was created to provide public servants across the federal bureaucracy with a common space in which to share and collaborate in the production of information, for example in developing briefing notes, creating background materials on programs, or discussing and consulting on internal corporate matters (e.g., human resources management).

One year later, in 2009, the CIOB launched GCconnex, a tool run on the open-source software Elgg and serving as a cross-government social networking platform. Like Facebook or LinkedIn, GCconnex allows users to build profile pages where they can upload a photo and detail their expertise and interests. The tool also features a Twitter-like function, called "The Wire," in which users can publish messages of 140 characters or less, to which others can reply or "like," and a blogging function. A "Bookmarks" function allows public servants to share weblinks of interest with other public servants, a "Chat" function supports instant messaging across the public service, and a tool called "Ideas" allows users to pitch proposals with a group who can then comment and vote on these proposed ideas. "Groups" and "Subgroups" allow users to segment the network into subject-specific topics, and they allow public servants to classify these "Groups" and "Subgroups" by the security level required to access them. Finally, a "Files and Folders" function allows users to upload documents onto the platform.[2]

GCTools were considered to be the first government-wide social network-ing tools ever developed globally and rendered the Government of Canada a world leader in this emerging area of practice.[3] They were created as a response to the emergence of new forms of collaboration and information sharing that had led to successful projects such as Wikipedia and that, as of the mid-2000s on, were promoted by popular technology writers, especially O'Reilly (2011), Shirky (2009, 2010), and Tapscott and Williams (2006), each of which was cited in a 2009 presentation on GCTools prepared by Jeff Bray-brook, then the deputy chief technology officer at the TBS. In his presentation, Braybrook (2009) argued that "Web 2.0 will change the way you work" and emphasized the tagline accompanying GCpedia – "collaboration is everything" – as a reflection of how today's successful organizations, such as Facebook, Google, and LinkedIn (all referenced in the presentation), produced and managed information and expertise. Braybrook went on to explain that GCTools were driven by five needs within the bureaucracy: (1) "deliver organ-ized information to a wide audience quickly"; (2) "aggregate knowledge across an enterprise and overcome organizational barriers to collaboration and sharing"; (3) "keep serendipitous interaction open across the enterprise, so that people can apply their different talents to a topic or problem"; (4) "replace inefficient point-to-point communications of e-mail with a centralized work-space"; and (5) "find ways to foster a more inclusive, less risk-averse organ-izational culture." Speaking more bluntly, one interviewee who had been involved in the creation of GCTools explained that these platforms emerged from the realization: "Oh, shit – the world is changing. We're government. We should change too" (I7).

These explanations emphasize that GCTools were inspired by the digital platforms that were fuelling impressive social networks and new forms of collaborative work outside the government. Yet the tools also responded to a much longer-standing recognition – common across previous reform efforts and the public management literature – that the bureaucracy suffered from a dearth of horizontality and collaboration across its silos and an equally stunted ability for information to move effectively and efficiently up and down vertical chains of command (Bakvis and Juillet 2004; Jarvis and Levasseur 2015; Peters 1998; Sproule-Jones 2000).

Thus, capitalizing on the affordances of digital social networks, and inspired by technology firms perceived as having defied the logic of hierarchies and silos in favour of "flatter," networked internal organizational structures, GCTools were developed to foster long-pursued – but difficult to achieve – systems-based work across the public service. The goal was to reduce the technical barriers that traditionally had rendered it difficult if not impossible for bureaucrats operating in different functions, policy and program areas, regions, and levels of authority to share and co-produce information or even to know that the other exists; prior to the creation of these tools, outside ad hoc networking opportunities, and scanning organizational charts, there was no way for a public servant to easily or systematically identify colleagues with the expertise that would render them a fruitful site for collaboration and information sharing. In this sense, the tools made possible novel forms of networking across the bureaucracy, for the first time providing spaces in which anyone in the public service, regardless of function or rank, could connect with each other and share information. This information might otherwise be restricted to a departmental or unit-exclusive intranet, ephemeral conversations at meetings, or individual desktop hard drives. In effect, then, GCTools provided a sort of digital, networked, and infinitely more populated "lunch table" to replace the literal space in which Savoie's (2003, 67) exclusive group of elite mandarins would foster systems-based collaboration in the "small village" of the public service past.

In addition to supporting horizontality in the bureaucracy, the creators of GCTools emphasized that part of their goal was to provide safe spaces for public servants to build the skills and comfort levels required to use social media effectively with the public. This perspective reflects a thoughtful appreciation for the traditions with which social media and networked information sharing can conflict. These traditions include the bureaucratic impulse to withhold information within defined, internal silos, public servant anonymity, and, as a corollary of this principle, centralization and top-down control of the official "government voice" on particular policy issues and programs by official, depersonalized spokespersons. Rather than simply adding these technologies to an existing culture steeped in these traditions, as was the case with departments' uptake of social media and in the open government initiative, GCTools were a half measure intended to socialize these disruptive technologies and to confront the challenges that they raise in the "safe spaces" provided by the government's firewalls. This theory of change – start internally to build capacity for external engagement – was captured in a comment from one frequent user of GCTools:

There's a giant fear to do external, but I think personally speaking, well, in my professional opinion, I don't think we're ready to do external yet because we have no idea what it actually means internally. I think we need to understand how to use the tools in our organizations to then actually foster conversation with the outside. Because, if we can't do it on the inside, we're just going to make giant jerks of ourselves on the outside, and I don't think we're at that stage yet. I think there needs to be, and I'm going to use the big word, *culture change* in the way we share information with each other on a day-to-day basis. (P1)

Another official remarked that "managers may just be a little hesitant, but I think it's the – and this is where I always see the importance of the internal networks – allowing them to see a dialogue and become more comfortable with it, I think, will start to help our external efforts" (C2).

GCTools thus far have been used in a number of ways. Some use the tools to support internal consultation. For example, the assistant deputy minister of Talent Management at the TBS used an online poll on GCconnex to get feedback from over 900 public servants on the development of key leadership competencies (Chief Information Officer Branch 2014). The former Department of Foreign Affairs and International Trade (DFAIT) used GCconnex to open up its policy research and development processes to public servants across the federal government. The Deputy Minister Committee on Policy Innovation, created in November 2012, used GCpedia to crowdsource its discussion papers. Clerk Wayne Wouters (2010) openly used his own GCpedia page to develop a document on workplace renewal in collaboration with other public servants. Beyond specific projects and tasks, public servants have used the tools to support their everyday work, sharing bookmarks (links to websites) and files, posting assignment opportunities, creating work spaces for teams, and soliciting quick feedback on documents being drafted. As described by one user,

I've repeatedly started a GCpedia page that's, like, four lines, linked to it on Twitter with the appropriate hashtag and a simple ask: "I need some input on this. This is what it's about." Nice, concise, sweet. Within minutes, five to ten to twenty comments, and ... it sounds small, but in the scale of things it's, like, imagine if there were more civil servants on it or tracking the hashtag on it ... The input would be huge. (P8)

This quotation points to an important dynamic at play in GCTools – disparity in the uptake and use of the tools across the bureaucracy. The tools are ultimately just that – a set of tools, a technical infrastructure. Those in the CIOB managing GCTools and public servants in line departments consistently emphasized that, though this technical infrastructure is a *necessary* condition to support large-scale information sharing and collaboration in the public service, the infrastructure itself is not *sufficient* as a driver of a more systems-based bureaucracy. As described by one official who managed the initial rollout of GCTools, "build it and they will come only works in the movies" (Androsoff 2016). Indeed, while a small group of champions and trainers of GCTools emerged across the bureaucracy, fewer than 5,000 employees registered an account on GCpedia between its launch in October 2008 and April 2009 (Chief Information Officer Branch 2014). And, despite Clerks Lynch, Wouters, and Charette espousing the benefits of internal wikis and GCTools in all but one of their annual reports to the prime minister between 2008 and 2015, as of August 2015 GCpedia counted only 60,000 users, roughly 25 percent of the population of the federal public service.[4]

What is more, a December 2015 GCconnex user study conducted by staff in the CIOB indicated that 87 percent of users had never contributed a comment on the platform (Chief Information Officer Branch 2015), though this should be interpreted with an appreciation for power laws in online contexts, which state that a smaller percentage of users will generally be responsible for the majority of the activity in web-based social networks (Johnson, Faraj, and Kudaravalli 2014). Still, the same 2015 study of GCconnex found that only a small percentage of users completed the "About Me" sections of their profiles (11 percent) and added their pictures to their profiles (21 percent). Fewer than 1 percent of GCconnex users (0.66 percent) had completed the "Skills" sections of their profiles, undermining the tool's utility as a platform for identifying and connecting expertise across the bureaucracy. Of the users who had engaged at least five times on the platform (a threshold set to avoid distorting the data with those who joined the platform but then never participated on it), only 13 percent had linked to other colleagues using GCconnex, and only 10 percent had joined a group (Chief Information Officer Branch 2015).

Some interviewees, including those who worked on GCTools, acknowledged that the tools were not widely used partly because of a lack of awareness among public servants about how such tools could be used and a perception that some of the tools' functionality was clumsy and ill designed (a reality not aided by the small budget allocated to GCTools, with only three full-time employees dedicated to their design, maintenance, training, and promotion).

But interviewees also revealed that their uptake was hindered by a lack of encouragement and leadership from executives. Certain managers did not understand what these tools were for, were unaware that they existed, or when they were aware of them actually banned or discouraged their employees from using them. This managerial response to GCTools illustrates how deeply the culture of information control can continue to mark the public service even in the face of tools that reduce the technical barriers to intragovernmental information sharing and collaboration and even when these tools are endorsed by the bureaucracy's highest ranking officer, the clerk of the Privy Council. In this context, GCTools have tended to be used and promoted most regularly and enthusiastically by atypical public servants comprising a grassroots network of generally mid- to lower-level innovators – often the same public servants engaged in Twitter networks such as #w2p – dubbed by David Eaves (2009) as the "Rat Pack of Public Service Renewal."

In addition to their low and uneven uptake across the bureaucracy proper (notably among the executive class), GCTools can be critiqued for failing to deliver on the theory of change that partly drove their initial development – to foster public servants' willingness and ability to engage with the public externally by experimenting with these technologies internally. No doubt because their use had proven to be spotty across the federal public service, and because when used internally these tools still allowed public servants to evade the complex issues of potential politicization, de-anonymization, and accountability that external bureaucrat-citizen interaction can invite and that must be resolved for wider external uptake of social media, GCTools as of 2015 had not generated a tolerance for more networked information sharing and engagement with the public. Social media and citizen engagement efforts were still largely managed through strict, top-down initiatives of communications and stakeholder engagement shops.

Two subsequent developments – Blueprint 2020 and a series of policy innovation initiatives – also attempted to tackle the cultural barriers to digital era open government; however, like GCTools, they too faced limitations upon implementation.

Blueprint 2020

Managed through a secretariat in the PCO, Blueprint 2020 was launched as an initiative of Clerk Wouters in June 2013, with the aim of supporting "a dialogue about the future of the Public Service" among federal public servants. The initiative began with a new "Vision for Canada's Federal Public Service" created by the clerk in consultation with senior deputies. The vision centred on five themes and was viewed over 125,000 times by public servants by November 2013, when the interim report on the progress of the initiative was published (Clerk of the Privy Council 2013b). The vision called for

1   an open and networked environment that engages citizens and partners for the public good
2   a whole-of-government approach that enhances service delivery and value for money
3   a modern workplace that makes smart use of new technologies to improve networking, access to data and customer service; and
4   a capable, confident and high-performing workforce that embraces new ways of working and mobilizing the diversity of talent to serve the country's evolving needs. (Clerk of the Privy Council 2013a)

The language and objectives invoked in these principles are significant. As with GCTools, Blueprint 2020 focused primarily on promoting an internal opening of the federal bureaucracy, with only the first principle mentioning the need to engage "citizens and partners." The remaining principles were inward looking, related to promoting "whole-of-government" approaches and the "smart use of new technologies" to support "networking" and "access to data" in the bureaucracy, along with generating a workforce that "embraces new ways of working and mobilizing [a] diversity of talent." In practice, Blueprint 2020 worked to move the federal bureaucracy from a culture of closed government to a culture of open government in three ways.

First, launched as an initiative of the clerk and mandated as a vision that deputy ministers were required to implement in their departments, Blueprint 2020 provided a top-level signal that at least rhetorically legitimized the need for the public service to tackle the excessively siloed, hierarchical, stagnant, and innovation-averse work models that had typically characterized life in the bureaucracy. If GCTools were somewhat marginalized as platforms that, despite having clerk-level support, were ultimately championed and used regularly only by a portion of the organization, the place of Blueprint 2020 as a central reform initiative, backed by a secretariat in the PCO and requiring departmental reporting, helped to mainstream GCTools' existing emphasis on creating whole of government, networked work processes that capitalize on the affordances of digital technologies.

Second, and moving from rhetorical signalling to practical implementation, the initiative sought to challenge closed government by inviting public servants to help refine the Blueprint 2020 vision and to propose initiatives that embodied this vision within their departments. GCTools served as a main site of information sharing and discussion throughout the initiative. GCpedia recruited roughly 250 users per week throughout the Blueprint 2020 initiative, and a Blueprint 2020 group on GCconnex recruited about 100 users per month, totalling 5,400 members as of November 2015 (Chief Information Officer Branch 2015). The Blueprint 2020 group thus became the largest and among the most active on GCconnex, albeit, again, a group representing only 2 percent of the federal public service. Nonetheless, demonstrating the roles that these tools could play in facilitating cross-government conversation among public servants, the GCconnex Blueprint 2020 group hosted active discussions on the Government of Canada's capacity to deliver the open, networked model of public service that the Blueprint vision, and broader narratives of digital era open government, promote. These discussions addressed the recruitment and retention of employees with the skills needed for a transformed governing context, issues of policy compliance (notably compliance with official languages policies), and new policy instruments such as behavioural insights, each of which was among the top ten most discussed topics in the Blueprint 2020 group (Chief Information Officer Branch 2015).

The initiative also broke from traditional models of public service reform in using Twitter and the hashtag "#GC2020" to organize a conversation among public servants on public service renewal, an unprecedented example of officially sanctioned public-facing, public servant–led conversation on the subject. Over one four-month period of study, the hashtag "#GC2020" was used 12,008 times by 1,162 unique Twitter users.[5] Although public facing and open to non-public servants, in many ways the conversation was focused on "inside baseball" public servant activities, with tweets in some cases including weblinks to internal sites inaccessible to those outside the government. In this sense, as GCTools intended, this online networking served as a sort of half step toward the fully fledged use of social media by individual public servants for decentralized public discussions (versus the norm of centralized, top-down, communications/spokesperson-controlled government use of social media). Through this Twitter conversation, departmental events, and engagement on GCTools, more than 110,000 public servants reportedly participated in internal Blueprint 2020 activities by May 2014, when a report titled *Destination 2020* was released, summarizing the results of the initiative over its first year of implementation (Clerk of the Privy Council 2014).

These initiatives and the conversations that Blueprint 2020 instigated revealed that public servants wanted "improved information sharing and more ways to connect and collaborate in the Public Service" (Clerk of the Privy Council 2013b). The consultation also revealed that employees wanted to "streamlin[e] internal red tape as well as approvals, planning and reporting, and administrative functions." The interim report concluded that "employees are looking for greater empowerment at the individual level and reduced hierarchy" (Clerk of the Privy Council 2013b), a sentiment echoed in the *Destination 2020* report. Demands for technology-enabled collaboration were also a strong theme in the Blueprint 2020 consultations. The interim report noted that, "to work better together, public servants are looking for a toolset the whole Public Service can use, and support for smart use of technologies such as social media," seen as useful tools for engaging internally but also externally, highlighting "a need for more risk tolerance to try out new ways of working and serving Canadians" through the web (Clerk of the Privy Council 2013b).

Of course, the challenges raised by these public servants were not new or unknown. A quick tour through the classics of Canadian public administration and the goals of previous reform efforts reveals that, albeit lacking the references to digital technologies that became prominent in the Blueprint 2020 consultations, the same set of complaints and concerns about hierarchy, silos, and risk aversion would likely have emerged from public servants of decades past. Unique here is that these complaints and concerns were solicited by the government as part of the first federal reform initiative to be shaped by a grassroots engagement exercise in which all members of the public service were encouraged to take part. The extent and variety of employee consultations under Blueprint 2020 represented a notable experiment in open, cross-governmental, and bottom-up engagement.

Third, Blueprint 2020 fostered an internal opening of the bureaucracy through a series of departmental employee engagement initiatives that deputy ministers across the government were required to host. This typically led to "Dragon's Den" forums in which employees could pitch their innovative ideas to senior executives to improve corporate processes, policies, programs, and services. For example, fulfilling Blueprint 2020 obligations, the Department of Fisheries and Oceans hosted a "Dragon's Den" in 2014 that attracted fifty-three submissions, 3,000 ideas and comments from the department, and the presentation of nine business cases from the winning submission to the Deputy Minister's Management Committee. Three ideas were selected for implementation. The first was a new human resources web portal that combined HR information and forms into one easy-to-find space. The second was a real-time collaboration tool that would use Microsoft OneDrive to test the effectiveness of simultaneous viewing, commenting on, and editing of documents internally, and (breaking from the primarily internal focus of other initiatives) consulting with external partners. Third, the "Dragon's Den" also resulted in the expansion of a mobile-friendly online poaching complaint form that had already been tested in Quebec (King 2014). To be sure, these ideas were not particularly mind blowing or cutting edge; they called the public service to take up tools and approaches already standard (or in some cases already dated) outside the government. Significant, however, is the bottom-up process that brought these ideas to senior management's attention, tackling the closed hierarchical relationship that has traditionally limited vertical information flows in the bureaucracy and that is emblematic of the closed government paradigm.

Yet, like GCTools, though Blueprint 2020 should be applauded for its admirable objectives and some of its demonstrated successes, the effort ultimately did not scale sufficiently or effect the substantive changes required to shift the culture of the public service meaningfully. Yes, almost half of the federal public service was reported to have participated in a Blueprint 2020 event, but some of the interviewees explained that these initiatives, whether a deputy minister "Dragon's Den" or some other departmental engagement effort, felt forced and relatively meaningless as one-time ventures in grassroots employee engagement. Others noted that the initiatives that their departments cited in their mandatory reports to the Blueprint 2020 secretariat were already under way as opposed to being inspired by the reform initiative. Still others argued that it was hard to "buy" the sincerity of the effort when their political leaders were otherwise infamous for encouraging information control and when media reports continued to reveal (and condemn) the bureaucracy for the lagged uptake of networked digital technologies, mirroring reactions to the official open government initiative, branded "a bit rich" by one interviewee (S5). Another interviewee suggested that the initiative was indeed recalibrating the public servant mindset: "Because of Blueprint 2020 and the clerk's support, now anyone with any ambition in the GC knows that they have to be on board with these tools, with this more open way of working, to rise up" (I9). Yet this interviewee also questioned whether the initiative was in part simply the clerk's "swan song," implemented merely to preface his eventual departure from his post as head of the public service (19). Other interviewees suggested that many of their colleagues (or they themselves) knew very little about Blueprint 2020 and that it had not actually arisen in any meaningful way in their work.

A third set of initiatives, in this case focused on promoting policy innovation, further attempted to shift the culture of the federal public service from one that defaulted to siloed information control, excessive hierarchy, and risk aversion, enjoying some success but also marred by the same scale and scope limitations that GCTools and Blueprint 2020 faced.

Policy Innovation

In December 2012, a new deputy minister committee was struck, titled the Deputy Minister Committee on Social Media and Policy Development. The committee's mandate was "to consider linkages between social media and policymaking, including new models for policy development and public engagement" (Deputy Minister Committee on Policy Innovation 2014, 1), thus attempting to reverse the trend whereby social media had been framed primarily as communication tools alone in departments. To this end, the committee initially focused on determining how new digital policy instruments related to social media could be applied to the work of the Government of Canada. These instruments included big data, open data, crowdsourcing, online collaborative tools, social media monitoring, open policy making, gamification, hackathons, behavioural insights, and deliberative polling.[6] The committee also explored a series of other policy instruments not exclusively linked to digital technologies, but which demanded that the bureaucracy adopt new forms of internal and external collaboration in policy design and service delivery, such as social finance, innovation hubs and labs, micro-assignments (term appointments by which public servants can be "loaned" to other units or projects within the bureaucracy), tiger teams (temporary task forces dedicated to addressing a specific challenge or project), interchanges with other sectors, prizes and challenges (competitions using monetary or other rewards to incentivize outsiders to contribute ideas and solutions to the government), academic partnership/engagement, and user-centred design.

In adopting this focus on digital policy instruments and open models of working, the interim report of the committee explained that they "sought to embody [their] mandate in [their] proceedings [by breaking] from the traditional DM Committee format ... [and] publishing discussion papers, agendas, and presentations for consultations by anyone in the public service; and curating crowdsourced input for Committee products from public servants across government" (Deputy Minister Committee on Policy Innovation 2014, 1).

This crowdsourcing effort was conducted using GCpedia, again illustrating GCTools' role as technical enablers of bottom-up, interdepartmental engagement across the public service. The committee also broke from the traditionally elite, top-down model of DM committees by sharing its meeting minutes on GCpedia, tweeting from the Twitter account @DMCPI, and including reverse mentors as full members of the committee. These reverse mentors were nonexecutive-level officials selected by each DM from his or her department, and they were invited to join the committee after its early meetings, when there was a general recognition that the committee's comparatively older members were not particularly well informed about the digital policy instruments that they intended to explore.

In November 2013, just under a year after the committee was first struck, it underwent a telling name change from the DM Committee on Social Media and Policy Development to the DM Committee on Policy Innovation (DMCPI). Although the original name focused on the adoption of new digital policy instruments (and even more specifically on social media), the new mandate, with its comparatively broader focus on policy innovation, signalled a recognition that the digital age brought with it new challenges that would demand a retooling of the traditional processes by which policies, programs, and services were developed and delivered in the bureaucracy. A deck prepared by the DMCPI in 2015 reflected this weightier, more complex remit, explaining that the committee's work would now focus on dramatic societal changes affecting the government's policy capacity, including

- increasing problem complexity ("wicked problems") fuelled by globalization and interconnectedness, stakeholder diversity and complexity, information uncertainty, and technology
- exponential growth in technology and unprecedented levels of information creation, storage, processing, and access/communication
- long-run fiscal constraints creating downward pressure on spending and the need to continually "deliver more with less"
- changing citizen expectations – from greater agency (peer-to-peer relationships and community-building) to demanding transparency, rapid responses, and greater participation in decision-making from government. (Deputy Minister Committee on Policy Innovation, 2015a)

Having catalogued these trends, the DMCPI concluded that "governments are adapting to these shifts by changing the way they do business and adopting new and innovative tools" (Deputy Minister Committee on Policy Innovation 2015a). In other words, the committee's change in mandate acknowledged that adjusting to the digital age is not simply a matter of adding new digital tools to a closed government. Rather, the expanded mandate was premised on the notion that the bureaucracy needed to undergo changes to its structures, worldviews, and tools to retain its policy capacity in the digital age. For the committee, this change would see the culture of government facilitate and reward smart risk taking and experimentation with new and in most cases more open and collaborative approaches to internal work processes, policy development, and service delivery.

In an effort to foster this culture, and following on the focus of GCTools and Blueprint 2020, the DMCPI first took aim at siloed, hierarchical models of information exchange in the bureaucracy, framing these silos and hierarchies as barriers to the free flow and scaling of innovative ideas emerging from across the bureaucracy and from all levels in the organizational chain of command. To this end, the DMCPI led its own "Dragon's Den," soliciting ideas for innovative proposals from across the government. The winning proposal led to a micro-assignment pilot that would use GCconnex to link employees with particular skills with units across the government in need of those skills. The assignment operates on a time-limited basis and represents a novel response to the long-standing recognition in the federal government that collaboration across functional areas of responsibility and policy expertise is much needed but difficult to facilitate given the large and disjointed bureaucratic machine within which pockets of expertise can easily be hidden and given the rigid human resource structures that typically have narrowly defined the scope of an individual employee's tasks.

The DMCPI also launched the Virtual Policy Challenge in the spring of 2014. The initiative was promoted at a deputy ministers' breakfast so that all DMs would then encourage participation in their departments. As Graham Flack, co-chair of the DMCPI and then deputy secretary to the cabinet at the PCO, described it, the Virtual Policy Challenge was

> an innovative, government-wide online policy discussion that invites employees to use GCconnex to identify medium-term trends, emerging issues and challenges facing Canada. The goal of this virtual challenge is to solicit input from across the public service to broaden

policy conversations, and surface new ideas and perspectives that can be harvested to support our policy work. Participants will be asked to identify issues, explain why they are important and propose how they could be further explored. (Flack 2014)

In follow-up emails discussing the Virtual Policy Challenge, the DMCPI co-chairs explained that the discussions and proposals received were so strong that, in lieu of selecting a few ideas as planned, they would propose a broader selection of ideas to take to policy committees (Flack and Pentney 2014). One idea emerging from the Virtual Policy Challenge was the need for further study of the sharing economy (populated by actors such as Uber and AirBnB), subsequently explored in a crowdsourced document prepared by a small group working on micro-assignment. Following on the Virtual Policy Challenge, the DMCPI – along with the PCO's Central Innovation Hub, Health Canada, the Public Health Agency of Canada, and Shared Services – also hosted a Public Service App Challenge in the summer of 2015, in which twenty-four departments submitted 500 ideas for apps.

But perhaps more significant than leading these experiments in horizontal policy work were the committee's efforts to diagnose the conditions that prevent innovation in the federal government. Part of this work focused on delineating why there had been interesting experiments in the use of more innovative, digital policy instruments in certain pockets but not in others. This spoke to the fact that the DMCPI did not emerge in an innovation vacuum. Rather, a number of units had already been applying new digital instruments and approaches to their work in innovative ways.

For example, as part of digital diplomacy initiatives and also within an initiative titled Open Policy Development, officials in the DFATD had been experimenting with social media as a tool of public diplomacy, consular service delivery, and information gathering (Department of Foreign Affairs and International Trade Canada 2012). In 2014, the Public Health Agency of Canada (PHAC) partnered with the CBC and the retailer Canadian Tire to crowdsource policy proposals that would support a more active population, invited external judges to rank the top six ideas, and then invited Canadians to vote online for the proposal that would receive a $1 million investment. In 2015, the PHAC, NRCan, and the Government of British Columbia partnered with the Heart and Stroke Foundation, the Canadian Diabetes Association, YMCA Canada, and an organization called Social Change Rewards to launch an initiative titled Carrot, which – using information cues, or "nudges" (Thaler and Sunstein 2009) and a mobile app – encourages healthy behaviours by linking them with established rewards programs, such as Aeroplan. Certain units, including the Canada Revenue Agency (CRA), ESDC, the DFATD, and Public Safety had been experimenting with big data in designing policies and services (Shared Services Canada 2015). The CRA in particular made notable advances in its online digital services and became a leader in the federal government in the use of behavioural insights and nudges.

In addition to departments' experimentation with new digital policy instruments, alongside the DMCPI dedicated innovation labs and hubs emerged in the ESDC, the former Industry Canada (now Innovation, Science and Economic Development Canada), and NRCan. And, emerging in part from requests for support and top-level cover in experimenting with new digital policy instruments as revealed in the Blueprint 2020 exercise, the PCO launched a Central Innovation Hub to guide departments in the use of new policy instruments, such as behavioural insights, big data, and design thinking.

But recognizing that these innovations had cropped up in an ad hoc, patchwork way, part of the DMCPI's work was analyzing why innovations had emerged in some places and not others and why specific initiatives were rarely scaled or mainstreamed to become more common across the government. As the committee observed, innovation in the use of new digital policy instruments was "still the exception, not the rule" (Deputy Minister Committee on Policy Innovation 2015a).

The DMCPI found that the uptake of unconventional, digital policy instruments was hindered by a series of factors well documented in theories of public sector innovation (Bason 2010; Bellafontaine 2013; Borins 2002; Schultz Larsen 2015). For example, the committee observed that traditionally the federal government had hired and rewarded those who operated in an environment that did not prioritize innovation, so innovation had not been "driven throughout organizations" or "made mission critical." According to the committee, innovation was not yet "democratized," reserved instead for particular elites working on files on which managers or the nature of the file itself (e.g., GCTools and Blueprint 2020) enabled public servants to experiment with new approaches to their work (Deputy Minister Committee on Policy Innovation 2015a). Targeting siloed organizational schemes and invoking the virtues of system-based, horizontal management, the committee critiqued how resourcing flowed along strict organizational lines versus being allocated by initiative, arguing that this stifled the flexibility and collaboration required to experiment with new policy instruments. Reflecting the closed government-outsider relationship, the committee noted that "key ideas, actors, expertise, and resources reside outside government, yet relationships with stakeholders/clients are limited and movement between sectors is challenging and disincentivized" (Deputy Minister Committee on Policy Innovation 2015a).

The TBS policy suite also came under attack. The committee found that certain rules overly handcuffed the public service. In other cases it was simply incorrect perceptions of rules among public servants that limited bureaucrats' willingness to experiment with new approaches to their work. This led a briefing on the DMCPI to the deputy minister of the ESDC to explain that the bureaucracy needed "myth busting" documents to clarify the rules on experimentation with new policy tools in the federal government (Employment and Social Development Canada 2015). In particular, the DMCPI highlighted that rules (real or perceived) related to grants and contributions, public opinion research, and data sharing were among those typically framed as barriers to the use of the digital policy instruments that the committee was advancing. This is unsurprising given that these activities involve government-outsider interaction and/or are information intensive, rendering them particularly relevant to new digital tools that involve networking, collaboration, and data exchange.

Chapters 3 and 4 provided concrete evidence to substantiate the committee's concern over the role that rules – real or perceived – play in stifling the public service's willingness to experiment in the digital age. TBS policy mission creep led to a dense set of guidelines and approval processes that ensured social media were not used as innovative tools for policy development or service delivery, and instead they merely digitized existing tightly managed communications and consultation models. The TBS rules on social media became so dense partly because of their creators' appreciation for executives' risk aversion. The rules were an attempt to appease this aversion by exhaustively detailing how social media could be squared with existing corporate policies. Yet the conversation on social media became much more one of rules and risks, and much less one on innovation and open engagement, fuelling rather than alleviating existing anxiety about these new tools of government-citizen interaction. Acknowledging this point, the DMCPI took aim at senior leaders, referring to their "unique role in setting tone, establishing demand and conditions for innovation, and creating space for safe risk-taking" (Deputy Minister Committee on Policy Innovation 2015a).

The role of management in propelling or halting innovation was a common theme in interviews. Almost universally, when asked why a particular initiative – such as the innovative use of data analytics in designing a service or an openness to partnerships with online communities – was launched, or more generally when asked what was required to experiment with new digital technologies, interviewees cited the courageous leadership of managers who trusted their staff members. As one interviewee put it, superiors need to provide "cover to take risks, I mean, obviously the leader, the director, needs to have confidence in the team that they will not hang – they will not get into trouble" (P7). In particular, interviewees suggested that it was often the personality of the particular manager, not the system or structure in which they operated, that determined the scope for innovative experiments with digital policy instruments, such that, when a courageous and trusting manager moved posts, often the innovations instituted under his or her watch were in peril.[7]

Other interviewees specified that middle managers in particular defined the scope for staff to experiment with new digital policy instruments. These interviewees suggested that, though at first executives in general were skeptical about digital technologies, over time *senior* executives tended to appreciate the potential gains that innovative engagement with digital technologies would offer the government. Operational middle managers, however, were cited as an enduring "clay layer" where good ideas go to die, that is, where enthusiasm for innovation among senior executives was lost on its way down to lower-level implementation. Speaking in 2012 about an early pilot project in the use of social media for Corrective Blogging on the controversial subject of the seal hunt, a communications manager in the former DFAIT explained that

> I've noticed the dialogue on social media in the social media circles has changed a lot, where I don't know if you've noticed but a couple years ago it was all about convincing the C-suite. "What's your return on the investment?" I don't notice that anymore at all ... So I found it interesting to see what has the conversation been about social media and government? And how has it shifted? So I think what you find, and this isn't just government, it's private sector as well, they [the C-suite] get it. It's the clay layer that's nervous, who think they won't want to do it, or "I don't want to look stupid" for whatever reason. But anytime I've gone up to the deputy level, they're signing off right away. You know, "Why aren't we doing more of this?" was one of the questions I had a deputy minister ask me. (C2)

Another official explained that, at the deputy minister level, encouraging innovation was comparatively safer since one had "already made it to the top" and had "less to lose." In contrast, he argued, middle managers seeking those high-level positions face greater pressures to stay the course and avoid any mistakes and fewer incentives to try something different given that it might fail (P8). The same perspective on middle management was expressed in a 2013 Twitter conversation among federal public servants. As described by one of the participants, "a quiet Wednesday night turned into a Twitter barn-burner on the topic of Canadian public sector renewal, innovation and the role of middle-management" ("Clay Layer" 2013). On one level, this debate served as a fascinating example of the largely internally focused but public-facing informal online discussions that public servants undertook on the subject of public service renewal as of the mid-2000s, as in the #gc2020 and #DMCPI Twitter networks. But pertinent to the issue of managers' roles in facilitating innovation, the Twitter exchange centred on a debate about where middle management begins and ends in the organizational hierarchy and on whether it is the people who occupy middle management, or the structures that they face, that limit innovation. Whatever the sticking points of the discussion, the common perspective was clear: the power to propel, or halt, innovation lay with those in the middle of the hierarchical chain of command.

Adding to this discussion, the DMCPI's report on the barriers to innovation concluded that senior managers nonetheless continue to play an important role in encouraging innovation among their staff, a task that "requires navigating [the] political/public service dynamic" (Deputy Minister Committee on Policy Innovation 2015a). This careful critique of senior leaders in the Government of Canada, and the cryptic reference to the political-administrative interface with which senior executives must grapple, have important undertones, implying what could be controversial to imprint in writing in a deck. Here the committee was stating, albeit in a guarded way, that innovation had been stifled partly because of a dearth of leadership from the committee members' colleagues in the executive class. But it had also been hindered by the reality that diversions from tried and tested methods – and the risk of failure that accompanied them – demanded cover and buy in from political leaders.

On this last point, the same DMCPI presentation offered another telling but implied suggestion that the Government of Canada had lacked the required political leadership to support innovative experimentation with these new policy instruments and open models of work, an argument substantiated by the findings in previous chapters. The committee referenced the effectiveness of "positive policies" that mandated experimentation with digital policy instruments in other jurisdictions, such as the US Executive Order on Streamlining Service Delivery and Improving Customer Service (White House 2011) and the UK 2012 Civil Service Reform Plan, which noted that "open policy-making will become the default" (Government of the United Kingdom 2012). As a telling illustration of the perceived illegitimacy of the official open government initiative, the government's 2014 directive on becoming "open by default" was not mentioned in the deck as an example of a potent "positive policy" in the federal government, even though technically it should have qualified as one (Treasury Board Secretariat 2014b). Having suggested that these policies are instrumental in promoting innovation, the message (however buried in subtext) was clear: the federal government needed political directives to combat the risk-averse, rule-bound culture that invariably emerges when public servants fear the public criticism and top-down sanctioning that they might attract by experimenting with unknown and potentially failure-ridden deviations from the status quo.

Like those revealed in Blueprint 2020, the conditions that the DMCPI catalogued as inhibiting innovation in the federal government are hardly novel discoveries; the "web of rules," risk aversion, and silos that the committee cited have long been the subject of criticism and the inspiration for public sector reforms in the federal government. Where the DMCPI added to this long-standing discussion was in linking these issues to digital technologies and, more broadly, to the exogenous pressures that necessitate open government in the digital age, including the need to meet changing citizen expectations and to capitalize on new information and data sources. And, acknowledging that a fear of public failure is one of the biggest inhibitors preventing experimentation with digital policy instruments, the DMCPI, like GCTools and Blueprint 2020, created a "safe space" within the bureaucracy in which open models of dialogue and information sharing could be tested and socialized.

Yet, as with other initiatives, the final diagnosis of the success of the policy innovation movement in the federal government – at least at the time period that this study covers – falls to a question of scale and scope of impact. The DMCPI and related policy innovation labs and hubs that emerged alongside it were created to expand access to novel digital policy instruments and approaches and to foster a flatter organizational culture more amenable to open innovation. However, as of the time of writing, their success in actually achieving this objective was minimal. As the DMCPI itself acknowledged and criticized in a 2015 report, the ability to engage in digital era policy innovation largely remained the exclusive prerogative of particular actors within the bureaucracy. Ultimately, beyond a few notable pilot projects and one-off ventures into networked, bottom-up policy making and the use of digital policy instruments, most of the DMCPI's early work consisted not of supporting policy innovation but of diagnosing why policy innovation was so rare.

This study's findings suggest that the committee was entirely accurate in appraising the conditions that complicate the public service's efforts to adapt to the digital age and its related policy pressures, instruments, and approaches. And, as I have argued consistently throughout this book, efforts to adapt to the digital age fail when they do not begin with a deep appreciation for the historical legacies and contemporary constraints at odds with the demands of digital era open government. In this sense, the diagnostic work undertaken by the committee was sensible and valuable. Yet, as with GCTools and the Blueprint 2020 reform effort, the policy innovation movement took baby steps at best toward the larger cultural transition from closed government to open government that I and those leading these initiatives argue is necessary to secure the resilience of the public service in the digital age.

The Limits of Incremental Public Servant–Led Reform

In a sense, GCTools, Blueprint 2020, and policy innovation initiatives themselves suffered from a lack of ambition and an excess of risk aversion. The initiatives promoted innovative forms of networked policy making and bottom-up engagement in the safe space of the bureaucracy, but they never truly opened up this work to the comparatively more ambitious and untested domain of external openings. This move would have forced the bureaucracy to resolve the much more thorny and fundamental dilemmas of de-anonymization, accountability, cross-/intradepartmental coordination, and public-facing failure that open policy making and service delivery can invite. We can also challenge the comparatively safe instruments by which these reforms were instituted. For instance, to promote a less bureaucratic model of policy development, deputy ministers somewhat ironically opted to strike a committee, an emblem of bureaucratic organization. To be fair, the DMCPI attempted to render itself less hierarchical and exclusive through the use of GCTools, Twitter, and reverse mentors, but the initiative in a sense used a flame to fight a fire. And, where these initiatives did spawn the innovative uptake of novel policy instruments, digital citizen engagement tactics, or partnerships with outsiders, they remained in the comparative safe zones of pilot projects and one-time initiatives as opposed to becoming standard practice.

On the other hand, these cautious, small-scale, and largely internal initiatives were perhaps the best possible solutions given the context in which they were rolled out. Their narrow impact and relative lack of ambition were products of the political climate at the time, with change being led with the levers that the public service had at its disposal – clerk- and DM-led initiatives, for example. These largely under-the-radar internal initiatives did not need to contend with a political leadership otherwise inclined to control information and limit public servants' individual agency (Clarke 2014c). It is extremely difficult if not impossible to build a culture more open to the risks that accompany the uptake of new and untested policy instruments and open policy-making approaches absent clear signals that the political leadership is open to these risks, a point Kevin Page noted when critiquing Blueprint 2020 at the close of his 2012 reflection on his time as parliamentary budget officer. Although not directly stifled or challenged by the prime minister and cabinet ministers, these initiatives nonetheless lacked their active, sustained involvement and support. And, as noted earlier, the initiatives were implemented even as the Harper government was regularly critiqued for adopting a draconian approach to information control and in some instances for ignoring advice and expertise from the bureaucracy in policy development, versus investing in its capacity to innovate in this domain (see Harris 2014; Marland 2016; Martin 2011; and Wells 2013).

This political support could have ensured that the initiatives received the financial and human resources needed to scale them to have greater impacts, such as investing in sustained ventures in innovative policy making and service delivery, versus one-time pilot projects, or providing more staff to support the expansion and functionality of GCTools. But more fundamentally, and as noted (however cryptically) by the DMCPI, political support was needed to alleviate the anxious risk aversion and impulse to information control at odds with these initiatives' ultimate goal of transforming the public service from a closed to an open institution. Without direct support from the political masters to whom bureaucrats must answer, public servant–led reform can go only so far, especially when one of the reform goals demands that the public service become more open to sharing information, engaging internally and externally, and treading the potentially failure-ridden territory of policy innovation, each of which might invite politically costly scrutiny of the minister in Question Period or unwelcome departmental coverage in a national newspaper.

Again the discussion falls on the crucial role that political leadership plays in enabling the public service to adapt to the pressures and opportunities of the digital age. The concluding chapter explores what this finding implies for the future of digital government in Canada in light of the changes in leadership and tone ushered in with the election of Justin Trudeau's Liberals in October 2015. The analysis thus far suggests that Trudeau's commitment to evidence-informed policy making, service improvement, experimentation, and a decentralized, pluralistic model of government-citizen engagement will at least provide the top-level leadership required to fuel digital innovation in the federal government going forward. But the analysis equally cautions that this leadership is only one of the conditions required to battle the bureaucracy's closed by default mentality and to narrow the time lag ensuring that the federal civil service is out of pace with changes arising quickly outside its walls. Indeed, though a lack of political investment constrained the scope of change that could be achieved by GCTools, Blueprint 2020, and various policy innovation initiatives, political leadership is not simply a silver bullet for the challenges plaguing the federal bureaucracy. These challenges include managers' attitudes, incentive structures, and excessive internal rules and processes. The next chapter considers one of the conditions that, alongside political direction and a range of administrative reforms, will be an essential driver of digital renewal in the Government of Canada and that of late has become a central preoccupation of governments globally: filling the digital skills gap in the public service.

6

The Digital Skills Gap in the Federal Bureaucracy

Imagine this scenario: encouraged by the clerk and the mandate of Blueprint 2020, given cover by a risk-tolerant minister demanding policy innovation, and facilitated by the departmental CIO's recent decision to open up access to social media sites and related analytical tools, a program manager decides that her team now has the right conditions to test which language cues and design elements on their webpage are more likely to encourage users to share information published on the page with their online social networks (thus greatly expanding the reach and impact of the information). The data generated by the page will allow the team first to adjust and improve the page iteratively in real time based on users' interactions with it and then to draw other insights from the page that might be relevant to program design and delivery, such as the time of day that users interact with the page or the source websites that lead them to it. Taking the analysis one step further, the team might explore how users who do share the link to the program page discuss it on their social networks. This would expose the language that users employ to describe the program, which the team could then use to create a more user-friendly description of the program on the original website. The team could also investigate how users describe the effectiveness or deficiencies of the program on social media and use this feedback to improve the program. The team might also use social network analysis to identify the most influential actors discussing the program. These individuals could provide fruitful insights in evaluations of the program, or they could be useful partners in communication campaigns related to the program. Finally, all the data generated from the site and the experiment with language and design changes could be stored using common data standards so that other units across the government could use them to support other policy, program, and service designs.

The problem, of course, is that, despite operating under the conditions that I suggest must be in place to engage in this type of work (e.g., top-level directives, political and administrative leadership, access to technology), the program officers and manager in this team likely will not be equipped to imagine how these digital policy instruments could be applied to their work, let alone possessing the skills required to wield these instruments in practice. This scenario exposes a key barrier inhibiting digital era open government in the federal public service: the digital skills gap.

The traditional social science curriculum and in-house training that inform policy analysts, program officers, and executives in the public service offer little preparation for adopting the tools that the open government initiative, Blueprint 2020, and DMCPI now promote, including A/B testing, big data, open data, crowdsourcing, gamification, deliberative polling, web-based service delivery, and collaboration platforms. Equally, the traditional skill sets and approaches found in government IT shops need to be refreshed and better embedded in the everyday policy work of the government if the bureaucracy is to bolster its digital policy capacity. In other words, though updating the bureaucracy for the digital age is not simply a technological challenge but also requires a much more fundamental turn from closed government to open government, this project will remain a nonstarter without access to the digital skills currently more likely to shape the work of Facebook and Twitter than the policies, programs, and services of government bureaucracies.

In this chapter I pick up on a trajectory that has seen leading digital government jurisdictions shift from initial enthusiasm for open data, crowdsourcing, big data, and other digital innovations to more sobering, tactical efforts to capitalize on a different breed of talent required to lead digital government reforms. In other words, in this chapter I shift from diagnosis to prescription, assessing the contracting, partnering, and recruitment strategies with which governments inside and outside Canada are now experimenting in order to fill the digital skills gap. In particular, I focus on the emergence of elite digital government units as the favoured solution globally, not simply as a vehicle to bring unconventional digital talent into the bureaucracy, but also to tackle – at a grander scale – the institutional barriers to digital era open government.

Defining the Federal Government's Digital Skills Gap

The previous chapters exposed the federal government's digital skills gap on a number of occasions. Recall, for example, Chapter 3's discussion of the basic and largely ineffective techniques that communications officials in ESDC employed when monitoring and attempting to draw insights from social media for the department. Likewise, officials demonstrated the limits of their traditional policy toolkits in implementing the open dialogue strategy. Well-established, talk-based models of consultation were digitized – as in the case of Tony Clement's Twitter townhall – producing mass amounts of text to which public servants applied manual analyses, a costly, time-consuming, and shallow approach that calls into question the marginal benefits of additional contributions to a consultation given the costs of traditional analytical techniques. The open dialogue initiative stalled as officials debated the procurement requirements for a common engagement platform in lieu of developing one themselves or informing an agile procurement strategy that would take advantage of open-source platforms upon which government-specific requirements could be built and that would allow for early user testing. Such an approach would have been equally useful in improving the usability and design of GCTools, in which limited functionality has hindered the broad uptake and use of these collaborative platforms. Likewise, the open data initiative has been hampered in part by public servants' lack of appreciation for the potential applications – digital and otherwise – of government data to policies and services. Initiatives produced through "Dragon's Dens" under Blueprint 2020 and the policy innovation banner were often years out of date, drawing on technologies and practices that are old hat outside the government.

Digital skills necessary in governments today include web development and user-centred design as well as a range of skills at play in the collection, interpretation, and application of massive amounts of data produced by social media, websites, mobile applications, and, increasingly, all digitized objects forming the Internet of Things (e.g., wearable technologies, sensors in cars). These skills include data visualization, social network analysis, machine learning, and automated classification techniques such as sentiment analysis, methodologies at the cutting edge of data science, and computational social science.[1]

Analysis of Canada's graduate programs in public policy and administration, a traditional source of public service recruitment (in particular to the Economics and Social Science Services and Program Administration classifications that staff the mainstream policy and program work of the public service), reveals that, beyond a few courses that merely provide an introduction to these tools, or references to their potential applications to policy, these technical skills are not represented in any of these programs' curricula (a similar trend is seen in American programs; see Hu 2017). In particular, courses in public policy and administration schools tend to focus on statistical literacy, which, though relevant to some of the analytical techniques required for digital policy work, falls short of the broader range of methodologies required to collect and analyze big data generated from the web, in particular in large-scale crowdsourcing or in social listening, or to wield policy instruments such as A/B testing, user-centred design, and behavioural insights. Given the relative newness of these techniques and their traditional places in schools of computer science, engineering, and design, one can reasonably hypothesize and at least anecdotally observe that other dominant feeder programs to the public service (e.g., undergraduate and graduate programs in political science, sociology, economics, and statistics, the last three of which are explicitly listed as required backgrounds for Economics and Social Science Services positions) also lack training in the technical digital policy skills listed here. With the advent of accessible training on coding and commercial and open-source tools that facilitate the collection and analysis of web data, the barriers in this field are waning.[2] But the point remains that the skills required to work with digital policy instruments and to interpret the data that they generate are in general absent from the toolkit that the conventional program officer and policy analyst bring with them to the federal bureaucracy.

Turning to the IT shops of federal departments, we find these skills equally lacking. Other than a few pockets of expertise, today's public service IT culture has not kept pace with trends emerging in the private and civic technology sectors. Rather, in the federal government, IT has traditionally been, and is still primarily, a game of managing large contracts with external providers offering proprietary IT solutions (though not exclusively so) and so-called waterfall approaches that draw on long-release development cycles, leave little room for small-scale, data-driven adjustments based on user experience, and that often cause the large-scale, costly IT failures that have haunted so many governments internationally (6 2007; Clarke 2017; Dunleavy et al. 2006). Embodied in the shift from the language of "e-government" to the language of "digital government," and summarized in Table 6.1, best practices in government IT today draw on trends in the tech start-up world, prioritizing agile, iterative, user-centred design; experimentation and risk taking; and in-house development combined with open-source technologies and smaller-scale contracting with small and medium-sized enterprises (SMEs). In addition, technology experts today combine their technical skills such as coding, design, and web development with data science skills such as big data analytics and data visualization, a trend that follows from the mass amounts of data that

Table 6.1

Traditional approaches to government IT versus digital era government IT

Traditional approaches to government IT ("e-government")	Current digital government orthodoxy
Waterfall design, the long-release cycle	Agile, iterative design
Government-centric (focused on adhering to internal government standards, processes, and needs)	User-centric (focused on identifying user needs and tailoring government standards and processes to those needs)
Limited reliance on data in decision making and design	Heavy reliance on data-driven decision making and design
Managing legacy contracts with a small number of big IT providers	Building in-house and procuring with a competitive, pluralistic marketplace
Favours proprietary solutions	Favours open-source solutions
Siloed ("one use," department/initiative specific project development and IT management)	Horizontal, platform models ("multiple use," whole of government project development and IT management)
Risk-averse, process-first, hierarchical organizational culture	Hacker, delivery-first, "flatter" organizational culture

digital technologies now produce and that inform constant, real-time tweaks to websites, mobile apps, social networks, and all digital technologies based on user experience. These cutting-edge data science skills would not have been in the standard university curriculum and on-the-job training of today's senior IT officials. Thus, the digital skills gap is not exclusively evident in the "meat and potato" policy and program shops that advise ministers, develop programs, and implement policy directives. It also exists in the workforce that the government currently turns to for its IT expertise.

How might the Government of Canada address the digital skills gap as it adjusts to the demands and opportunities of a digital age? I begin by introducing and swiftly dismissing an option often bandied about as key to addressing the digital skills gap – turning to millennials. This nonsolution at once overestimates the talents of young public service recruits and underestimates the severity of the digital skills gap that currently plagues the federal public service.

Just Wait for the Millennials? No

Some observers have suggested that governments, like all organizations facing a dearth of digital skills, need only wait for the "digital natives" or the "Net

Generation" (Palfrey and Gasser 2008; Tapscott 2009) – the label often applied to those born between 1982 and 2004 and the generations that follow – to join their ranks to ensure that they are ready to face the challenges and opportunities of the digital age.[3] We see this perspective advanced by firms such as IBM[4] and in texts such as *Growing Up Digital*, in which Don Tapscott (1998, 1–2) writes that

> to them [digital natives] the digital technology is no more intimidating than a VCR or toaster.
>
> For the first time in history, children are more comfortable, knowledgeable, and literate than their parents with an innovation central to society. And it is through the use of digital media that the N-Generation [Net Generation] will develop and superimpose its culture on the rest of society. Boomers, stand back.

Although there might be truth in the notion that an incoming fleet of younger public servants will be more accustomed to the everyday use of digital technologies, there is no reason to believe that they will fill the digital skills gap within the bureaucracy. The skills required in government today are not something that the average young person will acquire simply by being a relatively prolific user of digital technologies; mastering Snapchat does not render one a data scientist, user-experience expert, or proficient web developer. In fact, as Tom Steinberg, founder of mySociety and early digital government innovator, noted at the 2016 Digital Governance Forum (hosted in Ottawa), today's youth are so adept at using digital technologies partly because these technologies have become so easy to use, hiding any technical components or the need for user-initiated modifications to perform complex tasks. The three-year-old who can operate an iPad is not exhibiting the impressive digital literacy and talent that will render her a digitally capable public servant, yet this kind of reference is common in discussions on the roles that digital natives will play in renewing workplaces for the digital age going forward. In other words, though we might expect incoming public servants to be more conscious of the basic affordances of digital technologies (they are more likely to have a Facebook account, to have used an iPhone, and to have contributed to a crowdsourcing effort than their boomer deputy minister), this basic familiarity does not equate directly with the literacy and technical skills required to wield digital policy instruments or to scrutinize and apply the data outputs of these instruments to the processes of governing.

In practice, the faulty assumption that one's youth would render one equipped to "handle digital" leads to a common trend in government departments. New, young recruits are handed the task of managing social media in the communications shop, for instance, effectively siloing off these tools and any data emerging from them to a low-level, ill-equipped official and undercutting their broader and more substantive potential applications to the work of the government.

The perspective that views millennials as a solution to the government's digital skills gaps is particularly flawed given that it says little about the responsibilities of existing public servants outside the "digital native" category – the "digital immigrants," as they are labelled (Prensky 2001) – to bolster their own digital skills or about the need to recruit outside digital talent into senior executive positions. This is problematic considering that as of 2015 those aged forty to fifty-four comprised roughly 50 percent of the public service (Treasury Board Secretariat 2016c). These individuals are set to join the executive class that will lead any effort to build a capable digital government and will in turn hold much of the power in fuelling or halting digital innovation. Thus, even if the public service were to attract the subset of millennials with digital skills, that alone would not solve the digital skills gap given that these new recruits would contend with leaders from a public service generation that in general has not been compelled to understand the opportunities and challenges that accompany the use of digital policy instruments, new sources of data, and related approaches to the work of the government. Reflecting this point, in commenting on the digital illiteracy of executives in the federal government, one digitally savvy communications manager asked

> how do you teach managers who aren't involved with social media or educated about it? How do you teach them to talk to their staff? So if, all of a sudden, you know, if someone comes, you know, as a manager, someone comes to me and says, "Well, I have a Twitter account, and I'm thinking of doing this," I feel comfortable advising you because I'm aware of the policy and everything else, but there are going to be some who go "Twitter?!" (C2)

The digital skills gap will not simply solve itself through the recruitment of a younger generation of public servants alone. The first option by which this skills gap might be filled is through partnerships and contracting.

Tapping into Digital Talent through Externalization

Externalization – the act of transferring all or part of government activities to those outside the bureaucracy (Alford and O'Flynn 2012) – represents one option for the federal government in its efforts to fill its digital skills gap. For example, the government could access technical digital skills through collaborations with civic technology communities, typically facilitated through prizes and competitions that challenge outsiders to use new sources of data (often open government data) to develop web and mobile applications or other solutions to improve programs and services. Hackathons, such as the CODE events hosted by the federal government in 2014 and 2015, are another mechanism by which the government can tap into the technical digital skill sets of outside web developers and designers. In other cases, governments rely on private organizations that provide digital services in order to capture profit from doing so, as in the Canada Revenue Agency's reliance on Intuit, whose commercial TurboTax software, web, and mobile applications are now one of the primary ways that Canadians interact with the tax system. According to Intuit, since 2012 over 12 million returns have been filed electronically using TurboTax (TurboTax Canada 2015).

Although open data communities, hackathons, civic technology groups, and private sector partnerships are well-documented options for governments seeking digital expertise (see Johnson and Robinson 2014; Lathrop and Ruma 2010; and Noveck 2009), less discussed in the literature on digital era externalization is the role that academic partnerships can play in bolstering digital policy capacity in the bureaucracy. The former DFAIT adopted this approach when it worked with the Munk Centre of Global Affairs in 2013 to remotely monitor the Iranian elections using social media after having pulled diplomatic staff from the region. In the United Kingdom, the Oxford Internet Institute and the London School of Economics Government on the Web project used web-based experiments and big data to inform the design of government websites and e-petitions and piloted the use of social media as a source of data for designing and evaluating programs.[5]

Also largely absent from the literature, which has tended to focus on partnerships and voluntary actors' contributions to digital service delivery and policy development, the federal government can and already does rely on contracted private sector external actors offering the technical digital skills that the bureaucracy currently lacks. The number of players in the federal policy process has proliferated through the years, and we can add to the list of existing external policy actors – such as KPMG, the Public Policy Forum, the Fraser

Institute, the former Canadian Policy Research Network – a new list of digital policy consultants eager to offer advice and services to federal government departments. This includes the SecDev Group, which offers access to skills in social network analysis and social media data scraping. A number of social media consultants advise on digital communications and online citizen engagement strategies, including Mike Kujawski of the Centre for Excellence in Public Sector Marketing and Mark Blevis of Full Duplex. Other consultants promise custom-made online solutions for hosting online citizen consultations, including Thornley-Fallis, Ascentum, and Hill and Knowlton. And the Government of Canada already turns to big IT corporations such as IBM for data analytics and digital service delivery.

Although a mix of co-productive partnerships and contracted solutions will likely continue to play a role in addressing the digital skills gap in the federal government, some caution is warranted in turning to these external solutions alone. This is the same caution that should be heeded whenever governments turn to outsiders to support their activities and is passed down from experiences with alternative service delivery, in particular large-scale contracted service provision under New Public Management.

When reliance on outside actors ensures that government-citizen interactions are mediated through a third party, the government runs the risk of losing access to data on citizens that could usefully be applied to improve policies, programs, and services. Countries that relied heavily on external service providers under NPM, such as the United Kingdom, saw this effect. As more and more services became the preserve of nongovernmental organizations, the number of interfaces for direct citizen-to-government contact decreased significantly (Barnes, Newman, and Sullivan 2007). Insights on service users' experiences were held by the contracted provider, not the government department responsible for designing the policies and programs that underpinned those services. Canada did not separate policy from service delivery to the extent that NPM leaders did, a move said to have prevented a hollowing out of federal policy capacity (Lindquist 2006). Thus, the first lesson to draw from NPM in turning to external actors for digital skills capacity is the importance of building in feedback loops with the outsiders providing these skills.

Consider, for example, the case of a mobile service application developed by a nongovernmental actor. That application will generate immense amounts of data tracking citizens' interactions with the service (e.g., mistakes commonly made in a form, failure to complete a transaction, the time and location that citizens use the service). This interface could also serve as a platform for soliciting input from service users, whether through customer satisfaction polls or by integrating opportunities to provide real-time feedback to inform consultations and reviews of policies and programs. Turning to a current federal government example, if we look at the Intuit tax service described above, we can imagine that the company could capture rich data describing how Canadians interact with the tax system, such as the time of day or week that they tend to file their taxes, the tax credits that they often make errors in claiming, or language cues more or less effective in guiding people through their tax claims. Such data could meaningfully inform CRA communication strategies and other efforts to ensure that Canadians file their taxes properly and take advantage of any programs and credits available to them. How will these data make their way back to departments?

Contracted providers are likely to see the commercial value of the data that they generate from digital interactions with citizens and likely will not be motivated to share these data with the government actor at the other end of the contract. For instance, in one case, a nongovernmental transit app provider who used City of Ottawa open data sets to run the transit app, explained that, conscious of the value of the rich data that the app captured by tracking transit users' movements through the city, the provider would try to sell the data back to the city before they would offer them for free.[6]

I raise this example not to discourage the government from working with nongovernmental actors in delivering digital services but to underscore the importance of anticipating the potential data gaps that can arise when governments mediate their involvement in policy implementation and service delivery through nongovernmental actors. Such data gaps are even more likely to arise where externalization involves digital technologies given the high-value user data that they can produce. Departments could institute provisions for data sharing in any contracts with outside providers, or at least they should account for the costs of data loss when such provisions are not possible and the costs/benefits of developing an in-house solution for a digital policy, program, or service need are weighed against those of relying on external actors. Where externalization occurs outside a contract, or with actors lacking commercial incentives, as in the case for certain apps developed by civic technology groups via hackathons, departments need to build high-trust, collaborative partnerships with those that develop such apps to ensure that useful data generated are fed back to departments. The importance of building such relationships is a core prescription and preoccupation of the network governance paradigm. Although public administration scholarship in this field rarely addresses digital era phenomena, the literature has much to offer governments that turn to externalized solutions in the digital age (see Alford and O'Flynn 2012; Brandsen and Pestoff 2006; Joshi and Moore 2004; Phillips 2006).

In addition, as with any endeavour involving externalization, reliance on outside actors for digital expertise raises important accountability questions (Jarvis 2014a; Phillips and Howard 2012). Who holds the ring when an app managed by a nongovernmental actor fails or provides false information? How can the government ensure that externalized solutions for service delivery and information provision meet government service standards in areas such as official languages and accessibility for those with disabilities? Recalling the benefits of centralized communications and common federal identifiers, we can equally ask whether creating a varied ecosystem of nongovernmental providers of online services and information runs the risk of citizens not properly recognizing official and sanctioned sources of information compared with those that might mislead them (whether intentionally or not). In many instances, these concerns could be addressed either by writing provisions addressing them into contracts with external providers or by developing high-trust partnerships with strong feedback loops with those providers operating outside formal contracts so that design decisions can be informed by these considerations. In other cases, externalization might not be an option given the high-stakes risks that it can raise, most obviously in the case of policies and services that rest on access to, or collection of, citizen information that cannot be shared with nongovernmental actors under current legislation or that citizens might not want shared with private corporations given the sensitivity of the information. This concern has arisen in particular in "smart city" initiatives that rely on private sector investment and ownership over digital sensors and the data that they collect in city infrastructures and services (Wylie 2017).

Finally, the federal government must equip itself to be a "smart shopper" when relying on externalized solutions to address its digital skills needs. Evgeny Morozov (2016) has been particularly critical of the deception to which governments are victim when they turn to those with technical expertise hawking their services with commercial motivations: "Technology experts have joined economists as America's most useful idiots. There is always demand for their expertise, there is no risk in saying stupid things about complex matters (the majority won't understand them anyway), and there are plenty of corporations willing to foot the bill for this intellectual circus."

Morozov's critique follows on research finding that countries steeped in the NPM ethos largely blindly outsourced their IT capacity in the first wave of e-government in the 1990s (6 2007; Dunleavy et al. 2006). Lacking the in-house knowledge required to identify their needs and scrutinize the technological "solutions" that private firms offered to address these needs, governments were locked into long-term legacy contracts that produced poor services and in some cases massive policy failures. In 2011, this trend led the United Kingdom's Public Administration Select Committee to publish an audit of government IT management with the biting title "Government and IT – A Recipe for Rip Offs."

Canada's early digital government success in the late 1990s and early 2000s stemmed partly from the fact that it retained the in-house capacity required to be a good shopper in IT procurement (Borins 2007; Dunleavy et al. 2006), a history that has not repeated itself in the case of failed procurement under the Phoenix pay system. A fine illustration of the costs of the digital skills gap in practice, the system was procured despite its incompatibility with the complex demands of public service remuneration, leaving just under 500,000 members of the public service without pay, or with too much pay, for months on end. Having already cost $310 million over its seven-year rollout, the system would cost departments an estimated $540 million to be repaired (far from the government's plan to *save* $70 million annually with the new system) (Office of the Auditor General of Canada 2017).

Beyond service procurement, this in-house capacity is equally important when working with outsiders promising access to new data sources and analyses. Information asymmetries between public servants lacking data science skills and external providers claiming this expertise might render the government ill-equipped to scrutinize supposedly data-driven policy prescriptions and program and service evaluations offered by outsiders (Decker 2014). One consultant active in the cottage industry of big data analytics that has emerged in Ottawa remarked that, in meetings with federal officials, he could essentially suggest that the data pointed to "Conclusion A" or "Conclusion B" and that no one in the room would have the expertise to question his assessment.[7]

Thus, acknowledging the potential for knowledge gaps, accountability breaches, and procurement failures, the federal government should remain cautious of the impracticality of filling its digital policy capacity through externalization alone. Indeed, though initially the dominant thrust of digital government thinking in the mid-2000s prioritized hackathons, open data, and crowdsourcing, global trends now emphasize the need to build sufficient in-house capacity alongside an interest in better leveraging outside expertise and resources (as noted in Table 6.1 in describing the new digital government orthodoxy). Most obviously, we witness this emphasis on in-house capacity building in the reinterpretation of the term "government as platform" as implemented in the United Kingdom. O'Reilly's (2011) original use of this term prioritizes nongovernmental actors as the proper providers of services and information in the digital age. The UK government has instead interpreted government as a platform as something that – though reliant on user feedback, contracts with outside providers, and open-source principles – nonetheless demands massive in-house recruitment of digital talent and significant investment in whole of government infrastructure, such as developing common data repositories, common web-based transactional platforms, and top-of-class government websites that de-silo government services (Clarke 2016a).[8] Drawing on the experience in the United Kingdom, and on the experiences of other governments that have followed its lead in this latest wave of digital government capacity building, I next consider how the Government of Canada might build its own in-house digital talent moving forward.

Digital Talent Recruitment in the Government of Canada

In the early days of computing technology in the 1960s, the public sector was a cutting-edge hotspot of ICT innovation (Starr 2010), rendering government a competitive player in recruiting top talent in the field. However, as the private sector bound ahead of the public sector in its capacity to innovate, and its capacity to compensate workers, the public sector became a less attractive employer to the "best and brightest" working in the ICT sector (Dunleavy et al. 2006). Today's market for technical digital skills is fiercely competitive, in particular in the field of data science.[9] "Statistician" has been dubbed the "sexiest job of the 21st century" by Google's chief economist (Davenport and Patil 2012). Yet there is a dearth of trained ICT workers in Canada in particular.[10] These trends further complicate the federal government's efforts to attract talent relative to the private sector.

Consider, for example, how the leading ten computer science programs in Canada (as ranked by *Maclean's* in 2015) describe the career prospects that their students will be offered on graduation.[11] The University of Victoria offers a vague reference to careers in "government" and internships with the National

Research Council but primarily emphasizes careers in the private sector, such as banking, gaming, and software development, when marketing its programs to prospective students (Department of Computer Science, n.d.). The University of Waterloo's Department of Computer Science lists CGI, Google, and Microsoft as career destinations for its graduates (Cheriton School of Computer Science, n.d.). Queen's University lists IBM, BlackBerry, McAfee, and Nortel when discussing internships for computer science graduates (Queen's School of Computing 2014). The University of Toronto boasts of the "industry-based partnerships" to which its students have access. Simon Fraser University's Department of Computer Science notes that "Google, Hootsuite, Microsoft, Telus, Deloitte, Electronic Arts and others all regularly visit us for good reason. Our students have got what they're looking for" (Computing Science, n.d.). The Université de Montréal explains that "our graduate students consistently go on to lead successful careers in industry, industrial research, and academia," leaving "the government" out of this list (Department of Computer Science and Operations Research, n.d.). References to government and public policy are equally absent in McGill University's program pitch: "A university-level education in computer science will help you develop your analytical thinking and creative problem solving skills while studying a wealth of exciting topics with a wide range of applications (from medicine to business). An undergraduate education in computer science will also open the door to careers in a variety of companies (engineering, high-tech, pharmaceutical)" (McGill School of Computer Science 2016).

Notably, the University of British Columbia remarks that, in addition to developing technologies used when "posting to a Facebook wall, designing a building, making a movie, listening to an iPod ... [and] talking on the phone," a degree in computer science can equip one to help in "running political campaigns," but like other computer science schools it avoids highlighting the role that computer science can play in improving public services or supporting stronger policy analysis in government beyond a brief reference to careers in public health policy (Computer Science at UBC, n.d.). So, whether a university program marketing the potential career paths attached to a computer science degree, or a student enticed to join a computer science program in pursuit of these career paths, the public sector is far from mind.

Recognizing not only that traditional government policy shops and IT departments lack the appropriate skills and approaches required in the digital age, but also that those with these highly sought after skills and approaches do not tend to prize government careers relative to opportunities in the private sector, governments have recently adopted two main mechanisms to jumpstart digital talent recruitment. The first I label the parachute model, in which specialized, short-term recruitment mechanisms are used to bring technical digital skills to the public service.

Parachute Models of Digital Talent Recruitment

Parachute models of digital talent recruitment include the Presidential Innovation Fellows (PIFs) in the United States, created in 2012 and (since 2013) housed in the General Services Administration. The PIFs program hires individuals with technical digital skills to join government agencies on a full-time basis for twelve months to help tackle "issues at the convergence of technology, policy, and process" (White House 2015a). As of 2016, eighty-eight PIFs have been recruited, working on projects such as the Veterans Employment Center, a web service that provides support to veterans seeking employment; GeoQ, a platform that uses open-source technology to crowd-source geotagged photos that can be used to support disaster response efforts; and Uncle Sam's List, an internal platform that allows departments to piggy-back on existing IT contracts and services used by other agencies as opposed to the more costly route of procuring their own services (General Services Administration, n.d.a.).

Although managed as nonprofits separate from the government, a number of organizations linked through the Code for All network also support fellowships that fund those with technical digital skills to work in government departments on time-limited bases on specific technology projects. This includes Code for America, which funds fellowships in city, county, and state governments in the United States and is the first and most established of these organizations (created in 2009), and a series of other initiatives that followed its lead, including Code for Australia, Code for the Caribbean, Code for the Netherlands, and Code for Japan, among others (though not all of these initiatives are as focused on recruiting digital talent into the government as Code for America is – some are external civic technology groups).[12]

As exemplars of the parachute model of digital talent recruitment, the PIFs program and Code for America have overcome the recruitment challenge that governments face in part by the individuals and organizations leading them. The PIFs initiative was introduced with the promise of serving the White House and President Barack Obama, and Code for America was founded by key leaders in the American tech sector: Jennifer Pahlka, Leonard Lim, Tim O'Reilly, and Clay Johnson (Kamenetz 2010). These programs also benefit from branding that positions the work of fellows as "a peace corps for civic-minded geeks," as Code for America has been dubbed (Finn 2012), and as "tours of duty," as Obama himself described PIFs (White House 2015b), framing that elevates the significance of the work by linking technology to the public good. Both programs have become effective recruiters of digital talent for the government. The PIFs program states that it now recruits through "a competitive process that attracts thousands of interesting and capable candidates each year" (General Services Administration, n.d.b.). Code for America reports that 658 individuals applied in 2014 (Oshiro 2013).

In addition to the uptake of programs facilitating temporary, project-based fly-ins of digital talent, governments have begun to develop permanent, in-house hubs of digital expertise. These digital government units (DGUs) are currently the dominant trend in digital government globally and in particular among Canada's peer countries. They are typically rationalized not only as sources of digital talent recruitment but also as vehicles to instigate a culture amenable to digital era open government across government bureaucracies.

DGUs as Sources of Talent Recruitment and Culture Change

The United Kingdom's Government Digital Service (GDS) was the first DGU to be introduced and has become a model for others. In October 2010, Martha Lane Fox, titled the digital champion for the United Kingdom and a former dotcom entrepreneur, published an analysis of the UK government's central web presence, Directgov (the predecessor to GOV.UK). The review, titled "Directgov: Revolution Not Evolution," issued four recommendations for the UK government:

1   adopt a "digital by default" strategy that places all transactional services on the government's central web presence
2   mandate the release of APIs to third parties to "make Directgov a whole-saler as well as the retail shop front for government services & content"
3   create a central department to exercise supreme control over all government web content, commissioning contributions from departments; and
4   create a "CEO for Digital" with authority over all online user experiences and online spending. (Lane Fox 2010, 2)

With these last two recommendations in particular, Lane Fox's report reflected broadly accepted critiques of the UK government's model of web management and IT procurement. Unlike the Government of Canada, which had opted for a whole of government model of website development and digital service delivery with Service Canada, UK government departments as of 2011 had a costly mishmash of uncoordinated websites following wildly varied styles, colour schemes, organizational layouts, back-end platforms, and contents. And, as already discussed, a prime example of the unfettered adoption of NPM in the United Kingdom, the government had largely contracted out the IT function in the 1980s and 1990s, locking itself into long-term legacy contracts with a small number of private sector providers, resulting in many disastrous IT failures and huge cost overruns (6 2007; Dunleavy et al. 2006; Public Administration Select Committee 2011). To clean up this mess, the Government Digital Service was introduced in 2011 as the first organization with a whole of government mandate on digital services and procurement, responding to Minister for the Cabinet Office Francis Maude, headed by Mike Bracken (former lead of the *Guardian*'s digital transition) as executive director, backed by a group of digital innovators within and outside the public service (especially those involved with the civic technology firm mySociety), and supported by an advisory board of digital leaders in the private sector and academia.

Following on the work of GDS, in 2011 the Government of Ontario began developing a government-wide website, Ontario.ca, and it has since built a team in the Cabinet Office with a cross-government "digital transformation" mandate. In 2016, the Government of Ontario introduced the role of chief digital officer (at the deputy minister rank) and a minister of digital government to lead the unit's work. In 2014, the US government created two organizations that would serve as hubs of dedicated in-house digital expertise. The first was 18F, so named for its home in the General Services Administration, located at the corner of 18 and F Streets in Washington, DC. 18F dubs itself a "civic consultancy" and operates on a cost-recovery basis, charging agencies that recruit members of 18F to support digital projects. Following on 18F, but in this case managed through the White House and emerging from the failings of healthcare.gov, the US Digital Service (USDS) was built under the leadership of Jennifer Pahlka, then the deputy chief technology officer (and, as noted earlier, a founder/executive director of Code for America). Finally, in 2015, the Government of Australia introduced its Digital Transformation Office (DTO) (now termed the Digital Transformation Agency [DTA]), created as an executive agency managed within the Department of the Prime Minister and Cabinet.

DGUs are intended to serve four purposes in their respective governments, each of which addresses the digital skills gap in different but related ways: recruiting digital talent, creating insulated space for digital innovation, improving procurement practices, and fostering broader culture change in the bureaucracy.

The first of these goals – recruiting digital talent – is the most obvious way in which DGUs tackle the digital skills gap in government. As with the Presidential Innovation Fellows and Code for America, these units attract digital talent to government by branding themselves as offering opportunities to transform government for the better, adding gravitas to the significance of the work as a means of luring in talent with calls to action such as "*Change lives every day:* We need top technologists to serve tours of duty, working on the nation's biggest challenges" (US Digital Service, n.d.a.). Similarly, the Government of Ontario's digital team's unconventional recruitment call on LinkedIn begins with this: "Hey, do you want to work here and make government better? So do we." It explains that recruits will "ignite disruption and innovation in every corner, mobilize new ideas, start small, learn from mistakes, measure performance and build upon success" (Abdulla 2016a). In addition, DGUs attempt to attract digital talent to government by modelling themselves as atypical government units, free of the process, hierarchy, and risk aversion associated with the stereotypical bureaucracy. In doing so, DGUs can present an unconventional portrait of government work meant to appeal to those who might otherwise seek work in the tech sector.

For example, GDS in the United Kingdom is set off physically from the rest of Whitehall, in an office in the Holborn district of London, and, as one GDS official put it, "it's like a startup ... It's like Google" (O4). This is immediately apparent when one walks into the GDS office, with its open concept organization, Post-It–covered walls, MacBooks, and casually dressed employees. When I visited the office to conduct interviews in 2012, an interviewee pointed out a new, lower-level recruit situated next to his senior manager in a shared workspace, underscoring how the organization strove to tackle the hierarchy that normally shapes work and physical workspaces in bureaucracies. Describing GDS, an official in the United Kingdom explained that "this is an unusual initiative in government. I know we're trying to recruit people from Google and Facebook and all sorts of digital agencies. We're trying to get the message across: this is government but not as you know it. This is a completely different proposition" (O5).

DGUs also brand themselves as offering more casual, fun workplaces, likely feeding off the trend in tech firms to feature things such as slides, free food, and even LEGO rooms (Crowley 2013). For example, the USDS describes its team as "emoji, post-it, and sticker enthusiasts" (US Digital Service, n.d.b.), and on its FAQ for recruitment it advises this: "Don't worry – most days you can dress like you're at any other startup. Every now and then we dress up for important meetings, so it's good to have at least one formal outfit in your closet" (US Digital Service 2016). It is difficult to imagine a typical government recruitment campaign invoking any of these concepts or ideas in framing a career in the bureaucracy.

DGUs' branding efforts have been effective so far. In describing the initial call for applicants in 2015, the USDS explained that "we worried if ten people would even apply. 1000 did" (US Digital Service, n.d.b.). No doubt this response was aided by the fact that the call was issued by President Obama during his State of the Union address, a testament to the importance that leadership plays in recruitment, as noted in the case of the PIFs and Code for America. The USDS now houses 200 staff. In the United Kingdom, GDS has grown immensely. As of 2015, the organization employed 425 full-time staff and 210 contractors (Marrs 2015).

However, more than simply having recruited this talent by promising an unconventional, flatter, more innovative work experience in government, these hubs actually work to institute this culture in practice, creating an isolated space within government for those with digital expertise to operate outside the constraints that limit digital innovation in the bureaucracy proper (the same logic of innovation labs; see Carstensen and Bason 2012). That is, the second way that these units address the digital skills gap in government is by creating exclusive spaces (both physically and organizationally) for digital talent to be best leveraged once recruited. Commenting on GDS in the United Kingdom, a member of the Foreign and Commonwealth Office's digital team observed that

the idea is to give *a blank sheet of paper* (as others have said) to people who are approaching the conundrum, not the situation. The whole approach to the project was not "how do departments and agencies do this and how can we make it better?" but "what is the problem we are trying to solve?" And that disinterested approach (not uninterested, note, this team are a committed bunch) is the key to coming up with something that is a fresh way of doing things. (Leach 2011; emphasis added)

Writing on this "blank sheet of paper," these units intend to operate as organizations "born digital," unencumbered by the legacies of hierarchy, silos, and traditional bureaucratic processes at play in established government bureaucracies. In turn, DGUs claim that they have what the US Digital Service dubs "a bias for action, focusing on delivery above all else" (US Digital Service, n.d.c.). Embodying this philosophy, 18F eschews traditional government strategic planing and related written reports and documentation, explaining instead that, for them, "delivery is the strategy" (18F 2016a). Posters instructing staff to "work on stuff that matters" and "show the thing" are hung on the walls of Australia's DTA. And, in a 2016 LinkedIn post advertising new positions in the unit, the director of digital for the Government of Ontario noted that "our unit structure is fluid to enable team members to self-organize around work, deliver quickly and operate autonomously" (Abdulla 2016b). As explained by Mike Bracken (2013) in the United Kingdom, the GDS "strategy was to be disarmingly simple: to deliver," focusing on users of the service and not on what he criticized as "risk-averse" policies and internal government processes that serve the government's internal needs more than they prioritize the needs of citizens.

To support expedient delivery, DGUs prioritize agile development methodologies, which release products early as prototypes that are continually refined incrementally based on user experience. The prime public-facing example of this approach in action was the decision by GDS to release the new UK website, gov.uk, as an alpha and beta site. GDS tested and refined the website as users interacted with it and tracked the site's development (and the rest of the unit's work) in a blog authored by staff, adopting a casual, frank tone distinct from the official corporate communications style typical of government when discussing its work.

The emphasis on delivery over process, and on early experimentation versus long-term corporate planning, contrasts with the classic bureaucratic approach to digital technology, most starkly in the multiyear social media policy development that the TBS undertook, in layered tweet approval processes, and in the internal debate over POR rules and platform requirements that stalled progress on the development of a citizen engagement tool as part of the open dialogue commitment. More importantly, relying on prototypes, constant data-driven adjustments, and scaling of demonstrated successes, the agile approach adopted in these units limits the likelihood and cost of failure that accompany the traditional long-term development processes and finished product launches typical of all government work (not just digital products).

In this sense, we see in this agile model a practical, safe means of experimentation and innovation that Blueprint 2020 and policy innovation initiatives have attempted to advance in Canada's federal bureaucracy, efforts that have been hindered by a fear among public servants of costly failures.

The third way in which DGUs fill gaps in digital expertise in departments is by guiding smarter procurement practices. With in-house expertise governments become less vulnerable to the information asymmetries that rendered them blind shoppers in early phases of government IT procurement. In particular, DGUs offer guidance on working with open-source solutions, developing requests for proposals that include requirements for agile and user-centred design, breaking down complex contracts into individual components to scale down procurement, and creating lists of pre-vetted suppliers, all with a view to fuelling a competitive market of suppliers, including SMEs as opposed to large providers exclusively.[13]

Finally, the fourth rationale driving investment in DGUs as a source of digital talent is their role in ushering in broader "digital transformation" across the bureaucracy. This promise extends the mandate of the units from that of simply delivering digital talent; instead, it frames them as catalyzing culture change that would see their open, collaborative, agile approach to work spread across the bureaucracy proper. In essence, this fourth claim suggests that, by bringing in a fleet of technologists socialized to the open, collaborative, user-focused ethos of the tech sector, DGUs will help to usher in the shift from a closed culture of government to an open one, the challenge that the Government of Canada has attempted to meet through recent renewal initiatives, as discussed in Chapter 5.

DGUs claim to drive this change by working closely with departments to socialize their open models of working, demonstrating in concrete ways how the new digital government orthodoxy outlined in Table 6.1 can improve government operations while also passing along the skills and approaches necessary for them. As 18F explains, "we can embed a fully dedicated 18F team within your agency to work hand-in-hand with you to increase your internal digital capacity, help you form new digital habits, and ultimately drive organizational culture change" (18F 2016b). According to Ben Balter (2015), a former Presidential Innovation Fellow and an open government advocate at GitHub,

> 18F's secret sauce is that it is insistently dogmatic about collaborating in the open, and after expending a great deal of organizational

energy painting a picture of a citizen-centric future and doing their best to inspire agency stakeholders that the way 18F approaches technology is vastly superior to the status quo, they will simply refuse to work with an agency unless the agency agrees to adopt 18F's culture and workflow, at least for the project at hand ... Sure, it's leading by example, but it's also the teach-a-CIO-how-to-fish strategy, and for them, culture's a first-class deliverable right along side the open-source code that that very culture necessitates.

Showing how this culture transfer happens in practice, a manager from a line department working on a time-limited stint in the Australian Digital Transformation Agency explained in a blog post in 2016 that

I'm still excited about the weeks ahead at the [DTA] and utilising the agile way. I want to bring the ideas back to the department. I believe that many in the department want to share more openly, want to try new things, but are not sure how, or if they can. I am looking forward to helping them explore a new approach. (Keilar 2016)

In addition to demonstrating concretely the value of their open model of working in their interactions with departments, DGUs in certain cases inform digital recruitment strategies for departments, hoping to embed their approaches and technical skills in departments full time. For example, GDS has introduced a recruitment hub that provides template job descriptions and advice on salaries for departments and has taken an active role in governing all senior civil service–level technology hires. GDS must approve all job descriptions and appointments to these leadership positions with the intention of "getting in more leaders with experience of transforming big organisations through technology and driving culture change" (Greenway 2013).

The final way in which DGUs claim to foster a larger organizational shift toward open government amenable to high-performing digital government is by developing whole of government infrastructures that enable the bureaucracy proper to shift from its default mode of closed operation. In the United Kingdom, this included the introduction of corporate standards and policies, such as the government's Social Media Guidance and Social Media Playbook created by GDS (Government Digital Service, n.d.a.). These documents provide an infinitely more encouraging and enabling approach to guiding public servants in their use of social media than is found in the convoluted matrix of risk-conscious social media policies produced by the TBS in Canada. For example, in describing social media use, they advised

> at GDS, we're firm believers in accountability on the web. Once you start using social media to talk to your community and spread your story, you become accountable and have a responsibility to engage. You have to take part in the conversation, especially when people are asking you questions. If you don't have the resource to answer enquiries, then you don't have the resource to use the channel. (Government Digital Service, n.d.a.)

Beyond rules and guidance, DGUs produce platforms and common standards that support greater internal collaboration across the bureaucracy. One example is the work of GDS with the Foreign and Commonwealth Office in creating a common register of country names, a simple but essential standard to allow different data sets and platforms across the bureaucracy to work intelligently with each other, thus enabling joined-up policy design and service delivery (Worron 2014). This mirrors some of the work already conducted by the Government of Canada, albeit in more ad hoc ways, such as the creation of GCTools and the data standardization efforts emerging from the open data team in the TBS.

Although DGUs themselves claim to drive a larger cultural transformation within the government, early evidence suggests that, given their rebuke of traditional bureaucratic approaches to problem solving, and given their power to manage procurement and IT spending in some cases, they can instead generate resentment among public servants outside their walls. 18F and the USDS have faced resistance from other technology procurement bodies in the US government (Shueh 2016); moreover, given their unconventional and comparatively younger workforce, deliberately "disruptive" mentality, and habit of openly discussing and praising their work (driven by perpetual fears of having their budgets cut and of needing to demonstrate their value), DGUs have been framed as fuelling "tensions between the geeks and the lifers" (Levy 2016).

This tension has been particularly potent in the United Kingdom. GDS has ushered in cost savings (cited at £1.7 billion in 2014 alone) and built award-winning digital services.[14] Nonetheless, it is perennially rumoured to be under threat of dissolution as departments question its spending control and authority over digital projects in the government (potentially an acute problem in the United Kingdom given the government's traditionally decentralized approach to services and IT) (Glick 2016; Margetts 2016; Neville 2015). In 2013, Labour's shadow secretary for the Cabinet Office remarked that "[GDS] has taken an approach that has, at times, alienated people at the coalface of service delivery" and "staff in key Whitehall departments" (Onwurah 2013). Commenting on the capacity of GDS to drive broad cultural change in the government, one UK official dismissed it as being too distinct from the rest of the government to offer lessons that could enable its *modus operandi* to be adopted in other parts of the bureaucracy: "The Digital Service is a little bit maverick out there. Wizzy, quick, fast, doesn't need to be bogged down with any of the constraints that actually go along with being part of government" (O6). This perspective was shared by another British civil servant who had worked with GDS: "The bulk of the team were recruited from outside government so it might be that resistance will come from those who will respond to the Alpha.gov.uk prototype with a 'It's all very well for them to do that but ... '" (Leach 2011). Elaborating on this view, a digital communications manager in the UK public service remarked that

> they're not troubled by the twin demons of modesty and humility, let's put it that way ... They think they're doing God's work, and the atmosphere around it is a bit up itself. I think the difficulty is that, for people who are still doing digital in the departments, who aren't in this sort of golden team, those people who are doing very difficult jobs and are very good at what they do, and in lots of cases much better than some of these people doing jobs centrally, they are being told that they're rubbish and that they've been doing it wrong all these years. And they're sort of "It's okay, we're here now, we're here now." And you know it's very irritating, it's extremely irritating, to have someone come 'round and say, "Oh, oh, yeah, yeah, you did fine with your funny little website, but now we're going to do it properly." (O7)

Also expressing this sentiment, a member of the UK civic technology community who had worked on technology projects with the UK government observed:

> I think the interesting thing is, if you talk to civil servants who aren't kind of "GDSonites," then they say, "Oh, GDS is such arrogant

wankers coming in and telling us how to do our jobs." I mean, I'm sure you've come across – I'm sure you've experienced the reputation of – GDS within Whitehall as, you know, not entirely positive. You know they are seen to be arrogant. (O8)

This perceived arrogance and the resultant tension between GDS and the bureaucracy proper are the flipside of the "delivery over process," antibureaucratic mentality by which DGUs define themselves and recruit unconventional talent to the government. On the one hand, overtly underscoring that DGUs are different from the traditional government is what allows them to attract digital talent and to adopt more open, agile work models. On the other hand, if handled incorrectly, this overt rebuke of the government does little to endear the units to those with whom they will need to work in departments. Consider, for instance, how the Government of Ontario described its team in a tweet advertising job openings in 2016. "Come join our Rogue Squadron," it stated (Abdulla 2016b). This was a reference to the team of rebels who, led by Luke Skywalker, battled Darth Vader's evil Galactic Empire in *Star Wars*. A geeky reference, to be sure, but one that invokes for would-be applicants a sense that a career in the government will allow them to "fight the good fight," applying their technological skills to challenge the status quo in the bureaucracy for the collective good. This is part of the branding that allows DGUs to attract digital talent that might otherwise land at Shopify or Facebook, but the message to any civil servant not in this Rogue Squadron is not as appealing – in essence, it suggests that members of the bureaucracy are mindless Stormtroopers, aligned with Darth Vader.

In an effort to reduce this tension, DGUs' tone and approach have shifted over time, with fewer references to the inefficacy of the traditional bureaucracy and more references to listening, partnership building, and cross-governmental teamwork sprinkled throughout their public writings. Consider this blog post, titled "It's Not about Us, It's about Collaboration," from Director of GDS Mike Bracken in 2015, which noted that "the simple truth is: the best work happens when there's *collaboration between departments and the centre.* Everyone looking sideways, seeking help. All of our successes have been a direct result of collaboration with departmental teams, working together to build brand new services, redesign old ones, and reshape departments themselves" (Bracken 2015b).

Similarly, the USDS notes that "technology alone doesn't change things – it's the people who push our mission forward. Strong EQ [emotional intelligence], compassion, and tenacity are just as important as being a great technologist" (US Digital Service, n.d.c). However, even acknowledging that the potential for DGU-to-bureaucracy-proper tension can be mitigated by ensuring that digital talent recruited to the units couple tech savviness with appreciation for the soft skills that facilitate organizational change, there is reason to remain cautious about these DGUs' potency as a tool of broader cultural transformation across the government. Furthest along in their development, having been instituted in 2011, GDS offers insight in this regard.

Bracken and Maude acknowledged in a 2016 presentation that, though they had managed to deliver immense change in the areas of service, recruitment, and procurement, they had been less successful in their first five years in shifting the broader culture of Whitehall (Bracken and Maude 2016). Bracken's successor, Stephen Foreshew-Cain, reiterated this view in a 2016 blog post. He noted that, though initially "the strategy was simple: delivery," to shift culture across the government, to achieve the "digital transformation" that GDS was mandated to usher in, GDS now faces a much more complex and less technology-sensitive task. Foreshew-Cain commented on the first five years of operations:

> We learned that 19th century organisational models and 20th century technology were serious constraints to 21st century service demands.
>
> We learned that transforming separate, siloed services one-by-one will never be good enough, or fast enough.
>
> We learned that government needs to rethink how it works, and what sort of people it employs.
>
> And we learned that in order to make this big change – to transform the relationship between citizen and state – we need to collaborate. Everyone in government needs to work together.
>
> Government has been ruled by silos for too long. Not just organisational silos, not even just technical ones, but silos of knowledge and experience that make service delivery more difficult than it should be. (Foreshew-Cain 2016)

As reflected in these comments, the current focus of GDS on dismantling siloed models of work in the bureaucracy ties its mandate to a much longer-standing project of public sector reform. This project far predates the digital age and takes aim at the closed culture of government inherited from Max

Weber and Progressive-Era Public Administration in the late nineteenth century and early twentieth century, a culture entirely out of step with contemporary demands of governing. This reflection in 2016 on the path forward for GDS thus invokes language and objectives that could be taken from any of the internal capacity-building initiatives of the Government of Canada from the mid-2000s on and, indeed, almost any public sector renewal initiative or casual water cooler complaint session focused on the inefficacy of the closed culture of the bureaucracy. In this sense, though these units are a potent avenue for recruiting much-needed digital talent into the government, there is little evidence at this stage to suggest that they alone are sufficient to drive the shift from a closed culture to an open culture, which will require upending over 100 years of established processes, rules, and worldviews and delving into thorny questions of accountability and equity, the role of the public servant, and the dynamics of our current political culture.

Digital Talent: A Necessary but Not Sufficient Driver of Digital Government

The dearth of digital talent in the federal government is one factor that constrains the bureaucracy in its effort to adapt to the digital age. Canada is not alone in facing this digital skills gap, and its government can learn from the various strategies by which its peer governments have been integrating digital expertise into their respective bureaucracies.

What can the Government of Canada draw from the experiences of DGUs, parachute models, and externalization strategies in addressing its own digital skills gap? Beginning with externalization, Canada has a rich ecosystem of civic technology players to which it can turn when experimenting with new digital policy instruments and service approaches, including Open North, Ajah, and city-level initiatives such as Montréal Ouvert, Open Data Ottawa, Ottawa Civic Tech, and Civic Tech Toronto, groups that, along with others, formed the Canadian Open Government Civil Society Network in 2016. Although thus far this network endeavours to provide a central voice for civil society groups to inform the federal open government initiative, it could also serve as a gateway for the federal government in its efforts to better leverage the technical digital skills that civic technology communities and individual web developers and designers in Canada possess. Collaborations with these players will no doubt also be coupled with contracted solutions that turn to commercially motivated outside providers of services and expertise. Regardless of the actor involved, any externalization strategy should be crafted with an appreciation for the knowledge gaps, accountability risks, and information asymmetries accompanying externalization that I have flagged in this chapter. Most importantly, I have argued here that externalization alone will not be sufficient in addressing the skills gap in the bureaucracy, most obvious in the fact that in-house capacity is required to mitigate the very risks that arise when the government is entirely reliant on outsiders for digital expertise.

In building in-house capacity, the parachute model aligns with broader interest in encouraging more cross-sectoral interchanges in the federal bureaucracy, as has been promoted in several recent public service renewal reports as a solution to dwindling policy capacity and leadership in the federal government (Campbell 2014; Jarvis 2016). A "Prime Minister's Innovation Fellows" program or a "Code for Canada" represent concrete means of filling the digital skills gap in the federal bureaucracy in the immediate term, jump-starting innovative digital service, program, and policy improvements on a project-by-project basis and providing opportunities to expose the broader bureaucracy to tools and approaches shaping work in the tech sector. The Recruitment of Policy Leaders and Advanced Economist Training Program might provide a template for an equivalent Recruitment of Digital Leaders program, an approximation of which was introduced in 2017 with a newly created digital stream of the Government of Ontario's Internship Program.[15]

The creation of a permanent unit of digital expertise would follow international trends and likely prove to be a necessary pursuit should the Government of Canada hope to bake in digital expertise to policies, programs, and services on a full-time, sustained basis and if it hopes to refresh its IT workforce going forward. In addition, though I have focused in this chapter primarily on citizen-facing, business applications of digital technologies to the work of government, a DGU could also prove to be essential in addressing ongoing and preventing future failures in internal, corporate IT systems, notably those that have followed Shared Services Canada's corporate IT consolidation and the Phoenix pay-system disaster. Finally, done right – specifically avoiding the "us versus them" antagonism that plagued early pioneers of the DGU model – this hub could institutionalize a unit with whole of government digital clout. This could be done by reframing and prioritizing the mandate of the existing role of CIO or through the creation of a chief digital officer position (as the Government of Ontario has done). This individual would be focused less on "keeping the IT lights on" (as the CIO is) and more on providing leadership to allow digital skills and approaches to be prioritized, funded, and supported as central to achieving the government's broader mandate, not simply treated as a technological add-on to the "real work" of the government (Pahlka 2016). At present, there is no central unit or leadership structure with such a mandate in the Government of Canada.

Perhaps most importantly, though I have offered insights into tactics by which digital skills could be better integrated into the work of the federal government, I have equally cautioned against a strategy that would view these options as easy solutions for the larger project of digital era renewal in the federal government. Even with digital talent recruited into the bureaucracy, difficult questions and ongoing challenges remain. How can public servants empowered to shed their anonymity and engage openly with the public online balance their newfound public personas with their duties to political neutrality and given corporate policies premised on a siloed, top-down, controlled government-citizen relationship? Questions endure about the proper balance between rule adherence, equity, and accountability and the increasingly prioritized public service values of risk taking, innovation, and entrepreneurialism. How can we build a management culture that facilitates experimentation and rewards information sharing? And, finally, how can we encourage an open, digital-ready government in a context of permanent campaigning and in the face of "gotcha journalism" that incentivizes closed, status quo–oriented public management? These complex but crucial questions occupy the book's concluding chapter.

7

The Future of Digital Government

In October 2015, ninety-three years after Max Weber described his theory of bureaucracy in *Economy and Society*, Justin Trudeau was elected prime minister of Canada, becoming the twenty-third leader of the country's national bureaucracy, the federal public service. Early in its tenure, the new Liberal government committed to empowering public servants to engage the public, to collaborate internally, and to experiment with new sources of data and digital policy instruments. But newly minted President of the Treasury Board Secretariat Scott Brison, in his first briefing from public servants, discovered that this ambitious vision of an open, agile, innovative public service would be difficult to implement in practice. His briefing described the bureaucracy's default to "limited disclosure" and "insular policy making" and used a stock image of a turtle to illustrate the public service's lethargy. Offering a careful critique of former Prime Minister Stephen Harper's public management philosophy, the documents warned that the "cultural changes" that the new government intended to usher in "are not easy. They are radical departures from how the government has operated over the last decade" (Tunney 2016).

My findings suggest that this diagnosis is partially right, partially wrong. In building an open government fit for the digital age, political leadership matters. On this front, Trudeau's approach to public management could serve as a potent driver of digital capacity building in the federal public service. But building a collaborative and innovative public service demands a historical perspective that reaches beyond the election of Harper in 2006. A "radical departure" from sclerotic, insular government does not simply represent a U-turn from the ten years during which Harper was at the helm of the federal public service, the time period under examination in this study. Rather, Canada's model of closed government originates in late-nineteenth-century and early-twentieth-century theories of bureaucracy baked into perceptions of the role of the public servant, models of accountability, framings of the government-citizen relationship, and internal structures, processes, and rules shaping daily life in the federal government. In building a resilient, capable, digital era open government, we need to tackle the legacies of Weber and long-standing trends in Canada's Westminster system, not simply the legacy of Harper.

What's more, in confronting these historical and ongoing patterns, political and administrative leaders must account for a series of trade-offs, dilemmas, and potential costs that the necessary transition to digital era open government invites, ensuring that this project is more complex than simplistic theories of digital government have claimed thus far. Specifically, whereas dominant theories of digital government presuppose that established traditions of governing should simply be upended, I have found that core Weberian, PPA, and Westminster principles retain their relevance in the digital age. It is where theories of digital government are silent on the principles of equity, neutrality, and accountability, and the enduring value of appropriately applied silos and hierarchies, that they fail to provide holistic, practical, and responsible guidebooks for governments facing the challenges and opportunities of the digital age. Thus, instead of rejecting historical traditions of governing wholesale, their traditions must be updated such that they are compatible with the demands of governing in the digital age. Finally, all of this work is punctuated by a political culture that continues to rationalize closed government, rendering efforts to foster digital era open government ambitious and uncertain in spite of its importance for the broader health of Canadian democracy.

In this final chapter, I synthesize the core empirical and theoretical contributions emerging from the findings of my research. I identify five prescriptive insights for current and future governments grappling with the opportunities and challenges of the digital age. I then raise questions that this study points to, but does not fully address, and propose future research that should build on and test the propositions in this book. Throughout, I argue that current efforts to build a resilient, capable federal public service hinge on the complex task of building a digital era open government going forward, placing this book and its contributions at the centre of current debates on the future of the federal public service and in line with a longer history of texts calling for the renewal of this institution.

Existing Theories of Digital Government: Where They Get It Right, and Where They Get It Wrong

If we look to current theories of digital government, we find two commonly held views. First, at a normative level, these theories argue that the digital age demands a more participatory, collaborative, and agile form of government. In this argument, social media, open data, crowdsourcing, and big data should properly usher in open government externally, with citizens and public servants regularly interfacing, exchanging information, and co-producing policies and services (Lathrop and Ruma 2010; Margetts and Dunleavy 2013; Noveck 2009; O'Reilly 2011). And within the bureaucracy, theories of digital government argue that public servants should dissolve departmental silos and challenge strictly hierarchical decision making in order to make better use of data; to facilitate nimble, agile, and innovative policy making; and to produce policies and services tailored to the needs of those outside the state, not bureaucratic structures and processes (Dunleavy and Margetts 2015). Thus, despite having emerged primarily from outside the mainstream field of public administration, dominant theories of digital government proposed to date pick up on long-standing critiques of closed government among public administration scholars and practitioners and suggest that robust digital era governance demands an opening of siloed, hierarchical bureaucracies.

Second, existing theories of digital government move from the normative to the descriptive, positing that, though digital era open government is an imperative of robust contemporary public management (the correct path forward), this path is not easily followed, obstructed in many cases by the enduring legacies of closed government. In certain instances, this research came from the original normative theorists themselves (e.g., Dunleavy and Margetts 2015; Margetts and Dunleavy 2013; Noveck 2015), who observed in subsequent analyses that their early normative prescriptions were hampered on implementation by entrenched bureaucratic practices, worldviews, and structures. These findings again followed neatly on a healthy body of public administration research illustrating the stickiness of institutional legacies, a stickiness that ensures that reform efforts are more often a case of "institutional garden[ing]" than "institutional engineer[ing]" (Olsen 2006, 17). Reformers tend merely to change the public service at the margins, finding that their reforms are subject to historical layering as the hangovers of previous organizational structures, processes, rules, and attitudes linger.

In the case of digital era open government, Weber and PPA's silos and hierarchies have proven to be the most relevant and potent "hangover" of times past (much more than NPM), undermining bureaucrats' willingness and ability to share data internally and externally, to engage fluidly with the public, and to adopt systems-based, flatter organizational models amenable to networked digital technology and innovation.[1] In this way, empirical research on digital era government confirmed the suspicions of early critical and pragmatic appraisals, which – in evaluating the promises of theories of Wiki Government, government as a platform, and Digital Era Governance – were quick to remind scholars that on implementation these new governance paradigms would clash with the siloed, hierarchical model of government that has been resilient in the face of previous reform efforts (Grabosky 2013; Macnamara 2010; McNutt and Carey 2008; Roy 2008; Starr 2010).

So, in which ways are these existing theories of digital government accurate? Where do they fall short?

I find that existing theories of digital government are accurate in their descriptive observations. The Canadian experience supports the now commonly documented observation that current manifestations of Weberian bureaucracy, PPA, and the Westminster system prevent the public service from achieving the model of open government called for in the literature. Beyond notable but nonetheless limited advances on open data and certain rare exceptions, such as foreign service officers' use of social media and other innovative collaborations with outsiders, the Canadian government-citizen relationship has not become more open and collaborative in the digital age. Siloed and hierarchical approaches to managing government-citizen interactions limit the fluid, interactive use of social media in service delivery and policy consultation. Exposing elaborate tweet approval processes, explicit orders to avoid inspiring policy debates online, reliance on preapproved messaging, and, on the open data front, a culture of information management that showed little appetite for, or awareness of, the benefits that might accrue from others' use of government data, the study uncovers a largely walled organization, steeped in historical traditions that limit bureaucrats' willingness and ability to network and collaborate with outsiders.

Turning to the bureaucrat-bureaucrat relationship, the ideal of horizontal, systems-based governance still remains an "administrative Holy Grail" (Peters 1998) in Canada. For instance, GCTools offer a technical infrastructure that reduces the logistical barriers of collaboration across the silos and hierarchies of today's large federal bureaucracy, yet their low uptake and, in some cases, explicit managerial directives banning their use reveal that powerful cultural barriers to horizontality endure. The closed bureaucrat-bureaucrat relationship was equally evident in the bureaucratic impulse to silo off access to digital networking tools to designated functional areas (e.g., communications); in the low-trust, overly hierarchical chains of command that governed public servants' use of these tools; and in complaints about the innovation-halting limited discretion that micromanagers offered their subordinates. In other words, the Government of Canada was not "born digital" as a *tabula rasa* on which a culture of open engagement, information sharing, and agile, bottom-up innovation could simply be painted. Rather, the bureaucracy brought to the digital age heavy historical baggage from its closed government origins.

However, in exploring the conditions that limit the federal bureaucracy's capacity to implement digital era open government reforms, this book reveals that contemporary manifestations of Weber, PPA, and the Westminster model are not strictly to blame. In part, the uptake of new digital policy instruments – such as open data, crowdsourcing, and social listening – has been a nonstarter because the public service lacks the skills and knowledge required to wield them. More significant is that digital era open government is hampered by a political culture of permanent campaigning that incentivizes and drives closed government.

Public servants explained that their laborious social media protocols and TBS rules mission creep were partly inevitable responses to a vicious political communications culture in which the costs of public failure were seen to be too high to justify a more decentralized, fluid approach to government-citizen interaction. Similarly, fear of public exposé in some cases inspired public servants to put digital technologies to the service of information control, as in their use of BlackBerry Messenger as a "non-ATIPable" method of communication. The DMCPI cited a fear of public failure as a powerful barrier hindering experimentation with new digital policy instruments in the federal government.

Dense, elaborate, top-down approval processes, risk aversion, information control, and strictly defined and siloed responsibilities for particular tasks all respond to a context of hyperaccountability, but accountability of a particular brand, one that emphasizes "naming and blaming" and seeks to mitigate failures at all costs. Ministers demand "error-free government," a directive that in turn inspires a "cover your ass culture" (to quote several interviewees) anathema to open government and innovation more generally. Here it is instructive to recall that social media, open data, crowdsourcing, and calls for digital era open government emerged in the mid-2000s, hot on the heels of the HRDC grants and contributions "boondoggle," the Sponsorship Scandal, the Gomery Inquiry, and the launch of the Federal Accountability Act. In this context, Canada's public service entered the digital age as supremely risk averse and hyper-Weberian, prioritizing excessive internal process in the face of intense public scrutiny, top-down oversight, and a political climate fed on exposé, all the while ignoring the efficiency, effectiveness, and responsiveness costs associated with this process bias. The prevalence of permanent campaigning revealed in this study adds to descriptive theories of digital era open government an appreciation for the contemporary political realities that stand in the way of a more open, collaborative public service, compounding the historical legacies of Weber and PPA.[2]

This book thus supports current theories of digital era open government at a *descriptive* level, inasmuch as my research confirms that digital era open government has not materialized in practice in today's federal government. The book adds to these existing studies an appreciation for the digital skills gap and permanent campaigning as additional constraints on the uptake of digital era open government reforms. Where this book argues that these theories are wanting, however, is at a *normative* level.

Dominant approaches to digital government have been quick to presume that, to build a resilient public service, we must adopt wholesale shifts from closed government to open government, shifts framed as complicated only insofar as they are resisted by unresponsive, status quo–oriented public servants, political leaders, and bureaucratic structures. Rather, I have uncovered that the shift from closed government to open government is not strictly a cost-free (if difficult to implement) solution to the challenges of governing in the digital age. A wholesale shift from closed to open raises a series of complex dilemmas, trade-offs, and risks not properly addressed in the current set of prescriptions offered in our mainstream theories of digital government.

These theories advocate that we dissolve silos and hierarchies, yet such structures retain pragmatic value when used appropriately, allowing for coordinated, whole of government, and citizen-centric engagement and service strategies. Chapter 6 in particular challenges the assertion that the capacity for digital service and policy work should be acquired through open government's preference for externalization alone (via open data, crowdsourcing, challenges and apps, or more traditional procurement), instead highlighting the need to build the state's capacity to work with new digital technologies to avoid gaps in policy feedback, to prevent information asymmetries with outside providers, and to ensure equitable, consistent access to high-quality government services.

Indeed, in the United Kingdom, the Government Digital Service – the oft-mimicked darling of digital innovation globally – itself rejects the notion that digital governments can thrive by relying on outside expertise alone as part of an open government strategy. Instead, it has reinterpreted O'Reilly's government as a platform as a model of governance that demands significant financial investment in *government*-managed digital services. Here we see a return to the state versus dominant theories of digital government that to date have presumed that bureaucracies looking to build digital capacity should simply leverage the talents and resources of outsiders using tools such as open data and crowdsourcing (Clarke 2016a). Likewise, GDS and subsequent digital units modelled on it advocate the creation of whole of government digital strategies that, while opting for systems-based views (e.g., rejecting departmentally siloed service delivery), are *themselves hierarchical* inasmuch as they demand some degree of control over digital services, recruitment, and spending from the centre of government (in GDS' case, in the Cabinet Office). Far from being rejected, Weber thus rears his head again in this latest wave of digital government reforms sweeping the globe.

Further underscoring the enduring utility of bureaucracy in the digital age, I have illustrated that the rules, standards, processes, and top-down control that current models of open government decry cannot be entirely eliminated without inviting the risk of significant breaches of accountability, which can arise when governments do not carefully manage the information that they share with and draw from the public (e.g., ensuring that interactions do not exclude official language groups or those with disabilities and that they adhere to privacy legislation). The research comprising this book exposes a series of dilemmas, trade-offs, and risks that accompany a more open bureaucrat-citizen relationship in Westminster systems in particular, providing more reason to question the unchecked enthusiasm for all things "open" at play in dominant theories of digital government.

Thrusting public servants into the public eye on social media or inviting them to engage in politically contentious policy debates in open forums further erodes the already dwindling tradition of public servant anonymity – not a problem necessarily but a consequence not simply to be brushed over without concern. Specifically, without crafting an appropriate set of guidelines, training, and an updated public service bargain, these new efforts to de-anonymize the bureaucracy might ensure that public servants across a range of ranks and authorities are held publicly accountable for decisions properly attached to the minister, blurring vertical accountability structures at the heart of the Westminster model. This shift in practice might also call into question the perceived or actual political neutrality of the public service, in cases where an individual's personal online political life is blended with his or her online professional presence, where a public servant engages in promiscuous partisanship in support of the government of the day or expresses policy perspectives that do not accord with the views of the current government. Such breaches would threaten the integrity of the public service as a source of frank, nonpartisan advice and loyal implementation, corroding its institutional role in Canada's democratic system. But again, instead of grappling with these weighty questions or providing concrete risk-mitigation strategies, theories of digital era open government tend to presume that we must simply open the floodgates on government-citizen dialogue, framing these interactions as uncomplicated, depoliticized encounters between the government and a set of "users" with shared interests and with whom the government can interact in strictly benevolent, apolitical, and responsive ways.

Thus, having exposed the risks that a wholesale and reckless shift to digital era open government invites, this book challenges the normative orthodoxy that to date has framed scholarly analyses of digital era governance and, crucially, informed practitioners in their efforts to adapt to the digital age (influential as these theories of digital government have been in practice). More specifically, my findings suggest that, in embracing the opportunities and meeting the pressures of the digital age, theories of digital government have been too quick to dispense with the historical principles that underpin equitable, neutral, and accountable governance. Where Weber, PPA, and the Westminster traditions uphold these principles, they retain their relevance and utility in the digital age. Theories of digital era government will fail to provide robust, pragmatic, and democratically sound guidebooks for contemporary public administration if they ignore the core values and principles that these early traditions laid out.

But this raises the question: if current manifestations of these traditions are out of step with the demands of governing in the digital age, then how can these traditions be made compatible with these demands? In other words, if theories of digital government do not sufficiently account for the core principles of equitable, neutral, and accountable governance, then which normative approach should replace them? Where do we go from here?

Digital Era Open Government and the Risks of the Status Quo

A conservative interpretation of the findings in this book might lead one to conclude that, given the risks that digital era open government can invite (whether a lack of coordination across different units in the government, a gutting of state capacity, inequitable provision of services, or politicization of the public service), governments facing the uncertain terrain of the digital age should stay the course. They should rely on established approaches to internal management and external engagement – at most dabbling in incremental changes – for fear of the unintended consequences that diversions from the status quo might invite. In this view, the safest path to good governance in the digital age is the current path.

This is, in a sense, "the Canadian way"; Canada has historically adopted a tempered, conservative approach to public management reform (Brock 2000; Halligan 2004; Lindquist 2006; Phillips 2006). This has proven to be a great strength in some cases, as in the government's cautious approach to NPM that bore fruit as the lessons of this reform movement's shortcomings rolled in from other jurisdictions that had enthusiastically jumped on the NPM bandwagon in the 1980s and 1990s (true in particular where Canada avoided NPM-inspired outsourcing of IT services; see Dunleavy et al. 2006). By this logic, the small scale of change and careful experimentation with new policy instruments and approaches ushered in by GCTools, Blueprint 2020, and the DMCPI are not strictly or necessarily weaknesses but could be framed as strengths, protecting the public service from the unintended consequences and unforeseen risks that can stem from aggressive reforms. This view essentially suggests that the public service might be best served by a "wait and see" attitude and challenges the urgency with which advocates of digital era open government call for reforms to the machinery of the government, the culture of the public service, and the relationship between bureaucrats and citizens.

At the same time, there are compelling reasons to critique the assertion that Canada has been best served and will continue to be by an unwavering status quo bias. Others have already launched this critique, albeit outside the context of digital government reforms specifically. For instance, John Halligan has observed that Canada has been "dabbling in managerial reform for over thirty years without producing either comprehensive reform or the degree of change elsewhere," undertaking "a number of initiatives [that] petered out after a relatively short period of time, leaving only traces rather than the significant advances that had been predicted" (2004, 205–6). Likewise, Kathy Brock has observed that "there is a joke in Canadian policy circles that Canada is usually ten to twenty years behind Britain and the US in awakening to new policy realities and adopting innovative policy reforms" (2000, 1).

What's more, decades of scholarly and practitioner challenges launched against the inefficacy of the government's excessive silos and hierarchies, opacity, and risk aversion suggest that the status quo defaults of the Government of Canada have long been suboptimal, begging for ambitious, sustained reform. Indeed, past clerks' reports, reform initiatives, and Canadian public administration stock takes are a bit of a broken record; everyone complains of the same problems, yet the perennial emergence of these complaints attests to the fact that they have never earnestly been confronted and resolved. Perhaps "the Canadian way" of public administration is better described as one in which we diagnose problems but do little to tackle them meaningfully.

The findings in this book suggest that the time is ripe to break this tradition; in the digital age, an enduring culture of status quo–oriented closed government poses risks that we ignore at our peril. More to the point, unlike the *potential* risks of open government that drive the conservative, "wait and see" approach to the digital age (e.g., fears of equity breaches and politicization of the public service), we are already witnessing the risks of digital era closed government. Beyond pockets of innovators, the majority of the current public service already adopts this conservative approach to reform, at best engaging in incremental changes or pilot projects, in general opting to stay the course, whether that be in how they organize their work, manage their teams, engage with stakeholders, or wield policy instruments. These leaders might feel pressure to respond to new digital realities, but my findings indicate that in practice this has not led to substantive changes in the business of government, which has rolled on in its analogue-era habits. In this sense, an alternative framing of this book casts it as an empirical investigation of the status quo–oriented model of closed government at play in the federal bureaucracy. Detailing the risks and virtues of this approach, this research tests the veracity of the conservative thesis that has been either consciously or unconsciously adopted as the safest path to good governance by most of those in the current federal public service and by the political leaders at its helm.

In testing this thesis, I have provided compelling evidence that, even acknowledging that a shift to open government is not risk free or without uncertainty, the most immediate, tangible, and empirically demonstrable risks that we face arise from our unwavering commitment to the status quo. The risks of closed government demonstrated in this study call us to reject the conservative thesis as one that is failing the public service.

At a basic level, the lethargic pace of cultural change that the Government of Canada followed as of the mid-2000s has proven to be no match for the frantic pace of change characterizing the digital age. The public service is thus playing catch up in a world of rapidly evolving expectations (for service quality, responsiveness, accountability, and transparency), technological innovation, and new instruments and phenomena that governments are expected to capitalize on themselves and will be called to regulate and govern. The digital phenomena that the federal government finally came to terms with as of 2015 were largely old hat by that time, with a new fleet of technological developments – including artificial intelligence, automation, blockchain, drones, and wearable technologies (e.g., Fitbits) – coming downstream.

Facebook had reached 100 million users by 2008,[3] yet it took the Government of Canada until 2013 to dedicate a team of senior officials to consider systematically how these external social media platforms could be applied to policy making in ways beyond their use as mere communication tools. And, even with this committee struck, as of 2016 it was still rare to find an executive working to integrate digital media into the policy processes that she manages, except where these tools were included in a communications strategy. For instance, consider the following email exchange on the use of big data in policy making between the chairs of the DMCPI and Chief Statistician Wayne Smith in April 2014. Smith (2014) explained that they were "pursuing some modest pilots at Statistics Canada" and noted that "at this early stage we are seeking to learn more about the challenges and risks we would face in the development and use of such data sources in order to be able to more effectively identify and pursue real opportunities." The year 2014 was hardly an "early stage" in the emergence of big data, with the phenomenon having already informed a series of academic and consultancy publications exploring its implications for society generally and policy makers specifically (see boyd and Crawford 2012; Clarke and Margetts 2014; Manyika et al. 2011; Mayer-Schönberger and Cukier 2013; and McAfee and Brynjolfsson 2012). This exchange suggests a worrying lack of foresight and/or capacity to act on that foresight in Canada's national statistics agency, a body that of all government units should have been at the forefront of thinking on big data and its role in policy making and service delivery.[4]

At the level of basic technological infrastructure, as of 2015, the Government of Canada continued to operate in a censored Internet environment (as illustrated in Table 4.1), without wifi in many cases and on devices and operating systems well out of date. At a presentation at Queen's University, one official noted that even in 2015 it took him nearly six months to get permission to download presentation slides from the website SlideShare. As he explained, in jest, the publisher of the slides was a little-known organization of questionable repute: the White House (Anonymous Government of Canada official 2016).

In addition to ensuring that the government cannot keep pace with a rapidly changing external environment – missing the opportunities that this environment offers while failing to address sufficiently the challenges that it poses to governance – the status quo of closed government also invites human resource costs that should not be discounted. We might question whether a public service that blocks access to social networking and collaborative work tools, locks information to desktops, and restricts employees' capacity to build online professional profiles and networks will be an appealing workplace for new recruits – especially when the dated analogue tendencies of the government are regularly ridiculed in mainstream media. To be sure, it is important not to overstate this argument. Recent evidence suggests that millennials are attracted to careers in government, at least at the outset of their working lives; enrolment in graduate programs in public administration in Canada was up roughly 20 percent in 2016 (Ireton 2016), and studies of millennials indicate that their top career objectives – salary, team environment, and job security – are the same as those of their boomer predecessors (albeit valuing security last, versus boomers who rank it first) (Coletto 2012). A US study conducted by Deloitte in 2015 similarly debunked many commonly held myths about millennials' aversion to public service careers (Viechnicki 2015). We are not dealing strictly with a foreign entity in attracting millennials to the public service, and dwindling proportions of public servants aged thirty-five and younger are partly products of prohibitive public service hiring processes, which the Liberal government elected in 2015 has pledged to tackle in a bid to revive a second "golden age" of the public service (Wernick 2016).

However, though there is evidence that millennials are still seeking careers in government at the outset of their working lives, we might question whether the "best and brightest" of this generation – especially those with highly sought after digital skills – will remain and, more importantly, be fulfilled and best leveraged in a workplace that stubbornly refuses to update its infrastructure, culture, and processes for a digital age. This concern falls in line with longer-standing critiques of the public service's appeal to competitive job seekers (Aucoin and Bakvis 2005). In interviews conducted for this study, I spoke with young, digitally savvy public servants genuinely committed to improving government. Yet these individuals were consistently frustrated by working in an institution in which digital innovation is an uphill battle. As one public servant put it in a 2014 blog post, "the excessive value that our society is putting on startup culture is causing a serious brain drain for traditional institutions like government." Reflecting specifically on his experience in the Government of Canada, he remarked that

> I ha[ve] been living this exact scenario for the past year. Moreover, I am not alone. In the four years since I moved back to Ottawa to join the federal public service I have met countless passionate, dedicated, innovative public servants who to their very core want to improve how government works and serve the public. Yet almost to a person, they are battling a constant crisis of faith in a public service career and considering if they can accomplish more or be more fulfilled working outside of "the system." (Androsoff 2014)

Compounding these human resource costs, a public service stuck in the analogue age, clinging to closed government approaches, also invites costly program and policy failures. When a crisis hits and the federal government cannot access and act expediently and effectively on rich online information trails left by citizens turning to social media; when a program rollout fails from a poorly designed web interface or a weak online communications campaign; when commitments to horizontal policy issues prioritized by the government fail because of a dearth of interoperable data and a low uptake of intragovernmental collaboration platforms; and when the prioritization of top-down process and unmitigated risk aversion limits the scope for much-needed innovation, the sting of the government's digital deficiencies is felt.

Internationally, we have already witnessed governments suffer significant criticism and political costs as key policy priorities flopped in the wake of disastrous digital failures. In the United States, the disastrous launch of healthcare.gov shone a light on digital as the sleeping giant of contemporary policy implementation, only to be ignored at the policy maker's peril. The website's failure directly undermined Obama's flagship health care initiative, placing digital capacity building on the president's agenda, and spurring the creation of the US Digital Service. Similarly, the mounting costs of decades of failed IT projects led to significant investment in the Government Digital Service in Britain. In Canada, the government has not yet hit a critical juncture in its digital trajectory, instead facing a slow burn of digital failures that have inspired criticism from observers – articles critiquing the bureaucracy's clumsy social media accounts, for example – or that have affected internal affairs – the

Phoenix pay-system disaster – but have not yet overtly caused key policy files to fail because of a dearth of digital capacity. Without investing in the data, skills, and technical and cultural infrastructures required of resilient digital era governments, such a large-scale, public-facing failure is inevitably around the corner.

Beyond their immediate social and economic costs, these program and policy failures will induce crises of democratic legitimacy, calling into question the capacity of the public service to solve social problems effectively and to meet the expectations and demands of a digital citizenry. This is the most potent risk of closed government. By reinforcing stereotypes of the public service as ineffective, out of touch, and unresponsive, closed governments exacerbate a trend that already finds Canadians mistrusting their government (Edelman 2017; EKOS Politics 2017).[5] The gap between government and citizens is ever more troubling when Canadians are empowered to join forces and engage on government policy to an extent unimaginable in previous eras. In a context in which "mommy bloggers" discuss child benefit policies in online forums, hashtags, profile pictures, and online petitions offer new modes of collective action, and Indigenous peoples engage in an unprecedented cross-Canada online movement, it is difficult to defend the democratic responsiveness of a government that carefully scripts its public engagement exercises, deliberately attempts to stifle online debate in outreach exercises, primarily retweets itself, and blocks access to the online social platforms where Canadians are congregating.

Here it is useful to recall the 2007 public opinion research cited in Chapter 3, which found that Canadians viewed Web 2.0 technologies as "an opportunity to transform the 'face' of the Government of Canada, to make it appear more approachable, less remote, and more responsive to Canadians." The research also revealed that the public thinks that the uptake of these technologies would help to "increase access, to make information and services more convenient, to increase transparency, and to enable the GC to better reach youth. Some even said government use of these types of applications would increase their confidence in the government" (Phoenix Strategy Perspectives 2008, ii–iii). It has been over a decade since the government was alerted to this potential through its own public opinion research, yet this study indicates that the government has nonetheless done little to meet these citizen demands meaningfully. The digital age thus strikes Canadian democracy with a double-edged sword. New technologies and related social phenomena can invigorate the government-citizen relationship but, if ignored, they may simply widen the gap between the Ottawa machine and the realities of everyday digital Canadians.

The risks of closed government – whether the lethargic metabolic rate of change that it sustains or the human resource costs, policy failures, and legitimacy crises that it invites – represent real and ongoing threats to the resilience and relevance of the federal bureaucracy. Thus, though I have consistently argued that a wholesale shift to a tech sector–inspired paradigm of open government as naively offered in the mainstream theories of digital government to date itself contains a number of risks to be mitigated, ultimately my findings cannot support a conservative approach that would see excessively siloed, hierarchical, opaque, and risk-averse public management endure. This approach in a sense is the exact problem to be remedied, emblematic of a public service that at present is overcalibrated to avoid the potential risks of reform but underattuned to the risks that the status quo already manifests. Disruptions to Canada's tradition of closed government are long overdue and ever more appropriate in the digital age.

The challenge, then, lies not in strictly calling for a simplistic, wholesale embrace of digital era open government – the tack adopted by dominant theories of digital government to date – but in crafting a new set of directives to guide the public service as it balances the imperatives of open government with the principles of equitable, neutral, and accountable democratic governance. We need not, nor should we, throw out the core principles of Weber, PPA, and the Westminster system. Rather, we need to recalibrate perverse, overzealous, contemporary manifestations of these principles as embodied in today's overly siloed, hierarchical, and status quo–oriented bureaucracy.

This recalibration will not be easy or straightforward; the legacy systems in need of reform are deeply embedded in the structures, processes, incentives, and worldviews of the public service, and they are reinforced by a political culture that the public service has few levers to alter. When it comes to reforming the public service, there is no "reset button" by which existing traditions can be easily undone. Nonetheless, just because reform is difficult and necessarily constrained by layering effects and lingering legacies (in some cases for good reasons), this does not warrant a defeatist commitment to stagnation. Concrete steps can and should be taken to update the federal bureaucracy for the digital age.

In developing these reform strategies, governments and their observers need to avoid the folly of optimistic early writings on digital government and instead contend directly with the entrenched structures, processes, incentives, worldviews, and political dynamics that have long undermined efforts to open the federal bureaucracy; without doing so, treatises on the value and importance of digital era open government are of little practical use to the bureaucrats and political leaders meant to implement them. Put bluntly, we cannot simply bolt new technologies and commitments to "openness" onto our closed governments and expect those governments to act any differently than they have for decades.

With this imperative in mind, in the next section I present five recommendations that explicitly seek to avoid the naive, "bolt on," "technological solutionism" (Morozov 2014) that has plagued digital era open government theories and reform agendas to date. These recommendations are not silver bullets for the complex challenges uncovered in this book, nor do I claim to offer a holistic recipe for updating the public service for the digital age. Rather, these recommendations are starting points, drawing on the lessons uncovered in this research and aiming first and foremost to open the federal bureaucracy while respecting the core democratic principles that underpin its legitimacy as a governing institution.

These recommendations are also crafted with an appreciation for the early changes instituted under the new Liberal government since its election in October 2015 and up to the time of writing in 2017. As Clerk of the Privy Council Michael Wernick put it, Prime Minister Trudeau inherited a bureaucracy that was a "fixer upper" (May 2016b). Acknowledging this, the government committed to a public management reform agenda that, by Canadian standards, was aggressive, taking the reins in Ottawa with the ambition of shaking up the federal bureaucracy as one of its core governing deliverables. In doing so, the government has provided the requisite leadership and advanced some of the concrete reforms that I argue are crucial to building a resilient digital era federal government. Still, certain issues and imperatives remain absent from the federal scene, omissions that these prescriptions flag.

Building a Digital Era Open Government in Canada

INVEST IN DIGITAL TALENT, LITERACY, AND INFRASTRUCTURE

The Canadian public service currently lacks the in-house skills required to integrate new digital instruments and sources of data into policy work, corporate processes, and service delivery. Regardless of the other reforms ushered in, updating the bureaucracy for the digital age will be a nonstarter without also instituting this baseline of skills and capabilities. Indeed, initiatives such as Code for America and dedicated digital government units are testaments to an evolution in thinking in digital government practice, which saw initial enthusiasm for digital government "revolutions" in countries such as the United States and United Kingdom quickly followed by recognition among public managers that the public service needs a range of new talent and expertise to implement digital technologies effectively. Canada can draw from these digital government groundbreakers the lesson that its current efforts to build digital capacity will face similar barriers if not coupled with a robust talent recruitment strategy.

Thus far, the Liberal government has not laid forth a concrete plan to address Canada's digital skills gap, rendering the country an outlier among its peer countries, all of which are now investing considerable funding and energy to attract digital expertise. Clerk of the Privy Council, Michael Wernick, did flag this skills gap in his first report to Trudeau in 2016, noting that recruitment policy, strategy, and broad objectives should be developed centrally as a whole of government priority. Alongside this central direction, Wernick's report noted that the Public Service Commission's Appointment Policy and Appointment Delegation and Authority Instrument were being amended to ensure that deputy heads can recruit and monitor staff through more streamlined processes and with greater discretion (Public Service Commission of Canada 2016).[6] These changes might prove to be crucial in departments' efforts to recruit new digital talent.

The Liberal government also flagged the digital skills gap in Canada's first Information Technology Strategic Plan, released in 2016 by the Chief Information Office. The plan outlines commitments leading to 2020 and is a welcome venture into whole of government digital planning that suggests a more holistic, integrated view of digital government is emerging from the CIO. On the digital talent front, though, the document is wanting. The plan indicates that the federal government will invest in career development for existing CIOs and IT staff through resources on GCpedia and training from the Canada School of Public Service. In addition, the new Management Accountability Framework will include talent management indicators for CIOs and IT assistant deputy ministers (Chief Information Officer Branch 2016). Beyond these vague commitments on training for and evaluation of existing staff, the plan primarily discusses efforts to better diagnose the skills gap in the federal public service. Importantly, however, it does not actually commit the government to recruit new talent to fill this gap. Diagnosing the government's specific digital talent needs is a sensible first step toward addressing the skills gap, but the plan in its current form suggests that, at the close of its tenure in 2020, the government will simply be well acquainted with its digital skills needs, having done little to meet these needs by actively recruiting digital expertise to the public service.

Funding announcements thus far equally support the view that digital talent recruitment is not a high priority for the current government. The 2016 budget committed the government to invest a mere $11.5 million over five years to open government, enough to add a few new full-time employees to the open government team in the TBS but not to recruit a fleet of technologists to advance commitments on open data and online citizen engagement. The budget committed $17.8 million over five years to a new Clients-First Service Strategy, though this funding is allocated primarily to completion of the Canada.ca website. In contrast, the UK government recently committed £450 million to its Government Digital Service (amounting to £125 million annually over the spending allocation, up from the previous £58 million annual budget) and a total of £1.8 billion to "digital transformation." Although not exclusively allocated to full-time employees, much of the UK government's digital strategy focuses on talent recruitment and sustaining the 425 full-time staff and 210 contractors employed by GDS (Marrs 2015). Compared with this massive undertaking, under current funding plans, the Canadian government appears set to continue running tools such as GCpedia and GCconnex, releasing data, and managing other digital initiatives on a shoestring budget only marginally more generous than those in previous years. This is a significant deficiency in the government's current approach to digital capacity building, one that could be remedied by considering the talent recruitment options presented in Chapter 6 but that will ultimately rest on funding allocations that we have not yet seen.

Alongside efforts to recruit digital talent to the bureaucracy, the federal government needs to build broader digital literacy across its workforce, especially among the executives on whose leadership digital innovation will hinge. That is, though there is a need to recruit the hard computer science, data science, and technical skills required of digital era governments, the government must also institute basic digital literacy across the bureaucracy. Needed are public servants who understand new technologies and their applications to their work, even if they themselves cannot technically configure and apply these technologies in practice. Those with intimate knowledge of policies, programs, and services will be crucial collaborators for those with elite technical skills when they do enter the policy process. In order to inform the work of DGUs, external collaborators in the civic technology community, or contracted consultants, the average public servant now needs to understand how digital technologies could support their work. Which questions could big data scraped from Twitter answer that would be relevant to better designing a service? How could crowdsourcing be used to improve regulatory reporting? What kinds of data might a mobile app collect to improve program evaluation? As argued already, digital considerations need to be baked into every step of the policy process going forward, and this will require baseline digital literacy that public servants have not traditionally been required to develop.

On this front, the public service is already taking some important steps forward. Blueprint 2020, "Dragon's Dens," and clerks' annual reports have served as a digital government showcase, exposing public servants to the kinds of policy instruments and approaches that the digital age makes possible. The Information Technology Strategic Plan, for its part, specifically notes the need to promote broader digital literacy across the government, and not simply in the IT function, though it details exclusively the need to promote literacy in the use of digital collaboration tools such as GCpedia and GCconnex. To that end, it commits the government to training on the tools as part of standard employee onboarding. The Open Government Action Plan released in 2016 adopted a more expansive view of digital literacy, committing the TBS and the Canada School of Public Service to develop programming to support public servants' information management skills, open data literacy, and knowledge of digital approaches to public engagement (Treasury Board Secretariat 2016d). Also in 2016, NRCan's Innovation Hub introduced a New Policy Instruments portal on GCpedia, which provides basic primers on big data, gamification, open policy making, citizen science, hackathons, and a range of other novel digital policy approaches.

Going forward, the Government of Canada could build on these efforts by ensuring that mandatory training for executives and new public servants provides not only exposure to GCTools but also accessible introductions to and concrete examples of a broad range of digital policy approaches in action (potentially drawing on existing resources such as the NRCan New Policy Instruments portal). Equally, the government might consider a "duty to document" the processes and results of experiments with new digital policy instruments. Recorded and shared using GCTools, this documentation could provide a rich repository of examples and a network of actors to draw on when units attempt to adopt new digital instruments for the first time or in an untested way.

To support these efforts, traditional feeder programs to the public service, especially master's programs in public policy and administration, need to update their core curriculum offerings to ensure that their graduates enter the public service with a baseline knowledge of these new policy instruments and an appreciation for the broader trends in open governance emerging in the digital age. With few exceptions, most programs in the field have not been updated for the digital age, unsurprising given that the professors teaching in these programs are the same public administration and policy scholars who tend to marginalize IT in their own research and writing. Having acknowledged that its workforce faces a dearth of digital literacy, the federal government could fruitfully engage with bodies such as the Canadian Association of Programs in Public Administration to ensure that the skills, perspectives, and knowledge sets required of digital era public servants are adequately represented in the programs that feed into the federal workforce.

Finally, all of the skills and literacy advances in the world will do little if the federal government cannot "keep the (IT) lights on." Focused on the broader institutional reforms required to build a resilient digital government in Canada, I have not addressed the "nuts and bolts" IT infrastructure questions relevant to internal corporate IT services, such as government email, data centres, intranets, document management, and human resource systems, or the external IT infrastructures that underpin government service delivery, for example. I have touched on the government's IT infrastructure in discussing the "IT time warp" that public servants face, a time warp that can ensure public servants work with operating systems so out of date that they are not even compatible with the Internet browsers and software required for innovative digital policy work. Security concerns that limit the ability to download from the web, or that block access to websites altogether, equally represent deal-breakers for much of the innovative policy work made possible by digital technologies.

Shared Service Canada's cost overruns and delays and the disastrous Phoenix pay-system rollout illustrate that Canada's IT house is not in order (see Office of the Auditor General of Canada 2016a). To its credit, the government's current Information Technology Strategic Plan adheres to best practices by committing to agile design, cross-departmental platforms, data and information sharing, open-source technologies, consolidated contracts, and access to the tools required of a modern workplace. Notably, the government finally committed to rolling out wifi across all government buildings – the absence of which as late as 2017 provides yet another striking illustration of the federal IT time warp, compared with the proliferation of wifi in coffee shops, shopping malls, hospitals, universities, airplanes, and every other imaginable space in the digital age.

The 2016 budget allocated $383.8 million on a cash basis over two years to support IT infrastructure updates. This funding and the Information Technology Strategic Plan commitments suggest that the federal government is headed in the right direction and prioritizing IT renewal after years of letting its infrastructure age in neglect (see Office of the Auditor General of Canada 2010), and we will need to see sustained and expedient investment in this area going forward. The government still falls short in its lack of concrete commitment or strategy to recruit new digital talent. This expertise will be crucial to guide smart procurement and rollout of IT reforms across the government, as in other jurisdictions (notably the United Kingdom and United States), where the development of in-house talent is rationalized in part for its gains in informing strong procurement and partnering strategies for core IT services.

Continue to Foster Internal Openings

The Trudeau government has signalled that it will promote collaboration across the government as a cornerstone of its public management philosophy. The prime minister's mandate letters advised ministers that they should work closely with their cabinet colleagues, and in a presentation in 2016 at Canada 2020's open dialogue conference in Ottawa, Scott Brison, the TBS president, called for the "desiloization of government." Most prominently, the new Results and Delivery unit in the PCO, headed by Matthew Mendelsohn and mandated to implement Michael Barber's (2008, 2016) "deliverology" philosophy in the federal government, has prioritized inherently horizontal policy issues, including climate change and poverty reduction, giving top-level impetus for collaborative, horizontal policy work in the federal public service.

The GCTools, Blueprint 2020, and policy innovation initiatives offer an existing base on which future efforts to challenge silos and hierarchies in the Government of Canada could be built. However, even with this base in place, much work needs to be done before the federal public service operates with an "open by default" mindset among colleagues. At present, only a handful of public servants regularly use GCTools and participate in initiatives that seek to promote greater collaboration horizontally across the silos of the bureaucracy (e.g., micro-assignments) and vertically between the layers of superiors and subordinates (e.g., "Dragon's Dens" and internal policy crowd-sourcing). On this point, the government has taken some important steps to render open collaboration the default mode of work in the public service. As already discussed, the 2016 Information Technology Strategic Plan mandates training on GCTools for all new recruits. The plan also prioritizes open discussions on GCTools over closed email exchanges, and it notes that senior leaders in particular must "adopt an 'open first' attitude towards content creation and encourage their employees to participate in shared-knowledge and collaborative digital spaces" (Chief Information Officer Branch 2017). This speaks to my finding that, in certain cases, employees did not use GCTools because their managers discouraged or prevented them from doing so, preferring instead to hoard information within the safety of their siloed units.

To be sure, it is doubtful that managers' instinctive preference for information control will be undone by a dictate in an IT strategic plan, a document that many government executives, especially those outside the IT/IM world, will probably never read. In a siloed government such as that of Canada, information is power, whereas the benefits of collaboration and information sharing remain largely theoretical. Given this, the government needs to systematically incentivize the uptake of collaborative information sharing and horizontal working. In some cases, this will mean turning to traditional mechanisms of staff evaluations and advancement criteria, ensuring that to rise up in the public service one has a demonstrated record of collaborating across units and working openly. These mechanisms gain more teeth in the digital age, given that tools such as GCpedia leave behind a digital trail providing evidence of the extent to which an employee does indeed network and share information with others. Similarly, a rich GCconnex profile, which illustrates ties made across the bureaucracy and tracks one's record of participating in micro-assignments, for example, could be used to evaluate empirically how networked a public servant – or a team of public servants that one manages – is in ways that would not be possible without this digital footprint.

Finally, beyond adding creative digital twists to traditional incentives and rewards approaches, the government should apply the logic of behavioural insights to better understand the conditions under which public servants (managers and subordinates alike) are likely to collaborate and share information. Again GCTools are an excellent vehicle to advance this work. They are essentially a laboratory within which information cues and design elements could be systematically adjusted to determine how best to nudge collaboration and information sharing across silos and between levels of authority. Some of these interventions are already ripe for study, as in the introduction in 2016 of badges to gamify use of GCTools. These sorts of interventions should be rigorously evaluated and tweaked based on their impacts. Beyond these context-specific experiments, the government can draw inspiration from behavioural insights in tying the tools to established processes that public servants already need to participate in by default, as in processes associated with the HR system. On this front, a recently developed Career ConneXions Opportunities Platform that facilitates at-level mobility (e.g., job swapping and micro-assignments) could be expanded such that applications for internal job postings would be managed through one's GCconnex profile, giving all public servants a strong incentive to join the platform and become active members. This proposal picks up on the notable growth in GCconnex membership that followed the clerk's decision to run Blueprint 2020 activities through the tool, which gave employees a new incentive to become members.

These are just some of the steps that could be taken to ensure that the ambitious goal of building horizontal, joined-up government moves beyond rhetorical commitment. Should this initial base of collaboration scale such that the federal public service is regularly collaborating and sharing data across units, functions, and departments, the government will need to build capacity to support horizontal accountability as a supplement to the vertical model of accountability to which its internal structures, external communications, and worldviews are presently calibrated (Jarvis and Levasseur 2015; Phillips and Howard 2012). This shift will demand first and foremost ministerial commitment both to horizontal accountability and, importantly, to shared attribution for policy and program successes from ministers who, in a context of joined-up government, will increasingly find that they are sharing the stage with ministerial colleagues when demonstrating their successes and seeking the budgetary and political capital that these successes can earn. Issues of accountability and attribution are further complexities of horizontality that current theories of digital era open government overlook when calling for the dissolution of silos as a simple solution to the challenges of governing. At this stage, these issues are on the horizon; the immediate challenge for digitally enabled collaboration is actually doing it. I flag horizontal accountability only to highlight future challenges likely to arise should these internal openings scale and shape high-profile policy priorities moving forward.

Rethink the Government's Approach to External Openings

The federal government thus far has shown little progress in its efforts to engage better with Canadians in the digital age – to open itself externally to the public – a stated goal of the open dialogue initiative that has been in place since the first Open Government Action Plan was released in 2012 but that has produced little in terms of tangible outputs since. Instead, traditional bureaucratic models of government-citizen interaction were simply digitized when social media were added to the government's arsenal of communication and consultation tools. These models have not been reimagined for an age of rapid, informal, networked, and personalized peer-to-peer digital interactions.

The 2016 Open Government Action Plan released by the Liberal government falls in line with the two previous plans in terms of its commitments on digital engagement with citizens. The commitments are vague and thin, largely related to developing common principles, best practices, and evaluation standards for citizen engagement. They appear to be especially paltry compared with the detail and volume of commitments on open data; at this stage, it appears that under Trudeau that initiative is still the star of Canada's open government initiative, with Budget 2016 titling the section detailing open government commitments "Open Data," a telling cue that recalls the central place of open data in Harper's open(ish) government initiative.

Yet the Liberal government is clearly keen to engage Canadians in policy development, having launched a wide range of consultations in its first months in office (Delacourt 2016b) and having mandated each minister to support "constructive dialogue with Canadians, civil society, and stakeholders, including business, organized labour, the broader public sector, and the not-for-profit and charitable sectors" (Prime Minister's Office 2015a). Evidently, the web will play some role in advancing this vision of active public engagement, even if the current open government plan does not flesh out what this role is.

Where departments do take the traditional consultation model and host all or part of it online, managers need to think more carefully about the challenges and opportunities that arise at the close of these exercises, once their outputs need to be analyzed and integrated into policy development processes. As explored in the case of Tony Clement's Twitter townhall, a virtue of the web is its capacity to host many-to-many conversations and to scale participation at relatively low cost at the front end, when the consultation is actually under way. At the back end, however, when analysis of each participant's contributions is required, the costs of large-scale citizen engagement are considerable. The government has not yet adopted in any mainstream, regularized way novel analytical techniques such as machine learning, automated classifiers, sentiment analysis, social network analysis, and data visualization to draw intelligence more systematically and efficiently from large-scale engagement efforts online. This is again a symptom of the government's digital skills and literacy gap. As already noted, the 2016 Open Government Action Plan commits to developing skills that will support digital public engagement. Any programming in this area should include a dedicated focus on developing capacity in the use of these new analytical techniques, typically absent in the toolkit of stakeholder engagement and consultation teams.

There is also a need to explore entirely new models of digital public engagement in the federal government. In the digital age, the government is no longer as central in social and informational networks as it was presumed to be traditionally. Using a tools of government framework, we might say that, though in the digital age the tool of nodality – the capacity to give and get information in socio-informational networks – has become an ever more powerful tool of governing (Clarke and Craft 2017; Hood and Margetts 2007), governments are not necessarily the best placed to wield this instrument anymore. Instead, nongovernmental actors are often now better able to distribute and collect information than government, leading to a redistribution of nodal capital (Clarke 2014a, 2014b). Engaging with these comparatively more nodal actors and their networks will mean that the government cannot also expect to carefully craft and execute an engagement strategy on its own terms and through its own managed venues (e.g., departmental website or boardroom). Instead, the public service must go to platforms and forums where stakeholders and citizens are already congregating and where nongovernmental actors are the dominant players setting the terms of the conversation.[7] In Canada, departmental experiments in Corrective Blogging – as the former HRSDC undertook on student loans in student forums and the former DFAIT undertook on the seal hunt – were inspired by the recognition that, to engage effectively with a target population, public servants needed to go to the networks where this population was already engaged. This is in contrast to sharing information on a government website or social media account or hosting a departmental consultation. Going forward, much could be gained from rethinking how and where the government engages with stakeholders and in particular using social network analysis to identify key influencers online who could serve as partners in engaging the public or whose platforms (e.g., websites or blogs) provide a more effective space for public outreach than government platforms alone.

Of course, Corrective Blogging and other experiments in nontraditional online engagement have revealed that efforts to engage publicly outside tightly managed, top-down, department-controlled consultation models fail unless coupled with a concomitant commitment to empowering public servants to engage autonomously on behalf of their departments. The policy of "inject, correct, and direct [back to the department website]" employed by public servants engaging on student forums, explicit directions not to promote policy dialogue in Corrective Blogging, and preplanned messages employed in the case of ESDC's Online Skills Forum revealed that, in their efforts to engage more creatively with stakeholders online thus far, departments have not proven to be willing to loosen the reins on the individual public servants meant to participate in these outreach exercises.

Similarly, in the case of departmental social media accounts, the decision to designate communications professionals as the exclusive voices of departments limited the scope for interactive dialogue, given that the subject matter experts capable of responding to questions and engaging substantively on policy issues were not invited to interface directly with the public via these channels. Going forward, departments will need to acknowledge that any effort to engage robustly with stakeholders online demands a level of immediacy and substantive expertise that cannot be achieved through strict preplanning and via reliance on a narrow set of designated spokespersons. Instead, a more pluralistic approach to government-citizen engagement might see a range of public servants empowered to engage online for their departments – something that TBS guidelines on social media use have always allowed but that has not become a mainstream approach to public engagement in departments thus far.[8]

This decentralized approach to online engagement already occurs on the digital file in a number of jurisdictions, as in the UK Government Digital Service blog, which uses the real faces, names, and voices of individual public servants outside the official communications cadre to discuss its work. Blog posts conclude by encouraging the reader to follow their authors' personal social media accounts.[9] Similarly, the United Kingdom's Behavioural Insights Team and Denmark's innovation lab, called MindLab, allow their staff to blog openly about their work, using real faces and names to personalize the dialogues.[10] This is a model of network building, information sharing, and public engagement radically different from that in traditional government bureaucracies. It ensures that, for the community of stakeholders engaged in the UK government's digital services or behavioural insights work, or in Denmark those interested in learning about their government's innovation initiatives, it has perhaps never been easier to understand the government's policies and programs in the area and, crucially, to feed easily and directly in to this work.

One could imagine this approach generating a range of impressive online networks and communities of practice supporting regularized information exchange on a broad set of policy issues in the federal government – a blog on climate change policy, a set of public servants tweeting about innovation policies and building a stakeholder network that can be engaged episodically and informally as part of the regular policy cycle. Picking up on this potential, in 2016 the open government team in the TBS started a blog to discuss their work.[11] Although this move offers leadership to the rest of the public service, it is likely that – given their mandate and the types of employees they attract – the open government team's comfort with blogging is not widely shared across the bureaucracy. To socialize this practice more broadly, foreign service officers might provide a more accessible, and established, precedent to follow. As noted in Chapter 5, these public servants have always been "presumed competent" to engage publicly for the government, partly because of their elite skills and education but more directly because the time lag of telegraphs and mail historically rendered it impossible for these actors to check with superiors each time they needed to engage with outsiders while abroad. The immediacy of digital era communications presents a similar logistical driver of a pluralistic model of government communications and engagement but expands this logic to a range of policy areas and public servants, not just those engaged in foreign diplomacy.

This model acknowledges that in the digital age public servant anonymity is an ever more impractical objective. Moving toward a less top-down, siloed approach to government-citizen interactions entails that all public servants, not simply those designated to act as spokespersons or operating at high levels of authority, will develop public profiles attached to their work and be in positions to speak publicly for the public service and network with stakeholders, service users, and everyday citizens. This digital era breach of anonymity has already occurred. A quick search on LinkedIn provides easy access to a range of public servants that, in the analogue era, would have existed under the radar as per the original bargain. The government itself facilitates this de-anonymization through the Government Electronic Directory Service, now available as an open data set, rendering it ever easier to identify individual federal public servants. But what a new model of government-citizen relations offers is not merely a recognition of this de-anonymization but rather an effort to capitalize on it as a component of a more pluralistic approach to government-citizen relations, one that does not presume that the interactions between the public service and the public must be channelled through specific access points and governed through strict top-down processes.

The launch in 2016 of an external-facing version of GCconnex – titled GCCollab – responded to this imperative and represented an innovative model of digital external engagement in the federal government. The platform allows academics and students to connect with public servants via the social networking platform, and in doing so it finally delivers on the theory of change that saw GCTools initially justified in part for their potential role in socializing external online social networking in the bureaucracy. Tools such as GCCollab, and the more pluralistic approach to government-citizen engagement advocated here, reflect Jeffrey Roy's prescient observation that, "rather than conformance to rules and managing down hierarchically, much evidence points to collaborative skills and outward navigation as the pillars of the public servant of the future" (2008, 555), betraying the classical view that "the good civil servant is neither seen nor heard. The one who is made fully visible has failed" (Savoie 2003, 34).

This approach to government-citizen engagement will require that public servants receive communications training previously reserved for defined spokespersons, a designation eliminated in the 2016 update to the government's official communications policy (and a potential window to expand the set of departmental voices engaged online). This training will demand that public servants appreciate the unique equity and coordination considerations that should guide their public interactions, such as respecting rules on bilingualism where appropriate and ensuring that core government policy messages are upheld and coherent across various information channels. In particular, if the government encourages a fleet of new public servants to develop public personas and speak online for the government, then these new spokespersons will need to be ready to walk the fine and sometimes blurry line between explaining policy and engaging with the public neutrally, and overt or, even more difficult to locate, "promiscuous" partisanship (Grube 2013, 2015; Kernaghan 2014a) in which public servants praise the government (or critique its opposition) and thus betray their duty to neutrality. Public servants' initial online fawning over the new Liberal government – evident in selfies taken by public servants with the prime minister in the Lester B. Pearson building following the election and public servants' criticisms of the Harper government in several news reports covering their reactions to the new government's win – suggests that at least some portions of the current public service are ill-equipped to navigate their way appropriately between partisan promotion (or criticism) of the government and neutral public engagement in online spaces (Bonokoski 2016; Van Dusen 2015). Training in this domain could become a focus of the 2016 Open Government Action Plan's commitments on preparing public servants for innovative forms of public engagement.

In designing this new model of government-citizen interaction and related training and guidelines, the public service and elected officials will finally not simply acknowledge but also act on the reality that "anonymity" has been for a long time an ineffective instrument for securing public service neutrality and ministerial accountability. This framing of anonymity as an instrument is useful, for it reminds us that anonymity is not a core tenet of the Westminster system but a means by which core tenets of this system (public servant neutrality and ministerial accountability) were achieved historically. In turn, explicitly dispensing with anonymity does not necessarily mean that we are abandoning the Westminster model; rather, we are developing new instruments to replace the function that anonymity used to fulfill. Clear guidelines and training on appropriate online networking are part of this replacement and represent a much more sensible and pragmatic path forward for today's public service than impossible aspirations for anonymity.

Those fearing this embrace of de-anonymization should take solace in the fact that the foreign service's long-standing model of decentralized bureaucrat-to-outsider communications has been made compatible with the dictates of coordinated, nonpartisan communications and ministerial accountability – the Westminster system has not crumbled at the feet of speech-giving, networking, and tweeting diplomats. To an extent, this example suggests that, though sufficient training and guidance and an updated digital bargain are required to facilitate this shift safely, fears about the loss of anonymity – especially in the digital era – as expressed in recent texts might exaggerate the dangers that this evolution of the Westminster system raises (see Aitken 2017; Grube 2013, 2015).

Finally, in crafting a new approach to public engagement fit for the digital age, the government will benefit by coupling innovative models of dialogue, or talk-based engagement, with approaches that abandon dialogue altogether. That is, while demanding appropriate attention to citizens' privacy concerns and related legislative constraints, the government should turn to the web as a rich site of big data describing citizens' interactions with, perspectives on, and experiences of services, programs, and policies. This includes the passive collection of data trails on social media – social listening – such as collecting and analyzing all social media posts that use a particular hashtag relevant to a policy, service, or program or that reference a department. Tracking the spread of Facebook profile changes in the wake of a contentious policy debate, as in the use of rainbow filters to show support for LGBTQ communities, provides another innovative means to take the pulse of Canadians on policy issues. These data trails have the advantage of telling the government what Canadians actually did or said in relation to a given policy, service, or program as opposed to relying on public opinion research surveys and consultations, which contain the biases that come from individuals being asked to recall (and be honest about) what they did or said in relation to these government activities (Clarke and Margetts 2014).

In addition to social listening, the Internet of Things and the proliferation of mobile technologies and sensors in all aspects of society now provide a wealth of new data sources that the government can tap to inform policy formulation, implementation, and evaluation. A big data–driven approach to public engagement will require that the government think creatively about how to embed data collection into its interactions with citizens on its own digital platforms – websites, social media accounts, mobile apps – and during in-person service transactions. In addition, this big data–driven approach to public engagement will rely on partnerships or data-sharing agreements in cases in which the digital interface collecting these data is not managed by the public service but owned by a third party delivering or supporting a government service, or by a private actor not providing a government service but whose data have value for the government. For instance, one can imagine that data collected via digital sensors in cars could be useful inputs on traffic patterns to inform transportation infrastructure investments. Framed so far as primarily an exercise in supporting greater dialogue between the government and the public, these innovative, data-driven approaches to collecting insights from the public have not yet featured prominently in the Government of Canada's digital engagement strategies, leaving much potential untapped.

STREAMLINE OLD RULES AND DEVELOP NEW RULES

This study exposed the reality of TBS rules mission creep, a phenomenon by which public servants are inclined to presume that a set of TBS rules applies to an activity as a default, ensuring that experimentation with new digital policy instruments places public servants in a stifling maze of TBS policies, directives, and guidelines. The DMCPI found that in some cases public servants cite nonexistent or misinterpreted rules when explaining why they do not experiment with innovative policy approaches. This is unsurprising to anyone who has spent time reading the TBS policy suite, whose dense language, complex interrelated instruments, and emphasis on risk mitigation do little to inform and empower public servants effectively.

The TBS has been renewing its policies so that they are more accessible. The new *Policy on Communications and Federal Identity,* released in May 2016, is indeed a much more concise document at a total of 1,347 words versus the 12,606 words (not including appendices and references) of the previous policy (Treasury Board Secretariat 2016b). The new policy also reduces the number of policy instruments that public servants need to consult, combining the former *Communications Policy of the Government of Canada* with the *Federal Identity Policy* (though the policy still requires that public servants interpreting it do so while considering a lengthy list of related policies and directives). Further efforts to streamline and more clearly express what is and is not permitted by the TBS rules are required to avoid the "TBS rules trump card" from preventing the uptake of new digital policy instruments and approaches going forward.

To this end, the TBS or line departments could consider creating myth-busting documents that encourage public servants to experiment with innovative digital instruments and approaches and to clarify how TBS rules support such experimentation. These documents could be particularly useful in arming those challenging the gap between official TBS policies and departmental implementation of those policies, as in the 2011 TBS policy which stated that individual public servants outside the communications shop should be encouraged to use social media to engage with the public (not implemented in practice), and in the 2013 TBS directive to open access to all social media sites (again not implemented uniformly across the federal public service as illustrated in Table 4.1). An additional measure would see the TBS test the language of its policies and directives with managers throughout their development, using this process to highlight language that should be edited to avoid inspiring overly draconian, restrictive readings of these policies in practice.

In other cases, the Government of Canada needs to add yet more rules to the mix as new digital policy instruments come downstream, reflecting the assertion in this book that the solution to digital capacity building is not strictly or exclusively one of eliminating rules and hierarchical oversight, as simplistic theories of digital era open government imply. In particular, the government has not yet developed robust guidelines to govern public servants' use of social listening, which raises particularly pressing ethical and legal questions related to the collection and use of data on private citizens. In one interview, a public servant noted that he was hesitant to track the public's online activities knowing that doing so could be perceived to be "big brother" behaviour (S3). This hesitation is unsurprising given the public backlash to Edward Snowden's revelations about mass online surveillance at play in the Five Eyes intelligence alliance of which Canada is a part. Yet there are other legitimate and "above board" reasons for the public service to track the public's online behaviours, tapping into rich data that could improve policies and services, as discussed in the previous recommendation (Clarke and Margetts 2014). A clear policy statement and guidance on the use of social listening would spell out the conditions under which the instrument can be used and how. Without such a directive, public servants might presume that the instrument is not permitted, missing important opportunities to understand Canadians' needs and preferences better. Alternatively, they might apply existing TBS instruments to the tool, the most likely candidate being the POR procedures, whose protocols render them suitable for preplanned surveys but not for regular, agile collection of big data online – a point explicitly acknowledged in the POR policy but that might nonetheless be lost on risk-averse managers generating a mythical prohibitive rule. Finally, we might see public servants "going rogue," collecting data online in ways that might or might not align with legislative requirements and ethical standards.

Social listening is just one example of the new policy instruments that demand empowering but responsible corporate rules and that, in turn, demand that the Government of Canada – especially the TBS – becomes ever more agile in its ability to develop policies and guidelines on rapidly advancing digital technologies. Let us not forget the three-and-a-half-year saga of internal meetings and reports required before official social media guidelines were produced. Such time lags again illustrate the risks that result from the excessive focus in the public service on internal process and risk aversion, a focus that can ensure that public servants live in a policy and guidance vacuum for periods of time that far exceed the initial introduction and uptake of new policy instruments. In this sense, the problem is not strictly that the public service is handcuffed by an excess of oversight and top-down, risk-averse TBS rules. Rather, the public service must also become more agile in its ability to create whole new sets of rules and guidance to safely and ethically usher in the widespread uptake of digital tools and approaches coming downstream.

Although these new rules will need to battle TBS mission creep and risk aversion that can render top-down oversight an innovation killer, both public servants and the public will still need to acknowledge the legitimate costs that can come from loosening the rules that at present can prevent rapid digital advances in the public service. I have argued in this book that building a resilient digital government is not a simple matter of political will and bureaucratic capacity building. It also demands that we address head-on the unique accountability concerns that impose higher standards on government than on other actors operating in the digital age. Whether the government is adhering to rules that aim to prevent partisan interference in the work of the public service, that ensure public services are accessible to those with disabilities, or that respect citizens' privacy, the bureaucracy will be limited in its ability to adapt to new digital technologies at the same pace and to the same extent as other organizations.

To be sure, to date, the public service has been too keen to adopt a draconian interpretation of rules where reasonably it should not. A prime example is the decision to prevent the automatic uploading of all ATIP requests to a government website out of a conservative interpretation of the Official Languages Act that would call for all of these documents to be translated in advance of their public release. The balance between strict rule adherence and flexible adaptation to the digital age has fallen too far toward the former thus far, evident in a fearful and rules-obsessed federal public service. Yet, in streamlining old rules and developing new ones, public servants leading these efforts and observers offering critiques of them should keep in mind the complicated accountability and innovation trade-offs that in some cases might justify a more tempered embrace of technology in the public service. Part of striking this balance will involve instituting a stronger culture of accountability for learning as opposed to the current approach in Canada, which tends to favour accountability as a vehicle of risk mitigation and error reduction (Jarvis 2014b). This approach has inspired a proliferation of top-down rules to govern the use of new digital policy instruments as opposed to prioritizing the need to learn strategically from successes and failures in their use. Such strategic experimentation invokes the accountability-for-learning model that I recommend as being more fitting with the demands of innovative digital era government.

GENERATE A POLITICAL CULTURE THAT REWARDS INNOVATION
AND TOLERATES FAILURE

The name change of the Deputy Minister Committee on Social Media and Policy Development to the Deputy Minister Committee on Policy Innovation was telling, indicating that the public service's efforts to adapt to the digital age are fundamentally dependent on cultivating an innovative culture within the federal government. The digital age presents new challenges and opportunities at a pace that demands agility and a willingness to prototype, iterate, and adjust approaches rapidly in the face of new information and continual feedback. These approaches also demand that the public service embrace the potential for uncertainty and failure that accompanies any diversion from tried and tested methods.

The public service traditionally has not been agile or tolerant of failure for a range of reasons – including siloed work models, a restrictive hierarchy, a rules-obsessed culture, and draconian models of accountability – but equally innovation has been stifled by the plain reality that our political culture does not reward it sufficiently. Whether it is political leaders demanding error-free government, or opposition parties, journalists, academics, and citizens pouncing on any sign of failure in the government, the public service faces greater incentives to stay the course than it does to experiment with novel approaches to its work – even where status quo approaches are suboptimal and produce their own failures, following a "better the devil you know" logic.

This fear of failure cuts even deeper in the digital age given that many digital policy instruments are outward facing – crowdsourcing, social media, and open data, for example – ensuring that failures are on display for public consumption. Thus, a key takeaway from this book is that, if we want to build digital capacity in the federal government, then we need to generate a political culture that demands innovation and in turn tolerates the failures that it might generate. Ultimately, this requires that we tackle the permanent campaigning tactics fuelling a vicious political communications cycle in Canada. That renders public servants fearful of a fluid, open style of communications and of the potential risks that accompany experimentation with new digital policy instruments and work processes. This is a tall order, admittedly, the most ambitious prescription flowing from this book.

This project in part demands political leadership that encourages innovation, that tolerates the failures that might follow from it, and that does not revert to ever stricter oversight and top-down, "name and blame" accountability measures in the wake of politically costly scandals. Campaigning on the promise that he would abandon negative political attacks for a more positive, collaborative style of politics – for "sunny ways," as expounded in his acceptance speech – Prime Minister Trudeau pledged to foster a more open style of communications as a counter to the vicious political communications culture that rationalizes information control and risk aversion in the public service. Reasserting this promise in his first response to the media after being sworn in as prime minister at Rideau Hall, Trudeau explained that his government would be different from that of his predecessor because of its open, trusting relationship with Canadians and the media. This signal was more explicit in the creation of a Cabinet Committee on Open Transparent Government and Parliament and in ministerial mandate letters, released to the public for the first time. The mandate letters included in their preamble a commitment to openness and transparency, but more directly they supported experimentation by mandating President of the Treasury Board Secretariat Scott Brison to ensure that all departments dedicate "a fixed percentage of program funds to experimenting with new approaches to existing problems and measuring the impact of their programs" (Prime Minister's Office 2015b).

Some might reasonably retort that, though the TBS is likely the only body with the whole of government levers to enforce such a directive, it is hardly in a position to encourage experimentation given that its own rules and oversight mechanisms are frequently cited barriers to innovation in the public service. An alternative (and decidedly more hopeful) reading suggests that the new role of the TBS in mandating experimentation might signal a shifting emphasis in the department, from one that overprioritizes risk mitigation, dense rules, and status quo defaults to one that seeks to balance accountability and process with innovation. At the least, under the right leadership, the unit responsible for this directive might serve as a seed for this shifting culture in the TBS.

Whatever the potential perils (and paradoxes) of its placement within the TBS – and in part to mitigate the effects of an innovation-phobic culture that the TBS historically has helped to drive – the government has coupled the commitment to experimentation with directives that encourage a healthy risk tolerance among public servants. Mandate letters explicitly challenged the widely held perception in the bureaucracy that public-facing failures must be avoided at all costs for fear of the bad press that they might invite. The letters note that, "if we want Canadians to trust their government, we need a government that trusts Canadians. It is important that we acknowledge mistakes when we make them. Canadians do not expect us to be perfect – they expect us to be honest, open, and sincere in our efforts to serve the public interest" (Prime Minister's Office 2015a).

This statement directly rejects the call for "error-free government" lamented as a troubling trend in a series of analyses of the federal public service (Himelfarb 2005; Jarvis 2016; Lynch 2007, 2008; Savoie 2013). Instead, this section of Trudeau's mandate letters prioritizes the accountability-for-learning model cited already, a model acknowledging that "error-free administration is simply not possible and [instead highlights] the importance of learning from shortcomings as an 'engine' of positive change" (Jarvis 2014b, 459).

Finally, the Trudeau government has also offered less direct but nonetheless potent calls for innovation from the public service by prioritizing deliverology as a central guiding philosophy in implementing its agenda. Although some have criticized the government's decision to adopt Barber's model, noting its failings as applied in other jurisdictions (Reevely 2016), its core preoccupations with measuring outcomes using high-quality data and adjusting approaches iteratively in response to these data align neatly with the requirements (and possibilities) of governing in the digital age and of encouraging the culture of continual innovation that digital era government requires. To this end, the appointment of Matthew Mendelsohn in June 2016 as co-chair of the Deputy Minister Committee on Policy Innovation, and the decision to place the Central Innovation Hub under his leadership, send important signals to the bureaucracy that innovation is tightly linked to the government's public management agenda and core policy priorities, as advanced by the Results and Delivery Secretariat of the PCO that Mendelsohn heads.

These signals have not been lost on bureaucrats, in particular among pockets of innovators eager to receive these directives from their political masters. In a February 2016 deck following the election, the DMCPI cited the new government's focus on openness, digital government, and experimentation and concluded that the "'hit-the-accelerator' scenario materialized: government has ambitious 'how to govern' agenda." The deck also stated that the "opportunity to scale and drive into core business has increased considerably" and that "top-down demand for open, innovative approaches [is] expected to create natural, mainstreaming 'pull'" (Deputy Minister Committee on Policy Innovation 2016).

The challenge going forward is ensuring that this "pull" is felt throughout a hierarchical leadership structure that traditionally has not been rewarded for encouraging innovation and among managers and staff who might be skeptical of the government's true commitment to embracing failure, especially failure that is politically costly. In particular, in the federal government, top-down demands for innovation are often lost in translation once they hit the "clay layer" of middle management, a worrying trend considering research, which finds that middle managers are crucial to advancing many innovations in government, especially those that involve technology (Borins 2002). And, at the time of writing, it remains unclear whether the government's call for innovation has even been heard, let alone heeded, among the bureaucracy proper. For example, at a presentation in March 2017 that I delivered to a group of roughly 200 IT professionals in the Government of Canada, approximately five individuals raised their hands when asked if they had heard of the new commitment to experimentation introduced in 2015.

Reward structures – such as advancing public servants who encourage or lead experimentation with new policy instruments, the use of "failure reports" (as pioneered by Engineers without Borders[12]) that destigmatize trial and error approaches, the recruitment of outside managers not socialized in the risk-averse public service culture, and innovation prizes – could bear fruit in ensuring that the Trudeau government's enthusiasm for innovation moves beyond a top-level directive. In implementing these options, the government should adopt the same data-driven, iterative approach that its efforts seek to promote more generally, testing which measures actually encourage experimentation in practice and adjusting interventions in response to these findings. Part of this work will also rest on careful analysis of the precise and context-specific conditions that can limit innovation, work begun by the DMCPI. On this front, the Public Service Employee Survey should be amended to include more questions on innovation specifically; currently, there is only one question on innovation, which merely asks whether or not employees are encouraged to innovate, leaving aside the conditions that enable innovation, the level of management (e.g., immediate supervisor versus senior manager), and the personality traits and tactics of leaders that tend to facilitate innovation.

But encouraging innovation and the open culture of information sharing and trust that it requires does not rest solely with the political leaders calling for it or the managers tasked with implementing this call in practice. Parliament, opposition parties, journalists, and citizens can also propel, or halt, innovation in the public service by the signals that they send to bureaucrats. Whereas the other prescriptions detailed in this chapter focus on the levers at the disposal of the government itself, this final recommendation highlights the role that nongovernmental actors play in encouraging, or discouraging, an open, innovative, digital-ready public service.

For the most part, the Canadian media, Parliament, and opposition parties have done little to encourage innovation in digital government thus far, part of a larger trend in which federal public management is excluded from mainstream, well-informed public debates (Jarvis 2016). Where these actors do wade into the subject of digital government, it is often simply to expose supposed failures, "supposed" because these critiques often rest on shallow appreciations of digital technologies and their roles in governing today. For instance, journalists have had a field day with a Twitter bot that automatically publishes edits made to Wikipedia from anonymous government IP addresses (Crawford 2016; Fekete 2014). Although in some cases these edits are not work related (e.g., editing a sports team's result or an article on a chocolate bar), many of the edits are entirely legitimate, such as those that saw public servants at Heritage Canada editing articles on Canada's 150th anniversary. Yet these examples of creative, networked information sharing are not applauded as such; rather, they are critiqued as evidence of public servants wasting time on the public dime.

In another instance, public servants were wrongly criticized by opposition members and the media for requesting that Google clear its cache to ensure that web searches no longer lead individuals to out-of-date PMO webpages giving the impression that the Harper government was still in office (Canadian Press 2016; Thompson 2016). To their credit, certain journalists did correct the record on this issue, noting that the move was not a case of Soviet-style propaganda but an entirely legitimate effort to ensure that Canadians can find the right information on government webpages (Ireland 2016). Nonetheless, these are just two examples of public servants thinking creatively about the requirements of information distribution in the digital age, yet by lambasting their efforts media and opposition parties suffering from a dearth of digital literacy reinforced the problematic trend in which even entirely legitimate diversions from status quo operations are derided publicly and disincentivized in the public service.

This is not a plea to discourage valid critiques of the government by outside actors, essential as they are to a robust democracy. And in the case of the media, it is only fair to acknowledge that the need for deeper journalistic coverage of digital government coincided with the digital disruption that brought massive revenue shortfalls and newsroom cuts in Canada.[13] However, notwithstanding these challenges and acknowledging the benefits of substantive, well-founded scrutiny of digital government reforms, we must still condemn cheap, ill-informed attacks and "gotcha journalism" that undermine efforts to promote a more risk-tolerant, innovative culture in the public service. The media, political commentators, parties, and Parliament need to beef up their own digital literacy if they are to critique – responsibly and helpfully – the federal government's efforts to adapt to the digital age, as opposed to the current trend, in which even benevolent innovations are often ignored or dismissed as failures. To this end, the decision in July 2016 to host an emergency Standing Committee on Government Operations and Estimates meeting on the Phoenix pay system brought welcome and much-needed parliamentary scrutiny to the issue of IT management in the federal public service. If the United Kingdom is any example, then parliamentary scrutiny of this sort can put digital government on the political agenda and inspire significant investment and reform, with the 2011 "Government and IT – A Recipe for Rip Offs" report of the Public Administration Select Committee in part inspiring massive investment and political attention to digital capacity in the United Kingdom.

Finally, citizens too have a role to play in generating a political culture amenable to innovative digital government. Take, for instance, the public's reaction to the return of the long-form census in 2015, which saw the hashtag "#censusselfie" trending in Canada, garnering international media attention (Blevis 2016). Eaves (2016) argued that this revealed Canadians' commitment to "peace, order and good government," but even more relevant for digital government this enthusiasm signalled an appetite for evidence, data, and robust public policy making among the electorate. In government, as in many things, you get what you ask for, and such signals tell policy makers that the health of federal policy-making processes is an issue that resonates with the voting public. To make this signal ever more clear, the Canadian public must continue to demand digital innovation as part of the political push that could precipitate significant investment in this space by leaders conscious of their obligation to respond to public will or, more cynically, conscious of their need to appeal to voters at election time.

At the same time, as the public service moves forth and experiments with untested digital approaches, the public, like journalists and opposition parties, will need to demonstrate a thoughtful tolerance for the failures that this experimentation might create. To bolster this tolerance, the public service itself has work to do. A more open culture of communications, in which the public service would describe its efforts to experiment with new models of policy making and service delivery, and explain what has worked well and what still requires improvement, could generate an empathetic, trusting relationship with Canadians that reduces the risk of vicious public backlash to failure and, in turn, rationalizes risk aversion in the public service. This approach to public communications has already benefited two global leaders in public sector innovation – the United Kingdom's Behavioural Insights Team and Denmark's MindLab – which, as noted above, invite their staff to discuss their work in blogs on their corporate websites, using their real names and faces. In a panel discussion in 2015 on policy innovation, held in Ottawa, representatives from each organization noted that their licence to innovate was earned in part because they transparently communicate their successes and failures to the public (Clarke 2016b). Here Marcel Massé's observation in 1993 bears revisiting and holds ever more true today:

> Those who traditionally simply made decisions will have to spend much more of their time explaining situations, setting out the various options and trade-offs, and persuading those involved, before proposed solutions become acceptable. A good part of the present unpopularity of both politicians and public servants is due to our insufficient adaptation to these new requirements of our jobs. (quoted in Savoie 2003, 107)

To rebuild trust between the public and the public service, Massé presciently argued, "in the post-modern government the task of understanding, consulting, explaining and persuading must be shared between politicians and bureaucrats" (quoted in Savoie 2003, 107). On this front, the open model of digital public engagement, including the use of personalized blogging and decentralized, informal, online network building, will likely be a useful instrument in generating tolerance for, and informed public scrutiny of, the bureaucracy's forays into innovative digital policy approaches and, more broadly, in realizing the Trudeau government's intention to build a high-trust government-citizen relationship.

Future Research and Issues on the Horizon

In this book, I have tracked the early adoption phase in which tools such as social media and open data were first integrated into the federal public service, and I have detailed the early work undertaken by the bureaucracy to shift corporate culture to one more amenable to collaboration, information sharing, and innovation. This effort sets the groundwork for future studies on the progress – or lack thereof – of this early work. In particular, future research should track the outcomes of initiatives that, at the time of writing, are in their early stages of implementation, including innovation labs and micro-assignments.

I have flagged GCTools as potentially powerful enablers of horizontal government that have not yet been adopted on a large scale. Much more systematic research is needed to explore how, why, and to what end public servants currently use, or avoid, these tools, to understand the networks that they foster across the public service, and to determine the impact of internal digital social networking on the policy process and machinery of government.

In addition, while this book provides a whole-of-government view of the federal bureaucracy's early digital era adaptation (or stagnation in certain instances), future studies will add to my findings by focusing on the experiences of particular departments and units across the government. In particular, in Chapter 5, I flagged innovative initiatives that stand as exceptions to the general trend across the federal government. These exceptions indicate that under the right conditions public servants can take up novel digital policy instruments and new forms of internal and external collaboration. I suggested that the characteristics of individual managers play significant roles in fuelling or halting innovation, but other variables likely help to explain variation in policy innovation capacity across the public service, such as policy sector, proximity of the issue to the political agenda, nature of the stakeholders involved, and stage of the policy cycle in question. These variables could be usefully probed in future research.

The Twitter study that I presented in Chapter 3 draws on data from 2012, depicting the Government of Canada's early efforts to integrate social media into communication strategies. The research design could be replicated on current government Twitter accounts to explore if and how departments have shifted their approaches to the platform and to test whether they have become more amenable to sharing information and interacting with nongovernmental actors versus simply leading people back to government websites and engaging with other government departments. In general, the Government of Canada provides a good case to explore the influence of political leadership on digital government over time. The election of Justin Trudeau and his government's overt commitment to public engagement, data-driven policy making, and innovation contrasts starkly with the public management philosophy of Stephen Harper, who provided little credible leadership on his flagship digital government effort, the open(ish) government initiative.

Should a more pluralistic approach to government-citizen engagement emerge under Trudeau's leadership, as I recommend it should, future research should carefully scrutinize whether it avoids the risks flagged here (e.g., breaches to public servant neutrality or coordination and equity issues) while exploring its implications for the role of the individual public servant in Canada's Westminster system of government. In particular, this model of decentralized, public servant–led networking could represent a potent challenge to the centralization thesis advanced by Savoie (1999) and recent work on politicization of the public service (Aucoin 2012). The model could even swing the balance between political responsiveness and bureaucratic independence too far toward the latter, reincarnating a digital variant of the "Sir Humphrey" syndrome that saw an autonomous civil service impervious to the political dictates of its ministerial superiors in decades past (Bakvis 2000).

To insulate against these risks, the time is right to strike a new bargain – the digital bargain – that accounts for the public facing, networking, and self-directed risk taking that innovative digital bureaucrats undertake. In this bargain, political leaders might view this newfound bureaucratic personality and autonomy as key to advancing their policy agendas for the reasons detailed in this chapter (e.g., tapping into external expertise, building public trust, and recruiting top digital talent). Public servants, for their part, would gain from this bargain a newfound sense of freedom to innovate and a capacity to blend their networked public lives with their public service work. This opportunity might be of greater appeal to a generation of public servants who have grown up online and operate in a career marketplace that rewards a rich online presence as evidence of a networked, innovative, ambitious, prospective employee (Schawbel 2013). This new bargain might also be a necessary development given recent interest in intersectoral interchange (Campbell 2014; Jarvis 2016) and in particular the trend in which digital talent is "parachuted" in for temporary "tours of duty" in the public service. Ultimately, this digital bargain will reflect the long-waning practicality and value of anonymity and under-the-radar, behind-the-scenes modesty of previous generations of public servants. This approach reflects the fact that public service bargains are "neither absolute nor rigid – they are subject to renegotiation especially during times of political transition in Westminster systems" (Althaus and Vakil 2013, 478; see also Lindquist 2006; Lindquist and Eichbaum 2016; Lodge 2009; and Roy 2008).

If a new digital bargain is to be struck, then scholars, political leaders, and public servants alike need to ensure that it is not a backroom deal, developed without open debate on its merits and risks or without folding it into longer debates on the evolving bargains at play in the Westminster system. In particular, as with any attempt to redefine the relationship between political leaders and public servants, the digital bargain demands that we carefully consider how to respect the doctrines of public servant neutrality and ministerial accountability in a context of networking, public-facing, self-directed – but unelected – public servant innovators and spokespersons. Previous explorations of evolving public service bargains and the issues of anonymity and accountability that they raise – such as the Tait Report (Tait 1996) and more recent work on digital era values and ethics (Kernaghan 2014a) – will serve as useful guides for scholars and practitioners in defining and scrutinizing the digital bargain and its implications for Canadian democracy.

In addition, though I have addressed questions of appropriate conduct in professional uses of online networking, in building this new digital bargain we must also revisit the rules and guidelines governing the personal political activities of public servants: that is, the activities that they are permitted to engage in given their Charter-protected right to freedom of expression (the emergence of which from a series of court decisions again attests to the evolutionary nature of the bargain).[14] As public servants are thrust into public view, generating networked personal and professional profiles, their ability to conceal their partisan political preferences and activities – especially those that leave a digital trail, as in signing an e-petition or following a party leader's Facebook account – becomes much more strained. Current rules provide only vague and difficult to apply examples of offline acts prohibited because they either confirm or give the appearance of inappropriate political activity. In cases such as the highly partisan "Harperman" YouTube video released by federal public servant Tony Turner during the 2015 federal election, a line is clearly crossed. But it is less clear whether individual public servants can engage in a range of other activities online as private citizens and how allowances in this regard will change depending on the privacy settings of their accounts, their public profiles (especially among those who build a rich professional online presence on platforms such as Twitter), their ranks, and the files on which they work.

Until clear guidelines are offered to address these questions, public servants will operate in a grey zone in which they might be unduly restricting their Charter right to freedom of expression in online settings, a particularly problematic restriction given that so much political activity now takes place online, in some cases at the direction of the government itself, as in the use of online consultations and the introduction of e-petitions in the House of Commons. Alternatively, public servants operating without guidance might engage in online political activities that clearly breach their duty of loyalty to the government of the day. Negotiating this new facet of the bargain will involve addressing the fact that the few political rights that one used to give up as an average public servant might grow in number if one is expected to, or opts to, build a prominent public profile online, bumping the public servant into a class of officials whose political rights have always been more circumscribed given their status (e.g., deputy ministers or clerks). It is not clear that the often low- to mid-level career bureaucrats already engaging online in a professional capacity through networks such as the #w2p and #gc2020 Twitter communities and on unofficial blogs are aware of and prepared to accept the new and more onerous limitations that this activity likely imposes on their capacity to engage in partisan politics as private citizens. Again, a new digital bargain is emerging, and the risk at present is that this is happening without a transparent, thoughtful, and frank public discussion on the costs and benefits that this unconscious evolution raises. This is a significant issue in need of attention in Westminster jurisdictions (but see Clarke and Piper, 2018), one that Kent Aitken (2017) has suggested might even warrant parliamentary inquiry.

Future research should also investigate how digital technologies shape the work of exempt political staff, a topic that I have not addressed given my focus on the bureaucrats who comprise the federal civil service but that has been helpfully taken up in recent writing (Marando and Craft 2017). Building on this work, researchers could explore how political staff and ministers manage the varying requirements and objectives of political and ministerial communications online, as became an issue when certain ministers were investigated by the commissioner of official languages for tweeting unilingually, raising important questions about the fuzzy line between one's digital presence as an MP and as a minister of the Crown (Clarke and Dubois 2015). Future studies should also probe the extent to which the digital policy capacity issues flagged here apply equally to ministers' offices and the "boys in short pants" working in them. This work should attend in particular to the gap between the data and digital instruments that newly appointed ministers benefit from during the election period and the digital incapacity that they face once they take the helm of a department that does not benefit from the resources and comparatively more lax corporate policy requirements that party strategists enjoy when launching digital campaigns. Here again the Canadian government offers an ideal case study given the prominent role that big data and social media played in the Liberal Party's campaign in 2015 (Delacourt 2016a) and the digital time warp that these elected officials entered on their first day as ministers.

In addition, though I have focused on questions of digital era public administration, future studies should build on the findings here in focusing more closely on the implications of digital technologies for policy design. I have suggested that public policy scholars need to expand the subject area disciplines deemed relevant to government policy work. Policy capacity now hinges on access to expertise in user experience, software development, agile design, and data science, not simply expertise in law, political science, and economics. Even more fundamentally, I have suggested in this study that research on government policy work needs to stop marginalizing the role of information technology – both as an instrument of policy work and as a functional area – in government. Typically, IT is framed as solely relevant to a narrow range of implementation tasks, most commonly the delivery of online services, and back-end corporate functions (e.g., database management and human resource systems). In the digital age, IT – the data that it generates, the analysis that it renders possible, the networks that it fosters – can no longer be treated as a mere "add on" or an "afterthought" to the "real work" of policy making. Instead, digital technology needs to be integrated into all stages of the policy process – from agenda setting to evaluation – an approach demanding scholarship that explores how those with digital skill sets are or should be integrated into the daily work of traditional policy shops as opposed to existing in the marginalized silo of IT and entering the policy process only when it is time to develop a communications or online delivery strategy.

As new forms of digital expertise and unconventional policy instruments are embedded in the policy process, and as nodality rises in prominence in the digital age (as governments "become their websites," as some have predicted; see Hood and Margetts 2007; Margetts 1999; and Steinberg 2012), scholars might need to reconceptualize where power and influence lie in the policy process. Do they lie internally, among communications staff, IT officers, and digital government units, or externally, among civic technology groups and private firms with access to skills and data not found in the traditional policy advisory shops of the public service? Pointing to a further redistribution of nodal capital, I have flagged the emergence of new players in the nongovernmental sphere of policy actors that now influence decision makers, including social media consultants, big data analytics firms, and civic technologists working with government open data. These actors extend an existing trend toward pluralistic policy work in which the public service is but one provider of "truth" to "power" and in which the very concept of "truth" is more contested and "power" more diffuse (Prince 2007).

Studies of digital era policy design should equally explore the collision of the ideological, normative, and strategic political considerations shaping policy work with new digital policy instruments that promise unprecedented data-driven decision making. To date, the research on digital government has tended to treat policy work as an inherently objective, depoliticized function that can only become more evidence driven in the digital age as tools such as crowdsourcing and big data are applied to it. This perspective denies the values-based and strategic partisan influences that will continue to colour policy design in the face of new sources of data, however "big" and "open" (Clarke 2016a; Clarke and Craft 2018). Here Robert Coase's (1994) observation that, "if you torture the data long enough, it will confess" is ever more relevant, reminding scholars to consider how digital policy instruments and data promising "objective" analyses will continue to be informed by the subjective biases and self-interested agendas of those in power while benefiting from a new veneer of credibility granted by the novel – but nonetheless manipulated – data on which they rest (Bates 2012; Eaves and Wagner 2012).

Instead of grappling with the questions of power and representation at the heart of governing, theories of digital government thus far prefer simpler narratives borrowed from the tech sector that frame citizens as mere "users" of technology and governing as the simple process of acting on objective data describing user needs or of crowdsourcing optimal solutions. This approach works well when considering how to design and deliver digital services better where the goal is relatively noncontentious and easy to define – shortening the time that it takes to apply for a new passport, for example. On this front, tech companies such as Google, which follows the motto "focus on the user and all else will follow" (Google, n.d.), have much to offer a public sector that, reaching back to its Weberian roots, has proven to be more concerned with its own processes and dense organizational structures than with the citizens and service users affected by its work.

However, as with the deficiencies of earlier "consumer" and "customer" framings of citizens (Aberbach and Christensen 2005; Drewry 2005; Dutil, Howard, and Langford 2010; Jung 2010; Needham 2003; Pierre 1995), it is less clear how a user-centred approach defines the government's role in developing policy on divisive or value-laden issues that create winners of some and losers of others and where no easily discernible, universally applicable user satisfaction metric can define success (Clarke 2014b, 2016a; Clarke and Craft 2018; Shaw 2016). We have already witnessed the uneven impacts of new forms of data-driven decision making in the case of predictive policing, for example, in which big data can be used to anticipate crimes before they happen, with the effect that certain already marginalized populations are subject to ever greater surveillance and an ever greater likelihood of being arrested (Clarke and Margetts 2014; Mayer-Schönberger and Cukier 2013; Stroud 2014). Whose user satisfaction metric trumps in these cases? That of the citizen seeking reduced crime rates? Or that of the potential, but not yet culpable, "criminal" wishing to avoid disproportionate surveillance from authorities?

The user-centric tech sector ethos falls short in informing a holistic descriptive theory of digital era government given that it is silent on the politics of policy as manifest in the class-based, ideological, and strategic partisan dynamics that determine the policy issues that a government prioritizes and inform the policy options that a government pursues. User-centrism as a guiding principle of governance rests on the flawed assumption that the state shares a relationship with citizens no more power laden than the one that Google, Amazon, and the creators of Pokémon Go share with their "users." This assertion begs even greater scrutiny given what we know about the power that these companies wield in shaping the informational infrastructures that determine what we see and do not see when we access the web and ultimately that shape the everyday decisions that draw on the web's informational offerings.

In addition, beyond the narrow range of public service delivery tasks that federal bureaucrats take on, in particular in advising on and implementing government policy decisions, the concept of "user-centrism" sits uneasily with the model of accountability at the heart of the Westminster system. This model calls public servants to serve the democratically elected minister, not the public (defined as "user" or otherwise). User-centrism, in short, is at best a lazy interpretation and at worst a complete betrayal of public servants' role in Canada's democratic system, their relationship to the Canadian public, and the hierarchical accountability structure that links public servants to ministers. Again this calls for greater scrutiny of the new digital bargain that, at present, governments are sleepwalking into, guided by the soothing promises of the ahistorical, technological solutionism (Morozov 2014) that punctuates popular digital government narratives.

Finally, just as the public service will need to remain nimble and responsive in adapting to the rapid introduction of new technologies and related social phenomena, so too will scholars of public administration and public policy. Automation, robotics, the Internet of Things, and advances in data mining and monitoring will raise not only practical questions on the capacity of the public service to wield and regulate these phenomena but also new questions for scholarship on public sector accountability and ethics (Kernaghan 2014b). Far from keeping up to date with fast-arising digital trends, public administration scholarship has barely acknowledged the rise of digital technologies as a defining feature of contemporary society. Researchers continue to discuss policy capacity, service delivery reform, co-production, and network governance while rarely mentioning the digital realities that inevitably punctuate these phenomena as they unfold in today's governments.

In particular, in the Canadian literature in the past few years, scholars have been preoccupied with an apparent rise of politicization and permanent campaigning in the public service (especially during the Harper years; see Lindquist and Eichbaum 2016). Focused on these themes, Canadian public administration scholars have tended to account for digital era phenomena only in a negative light and narrowly so. They have discussed social media as a driver of short-termism, political marketing, and command and control governance, but they have not taken heed or contributed to a larger international literature focused on the broader range of pressures, dilemmas, and *opportunities* that the digital age presents to today's governments. As I argued at the start of this book, these themes have instead been addressed primarily by those outside the field of public administration, and thus they have not been scrutinized with the broader historical viewpoints and theoretical nuances that the field offers discussions of digital era governance. I was inspired to write this book in part to bring these two solitudes together and in part to bring the Canadian experience into an active international conversation on digital era public sector reform. Though I have argued that traditional public administration concepts and empirical research can enrich theories of digital government, the field of public administration – Canadian focused and otherwise – will still write itself out of relevance if it does not engage with the digital phenomena that those outside the field have rightfully identified as central to contemporary governance.

Digital Era Open Government in Canada:
Unfinished Project, Uncertain Future

One central takeaway from this book is that the public service can be impressively steadfast in evading the changes enabled by, and required of, the digital age. We might see small adjustments at the margins. However, without confronting complex questions of digital era accountability, striking an updated digital bargain, investing in a new set of skills, dismantling restrictive silos and hierarchies, fostering innovation, and rejecting a political culture that rewards closed government, the federal public service will remain in a time warp in the years to come, constrained by the worldviews, structures, and resources that I have argued are incompatible with the demands of the digital age. There is no inevitable march of progress toward an open, innovative, digital government. Instead, we face a set of defined challenges that political leaders, public servants, scholars, and citizens alike must tackle to ensure that the public service survives as a resilient institution in the digital age. This is how we should frame digital era open government – not as an inevitable outcome of the digital era but as an unfinished project with no guarantee of success.

At the same time, should administrative and political leaders earnestly heed this book's call for reform – a call also found in decades of writing that critiques excessive silos, hierarchies, and risk aversion in the public service – we can take solace in the reminder that the Canadian model of government is designed to accommodate such reform and to do so without necessarily abandoning the core principles of our democratic system. As John Tait noted in his 1996 report on public service values and ethics,

> it should be kept in mind that parliamentary government is an inherently evolutionary form of government, continually adapting to meet new circumstances, in contrast to more rigid, static and codified systems. And we do not see any reason, at this point, why it could not or should not evolve in ways that are largely consistent with the vital or essential principles of the past. (7)

Historically, as a cautious reformer, Canada has not tended to capitalize strategically on the "inherent evolutionary" potential that its system of government offers. Instead, where the public service has evolved, it has done so in an incremental, reactionary way, layering on new oversight mechanisms, strengthening silos, and emboldening a status quo bias despite evidence of the deficiencies that this trajectory invites, especially over the long term. I have explored in this book these long-documented trends, still manifest in the digital age, when the incompatibility of closed government with the demands of governing has perhaps never been so stark. In contemporary efforts to challenge closed government, my findings suggest that, far from abandoning the principles of Canada's Westminster system, the time is ripe to return to these principles and to acknowledge that their core preoccupation with effective, equitable, and accountable governance has been overshadowed incrementally by a creeping culture of excessive silos, hierarchies, and risk aversion. To break this cycle in the coming years, both practitioners and observers of Canadian public administration must advance to a point where they are not decrying but remedying the deficiencies of Canada's long-standing closed government traditions. The diagnoses and prescriptions that I have laid out in this book provide a point of departure to guide this complex but necessary project moving forward.

Appendix: Interview Index

A relatively small and well-acquainted group of federal public servants are involved in implementing digital policy instruments such as social media and open data and in the key digital initiatives explored in this study (open government, GCTools, Blueprint 2020, and initiatives related to policy innovation). In the interest of protecting the identities of interviewees, I use generic titles and do not provide the names of interviewees' departments/agencies where doing so would reveal their identities. In some cases, interviewees specifically requested that I use a generic department name to avoid revealing their identities (e.g., "line department" versus Health Canada or "central agency" versus the TBS), a request that I respected.

I have listed the date on which the initial interview took place. In many cases, contact with the interviewee continued via follow-up emails, subsequent face-to-face interviews, and phone calls in order to clarify points raised in the interview, to collect missing details, to fact-check basic details such as timelines, and to check in on initiatives that had advanced since the time of the interview. These follow-ups continued until August 2016.

External Advisers
A1 Adviser, open government, and former Government of Canada executive, April 4, 2012
A2 David Eaves, March 29, 2012

Communications
C1 Web communications manager, ESDC, April 5, 2012
C2 Web communications manager, DFAIT, April 11, 2012
C3 Web communications manager, ESDC, May 2, 2012
C4 Senior web communications manager, ESDC, May 8, 2012
C5 Web communications officer, line department, May 2, 2012

C6 Web communications officer, line department, May 2, 2012
C7 Web communications manager, line department, May 14, 2012

Stakeholder Engagement and Consultations
S1 Manager, PCO, April 3, 2012
S2 Manager, PCO, April 13, 2012
S3 Senior executive, line department, April 24, 2012
S4 Manager, line department, May 9, 2012
S5 Policy adviser, PCO, May 2, 2014

Policy and Program Development
P1 Policy analyst, line department, April 4, 2012
P2 Policy analyst, line department, April 24, 2012
P3 Senior executive, line department, April 24, 2012
P4 Policy analyst, DFAIT, April 26, 2012
P5 Policy analyst, line department, April 27, 2012
P6 Policy analyst, line department, May 8, 2012
P7 Program manager, line department, March 14, 2013
P8 Policy analyst, line department, March 27, 2013
P9 Policy analyst, line department, August 7, 2014

Information Management and Information Technology
I1 IM manager, line department, May 11, 2012
I2 IM staff, line department, June 20, 2012
I3 Senior IM/IT executive, TBS, April 17, 2013
I4 IM officer, line department, April 18, 2013
I5 IM officer, line department, April 18, 2013
I6 IM manager, line department, May 6, 2013
I7 IM/IT manager, TBS, July 18, 2013
I8 IM policy adviser, TBS, July 23, 2013
I9 IM policy adviser, central agency, April 18, 2014

Other
O1 Special adviser, Values and Ethics, line department, May 9, 2012
O2 Former senior adviser, Cabinet Office, UK government, May 23, 2012
O3 Former digital communications manager, Foreign and Commonwealth Office, UK government, May 22, 2012

O4 Senior executive, GDS, UK government, May 25, 2012

O5 Senior executive, GDS, UK government, July 8, 2012

O6 Senior digital engagement manager, Cabinet Office, UK government, July 3, 2012

O7 Senior digital communications manager, line department, UK government, August 6, 2013

O8 Citizen engagement consultant to the UK government and former Cabinet Office policy adviser, UK government, November 14, 2012

Notes

Chapter 1: Opening Government in the Digital Age

1 For example, see the UK Parliament's Education Committee Twitter feed at https://twitter.com/CommonsEd.

2 Canada does not benefit from a robust survey on national Internet use, making it difficult to draw conclusions about Canadians' access to and use of digital technologies. The Canadian Internet Use Survey (last conducted in 2012 and previously conducted biannually) offers no question on social media use. The General Social Survey (GSS) focused on information and communications technologies in its 2000 iteration, but this theme was retired after that survey was completed (particularly odd given that, from 2000 on, the impact of digital technologies on society only increased). The GSS does retain questions on cyber-bullying and Internet victimization as well as questions on online charitable giving and how Canadians use the Internet to participate in groups. Differently, the United Kingdom benefits from robust biannual surveys of Internet use, as conducted by the Oxford Internet Institute through the Oxford Internet Survey (see http://oxis.oii.ox.ac.uk/). The Pew Center offers similarly high-quality data tracking digital technologies and Internet use in the United States (see http://www.pewinternet.org/). These kinds of data are sorely needed in Canada, although recent survey-based research led by Ryerson University's Social Media Lab, as cited in Chapter 1, are helping to fill this data gap.

3 These statistics indicate that respondents have an account on the platform but do not reveal how frequently the respondents access the accounts.

4 Web 1.0 refers to the first generation of web technologies, which facilitated a one-way flow of information from website creator to website consumer. Temporally, it is associated with the web as it existed prior to the 2001 dot-com bubble burst, though many Web 1.0 applications endure and are produced today. Web 2.0 refers to the second generation of web technologies, which support interactivity and user modification, including social media, and frame the Internet as a platform; websites and services are perpetually "beta" (i.e., always adapting based upon user feedback and experience), rely on "long tail" economics that support a large number of niche audiences/products online, and facilitate crowdsourced production since many small contributions are aggregated at low cost (Anderson 2004; O'Reilly 2005).

5　Policy regimes consist of enduring "paradigms" or worldviews alongside entrenched problem-solving approaches, or "policy styles," that set bounds on the courses of action that a given government is able and willing to pursue (Hall 1993; Howlett and Ramesh 2003; Streeck 1995).

6　Unlike in other journals, in which authors cited Facebook pages in their reference lists, producing false hits not included in the count, "Facebook" did not even produce such false hits in the case of the *Journal of European Social Policy* – the term is not evident anywhere in the text of the journal.

7　See Chancellor of the Duchy of Lancaster (2007); Government 2.0 Taskforce (2009); and Orszag (2009) for three examples.

8　See United Nations (n.d.); Organization for Economic Co-operation and Development (2017).

9　China is criticized for suppressing political opposition, restricting civil liberties, and censoring Internet access and media, yet it has also been praised for its innovative uptake of digital government services (Rubinstein 2012). Singapore is ranked as "partly free" in Freedom House's 2015 "Freedom in the World" report and criticized for suppressing opposition online and limiting the scope for citizen engagement in government. At the same time, Singapore is regularly cited as a digital government leader, ranking fourth in the 2016 UN E-Government Survey, for example (United Nations and Department of Economic and Social Affairs 2016).

10　Donald Savoie is particularly critical of the impact that transparency standards facilitated by digital technologies have on government today, looping this criticism into his analysis of the decline of the traditional bargain and the golden age of the federal public service. Savoie writes that, "in the era of permanent election campaigns, access to information and the new media, the avoidance of sin is even more important than in past years" (2013, 225). In an earlier book, he observes that "television and its tendency to offer a ten- or thirty-second clip on the evening news to sum up major policy issues, or, more often, to report on something gone awry in government, have changed government operations. The media have become far more aggressive and less deferential to political power" (2003, 65).

11　Note that, in discussing the "equitable treatment of citizens," I refer to equal access to state resources and nondiscriminatory provision of public services. I do not mean that policies and services should be universal or "one size fits all." Rather, as has been noted by Clarke and Craft (2017) and Dunleavy and Margetts (2015), digital technologies make possible the unprecedented customization of policy interventions and service designs based upon individual citizen/user need. In this case, the equitable treatment of citizens might best be secured through diverse policy and service offerings tailored to individuals.

12　For the blogs, see *Canadian Public Sector Renewal* (http://www.cpsrenewal.ca/), *An Inconvenient Renewal* (https://sites.google.com/site/aninconvenientrenewal/), and *The Public Servant* (http://thepublicservant.ca/).

13　For example, in one case, I shared a timeline that I created tracking the various digital initiatives that the federal government undertook from the mid-2000s on. I uploaded this timeline to a wiki so that others – many of whom had directly worked on the initiatives and were better acquainted with their specific timing – could add to the document and correct or debate its information. In another instance, I used Twitter and the hashtag "#goc" to ask public servants to share a video of Prime Minister Trudeau speaking to public servants at the Canada School of Public Service. A public servant was able to release a publicly accessible link via Twitter within hours.

14 GCpedia is the Government of Canada's internal wiki, available only to officials within the Government of Canada firewall.

15 In the Appendix, I list the date on which the first interview with a given official took place. Follow-up interviews were conducted in many cases, and they continued until August 2016.

16 I developed an initial seed list of potential interviewees, drawing on names generated through Internet searches, informal contact with government employees, and references to individuals in documents reviewed (e.g., authors of reports, managers of particular initiatives, etc.). The Government Electronic Directory Service, Twitter, and LinkedIn were useful tools in identifying potential interviewees. In particular, public social media platforms provided novel insights into interviewees' professional networks within government (evident in the "connections" and "followers" attached to a given interviewee's account) and previous employment history. This information was helpful in preparing interview questions and interpreting interviewees' responses, and it was a useful means of identifying other interviewees through a given interviewee's online network. More conventionally, I followed a similar snowballing technique by asking interviewees to recommend the names of other individuals whom I should approach for the study.

17 For earlier empirical accounts of the first phase of Canada's digital government experience, see Borins et al. (2007); Dutil, Howard, and Langford (2010); and Roy (2006).

Chapter 2: Canada's Closed Government

1 On life in this "small village," Savoie (2003, 67) writes that "policy making was also a straightforward affair. The deputy minister was the key player, and anything of consequence was brought quickly to his office. The village was sufficiently small that there was no need for an elaborate consultative process to assess options. The relevant deputy minister might simply have lunch with a handful of interested individuals in other departments to explain or sort out a game plan."

2 The survey was completed between August 25 and October 3, 2014, and 182,165 employees across ninety-three federal departments and agencies responded to it. The response rate was 71.4 percent.

3 These figures and related analyses were adapted from content included in a previous draft of the Mowat Centre's 2016 report *Creating a High-Performing Canadian Civil Service against a Backdrop of Disruptive Change*, authored by Mark Jarvis, for which I served as a member of the advisory panel.

4 This distinction draws on the policy design literature, in which P.J. May (2003) distinguishes between designing policy at the formulation stage (verb) and the output of that process at the implementation stage (noun).

5 For the lecture series, see http://www.international.gc.ca/odskelton/index.aspx?lang=
    eng.
6 This section draws heavily from a comprehensive review of citizen engagement in
    the federal government conducted by Alison Van Rooy (2012) of the Canada School
    of Public Service, to whom I owe gratitude for sharing the review in support of this
    study.
7 The relevant judicial decisions laying out the duty to consult are *Haida Nation v.
    British Columbia (Minister of Forests)*, 2004 SCC 73, [2004] 3 S.C.R. 511; *Taku River
    Tlingit First Nation v. British Columbia (Project Assessment Director)*, 2004 SCC 74,
    [2004] 3 S.C.R. 550; *Mikisew Cree First Nation v. Canada (Minister of Canadian Heri-
    tage)*, 2005 SCC 69, [2005] 3 S.C.R. 388; *Rio Tinto Alcan Inc. v. Carrier Sekani Tribal
    Council*, 2010 SCC 43, [2010] 2 S.C.R. 650; *Beckman v. Little Salmon/Carmacks First
    Nation*, 2010 SCC 53, [2010] 3 S.C.R. 103.
8 See *Canada (Attorney General) v. Jodhan*, 2012 FCA 161.

Chapter 3: #Fail
1 Over the period examined in this study, the names of certain federal departments
    changed. I use the name of the department as it was known at the time of data col-
    lection or, when referring to a specific event, the name of the department when that
    event took place.
2 For examples of this more sophisticated form of social media monitoring as applied
    to the public sector specifically, see Bright et al. (2014).
3 I identified accounts using systematic Google searches (e.g., department name and
    "Twitter"), by scanning the "contact us" sections of departmental websites, and by
    referencing Twitter lists that other users had created of official Government of Can-
    ada Twitter accounts. I am grateful to Scott Hale of the Oxford Internet Institute, who
    wrote and executed the script that generated the Twitter archive. More information
    on the method by which the Twitter data was scraped, handled, and analyzed can be
    provided on request.
4 Before generating a sample and subjecting it to content analysis, I removed tweets
    originating from certain Government of Canada Twitter accounts, such as tweets
    from crown corporations. These institutions operate at arm's length from the govern-
    ment and are not always subject to the same bureaucratic dynamics as departments
    and agencies. Similarly, I excluded Twitter accounts administered by the Office of
    the Governor General, the Royal Canadian Mounted Police, and the Armed Forces,
    for these institutions also operate independently or quasi-independently and face
    different constraints than departments and agencies. In addition, I omitted tweets
    originating from the Canada Border Service Agency's Canada-US border wait time
    account. The account automatically updates as the latest information on border wait
    times becomes available and produces high numbers of tweets as a result. By includ-
    ing these tweets in the content analysis, I would run the risk of misrepresenting
    trends in government Twitter use across all departments, since these tweets would
    dominate the sample analyzed. Finally, to avoid duplication in the archive, I removed
    all French accounts, leaving only English and bilingual accounts. In accordance with

the *Policy on the Use of Official Languages for Communications with and Services to the Public* (Treasury Board Secretariat 2006b), English and French accounts mirror each other, the only exception being that information resulting from nonsubstantive interactions on one language's account are not always reproduced on the other (C1). Cross-referencing between accounts suggested that the risk of excluding French accounts in terms of omitting relevant data was low and far outweighed by the benefits of avoiding duplication in the population set.

5 The sample of 909 tweets gives a confidence level of 95 percent, ± 3 percent.

6 I hired three graduate student coders from Carleton University's Master of Arts in Public Administration program after distributing a job call through the School of Public Policy and Administration. I received over twenty applications. Using a training data set, I trained each coder in the use of the codebook using a sample of tweets and then gave the coders the same 10 percent random sample of tweets ($n = 91$) from the set of 909 tweets analyzed for the study. The coders then analyzed this set of tweets independently. Intercoder reliability was checked using ReCal3, a program that tests reliability across three or more coders (see http://dfreelon.org/utils/recal-front/recal3/). For this study, the most appropriate measure of reliability is Fleiss's kappa (κ), which ranges between 1 and −1 and can be used to measure intercoder reliability when multiple individuals code nominal data. A statistic between 0.60 and 0.74 signals intermediate to good agreement, any number below 0.40 indicates poor agreement, and any number 0.75 and over indicates excellent agreement (Fleiss, Levin, and Paik 2003).

7 To protect the identities of Twitter users whose usernames are included in the data set, I use @username as an anonymized user handle. I employed a combination of deductive and inductive methods to prepare the codebook used to categorize the content of tweets. Beginning deductively and drawing on an existing preoccupation with the distinction between informational digital government services and participatory digital government initiatives (see Allen et al. 2001; Brainard and McNutt 2010; and Layne and Lee 2001), I developed two initial broad categories for the codebook: informational tweets and participatory tweets. Moving from deductive to inductive category generation, I hand-coded a random sample of 100 tweets into these two broad categories, and I derived further subcategories as they emerged in the data. In line with the constant comparative method of content analysis (Glaser and Strauss 1967), I assessed all tweets in light of existing codes, deleting, merging, and creating new categories to reflect both the theoretical concerns of the research and the data under examination (Patton 2002). This process revealed a third type of message – amicable ties – that did not fit comfortably into either the informational or the participatory category initially set for the study.

8 This study's results are corroborated by another study of the Government of Canada's use of Twitter (Small 2012), which, using content analysis of a set of federal government tweets from 2011, also found that the majority of these tweets were informational versus soliciting citizen participation/engagement. The Twitter analysis presented in this book is innovative in its consideration of the types of messages published by the government (e.g., retweets versus original tweets) and in its

accounting of the weblinks and users referenced in government tweets, using these variables to measure the extent to which the government uses Twitter to engage with the network in more interactive ways than simply publishing "one-way" informational tweets.

9   For this variable (content categorization – informational, participatory, or amicable ties), the average pairwise agreement across the four coders was 87.4 percent, with a range of 78.0 percent to 93.4 percent. Fleiss's kappa averaged 0.63, signalling intermediate to good agreement but not excellent agreement (defined as ≥ 0.75). This reflects the subjective interpretations at play in determining whether a message is purely informational, engages users to participate in policy development or service delivery, or merely employs friendly and informal language. Still, a κ of 0.63 across four coders is sufficiently high to assume that the results are replicable and not the product of chance. We can thus interpret the conclusions with confidence. The original codebook also included a series of subcategories into which each tweet's content could be placed. These subcategories added more nuance to the three high-level categories presented in the analysis (e.g., breaking down informational tweets by the type of information that they share). When the reliability of these classifications was evaluated using Fleiss's kappa, the statistics did not fall into a satisfactory range, suggesting that my application of the codes was not robust, that the codebook detailing these various subcategories was weak, and/or that the three student coders did not sufficiently understand or accurately apply the codebook in the case of these subcategories. Given the low intercoder reliability scores for these variables, I did not include these results in the analysis.

10 The script used to archive the Twitter data set did not include metadata describing the category into which each tweet fell: that is, whether it was a tweet directed to another user via the mention convention (e.g., Hey @username) or via the native retweet button (i.e., the retweet function introduced by Twitter in 2009). I identified retweets by the presence of the letters "RT" or "VIA" (an alternative convention for retweeting) in the tweets, as manually added by the user. I identified @username mentions by an @username in the tweet (but without an "RT" or "VIA", and I identified tweets coded as "original tweets" by their lack of @ username or "RT/VIA": that is, without any direct effort to connect the tweet to other Twitter users.

11 The number of Twitter users was calculated using the average number of monthly active Twitter users over the first two quarters of 2012, the time period during which the data were collected from Twitter, as reported by Statista (2016a).

12 For this variable – the type of user referenced in federal government tweets – the average pairwise agreement was 80 percent, with a range of 76.9 percent to 90.1 percent. The Fleiss's kappa across the four coders was 0.70, suggesting near-excellent agreement among the coders and that the results are replicable and can be interpreted with high confidence.

13 Another means of evaluating the extent to which a Twitter user attempts to network with other users is to explore hashtags included in a user's tweets. For this study, I did not explore the hashtags that the Government of Canada included in

its tweets. This represents an interesting avenue for future research. Perhaps a more interactive, networked form of engagement with the Twitter platform is evident in the hashtags that departments use to link their tweets to larger conversations taking place on Twitter.

14 For this variable – the type of weblink included in Government of Canada tweets – the coders had to visit the website by accessing the link included in the tweet. When the site was no longer available, coders made a judgment based upon the URL in order to classify the site. The average pairwise agreement was 85.2 percent, with a range of 82.4 percent to 89.0 percent. The Fleiss's kappa across the four coders was 0.75, suggesting excellent agreement among the coders and that the results can be interpreted with high confidence.

15 Although the specific wording varied, I framed this question as follows: "Some argue that moves toward open government, and using tools like social media to engage the public, are paradoxical, or a non-starter, given the current government's reputation for information control. Do you have any thoughts on that perspective?" Acknowledging the risk that such a question could make interviewees uncomfortable, given that it could be perceived as asking for a partisan opinion or as a criticism of the government, I saved this question until the end of the interview (except when the interviewee raised Harper's leadership style in the course of the interview).

16 See *Canadian Public Sector Renewal* http://www.cpsrenewal.ca/.

17 Several lists have been compiled of federal public servants' accounts on Twitter. See GC2.0, which covers 432 public service employees' Twitter accounts (https://twitter.com/RyanAndrosoff/lists/gc2-0) and Government-Canada, which covers 552 public service employees' Twitter accounts (https://twitter.com/Lissansky/lists/government-canada).

18 See https://twitter.com/AndrewTreusch?

Chapter 4: Stephen Harper's Open(ish) Government Initiative

1 See https://www.opengovpartnership.org/.

2 See https://open.canada.ca/en/open-government-licence-canada.

3 The Auditor General provided further evidence of insufficient information management practices in the federal government in a 2016 report, uncovering persistent data entry errors and incomplete updates of the database used by Citizenship and Immigration Canada in processing applications for citizenship and immigration. See Office of the Auditor General of Canada (2016b).

4 Canada's OD150 project is part of the OD500 Global Network led by the GovLab, which also tracks how businesses use open data in Australia, Mexico, the United States, Italy, and Korea. Also see Davies (2010, 3) for a survey-based study of open data use in the United Kingdom, which found that "users of OGD [open government data] were overwhelmingly male (6-to-1 in survey results), and generally split between micro-enterprise and SME [small and medium-sized enterprise] business in the private sector, local and national public sector institutions, and academic institutions, with a very limited representation of voluntary sector workers."

5 For example, see http://landscape.ajah.ca/, which maps the locations of organizations receiving grants and contributions using government data sets.

6 See https://github.com/wet-boew/wet-boew.

7 See https://niagaraopendata.ca/showcase/niagara-minecraft-project.

8 See https://prophesy.herokuapp.com/#!/about.

9 "Authorized individuals" are defined in the policy as "individuals working with the Government of Canada, including employees of the federal government as well as casuals, contractors, students and other persons who have been authorized by the deputy head to access Government of Canada electronic networks and devices" (Treasury Board Secretariat 2013b).

10 Personal communication, Ottawa, June 2016.

11 See GC Infobase at http://www.tbs-sct.gc.ca/ems-sgd/edb-bdd/index-eng.html#start.

12 In its 2016 budget, the Liberal government claimed to double the existing open government budget to $11.5 million over five years (Government of Canada 2016a, 209). The $1 million annual budget estimate is based upon that claim.

13 The other founding OGP member countries are Brazil, Indonesia, Mexico, Norway, the Philippines, and South Africa.

14 The original job call for the director of digital engagement stated that "[digital engagement] would require Government and individual departments to change the way they do business – from consulting citizens to collaborating with them on the development of policy and how public services are delivered to them. It will involve supporting Ministers and senior officials in entering conversations in which Government does not control the message or the dialogue" (Civil Service Recruitment Gateway 2009, 2).

15 The federal public servant who had worked on the Twitter townhall offered this reflection during an Open Government Partnership Meet Up hosted by the former Department of Foreign Affairs and International Trade on April 17, 2012, in Ottawa.

Chapter 5: Internal Openings in the Federal Bureaucracy

1 A wiki (taken from the Hawaiian word for "quick") is a website that allows users to collaboratively edit the content and structure of a website directly from a web browser ("Wiki" 2016).

2 A third tool, GCForums, provided an online space for discussion forums and was retired in early 2015, with its content migrated to GCconnex.

3 For other examples of government wikis, see the US Department of State's Diplopedia (https://www.state.gov/m/irm/ediplomacy/115847.htm) and the Government of Ontario's OPSPedia (which, like GCpedia, is government wide versus department specific).

4 There was no reference to these tools in the 2012 annual report (by Clerk Wouters). The number of users was calculated using the population of the federal public service for 2015 (257,034; see https://www.canada.ca/en/treasury-board-secretariat/services/innovation/human-resources-statistics/population-federal-public-service.html) and the GCpedia user count on Wikipedia, regularly updated by the GCTools managers

(see https://en.wikipedia.org/wiki/GCpedia#Overview_of_Usage_Levels_from_August_31.2C_2015).

5 January 2–May 6, 2015, archived using Netlytic, https://netlytic.org.

6 Gamification refers to the use of game dynamics, such as points, scoring, and competition with others, to encourage certain behaviours and activities among individuals and groups.

7 Mark Jarvis (2014b), in a study of accountability practices in Australia, Canada, and the Netherlands, also uncovers the importance of the personal characteristics of individual managers.

Chapter 6: The Digital Skills Gap in the Federal Bureaucracy

1 See Borra and Rieder (2014); Hu, Farnham, and Talamadupula (2015); Lewis, Zamith, and Hermida (2013); Scharkow (2013); Shahin (2016); Veltri and Atanasova (2015); and Vraga et al. (2016).

2 Examples of such tools include Netlytic (https://netlytic.org/), NodeXL (https://archive.codeplex.com/?p=nodexl), Gephi (https://gephi.org/), and Google Analytics (which, unlike the others listed here, is not open source).

3 Including on occasion current TBS President Scott Brison; see May (2016a).

4 For an example of how millennials are framed as digital experts, see this 2016 IBM report, which states: "As digital natives, Millennials offer the skills and perspectives that can help re-imagine government for the digital era" (IBM 2016).

5 See http://www.governmentontheweb.org/; and Bright et al. (2014).

6 Personal communication with the author, December 2014.

7 Personal communication with the author, March 2014.

8 In a 2015 blog post, the former executive director of the UK Government Digital Service, Mike Bracken (2015a), wrote that "Government as a Platform is a phrase coined by Tim O'Reilly in a 2010 paper, although there are differences between the environment he describes and the one we face in the UK." The blog post then proceeds to discuss state-managed initiatives that support whole of government, horizontal services and data sharing (e.g., the gov.uk website and a platform called Gov.uk Verify that verifies service users' identities).

9 A report from Canada's Big Data Consortium (2015) found that "Canada's Big Data Talent Gap is estimated between 10,500 and 19,000 professionals with deep data and analytical skills, such as those required for roles like Chief Data Officer, Data Scientist, and Data Solutions Architect. The gap for professionals with solid data and analytical literacy to make better decisions is estimated at a further 150,000, such as those required for roles like Business Manager and Business Analyst."

10 In 2016, Canada's Information and Communications Technology Council noted that "the growth in digital jobs has outpaced the overall economy in the last two years by over 4 to 1, leading to a strong demand of 182,000 skilled ICT workers by 2019. Unfortunately, the domestic supply of ICT graduates and workers will be insufficient to meet this demand."

11 *Maclean's* top ten Canadian computer science schools in 2015 were (10) University of Calgary, (9) Queen's University, (8) University of Victoria, (7) Université de Montreal,

(6) McGill University, (5) Simon Fraser University, (4) University of Alberta, (tied for 2nd) University of Waterloo and University of British Columbia, and (1) University of Toronto.

12 See https://codeforall.org/.

13 The USDS created the Federal Acquisition Training Program to guide procurement; see https://medium.com/the-u-s-digital-service/congratulating-our-challenge-gov-winners-f6ec5deefbd6. In Australia, the DTO created a Digital Marketplace to support procurement. In the United Kingdom, GDS created a Digital Buyers Guide, a spending control policy, and a Technology Code of Practice. Similarly, 18F offers a request for proposal ghostwriting service, a blanket Agile Purchase Agreement, and a micropurchase platform to help departments buy small pieces of open-source code versus large contracted solutions. In these cases, DGUS helps to tackle the digital skills gap in the government by creating replicable standards and templates to guide technology decisions across departments that lack the in-house expertise to work intelligently with outside providers.

14 GDS breaks down this claim of £1.7 billion in savings in a 2015 blog post (see Foreshew-Cain 2015). In 2013, GDS received the Design of the Year Award from the UK Design Museum (see Terrett 2013).

15 See https://medium.com/ontariodigital/finding-new-digital-talent-ec601c4df682#.yvt83a2zd.

Chapter 7: The Future of Digital Government

1 Supporting this argument, though Dunleavy et al.'s influential 2006 text *Digital Era Governance: IT Corporations, the State, and E-Governance* initially framed its argument by contrasting DEG with NPM, the latest iteration of the DEG theory (described by Dunleavy and Margetts in 2015) is far more preoccupied with the enduring role of Weberian bureaucracy and Progressive-Era Public Administration in today's governments.

2 This finding is shared in *Smarter Citizens, Smarter State: The Technologies of Expertise and the Future of Governing*, in which, focused on the US context, Noveck observes that, even when operating under the leadership of Barack Obama, who enthusiastically supported digital government innovation and open government in the United States, the political climate remained a constraint during her years as deputy chief technology officer: "In the midst of two wars, facing widespread dissatisfaction at home about Wall Street malfeasance, congressional bailouts, partisan backbiting, and an economy in seeming free fall, there was little appetite for more radical institutional innovation. There was virtually none for admitting that government did not have all the answers" (2015, xiv).

3 The number of active monthly Facebook users globally in 2008 (Statista 2016b).

4 To cut some slack to Statistics Canada, with the elimination of the mandatory long-form census and grappling with deep budget cuts – amounting to a reduction of almost $30 million and 18 percent of its staff (Globe and Mail 2014) – the agency hardly had the leadership and concomitant investment that would allow it to keep pace with new trends in data collection and analysis.

5 Surveys that ask Canadians to rate their level of trust in the government often do not capture their perceptions of the public service specifically, but rather the government generally, with respondents grouping the public service together with Parliament and elected officials. Given this, it is possible that reported levels of trust in government would be different were respondents asked to comment on their trust in public servants and government departments specifically.

6 The policy change provides a shorter and simpler delegation instrument to deputy heads, reducing the policies involved in recruitment from twelve to one. The change also reduces reporting requirements, specifically eliminating the departmental staffing accountability report to allow human resources procedures to "focus less on rules and more on outcomes" (Public Service Commission of Canada 2016).

7 "The Power of Information Review" prepared by Ed Mayo and Tom Steinberg (of mySociety) for the UK government, provides a compelling argument in favour of public servants and politicians engaging with citizens in unconventional citizen-managed online spaces, such as parenting forums (e.g., MumsNet in the United Kingdom) and patient support sites (Chancellor of the Duchy of Lancaster 2007; Mayo and Steinberg 2007).

8 The 2011 Guideline for External Use of Web 2.0 and its subsequent update specify that individual public servants are permitted to use social media for professional networking and to discuss their work (Treasury Board Secretariat 2011c, 2013a).

9 See Qasem (2016), a blog post from GDS in which a public servant reflects on her work as a product manager there. The post concludes with "Follow Fajer on Twitter [hyperlinked to her Twitter account] and don't forget to sign up for email alerts."

10 See http://www.behaviouralinsights.co.uk/blog/; and http://mind-lab.dk/en/.

11 See https://open.canada.ca/en/blog.

12 See https://www.ewb.ca/en/about-us/governance/annual-report/.

13 For solutions to the challenges facing journalism in Canada, see Public Policy Forum (2017).

14 The relevant court decisions are *Fraser v. P.S.S.R.B.*, [1985] 2 S.C.R. 455; *Haydon v. Canada*, [2001] 2 F.C. 82; *Osborne v. Canada (Treasury Board)*, [1991] 2 S.C.R. 69; and *Haydon v. Canada (Treasury Board)*, 2004 F.C. 749, aff'd 2005 FCA 249, application for leave to appeal to the Supreme Court of Canada denied on January 19, 2006, [2005] S.C.C.A. No

References

6, Perri. 2007. "Don't Try This at Home: Lessons from England." In *Digital State at the Leading Edge*, 325–54. Institute of Public Administration of Canada Series in Public Management and Governance. Toronto: University of Toronto Press.

18F. 2016a. "Building Better by Building with the Federal Election Commission." https://18f.gsa.gov/2016/06/07/building-better-by-building-together-with-the-federal-election-commission/.

–. 2016b. "What We Deliver." https://github.com/18F/beta.18f.gov/blob/master/pages/what-we-deliver.md.

Abdulla, Zeena. 2016a. "Hey, Do You Want to Work Here ... " *LinkedIn Pulse*, June 1. http://www.linkedin.com/.

–. 2016b. "Only 2 Days Left, Apply to Join the Rogue Squadron." *LinkedIn Pulse*, June 8. https://twitter.com/hizeena/status/740616587150020608.

Aberbach, Joel D., and Tom Christensen. 2005. "Citizens and Consumers: An NPM Dilemma." *Public Management Review* 7 (2): 225–46.

Accenture. 2005. "Leadership in Customer Service: New Expectations, New Experiences." http://www.umic.pt/images/stories/publicacoes/leadership_cust.pdf.

Aitken, Kent. 2015. "Why Government Social Media Isn't Social." *Canadian Public Sector Renewal* (blog), December 16. http://www.cpsrenewal.ca/2015/12/why-government-social-media-isnt-social.html.

–. 2017. "Public Service Anonymity Is Dead, Long Live Public Service Anonymity." *Canadian Public Sector Renewal* (blog), March 1. http://www.cpsrenewal.ca/2017/03/public-service-anonymity-is-dead-long.html.

Alexa. 2018. "wikipedia.org Traffic Statistics." https://www.alexa.com/siteinfo/wikipedia.org.

Alford, John, and Janine O'Flynn. 2012. *Rethinking Public Service Delivery: Managing with External Providers*. Houndmills, UK: Palgrave Macmillan.

Allen, B.A., L. Juillet, G. Paquet, and J. Roy. 2001. "E-Governance and Government On-Line in Canada: Partnerships, People, and Prospects." *Government Information Quarterly* 18 (2): 93–104.

Althaus, Catherine, and Thea Vakil. 2013. "Political Transitions: Opportunities to Renegotiate the Public Service Bargain." *Canadian Public Administration* 56 (3): 478–90.

Anderson, Chris. 2004. "The Long Tail." *Wired*, October 1. https://www.wired.com/2004/10/tail/.

Androsoff, Ryan. 2014. "The Seduction of the Startup." May 24. http://ryanandrosoff.ca/?p=83.

–. 2016. "Digital Government Today: International Perspective and Lessons for the Future." Johnson Shoyama Graduate School of Public Policy, University of Regina, March 16. https://www.slideshare.net/randrosoff/digital-government-today-international-perspective-and-lessons-for-the-future.

Anonymous Government of Canada official. 2012. "List of GOC Social Media Accounts." Email to the author, February 12.

–. 2014. "Quoting You in My Thesis." Email to the author, August 31.

–. 2016. Queen's University Policy Forum 2016: Open Government. April 29.

Arnstein, Sherry R. 1969. "A Ladder of Citizen Participation." *Journal of the American Institute of Planners* 35 (4): 216–24.

Aslam, Salman. 2018. "Twitter by the Numbers: Stats, Demographics and Fun Facts." *Omnicore.* https://www.omnicoreagency.com/twitter-statistics/.

Aucoin, Peter. 1990. "Administrative Reform in Public Management: Paradigms, Principles, Paradoxes, and Pendulums." *Governance: An International Journal of Policy, Administration, and Institutions* 3 (2): 115–37.

–. 2006. "Improving Government Accountability." *Canadian Parliamentary Review* 29 (3): 21-26.

–. 2012. "New Political Governance in Westminster Systems: Impartial Public Administration and Management Performance at Risk." *Governance: An International Journal of Policy, Administration. and Institutions* 25 (2): 177–99.

Aucoin, Peter, and Herman Bakvis. 2005. "Public Service Reform and Policy Capacity: Recruiting and Retaining the Best and the Brightest." In *Challenges to State Policy Capacity: Global Trends and Comparative Perspectives,* edited by Martin Painter and Jon Pierre, 185–204. London: Palgrave Macmillan.

Aucoin, Peter, and Mark D. Jarvis. 2005. *Modernizing Government Accountability: A Framework for Reform.* Ottawa: Canada School of Public Service.

Aucoin, Peter, Lori B. Turnbull, and Mark D. Jarvis. 2011. *Democratizing the Constitution: Reforming Responsible Government.* EMP Political Perspectives Series. Toronto: Emond Montgomery Publications.

Auditor General of Canada, Office of the Auditor General of Canada. 2018. "Message from the Auditor General of Canada." May 29, 2018. http://www.oag-bvg.gc.ca/internet/English/parl_oag_201805_00_e_43032.html.

Axworthy, Thomas S., and Julie Burch. 2010. "Closing the Implementation Gap: Improving Capacity, Accountability, Performance, and Human Resource Quality in the Canadian and Ontario Public Service." Queen's University. http://www.queensu.ca/csd/sites/webpublish.queensu.ca.csdwww/files/files/publications/wps/Closing_Gap_Main.pdf.

Bakvis, Herman. 2000. "Rebuilding Policy Capacity in the Era of the Fiscal Dividend: A Report from Canada." *Governance: An International Journal of Policy, Administration, and Institutions* 13 (1): 71–103.

Bakvis, Herman, and Luc Juillet. 2004. "The Horizontal Challenge: Line Departments, Central Agencies, and Leadership." Canada School of Public Service. http://publications.gc.ca/pub?id=9.686919&sl=0.

Balter, Ben. 2015. "The Difference between 18F and USDS." *Ben Balter* (blog), April 22. https://ben.balter.com/2015/04/22/the-difference-between-18F-and-usds/.

Barber, Michael. 2008. *Instruction to Deliver: Fighting to Transform Britain's Public Services.* Rev. paperback ed. London: Methuen.

–. 2016. *How to Run a Government: So that Citizens Benefit and Taxpayers Don't Go Crazy.* London: N.p.: Penguin Books.

Barnes, Marian, Janet Newman, and Helen Sullivan. 2007. *Power, Participation, and Political Renewal: Case Studies in Political Participation.* Bristol: Policy Press.

Bason, Christian. 2010. *Leading Public Sector Innovation: Co-Creating for a Better Society.* Bristol: Policy Press.

Bates, Jo. 2012. "'This Is What Modern Deregulation Looks Like': Co-Optation and Contestation in the Shaping of the UK's Open Government Data Initiative." *Journal of Community Informatics* 8 (2).

Bellafontaine, Teresa. 2013. "Innovation Labs: Bridging Think Tanks and Do Tanks." Ottawa: Policy Horizons Canada. http://www.horizons.gc.ca/en/content/innovation-labs-bridging-think-tanks-and-do-tanks.

Benay, Alex. 2017. "What Is Digital Citizenship for Government?" *LinkedIn Pulse,* March 9. http://www.linkedin.com/.

Benkler, Yochai. 2006. *The Wealth of Networks: How Social Production Transforms Markets and Freedom.* New Haven, CT: Yale University Press.

Biddle, Sam. 2014. "Smiling Young White People Make App for Avoiding Black Neighborhoods." *Gawker.* http://valleywag.gawker.com/smiling-young-white-people-make-app-for-avoiding-black-1617775138.

Bixler, R. Patrick. 2014. "It's Not Just Who You Know, but Can You Tell a Story? The Role of Narratives in Network Governance." *Public Administration Review* 74 (2): 277–80.

Blanchfield, Mike, and Jim Bronskill. 2010. "Documents Expose Harper's Obsession with Control." *Toronto Star,* June 6. https://www.thestar.com/news/canada/2010/06/06/documents_expose_harpers_obsession_with_control.html.

Blevis, Mark. 2016. "Canadians Geeked Out on the 2016 Census." *Full Duplex Digital Public Affairs,* May 11. https://digitalpublicaffairs.com/canadians-geeked-2016-census/.

Bonokoski, Mark. 2016. "A Love-In, Bureaucracy Bias, and a Pink Slip." *Toronto Sun,* January 30. http://torontosun.com/2016/01/30/a-love-in-bureaucracy-bias-and-a-pink-slip?utm_source=facebook&utm_medium=recommend-button&utm_campaign=a.

Borins, Sandford F. 2002. "Leadership and Innovation in the Public Sector." *Leadership and Organization Development Journal* 23 (8): 467–76.

Borins, Sandford, Kenneth Kernaghan, David Brown, Nick Bontis, Perri 6, and Fred Thompson. 2007. *Digital State at the Leading Edge.* Institute of Public Administration of Canada Series in Public Management and Governance. Toronto: University of Toronto Press.

Borra, Erik, and Bernhard Rieder. 2014. "Programmed Method: Developing a Toolset for Capturing and Analyzing Tweets." *Aslib Journal of Information Management* 66 (3): 262–78.

Botsman, Rachel, and Roo Rogers. 2010. *What's Mine Is Yours: The Rise of Collaborative Consumption.* New York: Harper Business.

boyd, danah, and Kate Crawford. 2012. "Critical Questions for Big Data: Provocations for a Cultural, Technological, and Scholarly Phenomenon." *Information Communication and Society* 15 (5): 662–79.

boyd, d., S. Golder, and G. Lotan. 2010. "Tweet, Tweet, Retweet: Conversational Aspects of Retweeting on Twitter." *IEEE Xplore Digital Library.*

Bracken, Mike. 2012. "Why GOV.UK Matters: A Platform for a Digital Government." *Government Digital Service* (blog), October 17. https://gds.blog.gov.uk/2012/10/17/why-gov-uk-matters/.

–. 2013. "On Strategy: The Strategy Is Delivery. Again." *Digital Transformation* (blog), January 6. http://mikebracken.com/blog/the-strategy-is-delivery-again/#.UUQUApaf_Ag.twitter.

–. 2015a. "Government as a Platform: The Next Phase of Digital Transformation." *Government Digital Service* (blog), March 29. https://gds.blog.gov.uk/2015/03/29/government-as-a-platform-the-next-phase-of-digital-transformation/.

–. 2015b. "It's Not about Us, It's about Collaboration." *Government Digital Service* (blog), September 10. https://gds.blog.gov.uk/2015/09/10/its-not-about-us-its-about-collaboration/.

Bracken, Mike and Lord Francis Maude. 2016. "Keynote Address." Institute on Governance's Third Annual Digital Governance Forum, May 30, Ottawa.

Brainard, Lori A., and John G. McNutt. 2010. "Virtual Government-Citizen Relations: Informational, Transactional, or Collaborative?" *Administration and Society* 42 (7): 836–58.

Brandsen, Taco, and Victor Pestoff. 2006. "Co-Production, the Third Sector, and the Delivery of Public Services." *Public Management Review* 8 (4): 493–501.

Braybrook, Jeff. 2009. "Web 2.0 Will Change the Way You Work." http://www.nrc-cnrc.gc.ca/eng/resources/fptt_events/2009/national/doc/braybrook.ppt.

Bright, Jonathan, Scott Hale, Helen Margetts, and Taha Yasseri. 2014. "The Use of Social Media for Research and Analysis: A Feasibility Study." Department for Work and Pensions. https://assets.publishing.service.gov.uk/government/uploads/system/uploads/attachment_data/file/387591/use-of-social-media-for-research-and-analysis.pdf.

Brock, Kathy. 2000. "Sustaining a Relationship: Insights from Canada on Linking the Government and Third Sector." http://www.queensu.ca/sps/sites/webpublish.queensu.ca.spswww/files/files/Publications/workingpapers/01.pdf.

Bronskill, Jim. 2016. "On World Press Freedom Day, Here Are 10 Ideas for Improving Canada's Access to Information Law." *Ottawa Citizen,* May 3. http://ottawacitizen.com/opinion/columnists/on-world-press-freedom-day-here-are-10-ideas-for-improving-canadas-access-to-information-law.

Brown, David C.G. 2012. "The Administrative Dilemmas of Government Communications." Paper presented at the Annual Meeting of the Canadian Political Science Association, Edmonton, Alberta, June 13. https://www.cpsa-acsp.ca/papers-2012/Brown-DCG.pdf.

–. 2013. "Accountability in a Collectivized Environment: From Glassco to Digital Public Administration." *Canadian Public Administration* 56 (1): 47–69.

Campbell, Ailish. 2014. "Lessons from Cross-Sector Experience." *Public Sector Digest.* Fall: 7–12.

Canada. Parliament. 2018. House of Commons Standing Committee on Public Accounts. *Minutes of Proceedings.* 1st sess., 42nd Parliament, Meeting No. 104. http://www. ourcommons.ca/DocumentViewer/en/42-1/PACP/meeting-104/evidence June 1.

Canada's Big Data Consortium. 2015. "Closing Canada's Big Data Talent Gap." https:// smith.queensu.ca/ConversionDocs/MMA/big-data-gap.pdf.

Canadian Intergovernmental Conference Secretariat. 1999. "Agreement: A Framework to Improve the Social Union for Canadians." http://www.scics.ca/en/.

Canadian Press. 2014. "Government Tweets Sanitized through 'Super-Rigid Process.'" *CBC News,* February 3. http://www.cbc.ca/news/politics/government-tweets-sanitized-through-super-rigid-process-1.2520731.

–. 2016. "Liberals Ask Google to Update PM Website Search Results." *CBC News,* June 16. http://www.cbc.ca/news/politics/harper-deleted-pmo-google-1.3639065.

Cappe, Mel. 2016. "Government Scientists and the Management of Science in Government." *Policy Options,* March 8. http://policyoptions.irpp.org/magazines/march-2016/government-scientists-and-the-management-of-science-in-government/.

Carstensen, Helle Vibeke, and Christian Bason. 2012. "Powering Collaborative Policy Innovation: Can Innovation Labs Help?" *Innovation Journal* 17 (1): article 4. http:// citeseerx.ist.psu.edu/viewdoc/download;jsessionid=4EFF214AD5D9D94ECA1E7 6AED0750568?doi=10.1.1.299.6225&rep=rep1&type=pdf.

Catalyst. 2016. "Smartphone Behaviour in Canada and the Implications for Marketers in 2016." *Catalyst* (blog). http://catalyst.ca/2016-canadian-smartphone-behaviour/.

Chancellor of the Duchy of Lancaster. 2007. "The Government's Response to the Power of Information: An Independent Review by Ed Mayo and Tom Steinberg (2007)." https://www. gov.uk/government/uploads/system/uploads/attachment_data/file/243238/7157.pdf.

Charette, Janice. 2015. "Preparing Canada's Public Service to Meet the Challenge." *Policy Options,* July 6. http://policyoptions.irpp.org/magazines/clearing-the-air/charette/.

Charney, Nicholas. 2008. *Scheming Virtuously: A Handbook for Public Servants.* http:// www.cpsrenewal.ca/p/handbook-scheming-virtuously.html.

Cheadle, Bruce, and Jennifer Ditchburn. 2011. "'Harper Government' Not 'Government of Canada': Documents Reveal Working Directive, Contradict PMO." *Huffington Post,* November 29. http://www.huffingtonpost.ca/2011/11/29/industry-canada-documents-harper-government-communications_n_1118001.html.

Cheriton School of Computer Science. n.d. "Careers." https://cs.uwaterloo.ca/future-graduate-students/careers-0.

Chief Information Officer Branch. 2014. *Outside, Inside – Social Networks for the Government of Canada and Its Employees.* Ottawa: Treasury Board Secretariat of Canada.

–. 2015. "Analysis of the Blueprint 2020 Group on GCconnex." Ottawa: Treasury Board Secretariat of Canada.

–. 2016. "Government of Canada Information Technology Strategic Plan 2016–2020." http://www.tbs-sct.gc.ca/hgw-cgf/oversight-surveillance/itpm-itgp/it-ti/itsp-tips/gcitsp-tigcps-eng.asp.

–. 2017. "Government of Canada Strategic Plan for Information Management and Information Technology 2017 to 2021." https://www.canada.ca/en/treasury-board-secretariat/services/information-technology/strategic-plan-2017-2021.html#toc1.

Christiansen, Jesper. 2015. "Redesigning the Culture and Functionality of Government." *Design for Europe* (blog), May 13. http://designforeurope.eu/news-opinion/redesigning-culture-and-functionality-government.

Civil Service Recruitment Gateway. 2009. "Director of Digital Engagement." http://fm.typepad.com/files/director_of_digital_engagement.pdf.

Clarke, Amanda. 2014a. "Empirical and Theoretical Blindspots in the Study of Government-Citizen Relations on the Social Web: A Case Study of the Government of Canada." Paper presented at the Annual Meeting of the Canadian Association of Programs in Public Administration, Kingston, Ontario, May 22.

–. 2014b. "Government-Citizen Relations on the Social Web: Canada and the United Kingdom, 2006–2013" PhD diss., Oxford Internet Institute, University of Oxford.

–. 2014c. "One of These Things Is Not Like the Other: Bottom-Up Reform, Open Information, Collaboration, and ... the Harper Government." In *How Ottawa Spends, 2014–15 – The Harper Government: Good to Go?*, edited by G. Bruce Doern and Christopher Stoney, 125–38. Montreal: McGill-Queen's University Press.

–. 2016a. "The Evolution of Government as a Platform." Paper presented at the Annual Meeting of the Association for Research on Nonprofit Organizations and Voluntary Action, Washington, DC, November 16.

–. 2016b. "The Innovation Challenge: Modernizing the Public Service." *Policy Options*, May 11. http://policyoptions.irpp.org/magazines/may-2016/the-innovation-challenge-modernizing-the-public-service/.

–. 2017. "Digital Government Units: Origins, Orthodoxy, and Critical Considerations for Public Management Theory and Practice." https://papers.ssrn.com/sol3/papers.cfm?abstract_id=3001188.

Clarke, Amanda, and Jonathan Craft. 2017. "The Vestiges and Vanguards of Policy Design in a Digital Context." *Canadian Public Administration* 60 (4): 476–97.

–. 2018. "The Twin Faces of Public Sector Design." *Governance* 17 (1): online. https://onlinelibrary.wiley.com/doi/epdf/10.1111/gove.12342.

Clarke, Amanda, and Elizabeth Dubois. 2015. "Forced to Tweet in Both Languages, Ministers Lose Their Impact." *Globe and Mail*, February 19. https://www.theglobeandmail.com/opinion/forced-to-tweet-in-both-languages-ministers-lose-their-impact/article23070214/.

Clarke, Amanda, and Mary Francoli. 2014. "What's in a Name? A Comparison of 'Open Government' Definitions across Seven Open Government Partnership Members." *eJournal of eDemocracy and Open Government* 6 (3). https://jedem.org/index.php/jedem/article/view/227/289.

–. 2017. "Digital Government and Permanent Campaigning." In *Permanent Campaigning in Canada*, edited by Alex Marland, Anna Esselment, and Thierry Giasson, 241–58. Vancouver: UBC Press.

Clarke, Amanda, and Helen Margetts. 2014. "Governments and Citizens Getting to Know Each Other? Open, Closed, and Big Data in Public Management Reform." *Policy and Internet* 6 (4): 393–417.

Clarke, Amanda, and Benjamin Piper. 2018. "A Legal Framework to Govern Online Political Expression by Public Servants." *Canadian Labour and Employment Law* 21 (1): 1–50.

"The Clay Layer." 2013. https://storify.com/RyanAndrosoff/the-clay-layer (accessed August 10, 2014).

Clement, Tony. 2011. "Address by Tony Clement, President of the Treasury Board, at PSEngage." November 22.

–. 2012. "Speech by Tony Clement, President of the Treasury Board and Minister Responsible for FedNor, Presenting the Government of Canada's Action Plan on Open Government." April 17.

Clerk of the Privy Council. 2013a. "Blueprint 2020: Getting Started, Getting Your Views. Building Tomorrow's Public Service Together." https://www.canada.ca/en/privy-council/corporate/clerk.html.

–. 2013b. "What We've Heard: Blueprint 2020 Summary Interim Progress Report." http://publications.gc.ca/site/eng/9.802267/publication.html.

–. 2014. "Destination 2020." http://www.clerk.gc.ca/local_grfx/d2020/Destination2020-eng.pdf.

Coase, Ronald Henry. 1994. *Essays on Economics and Economists*. Chicago: University of Chicago Press.

Coleman, Stephen, and Giles Moss. 2011. "Under Construction: The Field of Online Deliberation Research." *Journal of Information Technology and Politics* 9 (1): 1–15.

Coletto, David. 2012. "R U Ready 4 Us? An Introduction to Canadian Millennials." *Abacus Data*. http://canadianmillennials.ca/wp-content/uploads/2012/01/R-U-Ready-for-Us-An-Introduction-to-Canadian-Millennials.pdf.

Computer Science. n.d. "Prospective Graduate Students." http://web.cs.toronto.edu/Graduate/prospective_gradwhy.htm.

Computer Science at UBC. n.d. "Prospective Undergrads." https://www.cs.ubc.ca/students/undergrad/prospective.

Computing Science. n.d. "Prospective Students." https://www.sfu.ca/computing/prospective-students.html.

Cooper, Terry L., Thomas A. Bryer, and Jack W. Meek. 2006. "Citizen-Centered Collaborative Public Management." *Public Administration Review* 66 (s1): 76–88.

Corporate Web. 2010. *A Protocol for Corrective Blogging by HRSDC Communicators Including a Rationale, Risk Assessment, and Standard Operating Procedures*. Ottawa: Human Resources and Skills Development Canada.

Craft, Jonathan. 2013. "The Promise and Paradoxes of Open Government in Canada." In *How Ottawa Spends, 2013–14 – The Harper Government: Mid-Term Blues and Long-Term Plans*, edited by G. Bruce Doern and Christopher Stoney, 209–22. Montreal: McGill-Queen's University Press.

Crawford, Alison. 2016. "Civil Servants Set Wikipedia Straight on Sexual Positions, Hockey." *CBC News*, May 13. http://www.cbc.ca/news/politics/wikipedia-edits-government-employees-1.3579273.

Crowley, Mark C. 2013. "Not a Happy Accident: How Google Deliberately Designs Workplace Satisfaction." *Fast Company*, March 21. https://www.fastcompany.com/3007268/where-are-they-now/not-happy-accident-how-google-deliberately-designs-workplace-satisfaction.

Danziger, James N. W.H. Dutton, Rob Kling, and Kenneth L Kraemer. 1982. *Computers and Politics: High Technology in American Local Governments*. New York: Columbia University Press.

Davenport, Thomas H., and D.J. Patil. 2012. "Data Scientist: The Sexiest Job of the 21st Century." *Harvard Business Review* October:. https://hbr.org/2012/10/data-scientist-the-sexiest-job-of-the-21st-century.

Davies, Tim. 2010. "The Potential of Open Government Data as a Tool in Democratic Engagement and Reform of Public Services: The Case of Data.gov.uk." MSc thesis, University of Oxford.

Decker, Paul T. 2014. "Presidential Address: False Choices, Policy Framing, and the Promise of 'Big Data.'" *Journal of Policy Analysis and Management* 33 (2): 252–62.

Delacourt, Susan. 2016a. *Shopping for Votes: How Politicians Choose Us and We Choose Them*. 2nd ed. Madeira Park: Douglas and McIntyre.

–. 2016b. "How Policy Is Being Made under the New Liberal Government." *Policy Options*, April 26. http://policyoptions.irpp.org/magazines/april-2016/how-policy-is-being-made-under-the-new-liberal-government/.

Department of Computer Science. n.d. "Co-Operative Education Program." https://www.uvic.ca/engineering/computerscience/co-op/index.php.

Department of Computer Science and Operations Research. n.d. "Graduate Programs." http://en.diro.umontreal.ca/programs/graduate-programs/#c36459.

Department of Foreign Affairs and International Trade Canada. 2012. *Open Policy Development*. Ottawa: Government of Canada.

Deputy Minister Committee on Policy Innovation. 2014. *Deputy Minister Committee on Policy Innovation Interim Report to the Clerk*. Ottawa: Government of Canada.

–. 2015a. *Advancing Policy Innovation: Conditions, Readiness, and the Path Ahead*. Ottawa: Government of Canada.

–. 2015b. "DMCPI Web Access Mini-Challenge (Round 1?) – June 25, 2015." Unpublished internal document.

–. 2016. "A Proposal for a Positive Policy in Support of Experimentation and Innovation." Unpublished internal document.

Digital Transformation Agency. 2015. "Government as a Platform." March 27. https://www.dta.gov.au/standard/design-guides/government-as-a-platform/.

Doern, G. Bruce. 1971. "Recent Changes in the Philosophy of Policy-Making in Canada." *Canadian Journal of Political Science* 4 (2): 243–64.

Drewry, Gavin. 2005. *Citizens as Customers-Charters and the Contractualisation of Quality in Public Services*. https://public-admin.co.uk/brochures/cutomers_charters_paper.pdf.

Dunleavy, Patrick, and Christopher Hood. 1994. "From Old Public Administration to New Public Management." *Public Money and Management* 14 (3): 9–16.

Dunleavy, Patrick, and Helen Margetts. 2015. "Design Principles for Essentially Digital Governance." http://eprints.lse.ac.uk/64125/1/Essentially%20Digital%20Governance.pdf.

–. 2006. *Digital Era Governance: IT Corporations, the State, and E-Government*. Oxford: Oxford University Press.

Dutil, Patrice A., Cosmo Howard, and John Langford. 2010. *The Service State: Rhetoric, Reality, and Promise*. Ottawa: University of Ottawa Press.

Eaves, David. 2009. "The Rat Pack of Public Service Sector Renewal." *Eaves.ca* (blog), June 23. https://eaves.ca/2009/06/23/the-rat-pack-of-public-service-sector-renewal/.

–. 2011a. "Canada Launches Data.gc.ca – What Works and What Is Broken." *Eaves.ca* (blog), March 17. https://eaves.ca/2011/03/17/canada-launches-data-gc-ca-what-works-and-what-is-broken/.

–. 2011b. "International Open Data Hackathon 2011: Better Tools, More Data, Bigger Fun." *Eaves.ca* (blog), October 11. https://eaves.ca/2011/10/11/international-open-data-hackathon-2011-better-tools-more-data-bigger-fun/.

–. 2011c. "The Canadian Government's New Web 2.0 Guidelines: The Good, the Bad, and the Ugly." *Eaves.ca* (blog), November 23. https://eaves.ca/2011/11/23/the-canadian-government-new-web-2-0-guidelines-the-good-the-bad-the-ugly/.

–. 2016. "Canadians Love for Census Says a Lot about Who We Are." *Toronto Star,* May 10. https://www.thestar.com/opinion/commentary/2016/05/10/canadians-love-for-census-says-a-lot-about-who-we-are.html.

Eaves, David, and Laura Wagner. 2012. "Lies, Damned Lies, and Open Data." *Slate,* September 7. http://www.slate.com/articles/technology/future_tense/2012/09/open_data_movement_how_to_keep_information_from_being_politicized_.html.

Edelman. 2017. "Trust in Government." https://www.edelman.com/trust2017/trust-in-canada/.

EKOS Politics. 2017. "Rethinking Citizen Engagement." http://www.ekospolitics.com/index.php/2017/03/rethinking-citizen-engagement-2017/.

Employment and Social Development Canada. 2013. "Update on the Online Skills Forum." Unpublished internal document.

–. 2015. "Deputy Minister Committee on Policy Innovation." Unpublished internal document.

Etherington, Darrell. 2016. "President Obama Explains Why You Can't Run the U.S. like a Startup." *TechCrunch* (blog), October 17. http://techcrunch.com/2016/10/17/president-obama-explains-why-you-cant-run-the-u-s-like-a-startup/.

Facebook Newsroom. 2016. "Company Info." https://newsroom.fb.com/company-info/.

Fekete, Jason. 2014. "Wikipedia Edits on Everything from the Stanley Cup to Scooby-Doo Traced to Parliament Hill Computers." *National Post,* August 15. http://nationalpost.com/news/canada/canadian-politics/httpnews-nationalpost-com20100714canadian-man-inveted-hawaiian-pizza-according-to-wikipedia-and-him.

Fereday, Jennifer, and Eimear Muir-Cochrane. 2006. "Demonstrating Rigor Using Thematic Analysis: A Hybrid Approach of Inductive and Deductive Coding and Theme Development." *International Journal of Qualitative Methods* 5 (1): 80–92.

Finn, Holly. 2012. "Code for America, a Peace Corps for Civic-Minded Geeks." *Wall Street Journal,* August 24. https://www.wsj.com/articles/SB10000872396390444270404577605622944527722.

Flack, Graham. 2014. "Virtual Policy Challenge/Défi de politique virtuel." Email, February 14.

Flack, Graham, and Bill Pentney. 2014. "Virtual Policy Challenge Conclusion and Next Steps/Défi de politique virtuel conclusion et prochaines étapes." Email, April 4.

Fleiss, Joseph L., Bruce Levin, and Myunghee Cho Paik. 2003. *Statistical Methods for Rates and Proportions*. 3rd ed. Wiley Series in Probability and Statistics. Hoboken, NJ: J. Wiley.

Ford, Robin, and David Zussman. 1997. *Alternative Service Delivery: Sharing Governance in Canada*. Toronto: Institute of Public Administration of Canada.

Foreshew-Cain, Stephen. 2015. "How Digital and Technology Transformation Saved £1.7bn Last Year." *Government Digital Service* (blog), October 23. https://gds.blog.gov. uk/2015/10/23/how-digital-and-technology-transformation-saved-1-7bn-last-year/.

–. 2016. "Where We're at, and Where We're Going." *Government Digital Service* (blog), April 8. https://gds.blog.gov.uk/2016/04/08/where-were-at-and-where-were-going/.

Fountain, Jane E. 2001. *Building the Virtual State: Information Technology and Institutional Change*. Washington, DC: Brookings Institution Press.

Francoli, Mary. 2014. "Canada Progress Report 2012–13." https://www.opengovpartnership. org/country/canada/progress-report/report.

–. 2016a. "Canada Progress Report: 2014–2015." www.opengovpartnership.org/sites/ default/files/1.Canada14-15_English_Final_0.pdf.

–. 2016b. "Engage Canadians on Open Government: Lessons Learned from Tony Clement." *Hill Times*, April 1.

Freedom House. 2015. "Singapore." *Freedom in the World 2015*. https://freedomhouse. org/report/freedom-world/2015/singapore.

Freeman, Gary P. 1985. "National Styles and Policy Sectors: Explaining Structured Variation." *Journal of Public Policy* 5 (4): 467–96.

"GCpedia." 2018. *Wikipedia*. https://en.wikipedia.org/w/index.php?title=GCpedia&ol did=858795442.

General Services Administration. n.d.a. "Projects." https://presidentialinnovationfellows. gov/projects/.

–. n.d.b. "FAQ." https://presidentialinnovationfellows.gov/faq/.

Glaser, Barney B., and Anselm L. Strauss. 1967. *The Discovery of Grounded Theory: Strategies for Qualitative Research*. Chicago: Aldine.

Glick, Bryan. 2016. "Revealed: The Battle for GDS – How Whitehall Mandarins Are Trying to Carve Up Digital Strategy." *Computer Weekly*, July 28. http://www. computerweekly.com/news/450301278/Revealed-The-battle-for-GDS-how-Whitehall-mandarins-are-trying-to-carve-up-digital-strategy.

Globe and Mail. 2014. "It's a False Economy to Cut Statscan's Budget." *Globe and Mail*, April 22. https://www.theglobeandmail.com/opinion/editorials/its-a-false-economy-to-cut-statscans-budget/article18113738/.

Gomery, John Howard. 2005. *Who Is Responsible?* Ottawa: Commission of Inquiry into the Sponsorship Program and Advertising Activities.

–. 2006. *Restoring Accountability*. Ottawa: Commission of Inquiry into the Sponsorship Program and Advertising Activities.

Goodsell, Charles T. 2004. *The Case for Bureaucracy: A Public Administration Polemic*. 4th ed. Washington, DC: CQ Press.

Google. n.d. "Ten Things We Know to Be True." https://www.google.com/about/.

Government 2.0 Taskforce. 2009. "Engage: Getting on with Government 2.0." https://www.finance.gov.au/sites/default/files/Government20TaskforceReport.pdf?v=1.

Government of Canada. 2012. "Canada's Action Plan on Open Government 2012–2014." https://open.canada.ca/en/canadas-action-plan-open-government.

–. 2014a. "The Road to Balance: Creating Jobs and Opportunities." https://www.budget.gc.ca/2014/docs/plan/toc-tdm-eng.html.

–. 2014b. "Canada's Action Plan on Open Government, 2014–2016." May 2. http://open.canada.ca/en/canadas-action-plan-open-government.

–. 2014c. "Canadian Open Data Experience [CODE] 2014 Event." *Open.canada.ca*, November 21. https://open.canada.ca/en/code-2014-event.

–. 2015a. "CODE 2015 – It's a Wrap!" *Open.canada.ca*, February 23. https://open.canada.ca/en/blog/code-2015-its-wrap.

–. 2015b. "12. Consulting with Canadians." *Open.canada.ca*, July 29. https://open.canada.ca/en/commitment/12-consulting-canadians.

–. 2016a. "Growing the Middle Class." https://www.budget.gc.ca/2016/docs/plan/budget2016-en.pdf.

–. 2016b. "Google Hangout, April 6." https://open.canada.ca/en/blog/google-hangout.

Government Digital Service. n.d.a. "Social Media Playbook." *Government Digital Service.* https://gdsengagement.blog.gov.uk/playbook/#accountability.

–. n.d.b. "#StartAtGOVUK." *Government Digital Service* (blog), accessed August, 2016. https://gds.blog.gov.uk/startatgovuk/ (accessed August 12, 2016).

Grabosky, Peter. 2013. "Beyond Responsive Regulation: The Expanding Role of Non-State Actors in the Regulatory Process." *Regulation and Governance* 7 (1): 114–23. https://doi.org/10.1111/j.1748-5991.2012.01147.x.

Granatstein, J.L. 1982. *The Ottawa Men: The Civil Service Mandarins, 1935–1957.* Toronto: Oxford University Press.

Greenway, Andrew. 2013. "Talent Scouting." *Government Digital Service* (blog), July 12. https://gds.blog.gov.uk/2013/07/12/talent-scouting/.

Grossman, Lev. 2006. "You – Yes, You – Are TIME's Person of the Year." *Time,* December 25. http://content.time.com/time/magazine/article/0,9171,1570810,00.html.

Grube, Dennis. 2013. "Public Voices from Anonymous Corridors: The Public Face of the Public Service in a Westminster System." *Canadian Public Administration* 56 (1): 3–25.

–. 2015. "Responsibility to Be Enthusiastic? Public Servants and the Public Face of 'Promiscuous Partisanship.'" *Governance: An International Journal of Policy, Administration, and Institutions* 28 (3): 305–20.

Gruzd, Anatoliy, Jenna Jacobson, Philip Mai, and Elizabeth Dubois. 2018. "The State of Social Media in Canada 2017." Ryerson University Social Media Lab. http://socialmedialab.ca/2018/state-of-social-media-in-canada/.

Hall, Peter A. 1993. "Policy Paradigms, Social Learning, and the State: The Case of Economic Policymaking in Britain." *Comparative Politics* 25 (3): 275–96.

Halligan, John, ed. 2004. *Civil Service Systems in Anglo-American Countries.* Civil Service Systems in Comparative Perspective. Cheltenham, UK: Elgar.

Hannay, Chris. 2013. "How Many Groups Does It Take to Craft a Tweet in This Government Body? Eight." *Globe and Mail*, February 6. https://www.theglobeandmail.com/news/politics/how-many-groups-does-it-take-to-craft-a-tweet-in-this-government-body-eight/article8283424/.

—. 2016. "Five Things I've Learned about How the Government Used BuzzFeed." *Globe and Mail*, February 12. https://www.theglobeandmail.com/news/politics/five-things-ive-learned-about-how-the-government-used-buzzfeed/article28741018/.

Hargittai, Eszter, and Heather Young. 2012. "Searching for a 'Plan B': Young Adults' Strategies for Finding Information about Emergency Contraception Online." *Policy and Internet* 4 (2): 1–23.

Harris, Michael. 2014. *Party of One: Stephen Harper and Canada's Radical Makeover.* Toronto: Viking.

Himelfarb, Alex. 2005. "Twelfth Annual Report from the Clerk of the Privy Council and Secretary to the Cabinet." https://www.canada.ca/en/privy-council/corporate/clerk.html.

—. 2012. "Governing in the Dark: Bargain Basement Citizenship." *Toronto Star*, October 9. https://www.thestar.com/opinion/editorialopinion/2012/10/09/governing_in_the_dark_bargain_basement_citizenship.html.

Honeycutt, Courtenay, and Susan C. Herring. 2009. "Beyond Microblogging: Conversation and Collaboration via Twitter." In *Proceedings of the Forty-Second Hawai'i International Conference on System Sciences (HICSS-42)*, 1–10. Los Alamitos, CA: IEEE Press.

Hood, Christopher. 1983. *The Tools of Government.* London: Macmillan.

—. 1995. "The 'New Public Management' in the 1980s: Variations on a Theme." *Accounting, Organizations, and Society* 20 (2–3): 93–109.

—. 2000. "Paradoxes of Public-Sector Managerialism, Old Public Management, and Public Service Bargains." *International Public Management Journal* 3 (1): 1–22.

Hood, Christopher C., and Helen Margetts. 2007. *The Tools of Government in the Digital Age.* Basingstoke, UK: Palgrave Macmillan.

Hood, Christopher, and Martin Lodge. 2006. *The Politics of Public Service Bargains.* Oxford: Oxford University Press.

Howard, Philip N. 2016. "Commentary: Facebook and Twitter's Real Sin Goes beyond Spreading Fake News." *Reuters*, December 7. https://uk.reuters.com/article/us-twitter-facebook-commentary-idUKKBN13W1WO.

Howlett, Michael. 2003. "Administrative Styles and the Limits of Administrative Reform: A Neo-Institutional Analysis of Administrative Culture." *Canadian Public Administration* 46 (4): 471–94.

Howlett, Michael, and M. Ramesh. 2003. *Studying Public Policy: Policy Cycles and Policy Subsystems.* Toronto: Oxford University Press.

Hu, Qian. 2017. "Preparing Public Managers for the Digital Era: Incorporating Information Management, Use, and Technology into Public Affairs Graduate Curricula." *Public Management Review* 20 (5): 766–87.

Hu, Yuheng, Shelly Farnham, and Kartik Talamadupula. 2015. "Predicting User Engagement on Twitter with Real-World Events." In *Ninth International AAAI Conference on Web and Social Media,* 168–77. Palo Alto: AAAI Press. http://yuhenghu.com/paper/icwsm15events.pdf.

Human Resources and Skills Development Canada. 2010. "HRSDC's Tiger Team on Social Media Establishing a Departmental Position for Consideration of the Portfolio Management Council." Unpublished internal document.

–. 2012. "Radar: Media Overview." Unpublished internal document.

–. n.d. "Tweet Approval Process." Unpublished internal document.

IBM. 2016. "Can the Millennial Generation Rescue Government? Leveraging Digital Natives in Your Transformation Efforts." https://www-01.ibm.com/common/ssi/cgi-bin/ssialias?htmlfid=GBE03756USEN.

Industry Canada. 2010. "Consultation – Digital Canada 150."

Information and Communications Technology Council. 2016. "Digital Talent: Road to 2020 and Beyond." https://www.ictc-ctic.ca/wp-content/uploads/2016/03/ICTC_DigitalTalent2020_ENGLISH_FINAL_March2016.pdf.

Internet World Stats. 2013. "Internet Users in Europe." https://www.internetworldstats.com/stats4.htm.

Ireland, Nicole. 2016. "Google Spat between Liberals and Tories Reveals Confusion about How Search Works." *CBC News,* June 18. http://www.cbc.ca/news/technology/google-search-results-pmo-explainer-1.3641336.

Ireton, Julie. 2016. "Liberal 'Sunny Ways' Could Be Leading to More Interest in Public Service." *CBC News,* May 11. http://www.cbc.ca/news/canada/ottawa/public-service-school-interest-increase-1.3576058.

Jarvis, Mark D. 2014a. "Hierarchy." In *The Oxford Handbook of Public Accountability,* edited by Mark Bovens, Robert E. Goodin and Thomas Schillemoans, 405–20. Oxford: Oxford University Press.

–. 2014b. "The Black Box of Bureaucracy: Interrogating Accountability in the Public Service." *Australian Journal of Public Administration* 73 (4): 450–66. https://doi.org/10.1111/1467-8500.12109.

–. 2016. *Creating a High-Performing Canadian Civil Service against a Backdrop of Disruptive Change.* Toronto: Mowat Centre.

Jarvis, Mark D., and Karine Levasseur. 2015. "The (Im?)possibility of Horizontal Accountability." Paper presented at the Annual Meeting of the Canadian Association of Programs in Public Administration, Toronto, Ontario, May 26. http://www.glendon.yorku.ca/cappa2015/wp-content/uploads/sites/22/Presentation-Jarvis-and-Levasseur-21may-CAPPA.docx.

Jay, Antony, and Jonathan Lynn. 1980. "Open Government." *Yes, Minister.* London: BBC.

Jeffrey, Brooke. 2011. "Strained Relations: The Conflict between the Harper Conservatives and the Federal Bureaucracy." Paper presented at the Annual Meeting of the Canadian Political Science Association, Waterloo, Ontario, May 17. https://www.cpsa-acsp.ca/papers-2011/Jeffrey.pdf.

Johnson, Peter, and Pamela Robinson. 2014. "Civic Hackathons: Innovation, Procurement, or Civic Engagement?" *Review of Policy Research* 31 (4): 349–57.

Johnson, Steven L., Samer Faraj, and Srinivas Kudaravalli. 2014. "Emergence of Power Laws in Online Communities: The Role of Social Mechanisms and Preferential Attachment." *Management Information Systems Quarterly* 38 (3): 795–808.

Joint Accord Table of the Voluntary Sector Initiative. 2002a. "A Code of Good Practice on Funding." http://www.vsi-isbc.org/eng/funding/funding_code.cfm.

–. 2002b. "A Code of Good Practice on Policy Dialogue." http://www.vsi-isbc.org/eng/policy/policy_code.cfm.

Jones, C., W.S. Hesterly, and S.P. Borgatti. 1997. "A General Theory of Network Governance: Exchange Conditions and Social Mechanisms." *Academy of Management Review* 22 (4): 911–45.

Joshi, Anuradha, and Mick Moore. 2004. "Institutionalised Co-Production: Unorthodox Public Service Delivery in Challenging Environments." *Journal of Development Studies* 40 (4): 31–49.

Jung, Tobias. 2010. "Citizens, Co-Producers, Customers, Clients, Captives? A Critical Review of Consumerism and Public Services." *Public Management Review* 12 (3): 439–46.

Kamenetz, Anya. 2010. "How an Army of Techies Is Taking on City Hall." *Fast Company*, November 29. https://www.fastcompany.com/1702210/how-army-techies-taking-city-hall.

Keilar, Nicholas. 2016. "Sticky Notes, Sticky Notes, and More Sticky Notes." *Digital Transformation Office* (blog), April 21. https://www.dta.gov.au/blog/govau-stickynotes/.

Kernaghan, Kenneth. 2010. "East Block and Westminster: Conventions, Values, and Public Service." In *The Handbook of Canadian Public Administration*, edited by Christopher Dunn, 289–304. Toronto: Oxford University Press.

–. 2014a. "Digital Dilemmas: Values, Ethics, and Information Technology." *Canadian Public Administration* 57 (2): 295–317.

–. 2014b. "The Rights and Wrongs of Robotics: Ethics and Robots in Public Organizations." *Canadian Public Administration* 57 (4): 485–506.

Khan, Jairus. 2011. "Guideline for Digital Oblivion." *Restraint* (blog), November 22. http://restraint.org/politics/2956/guideline-for-digital-oblivion/.

King, Matthew. 2014. "Memorandum for the Minister: Information on Blueprint 2020 Dragon's Den Initiatives." Department of Fisheries and Oceans.

Kitchin, Rob. 2013. "Four Critiques of Open Data Initiatives." *The Programmable City* (blog), November 9. http://progcity.maynoothuniversity.ie/2013/11/four-critiques-of-open-data-initiatives/.

Kozolanka, Kirsten, ed. 2014. *Publicity and the Canadian State: Critical Communications Perspectives.* Toronto: University of Toronto Press.

KPMG. 2017. "Alex Benay: Opening Canadian Government." https://home.kpmg.com/xx/en/home/insights/2017/11/alex-benay-opening-canadian-government.html.

Kvale, Steinar. 1996. *Interviews: An Introduction to Qualitative Research Interviewing.* Thousand Oaks, CA: Sage Publications.

Lane Fox, Martha. 2010. "Directgov 2010 and Beyond: Revolution Not Evolution." https://www.gov.uk/government/publications/directgov-2010-and-beyond-revolution-not-evolution-a-report-by-martha-lane-fox.

Lathrop, Daniel, and Laurel Ruma, eds. 2010. *Open Government: Collaboration, Transparency, and Participation in Practice.* Theory in Practice. Cambridge, MA: O'Reilly.

Lauriault, Tracey P., and Hugh McGuire. 2008. "Data Access in Canada: CivicAccess.ca." *Technology Innovation Management Review.* February. http://timreview.ca/article/120.

Layne, Karen, and Jungwoo Lee. 2001. "Developing Fully Functional E-Government: A Four Stage Model." *Government Information Quarterly* 18 (2): 122–36.

Leach, Jimmy. 2011. "The Power of the Disinterested." *Government Digital Service* (blog), May 9. https://gds.blog.gov.uk/2011/05/09/the-power-of-the-disinterested/.

Legault, Suzanne. 2015a. *2014/15 Annual Report.* Ottawa: Office of the Information Commissioner of Canada. http://www.oic-ci.gc.ca/eng/rapport-annuel-annual-report_2014-2015_1.aspx.

–. 2015b. *Striking the Right Balance for Transparency: Recommendations to Modernize the Access to Information Act.* Ottawa: Office of the Information Commissioner of Canada. http://epe.lac-bac.gc.ca/003/008/099/003008-disclaimer.html?orig=/100/201/301/ weekly_acquisition_lists/2015/w15-35-F-E.html/collections/collection_2015/ci-oic/ IP4-12-2015-eng.pdf.

Lenihan, Don. 2015. *Open Government in Transition: A Case Study of the Canadian Geomatics Community Round Table.* Ottawa: Public Policy Forum. https://www.ppforum.ca/ publications/open-government-in-transition-a-case-study-of-the-canadian-geomatics-community-round-table/open-government-in-transition-a-case-study-of-the-canadian-geomatics-community-round-table-ppf-report/.

Leskovec, Jure. 2013. "Web Data: Amazon Reviews." https://snap.stanford.edu/data/web-Amazon.html.

Levesque, Lisa. 2013. "Public Servant Use of Twitter Requires 9 Levels of Approval." *Canadian Government Executive,* February 28. https://www.canadiangovernmentexecutive.ca/category/item/1159-public-servant-use-of-twitter-requires-9-levels-of-approval.html.

Levinson King, Robin. 2015. "Muzzled Canadian Scientists Now Free to Speak with Media." *Toronto Star,* November 6. https://www.thestar.com/news/canada/2015/ 11/06/muzzles-removed-for-federal-scientists-at-department-of-fisheries-and-oceans.html.

Levitz, Stephanie. 2013. "Conservative Supporters Should Mind Their Tongues, Says Preston Manning." *Toronto Star,* March 9. https://www.thestar.com/news/canada/ 2013/03/09/conservative_supporters_should_mind_their_tongues_says_preston_ manning.html.

Levy, Steven. 2016. "Inside the Obama Tech Surge as It Hacks the Pentagon and VA – Backchannel." *Medium,* July 19. https://www.wired.com/inside-the-obama-tech-surge-as-it-hacks-the-pentagon-and-va-8b439bc33ed1.

Lewis, Seth C., Rodrigo Zamith, and Alfred Hermida. 2013. "Content Analysis in an Era of Big Data: A Hybrid Approach to Computational and Manual Methods." *Journal of Broadcasting and Electronic Media* 57 (1): 34–52.

Lindquist, Evert A. 2006. *A Critical Moment: Capturing and Conveying the Evolution of the Canadian Public Service.* Special Studies. Ottawa: Canada School of Public Service.

–. 2012. *Horizontal Management in Canada Ten Years Later.* Ottawa: Optimum Online.

Lindquist, Evert A., and Chris Eichbaum. 2016. "Remaking Government in Canada: Dares, Resilience, and Civility in Westminster Systems." *Governance: An International Journal of Policy, Administration, and Institutions* 29 (4): 553–71.

Lodge, Martin. 2009. "Strained or Broken? The Future(s) of the Public Service Bargain." *Policy Quarterly* 5 (1): 53–57.

Lodge, Martin, and Kai Wegrich. 2015. "Crowdsourcing and Regulatory Reviews: A New Way of Challenging Red Tape in British Government?" *Regulation and Governance* 9 (1): 30–46.

Longley, Carrick, and Douglas Zimmerman. 2011. "Practitioner Response to 'Beyond Smokestacks and Silos: Open-Source, Web-Enabled Coordination in Organizations and Networks.'" *Public Administration Review* 71 (5): 697–99.

Longo, Justin. 2011. "#Opendata: Digital-Era Governance Thoroughbred or New Public Management Trojan Horse?" *Public Policy and Governance Review* 2 (2): 38–51.

–. 2016. "BC Open Data Site, Internal Use." Email to the author, May 17.

Longo, Justin, and Tanya Kelley. 2016. "GitHub Use in Public Administration in Canada: Early Experience with a New Collaboration Tool." https://papers.ssrn.com/sol3/papers.cfm?abstract_id=2785874.

Lopez, L.K. 2009. "The Radical Act of 'Mommy Blogging': Redefining Motherhood through the Blogosphere." *New Media and Society* 11 (5): 729–47.

Lynch, Kevin G. 2007. "Fourteenth Annual Report to the Prime Minister on the Public Service of Canada." https://www.canada.ca/en/privy-council/corporate/clerk.html.

–. 2008. "The Public Service of Canada: Too Many Misperceptions." February 18. https://www.canada.ca/en/privy-council.html.

Maclean's. 2015. "University Rankings: Canada's Top 10 Universities for Computer Science." November 5. http://www.macleans.ca/education/top-10-computer-science-universities/.

Macnamara, Jim. 2010. "The Quadrivium of Online Public Consultation: Policy, Culture, Resources, Technology." *Australian Journal of Political Science* 45 (2): 227–44.

Maheshwari, Sapna, and Alexandra Stevenson. 2017. "Google and Facebook Face Criticism for Ads Targeting Racist Sentiments." *New York Times,* September 15 https://www.nytimes.com/2017/09/15/business/facebook-advertising-anti-semitism.html.

Manasan, Althea. 2015. "FAQ: The Issues around Muzzling Government Scientists." *CBC News,* May 20. http://www.cbc.ca/news/technology/faq-the-issues-around-muzzling-government-scientists-1.3079537.

Manyika, James, Michael Chui, Brad Brown, Jacques Bughin, Richard Dobbs, and Angela Hung Byers. 2011. *Big Data: The Next Frontier for Innovation, Competition, and Productivity.* McKinsey Global Institute.

Marando, Dylan, and Jonathan Craft. 2017. "Digital Era Policy Advising: Clouding Ministerial Perspectives?" *Canadian Public Administration* 60 (4): 498–516.

Margetts, Helen. 1999. *Information Technology in Government: Britain and America.* London: Routledge.

–. 2010. "Modernizing Dreams and Public Policy Reform." In *Paradoxes of Modernization: Unintended Consequences of Public Policy Reform*, edited by Helen Margetts, Perri 6, and Christopher Hood, 3–43. Oxford: Oxford University Press.

–. 2016. "Back to the Bad Old Days, as Civil Service Infighting Threatens UK's Only Hope for Digital Government." *The Conversation*. http://theconversation.com/back-to-the-bad-old-days-as-civil-service-infighting-threatens-uks-only-hope-for-digital-government-47683.

Margetts, Helen, and Patrick Dunleavy. 2013. "The Second Wave of Digital-Era Governance: A Quasi-Paradigm for Government on the Web." *Philosophical Transactions of the Royal Society A: Mathematical, Physical, and Engineering Sciences* 371, 1987.

Margetts, Helen, Peter John, Scott Hale, and Taha Yasseri. 2016. *Political Turbulence: How Social Media Shape Collective Action*. Princeton, NJ: Princeton University Press.

Marland, Alex. 2016. *Brand Command: Canadian Politics and Democracy in the Age of Message Control*. Vancouver: UBC Press.

Marland, Alex, Thierry Giasson, and Anna Esselment, eds. 2017. *Permanent Campaigning in Canada*. Vancouver: UBC Press.

Marrs, Colin. 2015. "Spending Review 2015: George Osborne Unveils Surprise Boost for Government Digital Service / Civil Service World." *Civil Service World*, November 25. https://www.civilserviceworld.com/articles/news/spending-review-2015-george-osborne-unveils-surprise-boost-government-digital-service.

Martin, Lawrence. 2011. *Harperland: The Politics of Control*. Toronto: Penguin Canada.

May, Kathryn. 2016a. "Brison Says Millennials Will Staff Next 'Golden Age' of Public Service." *Ottawa Citizen*, February 16. http://ottawacitizen.com/news/national/brison-says-millennials-will-staff-next-golden-age-of-public-service.

–. 2016b. "PS Needs to Pick Up Pace of Reforms: Privy Council Clerk." *Ottawa Citizen*, March 25. http://ottawacitizen.com/news/local-news/ps-needs-to-pick-up-pace-of-reforms-privy-council-clerk.

May, P.J. 2003. "Policy Design and Implementation." In *The Handbook of Public Administration*, edited by B. Guy Peters and Jon Pierre, 223–33. Beverly Hills: Sage.

Mayer-Schönberger, Viktor, and Kenneth Cukier. 2013. *Big Data: A Revolution that Will Transform How We Live, Work, and Think*. London: Murray.

Mayo, Ed, and Tom Steinberg. 2007. "The Power of Information: An Independent Review by Ed Mayo and Tom Steinberg." http://www.opsi.gov.uk/advice/poi/power-of-information-review.pdf.

McAfee, Andrew, and Erik Brynjolfsson. 2012. "Big Data: The Management Revolution." *Harvard Business Review* 90 (10): 60–68.

McGill School of Computer Science. 2016. "McGill School of Computer Science." https://www.cs.mcgill.ca/prospective/whycs.

McNutt, Kathleen. 2014. "Public Engagement in the Web 2.0 Era: Social Collaborative Technologies in a Public Sector Context." *Canadian Public Administration* 57 (1): 49–70.

McNutt, Kathleen, and Meaghan Carey. 2008. *Canadian Digital Government*. Regina: Government of Saskatchewan.

Meijer, Albert. 2007. "Why Don't They Listen to Us? Reasserting the Role of ICT in Public Administration." *Information Polity* 12 (4): 233–42.

Meijer, Albert, Kees Boersma, and Pieter Wagenaar, eds. 2009. *ICTs, Citizens, and Governance: After the Hype!* Amsterdam: IOS Press.

Meijer, Albert, and Marcel Thaens. 2010. "Alignment 2.0: Strategic Use of New Internet Technologies in Government." *Government Information Quarterly* 27 (2): 113–21.

Mendelsohn, Matthew. 2015. *Results and Delivery in a Digital Context.* https://www.youtube.com/watch?v=JFKs42E82DQ&feature=youtu.be.

Mergel, Ines, and Kevin C. Desouza. 2013. "Implementing Open Innovation in the Public Sector: The Case of Challenge.gov." *Public Administration Review* 73 (6): 882–90.

Meyer, David. 2012. "How the German Pirate Party's Liquid Democracy Works." *TechPresident*, May 7. http://techpresident.com/news/wegov/22154/how-german-pirate-partys-liquid-democracy-works.

Morozov, Evgeny. 2014. *To Save Everything, Click Here: The Folly of Technological Solutionism.* New York: PublicAffairs.

–. 2016. "They Made Him a Moron: The Strange Career of Alec Ross." *The Baffler* 30 (March). https://thebaffler.com/salvos/made-a-moron.

Needham, Catherine. 2003. "Citizens as Consumers: The Government-Citizen Relationship in England, 1997–2003" PhD diss., University of Oxford.

Newman, Nic, with Richard Fletcher, Antonis Kalogeropoulos, David A.L. Levy, and Rasmus Kleis Nielsen. 2017. "Reuters Institute Digital News Report 2017." *Reuters Institute for the Study of Journalism.* https://reutersinstitute.politics.ox.ac.uk/sites/default/files/Digital%20News%20Report%202017%20web_0.pdf.

News Media Canada. 2017. "2017 Freedom of Information Audit." https://nmc-mic.ca/public-affairs/freedom-of-information/2017-freedom-information-audit/.

Neville, Sarah. 2015. "Government Digital Service Faces Diminished Role." *Financial Times*, October 11. https://www.ft.com/content/e00b2134-6eaf-11e5-8171-ba1968cf791a.

Noeftle, Tracie, and Adrian Cloete. 2010. "Corrective Blogging: 'Writing' the Wrongs of Internet Information." Paper presented at the International Council for Information Technology in Government Administration, Washington, DC, November 24. https://prezi.com/ufj3qjxqhx9u/blogging-writing-the-wrongs-of-internet-information/.

Norris, Donald F., and Christopher G. Reddick. 2013. "Local E-Government in the United States: Transformation or Incremental Change?" *Public Administration Review* 73 (1): 165–75.

Noveck, Beth Simone. 2009. *Wiki Government: How Technology Can Make Government Better, Democracy Stronger, and Citizens More Powerful.* Washington, DC: Brookings Institution Press.

–. 2015. *Smart Citizens, Smarter State: The Technologies of Expertise and the Future of Governing.* Cambridge, MA: Harvard University Press.

O'Reilly, Tim. 2005. "What Is Web 2.0?" September 30. http://www.oreilly.com/pub/a/web2/archive/what-is-web-20.html.

Obama, Barack. 2009. "Transparency and Open Government." https://obamawhitehouse.archives.gov/the-press-office/transparency-and-open-government.

Office of the Auditor General of Canada. 2010. "2010 Spring Report of the Auditor General of Canada." http://www.oag-bvg.gc.ca/internet/English/parl_oag_201004_01_e_33714.html.

–. 2016a. "Report 4 – Information Technology Shared Services." http://www.oag-bvg. gc.ca/internet/English/parl_oag_201602_04_e_41061.html#ex1.

–. 2016b. "Report 2 – Detecting and Preventing Fraud in the Citizenship Program." http:// www.oag-bvg.gc.ca/internet/English/parl_oag_201602_02_e_41246.html#hd3a.

–. 2017. "Report 1 – Phoenix Pay Problems." http://www.oag-bvg.gc.ca/internet/English/ parl_oag_201711_01_e_42666.html.

–. 2018. "Reports of the Auditor General of Canada to the Parliament of Canada." http:// publications.gc.ca/collections/collection_2018/bvg-oag/FA1-27-2018-1-0-eng.pdf.

Office of the Information Commissioner of Canada. 2013. "Instant Messaging Putting Access to Information at Risk." http://www.oic-ci.gc.ca/eng/pin-to-pin-nip-a-nip.aspx.

–. 2017. Failing to Strike the Right Balance for Transparency – Recommendations to improve Bill C-58: An Act to Amend the *Access to Information Act* and the *Privacy Act* and to Make Consequential Amendments to Other Acts. http://www.oic-ci. gc.ca/eng/rapport-special-c-58_special-report-c-58.aspx.

Olsen, J.P. 2006. "Maybe It Is Time to Rediscover Bureaucracy." *Journal of Public Administration: Research and Theory* 16 (1): 1–24.

Onwurah, Chi. 2013. "Chi's Speech to the Digital Leaders Conference 2013." *Chi Onwurah MP* (blog), December 5. https://chionwurahmp.com/2013/12/chis-speech-to-the-digital-leaders-conference-2013/.

OpenMedia. n.d. "A Look Back at Our Stop the Meter Campaign." https://openmedia. org/en/ca/look-back-our-stop-meter-campaign.

–. 2011. "Government as a Platform." *Innovations* 6 (1): 13–40.

Organization for Economic Co-operation and Development. 2017. "Open Government." http://www.oecd.org/gov/open-government.htm.

Orszag, Peter R. 2009. "Open Government Directive." https://obamawhitehouse.archives.gov/ open/documents/open-government-directive.

Oshiro, Dana. 2013. "The 2014 Fellowship Applicants," *Code for America* (blog), August 1. https://www.codeforamerica.org/blog/2013/08/01/2014_fellows_applications/.

Owen, Taylor, and Edward Greenspon. 2017. "'Fake News 2.0': A Threat to Canada's Democracy." *Globe and Mail,* May 28. https://www.theglobeandmail.com/opinion/ fake-news-20-a-threat-to-canadas-democracy/article35138104/.

Page, Christopher. 2006. *The Roles of Public Opinion Research in Canadian Government.* Institute of Public Administration of Canada Series in Public Management and Governance. Toronto: University of Toronto Press.

Page, Kevin. 2012. *Unaccountable: Truth, Lies, and Numbers on Parliament Hill.* Toronto: Viking.

Pahlka, Jennifer. 2016. "The CIO Problem, Part 1." *Code for America* (blog), May 17. https://medium.com/code-for-america/the-cio-problem-part-1-678ae2e9d0bf.

Palfrey, John G., and Urs Gasser. 2008. *Born Digital: Understanding the First Generation of Digital Natives.* New York: Basic Books.

Patton, Michael Quinn. 2002. *Qualitative Research and Evaluation Methods.* 3rd ed. Thousand Oaks, CA: Sage Publications.

Peters, Guy. 1998. "Managing Horizontal Government: The Politics of Co-Ordination." *Public Administration* 76 (2): 295–311.

–. 2010. "Bureaucracy and Democracy." *Public Organization Review* 10 (3): 209–22.

Peters, Joseph, and Manon Abud. 2009. "E-Consultation: Enabling Democracy between Elections." http://irpp.org/wp-content/uploads/assets/research/strengthening-canadian-democracy/e-consultation-enabling-democracy-between-elections/vol15no1.pdf.

Phillips, Susan, and Karine Levasseur. 2004. "The Snakes and Ladders of Accountability: Contradictions between Contracting and Collaboration for Canada's Voluntary Sector." *Canadian Public Administration* 47 (4): 451–74.

Phillips, Susan D. 2006. "The Intersection of Governance and Citizenship in Canada: Not Quite the Third Way." *Policy Matters* 7 (4): 2–33.

Phillips, Susan D., and Cosmo Howard. 2012. "Moving Away from Hierarchy: Do Horizontality, Partnerships, and Distributed Governance Really Signify the End of Accountability?" In *From New Public Management to New Political Governance: Essays in Honour of Peter C. Aucoin,* edited by Herman Bakvis and Mark D. Jarvis, 314–41. Montreal: McGill-Queen's University Press.

Phillips, Susan D., and Jane Jenson. 1996. "Regime Shift: New Citizenship Practices in Canada." *International Journal of Canadian Studies* 14: 111–36.

Phillips, Susan D., and Michael Orsini. 2002. "Mapping the Links: Citizen Involvement in Policy Processes." Canadian Policy Research Networks. http://citeseerx.ist.psu.edu/viewdoc/download?doi=10.1.1.488.8565&rep=rep1&type=pdf.

Phoenix Strategy Perspectives. 2008. "New Technologies and Government of Canada Communications." http://epe.lac-bac.gc.ca/100/200/301/pwgsc-tpsgc/por-ef/agriculture_agri-food/2008/130-07-1/report.doc.

Pierre, Jon. 1995. "The Marketization of the State: Citizens, Consumers, and the Emergence of the Public Market." In *Governance in a Changing Environment,* edited by B. Guy Peters and Donald J. Savoie, 55–81. Ottawa: Canadian Centre for Management Development.

Pilieci, Vito. 2017. "Meet the Public Service's New Top Tech Boss, Who's Not Afraid to Speak His Mind." *The Ottawa Citizen.* August 6, 2017. http://ottawacitizen.com/news/local-news/meet-the-public-services-new-top-tech-boss-whos-not-afraid-to-speak-his-mind.

Pitfield, Michael. 1976. "The Shape of Government in the 1980s: Techniques and Instruments for Policy Formulation at the Federal Level." *Canadian Public Administration* 19 (1): 8–20.

Porway, Jake. 2013. "You Can't Just Hack Your Way to Social Change." *Harvard Business Review,* March 7. https://hbr.org/2013/03/you-cant-just-hack-your-way-to.

Power, Michael. 1994. "The Audit Explosion." https://www.demos.co.uk/files/theauditexplosion.pdf.

Prensky, Marc. 2001. "Digital Natives, Digital Immigrants Part 1." *On the Horizon* 9 (5): 1–6.

Prime Minister's Office. 2015a. "Ministerial Mandate Letters." November 12. https://pm.gc.ca/eng/ministerial-mandate-letters.

–. 2015b. "President of the Treasury Board of Canada Mandate Letter." https://pm.gc.ca/eng/president-treasury-board-canada-mandate-letter.

Prince, Michael J. 2007. "Soft Craft, Hard Choices, Altered Context: Reflections on Twenty-Five Years of Policy Advice in Canada." In *Policy Analysis in Canada: The State of the Art,* edited by Laurent Dobuzinskis, Michael Howlett, and David H. Laycock, 163–85. Toronto: University of Toronto Press.

Public Administration Select Committee. 2011. "Government and IT – 'A Recipe for Rip-Offs': Time for a New Approach." https://publications.parliament.uk/pa/cm201012/cmselect/cmpubadm/715/71502.htm.

Public Policy Forum. 2017. "The Shattered Mirror: News, Democracy, and Trust in the Digital Age." https://shatteredmirror.ca/download-the-report/.

Public Service Commission of Canada. 2016. "Video: New Direction in Staffing – Transcript." March 18. https://www.canada.ca/en/public-service-commission.html.

Qasem, Fajer. 2016. "A New Road: My First Month at GDS." *Government Digital Service* (blog), June 21. https://gds.blog.gov.uk/2016/06/21/a-new-road-my-first-month-at-gds/.

Queen's School of Computing. 2014. "Internship Program." http://www.cs.queensu.ca/students/undergraduate/faq/internship.html.

Rasmussen, Ken. 1999. "Policy Capacity in Saskatchewan: Strengthening the Equilibrium." *Canadian Public Administration* 42 (3): 331–48.

Rasmusson, Jonathan. n.d. "Agile vs Waterfall." http://www.agilenutshell.com/agile_vs_waterfall.

Raymond, Eric S. 1999. *The Cathedral and the Bazaar: Musings on Linux and Open Source by an Accidental Revolutionary.* Cambridge, MA: O'Reilly.

Reevely, David. 2016. "Ontario's Experience Shows Serious Flaws in 'Deliverology' Governance." *National Post,* April 28. http://nationalpost.com/full-comment/david-reevely-ontarios-experience-shows-serious-flaws-in-deliverology-governance.

Reimsbach-Kounatze, Christian. 2015. "The Proliferation of 'Big Data' and Implications for Official Statistics and Statistical Agencies." OECD Digital Economy Papers 245. http://www.oecd-ilibrary.org/science-and-technology/the-proliferation-of-big-data-and-implications-for-official-statistics-and-statistical-agencies_5js7t9wqzvg8-en. https://doi.org/10.1787/20716826.

Rhodes, R.A.W. 1997. *Understanding Governance: Policy Networks, Governance, Reflexivity, and Accountability.* Public Policy and Management. Buckingham, UK: Open University Press.

Rice, P., and D. Ezzy. 1999. *Qualitative Research Methods: A Health Focus.* Melbourne: Oxford University Press.

Roberts, Nancy C. 2011. "Beyond Smokestacks and Silos: Open-Source, Web-Enabled Coordination in Organizations and Networks." *Public Administration Review* 71 (5): 677–93.

Robinson, David G., Harlan Yu, William P. Zeller, and Edward W. Felten. 2008. "Government Data and the Invisible Hand." *Yale Journal of Law and Technology* 11 (1): Article 4.

Roy, Jeffrey. 2006. *E-Government in Canada: Transformation for the Digital Age.* Governance Series. Ottawa: University of Ottawa Press.

–. 2008. "Beyond Westminster Governance: Bringing Politics and Public Service into the Networked Era." *Canadian Public Administration* 51 (4): 541–68.

Rubinstein, Carl. 2012. "China's Government Goes Digital." *The Atlantic*, November 29. https://www.theatlantic.com/international/archive/2012/11/chinas-government-goes-digital/265493/.

Salamon, Lester M., and Odus V. Elliott, eds. 2002. *The Tools of Government: A Guide to the New Governance*. Oxford: Oxford University Press.

Savoie, Donald J. 1999. *Governing from the Centre: The Concentration of Power in Canadian Politics*. Toronto: University of Toronto Press.

–. 2003. *Breaking the Bargain: Public Servants, Ministers, and Parliament*. Toronto: University of Toronto Press.

–. 2004. "Searching for Accountability in a Government without Boundaries." *Canadian Public Administration* 47 (1): 1–26.

–. 2013. *Whatever Happened to the Music Teacher? How Government Decides and Why*. Montreal: McGill-Queen's University Press.

Scharkow, Michael. 2013. "Thematic Content Analysis Using Supervised Machine Learning: An Empirical Evaluation Using German Online News." *Quality and Quantity* 47 (2): 761–73.

Schawbel, Dan. 2013. "My 10 Best Pieces of Career Advice for Millennials." *Forbes*, October 17. https://www.forbes.com/sites/danschawbel/2013/10/17/my-10-best-pieces-of-career-advice-for-millennials/.

Schindeler, Fred, and C. Michael Lanphier. 1969. "Social Science Research and Participatory Democracy in Canada." *Canadian Public Administration* 12 (4): 481–98.

Schultz Larsen, Troels. 2015. "The Ambivalent Relations between Bureaucracy and Public Innovation: The Case of the Successful Failure of Dial Police." *International Journal of Public Administration* 38 (2): 92–103.

Shahin, Saif. 2016. "When Scale Meets Depth: Integrating Natural Language Processing and Textual Analysis for Studying Digital Corpora." *Communication Methods and Measures* 10 (1): 28–50.

Shared Services Canada. 2015. "Big Data @ SSC." June 18. http://ssc-spc.gc.ca/pages/itir-triti/itir-triti-afac-030615-pres1-eng.html.

Shaw, Emily. 2016. "Debugging Democracy – from mySociety." *Medium*, January 9. https://medium.com/from-mysociety/debugging-democracy-bfa68e37967b.

Shirky, Clay. 2009. *Here Comes Everybody: How Change Happens When People Come Together*. London: Penguin.

–. 2010. *Cognitive Surplus: Creativity and Generosity in a Connected Age*. London: Allen Lane.

Shueh, Jason. 2016. "Former GSA Head: Internal Procurement Groups Were against 18F from the Start." July 8. http://www.govtech.com/data/Former-GSA-Head-Internal-Procurement-Groups-Were-Against-18F-from-the-Start.html.

Small, Tamara A. 2012. "E-Government in the Age of Social Media: An Analysis of the Canadian Government's Use of Twitter." *Policy and Internet* 4 (3–4): 91–111.

Smith, Wayne. 2014. "Deputy Minister Committee on Policy Innovation." April 14.

Sproule-Jones, Mark. 2000. "Horizontal Management: Implementing Programs across Interdependent Organizations." *Canadian Public Administration* 43 (1): 93–109.

Standing Committee on Government Operations and Estimates. 2016. *Minutes of Proceedings*. 1st sess., 42nd Parliament, Meeting No. 24.

Starr, Paul. 2010. "The Liberal State in a Digital World." *Governance: An International Journal of Policy, Administration, and Institutions* 23 (1): 1–6.

Statista. 2016a. "Twitter: Monthly Active Users 2010–2016." https://www.statista.com/statistics/282087/number-of-monthly-active-twitter-users/.

–. 2016b. "Facebook Users Worldwide 2016." https://www.statista.com/statistics/264810/number-of-monthly-active-facebook-users-worldwide/.

Stein, Joseph. 1964. *Fiddler on the Roof.* New York: Limelight Editions.

Steinberg, Tom. 2012. "Governments Don't Have Websites: Governments Are Websites." *mySociety*, July 18. https://www.mysociety.org/2012/07/18/governments-dont-have-websites-governments-are-websites/.

Streeck, Wolfgang. 1995. "Neo-Voluntarism: A New European Social Policy Regime?" *European Law Journal* 1 (1): 31–59.

Stroud, Matt. 2014. "The Minority Report: Chicago's New Police Computer Predicts Crimes, but Is It Racist?" *Verge*, February 19. https://www.theverge.com/2014/2/19/5419854/the-minority-report-this-computer-predicts-crime-but-is-it-racist.

Sutherland, Sharon L. 2001. "'Biggest Scandal in Canadian History': HRDC Audit Starts Probity War." Queen's University School of Policy Studies Working Paper 23.

Tait, John. 1996. *A Strong Foundation: Report of the Task Force on Public Service Values and Ethics.* Ottawa: Canadian Centre for Management Development.

Tapscott, Don. 1998. *Growing Up Digital: The Rise of the Net Generation.* New York: McGraw-Hill.

–. 2009. *Grown Up Digital: How the Net Generation Is Changing Your World.* New York: McGraw-Hill.

Tapscott, Don, and Anthony D. Williams. 2006. *Wikinomics: How Mass Collaboration Changes Everything.* New York: Portfolio.

Task Force on Horizontal Issues. 1996. *Managing Horizontal Policy Issues.* Ottawa: Government of Canada. http://publications.gc.ca/collections/Collection/SC93-8-1996-3E.pdf.

Taylor, Frederick Winslow. 1967. *The Principles of Scientific Management.* New York: Norton.

Terrett, Ben. 2013. "GOV.UK Wins Design of the Year 2013." *Government Digital Service* (blog), April 17. https://gds.blog.gov.uk/2013/04/17/gov-uk-wins-design-of-the-year-2013/.

Terry, Larry D. 2005. "The Thinning of Administrative Institutions in the Hollow State." *Administration and Society* 37 (4): 426–44.

Thaler, Richard H., and Cass R. Sunstein. 2009. *Nudge: Improving Decisions About Health, Wealth, and Happiness.* New York: Penguin.

Thompson, Elizabeth. 2011. "Twitter, Facebook, and Social Media 'Critical' to Government, Clement Says." *iPolitics* (blog), October 27. https://ipolitics.ca/2011/10/27/twitter-facebook-and-social-media-critical-to-government-clement-says/.

–. 2016. "Un-Googled: Trudeau Government Had Harper Web Pages Removed from Search Results." *iPolitics* (blog), June 16. https://ipolitics.ca/2016/06/16/un-googled-trudeau-government-had-harper-web-pages-removed-from-search-results/.

Torfing, Jacob. 2005. "Governance Network Theory: Towards a Second Generation." *European Political Science* 4 (3): 305–15.

Treasury Board Secretariat. 2003. "Federal Identity Program." https://www.canada.ca/en/treasury-board-secretariat/services/government-communications/federal-identity-program.html.

–. 2006a. "Communications Policy of the Government of Canada." http://www.tbs-sct.gc.ca/pol/doc-eng.aspx?id=12316.

–. 2006b. "Policy on the Use of Official Languages for Communications with and Services to the Public." http://www.tbs-sct.gc.ca/pol/doc-eng.aspx?id=12526.

–. 2011a. "Minister Day Announces Expansion of Open Government." News releases. https://www.canada.ca/en/news/archive/2011/03/minister-day-announces-expansion-open-government.html.

–. 2011b. "Standard on Web Accessibility." https://www.tbs-sct.gc.ca/pol/doc-eng.aspx?id=23601.

–. 2011c. "Guideline for External Use of Web 2.0." http://www.tbs-sct.gc.ca/pol/doc-eng.aspx?id=24835.

–. 2011d. "Values and Ethics Code for the Public Sector." https://www.tbs-sct.gc.ca/pol/doc-eng.aspx?id=25049.

–. 2012a. "Speech by Tony Clement, President of the Treasury Board of Canada, to Regina and District Chamber of Commerce." April 12.

–. 2012b. "Minister Clement Participates in Tweet Chat on Proposed Open Government Licence." December 11.

–. 2013a. "Guideline on Acceptable Network and Device Use." https://www.tbs-sct.gc.ca/pol/doc-eng.aspx?id=27907.

–. 2013b. "Policy on Acceptable Network and Device Use." http://www.tbs-sct.gc.ca/pol/doc-eng.aspx?id=27122&section=HTML.

–. 2013c. "Open Government Consultation Report." https://open.canada.ca/en/open-government-consultation-report.

–. 2014a. "2014 Public Service Employee Survey." http://www.tbs-sct.gc.ca/pses-saff/2014/results-resultats/bq-pq/00/org-eng.aspx.

–. 2014b. "Directive on Open Government." http://www.tbs-sct.gc.ca/pol/doc-eng.aspx?id=28108&section=HTML.

–. 2016a. "Population of the Federal Public Service." https://www.canada.ca/en/treasury-board-secretariat/services/innovation/human-resources-statistics/population-federal-public-service.html.

–. 2016b. "Policy on Communications and Federal Identity." https://www.tbs-sct.gc.ca/pol/doc-eng.aspx?id=30683.

–. 2016c. "Demographic Snapshot of the Federal Public Service, 2015." https://www.canada.ca/en/treasury-board-secretariat/services/innovation/human-resources-statistics/demographic-snapshot-federal-public-service-2015.html.

–. 2016d. "Third Biennial Plan to the Open Government Partnership." https://open.canada. ca/en/content/third-biennial-plan-open-government-partnership.

Tunney, Catherine. 2016. "'Cultural Change' Needed to Speed Turtle's Pace of Public Service, Brison Warned in Briefing Notes." *CBC News*, March 8. http://www.cbc.ca/news/canada/ottawa/public-service-cultural-change-brison-1. 3474660.

TurboTax Canada. 2015. "Tax Filing Guide for Canadian Taxpayers." https://turbotax. intuit.ca/tax-software/how-to-file-taxes.jsp.

Turner, Chris. 2013. "Harper's War on Science Continues with a Vengeance." *Toronto Star,* October 13. https://www.thestar.com/opinion/commentary/2013/10/13/ harpers_war_on_science_continues_with_a_vengeance.html.

United Nations. n.d. "Open Government Data and Services." https://publicadministration. un.org/en/ogd#popup.

United Nations and Department of Economic and Social Affairs. 2014. *United Nations E-Government Survey 2014: E-Government for the Future We Want.* New York: United Nations.

–. 2016. "UN E-Government Survey 2016." https://publicadministration.un.org/egovkb/ en-us/reports/un-e-government-survey-2016.

US Digital Service. 2016. "Dress Code." https://www.usds.gov/join#dress-code.

–. n.d.a. "About Us." https://www.usds.gov/about.

–. n.d.b. "Our Story." https://www.usds.gov/story.html.

–. n.d.c. "Our Values." https://www.usds.gov/values.html.

Van Audenhove, L. 2007. "Expert Interviews and Analysis: Techniques for Policy Analysis." http://www.ies.be/files/060313%20Interviews_VanAudenhove.pdf.

Van Dusen, Julie. 2015. "Justin Trudeau Joyfully Mobbed by Federal Civil Servants." *CBC News*, November 6. http://www.cbc.ca/news/politics/trudeau-dion-duncan- civil-servants-cheered-pearson-1.3308271.

Van Rooy, Alison. 2012. "A History of Public Engagement in the Government of Canada: A Discussion Paper." Canada School of Public Service.

Veltri, Giuseppe A., and Dimitrinka Atanasova. 2015. "Climate Change on Twitter: Content, Media Ecology, and Information Sharing Behaviour." *Public Understanding of Science* 36 (6): 721–37.

Viechnicki, Peter. 2015. "Understanding Millennials in Government: Debunking Myths about Our Youngest Public Servants." https://www2.deloitte.com/insights/us/en/ industry/public-sector/millennials-in-government-federal-workforce.html?id=us: 2el:3dc:dup1450:eng:dup.

Voluntary Sector Initiative. 2014a. "Policy Development." http://www.vsi-isbc.org/eng/ policy/policy_guide/doc13.cfm.

–. 2014b. "Voluntary Sector Initiative: Partnering for the Benefit of Canadians." http:// www.vsi-isbc.org/eng/relationship/accord.cfm.

von Hippel, Eric. 2005. *Democratizing Innovation.* Cambridge, MA: MIT Press.

Vraga, Emily K., Leticia Bode, Anne-Bennett Smithson, and Sonya Troller-Renfree. 2016. "Blurred Lines: Defining Social, News, and Political Posts on Facebook." *Journal of Information Technology and Politics* 13 (3): 272–94.

Weber, Max. 1994. *Weber: Political Writings*. Cambridge Texts in the History of Political Thought. Cambridge, UK: Cambridge University Press.

Wells, Paul A. 2013. *The Longer I'm Prime Minister: Stephen Harper and Canada, 2006–*. Toronto: Random House Canada. http://search.ebscohost.com/login.aspx?direct=true&scope=site&db=nlebk&db=nlabk&AN=719095.

Wernick, Michael. 2016. "Twenty-Third Annual Report to the Prime Minister on the Public Service of Canada." https://www.canada.ca/en/privy-council/corporate/clerk.html.

The White House. 2011. "Executive Order 13571: Streamlining Service Delivery and Improving Customer Service." *Whitehouse.gov*, April 27. https://obamawhitehouse.archives.gov/the-press-office/2011/04/27/executive-order-13571-streamlining-service-delivery-and-improving-custom.

–. 2015a. "About the Fellowship." *Whitehouse.gov*, June 23. https://presidentialinnovationfellows.gov/about/.

–. 2015b. "Meet the Presidential Innovation Fellows." *Medium*, August 17. https://medium.com/@ObamaWhiteHouse/meet-the-presidential-innovation-fellows-194dec20442b.

"Wiki." 2016. *Wikipedia, the Free Encyclopedia*. https://en.wikipedia.org/w/index.php?title=Wiki&oldid=732435520.

Wikimedia Statistics. 2018. "Total Page Views Daily." https://stats.wikimedia.org/v2/#/en.wikipedia.org/reading/total-page-views.

Williams, Brian N., Seong-Cheol Kang, and Japera Johnson. 2015. "(Co)-Contamination as the Dark Side of Co-Production: Public Value Failures in Co-Production Processes." *Public Management Review* (November): 1–26.

Worron, Tony. 2014. "Spreading the Word (and Data) on Country Names." *Foreign and Commonwealth Office* (blog), February 11. https://blogs.fco.gov.uk/guestpost/2016/02/11/spreading-the-word-and-data-on-country-names/.

Wouters, Wayne. 2010. "Seventeenth Annual Report to the Prime Minister on the Public Service of Canada." https://www.canada.ca/en/privy-council/corporate/clerk.html.

–. 2013. "Blueprint 2020." June 24. https://www.canada.ca/en/privy-council/corporate/clerk.html.

Wylie, Bianca. 2017. "Smart Communities Need Smart Governance." *Globe and Mail*, December 5. https://www.theglobeandmail.com/opinion/smart-communities-need-smart-governance/article37218398/.

Yu, Harlan, and David G. Robinson. 2012. "The New Ambiguity of "Open" Government." *UCLA Law Review Discourse* 178–208. https://www.uclalawreview.org/pdf/discourse/59-11.pdf.

Index

18F, 173–74; Agile Purchase Agreement, 244*n*13

Access to Information Act/Privacy Act: Open Government Action Plans and, 108–9; and open information, 107–9; in TBS Guideline, 75; TBS training modules, 108
Access to Information and Privacy (ATIP): and anonymity, 53; BlackBerry Messenger vs, 109, 186; culture of secrecy/information control vs, 63, 113; initiation of requests within bureaucracy, 42–43, 100; modernization of, 108–9; open data emphasis vs reform of, 106; open government and, 7–8, 27, 28, 109; and open.canada.ca site, 107; prevention of automatic uploading to government website, 214; reporting burdens and, 49; thwarting of requests under, 128; and withholding information vs informed citizenry, 63
accessibility: accountability for, 214; of communications, 66; consultations and, 66; externalization and, 163; of government-citizen relationship, 70–71; of information sharing, 70–71; social media and, 89, 90
Accord between the Government of Canada and the Voluntary Sector, 54, 56

accountability: for accessibility, 214; anonymity and, 188; for citizens' privacy, 214; and closed government, 7; decentralized service providers and, 22, 163; digital era governance and, 26; digital government theories and, 20; enduring relevance of, 29; for equity, 214; and error-free government, 186, 214; explosion in, 61; externalization and, 22, 163; and failure mitigation, 186–87; for-learning model, 214, 217; GCTools and, 136; GDS and, 175; and government-citizen relationship, 66, 67, 68, 88–89; hierarchies and, 19–20, 40–41, 45, 49, 52, 68, 69; historical principles underpinning, 189; horizontal, 204; and information management, 188; information sharing and, 93, 188; innovation and, 50; and learning from failure, 50, 214, 217; ministerial, 7, 20–21, 41, 45, 210, 223–24; naming/blaming, 215–16; and Open Government Action Plan, 109; open government and, 7; open government initiative and, 129; and open vs closed government, 97; and partisanship, 214; pluralistic online government-citizen interactions and, 20; PPA and, 7; for public funds, 66; and public service bargain, 20–21, 51, 188–89, 209–10, 223–24, 229, 230; reporting/rules/oversight and, 49–50; and risk aversion,

50, 214; and rule adherence vs flexible adaptation, 214; silos and, 19–20, 40–41, 44–45, 68, 69, 204; social media and, 88–89, 90, 96; user-centrism vs, 228–29; vertical, 188, 204; Weber and, 7
Advertising Standards Authority (UK), 65–66
Aitken, Kent, 92–93, 210, 225
Ajah, 100–1, 179
Amazon, 3, 4
anonymity: Access to Information and Privacy requests and, 53; and accountability, 188; bureaucrat-citizen relationship and, 68; foreign service and, 58, 125–27, 208–10; GCTools and, 136; government de-anonymization, 53; Government Electronic Directory Service vs, 208–9; government-citizen relationship and, 58, 94, 208–9; information sharing vs, 133; media coverage and, 53; and ministerial accountability, 20, 210; and neutrality, 20, 210; online consultations and, 128; and open dialogue, 125, 128; open government vs, 29; personal blogs and, 93; and public service bargain, 20–21, 51, 188–89, 209–10, 223–24, 229, 230; selective de-anonymization, 58; senior officials and, 93; social media vs, 93–94, 133, 188; spokespersons and, 87; in Westminster system, 7, 20, 38, 51, 91, 210
Ascentum, 161
Aucoin, Peter, 22, 62–63, 93
Australia: Australia.gov.au, 65; Department of the Prime Minister and Cabinet, 169; Digital Marketplace, 244n13; Digital Transformation Agency (DTA), 172, 174; Digital Transformation Office (DTO), 169; government as a platform and, 18

Bakvis, Herman, 43–44
Balter, Ben, 173–74
Barber, Michael, 202, 217

Bason, Christian, 48
behavioural insights, 138, 203–4
Behavioural Insights Team, 207, 221
Benay, Alex, ix, 18
Berners-Lee, Sir Tim, 116
big data: and dearth of information management across silos, 12; digital skills and, 156; and government-citizen relationship, 211; guidelines/policies for, 213; in Liberal campaign, 226; and policy development, 10, 227; Statistics Canada pilots, 192; uses of, 145
Big Data Consortium, 243n9
BlackBerry Messenger, 109, 186
Blevis, Mark, 161
Blueprint 2020: about, 130, 136–41; as base for challenges to silos/hierarchies, 202; carefulness in applying, 190; and closed vs open government, 137; criticisms of, 140–41; DCMPI and, 143, 149; as digital government showcase, 200; and digital skills gap, 154; and "Dragon's Den" forums, 139–40, 155, 200; employee consultations under, 138–39; #GC2020, 138–39, 148, 225; and internal opening of bureaucracy, 137; introduction of, 46; launch, 136; participation rate, 140; and PCO's Central Innovation Hub, 145; and policy innovation, 150, 153; results, 140–41; and risk aversion, 150–51; and social media, 139; uses, 138–39; "Vision for Canada's Federal Public Service," 136–37
Bourgon, Jocelyn, 57
Bracken, Mike, 169, 172, 177, 178, 243n8
branding: through communications standardization, 64; DGUs and, 169, 170, 171, 177; open data and, 113–14; PIF/Code for America and, 168; public administration and, 62
Braybrook, Jeff, 132
Brison, Scott, 182, 202, 216
British Columbia, Government of, 99, 144; open data portal, 100

British Columbia, University of, 166
Brock, Kathy, 190
Brown, David C.G., 28–29
Brown, Gordon, 116
bureaucracy/bureaucrats. *See* public
service
bureaucrat-bureaucrat relationship:
about, 39–40; and bureaucrat-
citizen relationship, 92; closed,
39–42, 58, 63–64, 92, 100; competitive
communications culture and, 63–64;
GCTools and, 133; horizontality in,
185–86; open, 15; silos/hierarchies
and, 6
bureaucrat-citizen relationship. *See*
government-citizen relationship

Cabinet Committee on Open Transparent
Government and Parliament, 216
Canada Revenue Agency (CRA), 145,
160, 162
Canada School of Public Service, 102,
198, 200
Canada Student Loans Program, 124
Canada.ca, 65, 107
Canada's Communications Community
Office (CCCO), 74; "Considerations
for the Government of Canada's Use
of Social Media to Communicate with
and Engage the Public," 74
Canadian Association of Programs in
Public Administration, 201
Canadian Council for International
Cooperation, 57
Canadian Diabetes Association, 144
Canadian Environmental Network, 57
Canadian Environmental Protection Act
(1999), 56
Canadian Exhibition Commission, 62
Canadian Manufacturers and
Exporters, 123
Canadian National Parks Act (2000), 56
Canadian Open Data Experience
(CODE), 101, 160

Canadian Open Government Civil
Society Network, 179
Canadian Policy Research Network, 56, 161
Canadian Tire, 144
Career ConneXions Opportunity
Platform, 204
Carrot, 144–45
Central Innovation Hub, 144, 145, 217
centralization: of communications, 64–65,
87–90, 163; of control over social
media, 88; and effective governance, 64;
and equity, 67; of information control,
84; pluralistic government-citizen
relationship vs, 223
Centre for Excellence in Public Sector
Marketing, 161
Charette, Janice, 135
Charter of Rights and Freedoms, 59, 66,
89, 224–25
chief digital officer position, 169, 180–81
Chief Information Officer (CIO):
and government as a platform, 18;
Information Technology Strategic Plan,
198–99; talent management indicators
for chief information officers, 198;
whole of government commitment to
open data, 99
Chief Information Officer Branch
(CIOB): about, 32; and GCTools, 131,
135; and open data, 114, 115, 117–18; open
data team, 100; and open government
initiative, 97, 112; and social media, 74
China, digital services vs accountability
in, 25–26
Chrétien, Jean, 67
citizen-government relationship. *See*
government-citizen relationship
citizen-/user-centrism: digital
government theories and, 21;
limitations/inaccuracies of, 227–29;
policies/services based on experiences,
9; Service Canada and, 43; in tech
sector vs governments, 23–24; in web-
based communications, 64–65

Civic Tech Toronto, 179

Clement, Tony: on crowdsourcing, 114; mandatory long-form census cancellation, 113; and open data, 114, 115, 116; and open government, 110–11, 113; TBS policy on use of social media, 74, 85; Twitter townhall, 106, 120, 122, 127, 155, 205; as Twitter user, 85

Clients-First Service Strategy, 199

Climate Change Secretariat, 44

closed government: and accountable governance, 7; bureaucrat-bureaucrat relationship in, 39–42; bureaucratic arrogance and, 118; cost of failures, 194; costs of, 29; and crises of confidence in state, 25; as default, 12, 95, 119, 174; human resource costs, 25, 94; information management and driver/ symptom, 117; networked, digital technologies vs, 69; origins, 182–83; permanent campaigning and, 27–28, 39; and policy/program/operational failures, 25; and rate of change/ reform, 25; reasons against, 24–25, 69; reasons for endurance, 39; recruitment of talent, 25; and reinforcement of stereotypes, 195; resilience of, 11–17; risks of, 24–25, 29, 90, 94–95, 191, 195, 196; social media and ineffectiveness of, 96; Weberianism/PPA and, 28–29; wholesale shift from, 187–89

closed vs open government. See open vs closed government

Coase, Robert, 227

Code for All network, 167

Code for America, 167–68, 169, 170, 198

"Code for Canada," 180

Code of Good Practice on Funding, 54, 56, 61

Code of Good Practice on Policy Dialogue, 56

collaboration: and accountability, 44–45; behavioural insights and, 203–4; benefits of, 203; Blueprint 2020 and, 139; bureaucrat-bureaucrat, 202–3; DGUs and, 175; externalization and, 179; GCTools and, 132, 133, 185; horizontal, 202–3; and horizontal accountability, 204; with nongovernmental organizations, 54; permanent campaigning vs, 27; on policy design/development, 10, 44, 105, 141; and policy innovation initiatives, 143, 145–46; promotion of cross-government, 202; silos vs, 44, 132, 202–3; social media and, 74, 80, 81; Trudeau and, 216; vertical, 203; wicked policy problems and, 26. See also consultation(s); coordination

command and control governance: default to, 12; digital era governance and, 26; Gomery Commission and, 49

commissioner of lobbying, 49

Common Look and Feel Standard, 59

communications: accessibility of, 66; centralization of, 64–66, 87–90, 163; citizen-centric, 64–66; Communications Policy of the Government of Canada, 59, 75, 212; competitive, 63–64; consultants, 161; consumerization of, 62; coordination of, 64; error-free government and, 90; failure intolerance and, 215; and government-citizen relationship, 20, 91; and hierarchies, 20; history as public service function, 53; message consistency, 62–63; ministers' online, 225; nonpartisanship of, 66–67; official languages and, 66; open culture and, 221; permanent campaigning and withholding of information, 63–64; pluralistic model of, 208; and public service impartiality, 62–63; rationalization/standardization of, 64–66; and silos, 20; and social media, 71, 72, 74–75, 77, 92, 94, 95, 141, 192, 207; training, 209–10; Trudeau and open style of, 216; whole of department/ government strategies, 88

conflict of interest and ethics
commissioner, 49
"Considerations for the Government
of Canada's Use of Social Media to
Communicate with and Engage the
Public" (CCCO), 74
consultation(s): accessibility, 66; on
Blueprint 2020, 138–39; Consulting
with Canadians, 106; and data
management, 121; digitization
of, 120–28; government-citizen
relationship and, 121–22; hierarchies
and, 125, 127; hybrid model of openness,
68; obligatory, 55–56; official languages
and, 66; and open data, 100; open
dialogue and, 102–6, 120, 121–22; policy,
64, 127, 185; preplanning for, 121–22;
siloing of, 125; social listening and, 121;
social media and, 74, 120–21; top-down
guidance/rules for, 60, 66; traditional
analytical techniques for, 155
Consulting with Canadians, 106
coordination: of communications, 64;
and credibility of information, 65–66;
of information sharing, 88; as key
objective of bureaucracy, 64; online
consultations and, 128; and open data,
100; and open vs closed government,
97; of policy consultations, 64; on
policy issues, 44; of service delivery,
88; in use of social media, 96. See also
collaboration
Corrective Blogging, 124–25, 127, 147,
206–7
corruption: ATIP vs, 7; PPA and, 52;
service delivery contracts vs, 66
court government, 62
Craft, Jonathan, 236n11
crowdsourcing: Challenge.gov, 115;
Clement on, 114; as digital policy
instrument, 10; digital skills gap and,
186; GCpedia and, 142; Icelandic
constitution, 3; and in-house capacity
building, 165, 188; internal policy, 203;

open dialogue and, 102, 106; of policy
proposals, 144; and policy work, 227;
questions raised by, 22; sharing/gig
economy and, 3; and statistical literacy,
156; *Time* and, 4

data: collection/trails from social
media, 211; commercial value of, 162;
digital technologies and production
of, 5; driving decision making, 227;
externalization, and loss of access to,
161–63; gaps, 162; guidelines/policies
for collection/use, 213; long-form
census, 113, 220; partnerships/sharing
agreements, 211; policy analysis, and
accessibility to social media data,
94; potential applications, 118, 128;
produced by consultations, 121; shallow
bureaucratic awareness/appreciation,
120; sharing, 162; siloing of, 117–18, 120;
tech firms and, 5. See also big data
datadotgc.ca, 99
data.gc.ca, 98
Day, Stockwell, 18, 35, 97, 99, 114, 116
Deficit Reduction Action Plan, 112
Delacourt, Susan, 62
deliverology, 202, 217
Deloitte, 193
democratic governance: failures and
legitimacy of, 195; and opening of
government, 29; and parochialism/
resistance to change, 23–24
Deputy Minister Committee on Policy
Innovation (DMCPI): about, 142–44;
attempt to be less hierarchical/
exclusive, 150; and big data in policy
making, 192; change of name from
Deputy Minister Committee on Social
Media and Policy Development, 142,
215; diagnosis of conditions preventing
innovation, 144; and digital skills gap,
154; #DMCPI Twitter network, 148;
exploration of Internet access, 103; on
fear of failure, 186; and innovation labs/

hubs, 145; and leadership from Trudeau government, 217; and rate of uptake of initiatives, 145–46; report on barriers to innovation, 148–50; and reverse mentors, 142; and siloed/hierarchical information exchange, 143; on societal trends, 142–43; use of GCpedia, 134; Virtual Policy Challenge, 143–44

Deputy Minister Committee on Social Media and Policy Development: about, 141–42; change of name to Deputy Minister Committee on Policy Innovation (DMCPI), 215

Destination 2020, 139

digital bargain: about, 223–24; accountability and, 229; and anonymity, 210, 223; and partisanship, 224–25; and political activity rules/guidelines, 224–25; user-centrism vs, 229; Westminster system and, 224

Digital Era Governance (DEG), 9, 12, 13–14, 18, 36, 185, 245n1

Digital Governance Forum 2016, 158

digital government theories: and accountability, 20; and citizens as "users," 227–29; and closed vs open government, 7–8; and coordination, 20; and costs of open government, 36; and DEG model, 9; and depoliticization of public service context, 21; descriptive, 184, 185–87; dispensing with historical principles, 189; and dissolution of hierarchies/silos, 8, 184; and externalization, 22–23; and government as platform, 8–9; and government-citizen relationship, 8–9, 189; governments' invocation of, 18; on incompatibility of closed government, 11; and layering effects, 13–14; nonpartisanship vs, 189; normative, 18, 183–84, 187; and NPM, 15–16; and open data, 10; and permanent campaigning, 22; and possibility vs desirability of open government, 17; problems with,

17; public administration research vs, 17, 19; as replacing Weber/PPA/Westminster narratives, 8; and retreat to closed government, 21–24; source of mainstream, 16–17; and stickiness of institutional legacies, 184; and transformations of government machinery/culture, 7–8; Trudeau and, 19; and uptake of new digital policy instruments, 10; wholesale shift to open government, 189; and wikis, 9

digital government units (DGUs): about, 168; agile development methodologies, 172; in Australia, 169, 172, 174; branding by, 169, 171, 177; and broader "digital transformation," 173–74; Canadian creation of, ix, 180; and closed vs open government, 173; and collaboration, 175; and culture change, 173–74, 178; delivery vs process emphasis, 172–73; and dismantling of silos, 178–79; GDS, 168–69; in Ontario, 169, 170, 172; platform/common standards production, 175; procurement practices, 173; recruitment of talent, 170–71, 178; resistance/resentment against, 175–78; and social media, 174–75; tone/approach shift over time, 177–78; in UK, 172, 174–75, 175–77; in US, 169, 170, 175; and whole of government infrastructures, 174–75

digital skills: absence of, 35; acquisition, 28; big data and, 156; Blueprint 2020 and retention of employees with, 138; bolstering of, 159; competitive market for, 165; computer science programs, 165–66; contracting, 160–61; creation of permanent unit of digital expertise, 180–81; dearth of, 28, 179; in departmental IT shops, 156–57; executives/managers and, 159; external vs internal, 22; and externalization/contracting consultants, 163–64, 165, 200, 202; and information asymmetries

between public servants and external providers, 164, 173; in-house capacity building, 22, 165, 168, 179, 187–88, 199, 202, 212–13; investment in, 197–202; literacy building, 199–200; millennials and, 157–59; on-the-job training, 157; and open government initiatives, 154; in policy work, 226; in public policy/administration programs, 155–56, 201; in public vs private sectors, 165–67; recruitment of outside talent, 159; statistical literacy vs, 156; as technical and data science skills, 156–57; training in, 156; in university curricula, 157
digital skills gap: academic partnerships and, 160; as barrier to digital government, 36, 154; contracting and, 159; and crowdsourcing, 186; data management, 121; DGUs and, 171–73; diagnosing needs for, 198–99; and externalization, 160, 161–62, 164–65; Information Technology Strategic Plan, 198–99; for large-scale government-citizen engagement analysis, 206; millennials and, 157–59; need for plan, 198–99; and open data, 186; partnerships and, 159; and Phoenix pay system procurement, 164; social listening, 121. *See also* recruitment of digital talent
Digital Transformation Agency (DTA), 172, 174
Directgov, 168
"Dragon's Den" forums, 139–40, 143, 155, 200, 203
Dunleavy, Patrick, 9, 13–14, 18, 184, 236*n*11; *Digital Era Governance*, 244*n*1

Eaves, David: and datadotgc.ca, 99; on Harper's open government initiative, 111; on long-form census, 113, 220; and open data, 99; on open data, 10, 114; on public service Twitter users, 136; on TBS Guideline for social media, 76;

and TBS open data strategies, 18; and Vancouver open data initiative, 18
Economic Action Plan, 35, 66, 111
Economy and Society (Weber), 182
electronic/e-government, 12–13, 19–20, 43, 64–65, 156–57, 164
Employment and Social Development Canada (ESDC), 32, 105, 145, 146, 154–55; Online Skills Forum, 123–24, 127, 207
Engineers without Borders, 218
Environmental Assessment Act (Canada), 56
e-petitions, 3–4, 10, 115, 195, 224, 225
equity: accountability for, 214; centralization and, 67; defined, 236*n*11; enduring relevance of, 29; and government-citizen interactions, 66; historical principles underpinning, 189; online consultations and, 128; and open information, 108; and open vs closed government, 97; and parochialism/resistance to change, 23; pluralistic online government-citizen interactions and, 20; PPA and, 38; silos/hierarchies and, 68, 69; social media and, 90; in treatment of citizens, 66
error-free government: accountability and, 186, 214; accountability-for-learning model and, 217; communications and, 90; failure vs, 215; innovation vs, 49–50, 186; ministerial mandate letters vs, 217; permanent campaigning and, 21, 49; social media and, 86
experimentation: with digital technologies, 147; open communications culture and, 221; and policy innovation initiatives, 143; reward structures for, 218; TBS rules/policies vs, 146, 216. *See also* innovation
externalization: about, 179–80; and accessibility, 163; and accountability, 22, 163; and centralized communications,

163; collaboration and, 179; and coordination, 22; and data collection, 211; and data sharing, 162; defined, 15, 160; digital government theories and, 22–23; digital literacy skills and, 200; digital skills gap and, 160, 161–62, 164–65; failed, 22–23; and feedback loops, 161–62; in-house digital skills and, 165, 202; in-house expertise development vs, 187–88; and loss of access to data, 161–63; network governance and, 15; and official languages, 163; and open data, 188; open government and, 187; partnerships, 159, 162–63; in policy process, 160–61; in public administration literature, 163; of service delivery, 53–54, 56; "smart shopping" in, 163–64; and value of data, 162
Extractive Sector Transparency Measures Act, 107

Facebook, 4, 16–17, 72, 84, 192
failure(s): accountability and mitigation of, 186–87; communications vs, 215; cost of closed government, 194; costs of, 186; and democratic legitimacy, 195; DGUs and prevention of, 180; digital, 194–95; embrace of, 218; error-free government vs, 215; information sharing vs, 215; of innovations, 48; learning from, 50; ministerial mandate letters vs, 216–17; need for public tolerance of, 220–21; nongovernmental actors and exposure of, 219; open government and public-facing, 21; permanent campaigning and, 27, 39, 215; political culture tolerating, 215–21; public service role in tolerance for, 220–21; reports, 218; status quo vs, 215
Federal Accountability Act (FAA), 49, 67, 186
Federal Economic Development Agency for Southern Ontario, 112

Federal Identity Policy, 212
Federal Identity Program (TBS), 59, 64, 75, 89
Five Eyes Intelligence consortium, 26, 213
Flack, Graham, 143–44
Foreign Affairs, Trade and Development, Department of (DFATD): and big data, 145; online dialogue, 125; Open Policy Development, 144; and social media, 144
Foreign Affairs and International Trade and Development, Department of (DFAIT): academic partnerships, 160; Corrective Blogging, 206–7; and social media, 73, 144, 147; use of GCconnex, 134
Foreign and Commonwealth Office (UK), 126–27, 171; register of country names, 175
foreign service: de-anonymization of, 58; model of government-citizen relationship, 210; presumption of competence to engage in social media, 208
Foreshew-Cain, Stephen, 178–79
Francoli, Mary, 108–9, 111
Fraser Institute, 160–61
Full Duplex, 161

G8 countries, Open Data Charter, 18
GCCollab, 209
GCconnex: about, 131; Blueprint 2020 and, 138, 204; and digital literacy, 200; "Dragon's Den" forums and, 143; funding, 199; GCCollab, 209; introduction of, 131; membership growth, 204; profiles, 203, 204; users/uses, 134, 135
GCDocs, 108
GCForums, 242n2
GCpedia: about, 131, 237n14; and Blueprint 2020, 138; collaboration and, 132; crowdsourcing and, 142; and digital literacy, 200; digital skills investment

through, 198; funding, 199; numbers of accounts, 135; uses of, 134

GCTools: about, 130, 131–36; as base for challenges to silos/hierarchies, 202; Blueprint 2020 and, 138; budget allocation, 135; carefulness in applying, 190; and collaboration/information sharing, 185, 203–4; creation of, 175; DCMPI and, 143; and "duty to document" digital policy instruments, 200–201; enabler of bottom-up, interdepartmental engagement, 142; failure to deliver on theory of change, 136; gamifying use of, 204; and horizontal government, 222; and information sharing, 136; and innovation, 145; internal capacity building for external engagement, 133–34; and internal opening of bureaucracy, 137; lack of political investment constraining scope of change, 152; limited functionality and, 155; and networking, 132–33, 222; policy innovation movement compared, 150; potential role in socializing external online social networking, 209; rate of usage, 134–36, 137, 202–3; results, 140; and risk aversion, 150; as "safe space" for dialogue/information sharing, 149; and silos/hierarchies, 185; and social media use, 133–34; staff for, 151; training in, 200, 203; uses of, 134, 185

GeoQ, 167

GitHub, 101, 173

Glassco Commission of 1960, 46, 49

Global Affairs Canada, 53

Globe and Mail Test, 63

Gomery Commission of Inquiry, 49, 67, 186

Google, 4, 93, 227; Hangouts, 106

Government 2.0, 8

"Government and IT – A Recipe for Rip Offs" (Public Administration Select Committee), 164, 220

Government Digital Service (GDS): award-winning digital services, 175; blog, 207; and cost savings, 175; costs of failed IT projects and investment in, 194; creation of, 18; on credibility of website information sources, 65; criticisms of, 176–77; Digital Buyers Guide, 244*n*13; dissolution threat, 175–76; as first DGU, 168; funding, 199; and government as a platform, 188; gov.uk, 172; growth of, 171; introduction of, 168–69; numbers of staff, 199; recruitment hub, 174; register of country names, 175; rejection of reliance on outside expertise, 187–88; Social Media Guidance, 174–75; Social Media Playbook, 174–75; strategy, 172; whole of government mandate, 169

Government Electronic Directory Service, 53, 208–9

Government Online, 43

government as a platform, 8–9, 12, 18, 36, 165, 185, 188, 244*n*8

government-citizen relationship: accessibility, 70–71; accountability and, 66, 67, 68, 88–89; aims of, 14; analytical techniques, 206; and anonymity, 58, 68, 94, 208–9; and "bargain basement citizenship," 63; big data from, 211; bureaucrat-bureaucrat relationship and, 92; citizens as consumers/clients in, 15, 228; citizens as "users," 227; closed, 51–52, 53, 58; closed government, and mistrust of government, 195; communications and, 91; costs of, 205–6; culture of secrecy and, 63–64; decentralization, and policy debates, 20–21; decentralized vs centralized approach to, 64, 186; digital communication technologies in, 20; digital government theories and, 8–9, 189; in digitized consultations, 121–22; empowerment of public services to engage online in, 207; equity and, 66;

exploration of new models, 206–7; foreign service model, 210; funding, 199; funding of external organizations in, 56–57; GCTools and, 136; GDS and, 18; and growth of public service functions, 53; hierarchies and, 59, 62, 68, 96, 128, 185; hybrid model/managed openness, 68; information control and, 71, 94; innovation and, 89, 220–21; innovative models of dialogue in, 210–11; large-scale engagement, 205–6; as low-trust, 7; marginalization of, 51–52; meaningful online engagement, 95; mediation through third party, 161; nongovernmental organization service delivery, 161; NPM and, 53–54; online challenges/opportunities, 205–6; open data and, 101, 117–18, 119; open government initiative and, 116; openings of, 53–58; permanent campaigning and, 61–62, 64; pluralistic approach, 20, 207–8, 209, 223; in policy development, 54–57, 103, 105, 205; POR, 59–60; power in, 228; PPA and, 28, 52; presumption of competence and, 208; quasi-open, 58–61, 64, 68; risk aversion and, 84–85; royal commissions and, 55; silos and, 62, 91, 96, 185; social media and, 11–12, 70, 79, 81–82, 103, 105, 205; transparency in, 71; in UK, 117–18; Web 2.0 technologies and, 195–96; Weber and, 63; under Westminster system, 6–7, 51, 63, 87, 188
GovLab, 9, 100
Growing Up Digital (Tapscott), 158
Guideline for the External Use of Web 2.0 (TBS), 74–76, 77, 89, 102, 245n8

hackathons, 10, 22, 101, 160, 162, 165
Halligan, John, 190
Harper, Stephen: and closed by default bureaucracy, 97–98; closure of government to public, 33; and command and control governance,

26; and consumerization of communications, 62; control of government communications, 35; and culture of secrecy/information control, 113; Economic Action Plan, 66; and Federal Accountability Act, 49, 67; as first digital-era prime minister, 35; and government communications, 66–67; ignoring bureaucracy advice/expertise, 151; information control, 111, 151; lack of commitment to open culture, 111; leadership style, 26, 30, 111, 128–29, 182, 223; legacy of, 183; limiting media access, 111; and open government, 128–29; and Open Government Action Plans, 117; and open(ish) government, 35, 98, 205; and parliamentary budget officer, 35; and permanent campaigning, 27–28, 61, 84, 86; politicization of communications, 111; politics of open government initiative, 116; proroguing Parliament, 35, 111; public service renewal under, 35; and risk-averse management, 84–86, 128; and scientists, 58, 111; social media approach, 84–87
"Harperman" YouTube video, 224
healthcare.gov, 169, 194
Heart and Stroke Foundation, 144
Heritage Canada, 219
hierarchies: about, 40, 68; and accountability, 19, 40–41, 45, 49, 52; advantages of, 19–20; in bureaucrat-citizen relationship, 59, 68; challenges against, vs status quo, 190–91; characteristics of, 46; and consultations, 60, 125; and corruption reduction, 52; and cross-cutting policy issues, 47; decrying culture of, 14; digital communication and, 20; digital government theories and dissolution of, 184; "Dragon's Den" forums vs, 139–40; endurance of, 67, 68, 69; and failure intolerance, 215; GCTools and, 132–33,

185; in government-citizen relationship, 62, 96, 128, 185; history of, 41–42; horizontality and, 19–20, 38; information control and, 87; and information sharing, 46–48, 132, 140; innovation vs, 48–51, 217–18; and internal openness, 130; joined-up government and, 19–20; and knowledge gaps, 48; legitimacy of, 19; new governance paradigms vs, 185; and open vs closed government, 184–85; permanent campaigning and, 39; and policy consultations/engagement, 60, 127; PPA and, 6, 40; reporting mechanisms, 46–48; and risk aversion, 49; and social media, 74, 83, 86, 87, 88–89, 94, 185; Westminster system and, 6; whole of government strategies as, 188

Hill and Knowlton, 161

Himelfarb, Alex, 63

Hootsuite, 72

horizontality: and accountability, 204; auditing vs, 61; bureaucracy as ill-equipped for, 44; in bureaucrat-bureaucrat relationship, 185–86; and centralization, 64; collaboration/cross-silos, 202–3; cultural barriers to, 185; e-government and, 43; fostering of internal openings, 202–4; GCTools and, 132–33, 222; and hierarchies, 19–20; incentivization of, 203; and innovation, 145–46; and ministerial accountability/attribution, 45; network governance and, 15; in policy issues, 44; in policy making, 57, 143–44; prioritization of, 202; as public administration objective, 14, 43–44; Shared Services Canada and, 43; and sharing of ministerial attribution, 204; silos vs, 15, 42, 132; stickiness of historical legacy vs, 39; task forces on, 44. See also joined-up government; whole of government

human resources: costs, 25, 94, 193–94. See also digital skills; recruitment of digital talent

Human Resources Development Canada (HRDC) Grants and Contributions program, 61, 186

Human Resources and Skills Development Canada (HRSDC): Corrective Blogging, 124–25, 127, 206–7; media roundup, 73, 92; on social media, 80, 82, 94; "Tweet Approval Process," 76–78; Twitter account, 91–92

human rights: digital era governance and, 26. See also equity

IBM, 158, 161

Industry Canada: innovation lab, 145; tweet approval process, 78

InfoBase, 107

information and communications technology (ICT): public sector as cutting-edge innovation hotspot, 165; and reinforcement vs reversal of status quo, 12–13. See also digital technologies; information technology (IT)

Information and Communications Technology Council, 243n10

information control: centralized, 84; and closed government, 68; decrying culture of, 14; digital age and democratization of, 4–5; digital era open government vs, 130; fear of failure and, 186; and GCTools use, 136; and government-citizen relationship, 71, 94; Harper and, 111, 113, 151; innovation vs, 68, 151; open communications style vs, 216; and open government initiative, 113, 129; permanent campaigning and, 27; silos/hierarchies and, 87, 203

information management (IM): and accountability, 188; and driver/symptom of closed government, 117; and open data strategy, 117, 119

information sharing: accessibility of, 70–71; and accountability, 93, 188; anonymity vs, 133; behavioural insights and, 203–4; benefits of, 203; Blueprint

2020 and, 139; coordination of, 88; decentralized vs centralized, 96, 207–8; failure vs, 215; GCTools and, 132, 133, 136; hierarchies and, 46–48, 132, 140; and horizontal accountability, 204; incentivization of, 203; and neutrality, 93; in pluralistic online interactions, 207–8; social media and, 73, 80, 82–83, 153; TBS open government initiative and, 97; traditions conflicting with, 133–34; vertical, 140

information technology (IT): infrastructure building/maintenance, 201–2; marginalization in public administration research/theory, 16–17, 163, 229–30; marginalization of, 16–17, 226. *See also* digital technologies

Information Technology Strategic Plan, 198–99, 200, 201, 202, 203

innovation: accountability and, 50; analysis of conditions limiting, 218; citizens' role in, 220–21; conditions preventing, 144; defined, 48; deliverology, 217; digital bargain and, 223; digital policy, 130; error-free government vs, 49–50, 186; failed, 48; in government-citizen interaction, 89; hierarchies vs, 48–51, 217–18; horizontality and, 145–46; information control vs, 68, 151; and information flows, 48; management and, 147–50; media and, 219–20; micromanagement vs, 49; middle management and, 147–48, 218; nongovernmental actors and, 218–19; permanent campaigning vs, 27, 50–51; political culture rewarding, 215–21; political leadership and, 151–52, 215–16; in Public Service Employee Survey, 218; and "pull," 217–18; rate of uptake of initiatives, 145; recruitment of outside managers for, 218; risk aversion vs, 50, 51, 68, 150, 151, 214; and rule adherence vs flexible adaptation, 214; silos and, 145–46; social media and,

146; TBS rules/policies vs, 212, 214, 216. *See also* experimentation

Innovation, Science and Economic Development Canada, 145

Innovation Strategy, 44

Institute for Research on Public Policy, 57

Internet: Canadians' use of, 4; departmental use, 103–5, 192–93; document-sharing services, 103; firewalls, 73; General Social Survey (GSS) and use of, 235*n*2; Pew Center surveys, 235*n*2

Intuit, 160, 162

Jarvis, Mark, 237*n*3

Johnson, Clay, 167

joined-up government: fostering of internal openings, 202–4; and hierarchies, 19–20; and open data, 120; as public administration objective, 14. *See also* horizontality; whole of government

Journal of European Social Policy, 17

Juillet, Luc, 43–44

Kernaghan, Kenneth, 29

KPMG, 160

Kujawski, Mike, 161

Lane Fox, Martha, 168; "Directgov: Revolution Not Evolution," 168–69

Laurier, Wilfrid, 62

Legault, Suzanne, 63, 108, 109, 110

Lenczner, Michael, 100

Levasseur, Karine, 61

Liberal Party: campaign use of big data/social media, 226; and early record on digital government, ix–xi; and open government, 26. *See also* Trudeau, Justin

Library and Archives Canada, 60, 67, 108

Library of Parliament, 60

Lim, Leonard, 167

LinkedIn: Canadians' use of, 4; de-anonymization of public servants, 208; Ontario and, 170
Linux operating system, 8, 9
London School of Economics, Government on the Web, 160
Lynch, Kevin, 50–51, 70–71, 73, 135

Maclean's, 165
Management Accountability Framework, 198
Margetts, Helen, 9, 14, 18, 184, 236*n*11, 244*n*1
Marland, Alex, 62
Massé, Marcel, 54–55, 221
Matthews, Deb, 169
Maude, Sir Francis, 169, 178
McGill University, 166
media: 24/7 environment, 63; and anonymity, 53; cycle, 21–22; denial of access to, 35; departmental communications roundups of, 72–73, 92; and "gotcha" journalism, 51, 110, 220; and innovation, 219–20; and limiting access to ministers, 111
Mendelsohn, Matthew, 202, 217
millennials, 157–59, 193–94
MindLab, 207–8, 221
Minecraft, 101
ministerial accountability: anonymity and, 20, 210; and digital bargain, 224; and ministerial attribution, 45; open government vs, 29; public servant accountability vs, 188; in Westminster system, 7, 41, 51, 95
ministerial attribution: ministerial accountability and, 45; sharing, 204
"mommy blogging," 4, 195
Montréal, Université de, 166
Montréal Ouvert, 179
Morozov, Evgeny, 163–64
Mozilla Firefox, 8
Munk Centre of Global Affairs, 160
mySociety, 158, 169

National Security Agency (US), 26
National Trading Standards Board (UK), 65–66
Natural Resources Canada (NRCan): and Carrot, 144; common geospatial data standards, 98; Innovation Hub, 145, 200; New Policy Instruments portal, 200; wiki, 131
neoliberalism: and consumerization of communications, 62; and open data, 35, 114. *See also* New Public Management (NPM)
network governance, 15–16, 57
networking: Blueprint 2020 and, 138; closed government vs, 69; GCconnex and, 131; GCTools and, 132–33, 222; increasing common interest participation, 4; and open government, 7–8; and pluralistic online interactions, 207–8; silos, and deficiency in, 43; social media and, 73; social movements and, 3–4; *Time* and, 4
neutrality: anonymity and, 20, 210; in communications training, 209–10; and digital bargain, 224; enduring relevance of, 29; historical principles underpinning, 189; information sharing and, 93; online consultations and, 128; of policy work, 227; social media and, 22, 188–89; Westminster system and, 95. *See also* partisanship/nonpartisanship
New Political Governance, 62–63
New Public Management (NPM): and accountability/auditing explosion, 61; and agencification of government, 9; alternative service delivery under, 161; in bureaucrat-citizen relationship, 53–54; Canadian government and, 190; challenges/resistance by bureaucracy, 15–16; and citizens as consumers, 62; DEG contrasted with, 244*n*1; individual citizens under, 16; and lessons for digital era externalization, 161–65; and open data, 114; outsourcing IT

capacity under, 164; persistence of silos/hierarchies compared to, 184; separation of policy from service delivery, 161; setbacks resulting from, 23; and silos, 9; in UK, 169

New Zealand, gov.nz, 65

nodality, 206, 226, 227

nongovernmental actors: and alternative models of service delivery, 53–54; collaboration with, 54; data use through externalization, 162; and decrease in direct citizen-government contact, 161; exposure of public service failures, 219; government as platform and, 165; influence of, 227; information distribution/collection, 206; and innovation, 218–19; open data and, 118–19; service delivery, 15

Norris, Donald, 13

Noveck, Beth, 9, 184; *Smarter Citizens, Smarter State,* 244n2; *Wiki Government,* 14

Nuclear Fuel Waste Act (2002), 56

Obama, Barack: campaign promise of open government, 14; enthusiasm for digital government innovation/open government, 244n2; on government vs Silicon Valley, 23–24; and healthcare.gov, 194; Memorandum on Transparency and Open Government, 115; Noveck and, 9, 14; open government initiative, 18; PIF program and, 167, 168; social media use, 115; and USDS, 171

official languages: communications and, 66; in communications training, 209; consultations and, 66; externalization and, 163; ministerial online communications and, 225; and open information, 108; and social media, 89, 90

Official Languages Act, 49, 55–56, 59, 89, 214

Olsen, J.P., 67

Online Skills Forum, 123–24, 127, 207

Ontario, Government of: chief digital officer, 169, 180; digital team's recruitment call on LinkedIn, 170; Internship Program, 180; job openings advertising, 177; minister of digital government, 169; Ontario.ca, 65, 169

open vs closed government, 25; accountability and, 97; coordination and, 97; and democratic governance, 26; DGUs and, 173; digital era governance and, 25–26; digital government activity and, 26–27; digital government theories and, 7–8; equity and, 97; open government initiative and, 97–98; permanent campaigning and, 186, 187; risks, 29–30; silos/hierarchies and, 184–85; and social media, 96; wicked policy problems and, 26

Open Contracting Data Standards, 107

open data: about, 98–102, 113–17; and Access to Information Act/ATIP, 107; Ajah, 100–1; BC government and, 100; and branding, 113–14; bureaucratic arrogance and, 118; Citizens for Open Access to Civic Information and Data, 98–99; Citizenship and Immigration Canada, 100–1; closed government vs, 128; CODE, 101; common data standards and, 100; consultation on digital economy (2010), 99; data coordination and, 100; data users/uses, 100–1; data.gc.ca, 99; and dearth of information management across silos, 12; digital government theories and, 10; early initiatives, 98–99; and economic growth, 115, 116; Environment Canada initiative, 99, 100; externalization and, 188; and fear of culpability, 119; flaws in sets, 99–100; funding, 199; and geospatial data, 119; Government Electronic Directory Service as, 53, 209;

government use, 100; government-citizen relationship and, 101, 117–18, 119; https://open.canada.ca/en/apps, 100; information management and, 117, 119; interjurisdictional data and, 100; joined-up systems thinking and, 120; and lack of skills/knowledge, 186; literacy, 200; neoliberalism and, 35; NRCan and, 98–99; numbers of data sets, 99; OGP and, 97; open dialogue vs, 106; open information compared, 110; permanent campaigning and, 113; potential benefits, 119–20; prioritization of, 165; sets as informational service, 101; silos vs, 10; standardization of, 175; in UK, 115–16, 117–18; in US, 117–18; web/mobile apps, 100–1; Westminster historical default vs, 101; whole of government commitment to, 99

Open Data Charter, 18

Open Data Institute (Waterloo), 112

Open Data Ottawa, 179

open dialogue: about, 102–6; aim, 102; anonymity and, 125, 128; communications and social media vs, 207; and consultations, 102–6, 120, 121–22, 127–28; and Consulting with Canadians, 106; crowdsourcing, 106; departmental use of Internet/social media, 103–5; in government-citizen relationship, 120; hierarchies and, 128; innovative citizen engagement, 123–25; limits of traditional policy toolkits in, 155; OGP and, 97; online platform development for, 105–6; open data vs, 106; and Open Government Action Plans, 205; and social media, 102, 120; and Web 2.0 tools, 102

open government: and accountability, 7; anonymity vs, 29; and ATIP, 7–8; broader interpretation of, 27; as default, 7, 149, 202–3; democratic governance and, 29; DGUs and, 168; digital government literature vs earlier interpretations of, 7–8; fostering internal openings, 202–4; freedom of information and, 7, 27; leading to opaque public administration, 21–22; media cycle and, 21–22; ministerial accountability vs, 29; networked digital technologies and, 7–8; political leadership and credibility of, 35; possibility vs desirability of, 17; public service bargain vs, 29; and public-facing failure, 21; rethinking approach to external openings, 205–11; and risk aversion, 21, 22; risks of, 189–90; tension between traditional vs digital framings of, 109; traditional public administration vs, 24; and transparency, 7; wholesale shift to, 187–89, 196

Open Government Action Plans: and ATIP, 108–9; on data skills gap, 121; on digital literacy, 200; and digital skills, 206; and government-citizen engagement, 205; lack of evidence of digital era in, 102; and open dialogue, 106, 205; and open information, 108–10; and open(ish) government, 117; releases of, 97

Open Government Directive, 97

open government initiative: as "bolt-on solution," 129; budget, 112; culture of secrecy vs, 110, 113; departmental resources for, 112; Harper's leadership style vs, 111, 116; information control vs, 113; introduction of, 97; OGP and, 112–14; open data, 98–102, 113–17; open dialogue, 102–6; open information, 107–10; political leadership and, 128–29; results, 128; rhetoric vs practice, 97–98; role of political culture, 110; three themes of, 97; in UK, 115–16; workforce cuts and, 112

Open Government Licence, 99

Open Government Partnership (OGP), x, 18, 97, 108, 110, 111, 112–14

open information: about, 107–10; and Access to Information Act/ATIP,

107–8; culture of secrecy vs, 128; OGP and, 97; open data compared, 110; Open Government Action Plans and, 108–10; open.canada.ca, 107; virtual library, 107

Open North, 179

Open Policy Development, 144

Open Source Governance, 8

open.canada.ca, 98, 107

O'Reilly, Tim, 8–9, 18, 132, 165, 167, 188

Organization for Economic Cooperation and Development, 18

Ottawa: Civic Tech, 179; nongovernmental transit provider, 162

Oxford Internet Institute, 160

Page, Kevin, 35, 151

Pahlka, Jennifer, 167, 169

partisanship/nonpartisanship: accountability and, 214; of communications, 66–67; communications and, 62–63; in communications training, 209–10; digital bargain and, 224–25; in government advertising contracts, 67; government advertising contracts and, 67; "promiscuous" partisanship, 63, 93, 189, 209; and social media, 77, 89, 90, 93, 189. See also neutrality; politicization

permanent campaigning: and closed bureaucrat-citizen relationship, 64; and closed government, 27–28, 39; and closed government-citizen relationship, 61–62; collaboration and, 27; digital government theories and, 22; and error-free government, 21, 49; and failure toleration, 215; and fear of public-facing failure, 27; and information control, 27; innovation vs, 27, 50–51; and open data, 113; and open vs closed government, 186, 187; public administration scholarship and, 229; and risk aversion, 27, 84–86; and silos/

hierarchies, 39; and withholding of information, 63–64

Pest Control Act (2002), 56

Peters, Guy, 44

Phillips, Susan, 61

Phoenix pay system, x, 164, 180, 195, 201, 220

Pitfield, Michael, 42

policy: and accessibility to social media data, 94; digital bargain and, 223; digital capacity, 154; NPM and capacity setbacks, 23; and open vs closed government, 26; uptake of new digital instruments, 10; wicked problems, 26, 42

Policy on Acceptable Network and Device Use (TBS), 102, 103

Policy on Communications and Federal Identity (TBS), 59–60, 212

policy consultation(s): about, 60; coordination of, 64; on design/development, 121–22; hierarchies and, 127; and policy development, 121–22, 205; social media and, 185

policy design/development: big data and, 10; collaboration and, 10, 105, 141, 143; digital technologies and, 226; externalization and, 160–61; government as a platform and, 9; government-citizen relationship in, 54–57, 103, 105, 205; legacy of PPA/Weber in, 14; pluralistic, 54–55; public consultations, 205; public engagement, 141; social media and, 79–80, 103, 105; user-centrism and, 228; whole of government and, 103, 105

policy issues: collaboration/coordination on, 44; cross-cutting, 47; data collection/trails from social media for, 211; decentralization of government-citizen relationship and debates over, 20–21; hierarchical decision making and, 47; horizontal, 44; networking and, 57; silos vs horizontality in cross-cutting, 42; user-centrism in divisive, 228

policy making: citizenry informing, 15; and data-driven decision making, 227; digital skills in, 226; digital technologies and, 12; external actors in, 160–61; horizontality in, 143–44; location of power/influence in, 226–27; open communications culture and experimentation with, 221; pluralistic, 57, 227; skill sets for, 154; social media and, 141, 192; strategic partisan influences over, 227

Policy on Official Languages, 75

Policy Research Institute, 57

politicization: digital government theories' depoliticization of public service context, 21; GCTools and, 136; pluralistic government-citizen relationship vs, 223; of public service, 229. *See also* New Political Governance; partisanship/nonpartisanship

Presidential Innovation Fellows (PIFs), 167–68, 170

"Prime Minister's Innovation Fellows" program, 180

Prime Minister's Office (PMO): court government, 64; out-of-date webpages, 219; and social media guidelines/policies, 84

Prince, Michael, 57

Privacy Act, 59

Privy Council Office (PCO): and Blueprint 2020, 136–37, 139; Central Innovation Hub, 144, 145; and centralization of communications, 87–88; Clerks, 14, 57, 134, 135, 136, 137; Communications and Consultations Secretariat, 60, 88, 122; and horizontality, 43, 44; preapproval of stakeholder roundtable subjects, 60; and public opinion research, 60; Results and Delivery unit, 202, 217; review, 89;

review of social media accounts, 88; "The Task Force on Horizontal Issues," 44; task forces on horizontality, 44

Procedures for Planning and Contracting Public Opinion Research (TBS), 59

Progressive-Era Public Administration (PPA): and accountability, 7, 40–41, 88–89; and closed government, 127, 179; digital open government theories vs, 8; government-citizen relationship in, 28, 51–52, 57, 58, 63, 68; hierarchical accountability mechanism, 41; and inequity, 38; legacy of, 14, 16; prevention of open government, 185; and principal-outsider relationship, 52; and reduction of government corruption, 52; relevance of core principles, 30, 183, 189, 196; and silos/hierarchies, 6, 38, 40, 68; state-centric vision vs NPM's alternative service delivery, 53; traditional public administration principles, 30; as traditional/old public administration, 40–41; Weber's theories and, 40; wholesale upheaval of, 19

proliteracy.ca, 101

public administration scholarship: marginalization of digital technologies, 16–17, 36–37, 229; on permanent campaigning, 229; on politicization of public service, 229; relevance of, 229–30; on social media, 229

Public Administration Select Committee (UK), "Government and IT – A Recipe for Rip Offs," 164, 220

Public Health Agency of Canada (PHAC), 144–45

public opinion research (POR), 59–60, 66, 67, 68, 70, 172, 213

Public Policy Forum, 105, 160

Public Safety Canada, 145

public sector integrity commissioner, 49

public servant-public relationship. *See* government-citizen relationship

public service: golden age of, 28, 42,
236*n*10; history of, 41–42; naming/
blaming of public servants, 53,
215–16
Public Service 2000 (PS2000), 46, 112
Public Service App Challenge, 144
public service bargain(s): anonymity in,
20, 94; government-citizen relationship
in, 57, 58, 63, 87; open government vs,
29; as renegotiable, 223–24; Schafferian
bargain, 51; traditional, 236*n*10
Public Service Commission: Appointment
Delegation and Authority Instrument,
198; Appointment Policy, 198
Public Service Employee Survey:
amendment re innovation, 218; on
approval states, 50; employee-supervisor
relationships in, 47
Public Services and Procurement Canada:
and horizontality, 43; and POR, 60

Queen's University, 166

Radian6, 72
Rasmussen, Ken, 45
Recruitment of Digital Leaders
Program, 180
recruitment of digital talent: about,
165–67; Blueprint 2020 and, 138; closed
government prevention of, 25; dearth
of digital skills and, 28; DGUs and,
168–79, 170–71, 178; digital skills gap
and, 159; into executive positions,
159; funding, 199; and government
as appealing workplace, 193–94;
government as platform and, 165;
lack of commitment, 202; millennials,
193–94; parachute models, 167–68, 180,
223; strategy for, 198–99; in UK, 199.
See also digital skills
Recruitment of Policy Leaders and
Advanced Economist Training
Program, 180
Reddick, Christopher, 13

Reform Party, 114
La Relève (1995), 46
Reuters Institute for the Study of
Journalism, 4
risk aversion: accountability and, 50, 214;
Blueprint 2020 and, 139; challenges
against, vs status quo, 191; and closed
government, 68; decrying of culture of,
14; digital era open government and,
130; and diversion from status quo, 88;
in government-citizen relationship,
84–85; hierarchy and, 49; innovation vs,
50, 51, 68, 150, 151, 214; media and, 21–22,
220; open communications culture/
style vs, 216, 221; open government and,
21, 22; and open government initiative,
129; permanent campaigning and, 27,
84–86; risks from focus on, 213–14;
social media and, 84–86, 175; and status
quo, 196; TBS guidelines/policies
and, 146
risks: of closed government, 24–25, 29, 90,
94–95, 191, 195, 196; of not using social
media/Web 2.0, 70; in online forums,
123–25; of open government, 189–90;
in open vs closed government, 29–30;
in pluralistic government-citizen
relationship, 223; policy innovation
initiatives, 143; of status quo, 189–97;
tolerance, and policy innovation, 153
Roy, Jeffrey, 28–29, 209
Royal Commission on the Economic
Union and Development Prospects for
Canada (Macdonald Commission), 55
Royal Commission on the Future of
Health Care in Canada (Romanow
Commission), 55

Saguenay–St. Lawrence Marine Park
Act, 56
Savoie, Donald, 41–42, 45, 133, 223, 236*n*10
SecDev Group, 161
secrecy, culture of, 63–64, 110, 113, 128
Service Canada, 41, 43, 64–65, 169

service delivery: alternative models/ arrangements, 53–54, 68, 161; citizens as consumers/clients, 15; collaboration in, 54, 143; contracts for, 66; coordination of, 88; digital technologies and, 12; externalization and, 15, 53–54, 56, 160–61; government as a platform and development of, 9; history of, 41; IT corporations and, 161; legacy of PPA/Weber in, 14; nongovernmental providers, 15; NPM and, 15, 53–54; NPM and failures of, 23; open communications culture and experimentation with, 221; social media and, 79–80, 81, 185; whole of government model, 169

Shared Services Canada: corporate IT consolidation, 180; cost overruns/ delays, 201; integration of services, 43; and Public Service App Challenge, 144

Shirky, Clay, 18–19, 132

silos: about, 68; and accountability, 19, 40–41, 204; advantages of, 19–20; challenges against, vs status quo, 190–91; collaboration vs, 44, 132; and consultations, 125; and coordination, 19–20; and corruption reduction, 52; cross-silo collaboration and accountability, 44–45; data, 117–18, 120; decrying culture of, 14; defined, 40; "desiloization of government," 202; DGUs and dismantling of, 178–79; digital communication and, 20; digital government theories and dissolution of, 184; disadvantages of, 42, 44–46; dissolution of, 8, 9, 187, 204; endurance of, 45–46, 67, 68, 69; and failure intolerance, 215; GCTools and, 132–33, 185; and government-citizen relationship, 62, 91, 96, 185; hierarchical chains of information and, 47; history of, 41–42; horizontality vs, 15, 42, 132; information across, 12; information control and, 87, 203;

and innovation, 145–46; and internal openness, 9, 130; legitimacy of, 19; and ministerial accountability/attribution, 45; networking deficiency and, 43; new governance paradigms vs, 185; open data vs, 10; and open vs closed government, 184–85; permanent campaigning and, 39; PPA and, 6, 38, 40; resistance toward, 43; and social media, 72–73, 83, 86, 87, 88–89, 94, 185; Weber and, 38; Westminster system and, 6; and whole of government management, 19

Simon Fraser University, Department of Computer Science, 166

Singapore, digital services, and accountability in, 25–26

Skelton, O.D., 53

SlideShare, 192–93

Smarter Citizens, Smarter State (Noveck), 244n2

smartphones, 4, 105, 109; Apple iPhone, 9; BlackBerry Messenger, 109, 186

Smith, Wayne, 192

Snowden, Edward, 26, 213

Social Change Rewards, 144

social listening, 121, 156, 186, 211, 213

social media: and accessibility, 89, 90; accountability in use of, 88–89, 90, 96; and anonymity, 93–94, 133, 188; "authorized individual" access to, 102; barriers to use of, 84; blocked access to, 105; Blueprint 2020 and, 139; Canadians' use of, 4; centralization of control over, 88; closed government model and loss of credibility, 94–95; and collaboration, 74, 80, 81; as communication tools, 141; communications and, 71, 72, 74–75, 77, 92, 94, 95, 192, 207; consultants, 161; consultations and, 74, 120–21, 185; coordination in use of, 96; and costs of public failure, 186; custom terms of service, 89; data collection/trails, 161, 211; decentralized vs centralized approach to, 84, 91, 92–93, 125–27; departmental blocking of access to, 102–3; departmental corporate accounts, 72; departmental corporate vs individual accounts, 74–75; departmental use, 103–5; DFATD and, 144; DGUs and, 174–75; and equity, 90; foreign service use of, 125–27; GCTools and, 130, 133–34; and government-citizen relationship, 11–12, 70, 79, 81–82, 103, 105, 205; guidelines/policies for, 213; Harper government and, 35; hierarchies and, 74, 83, 86, 87, 94, 185; HRSDC tweet approval process, 76–78; increasing participation in, 4; individual, personal accounts, 74–75, 92–93; and ineffectiveness of closed government, 96; information collection from, 72–73; and information sharing, 73, 80, 82–83, 153; and innovation, 146; Internet firewalls and, 73; introduction of, 71; leadership style and, 84; in Liberal campaign, 226; marginalization of, 71; millennials and, 159; and networking, 73; and neutrality, 22, 188–89; Obama's use of, 115; official languages and, 89, 90; open dialogue and, 102, 120; in open vs closed government, 96; partisanship and, 89, 90, 93, 189; PCO review of accounts, 88; personal blogs, 92–93; place within communications media roundups, 72–73; policy analysis, and accessibility to data, 94; policy considerations, 75–76; and policy consultations, 185; and policy development, 79–80, 103, 105, 141, 192; and politicization of public service, 22; POR on use of, 70; public administration scholarship on, 21–22, 229; risk aversion and, 84–86, 175; security risks, 89, 90; and service delivery, 79–80, 81, 185; siloing of, 72–73, 83, 86, 87, 88–89, 94, 185; spokespersons for,

87, 133; standardization and, 88; TBS guidelines/policies, 74–76, 102, 146, 212; traditions conflicting with, 133; training in use of, 102; users of, 81–82; whole of government access to, 102–3
Social Media Community of Practice, 102
Social Media Guidance (GDS), 174–75
Social Media Playbook (GDS), 174–75
Social Sciences and Humanities Research Council, 57
Social Union Framework Agreement (1999), 56
spokespersons, 58, 87, 133, 209
Sponsorship Scandal, 49, 67, 186
Standard on Web Accessibility (TBS), 75, 89
Standing Committee on Government Operations and Estimates, 220
Statistics Canada, big data pilots, 192
Steinberg, Tom, 158

Tait Report, 224, 230
Tapscott, Don, 18–19, 132; *Growing Up Digital*, 158
"The Task Force on Horizontal Issues" (PCO), 44
Thorney-Fallis, 161
Time, "Person of the Year," 4
top-down management. *See* hierarchies
Toronto, University of, 166
transparency: digital era governance and, 26; digital technologies and, 236*n*10; in government-citizen interactions, 71; Obama and, 115; and Open Government Action Plan, 109; open government and, 7
Treasury Board Secretariat (TBS): and accountability, 49; ATIP training modules, 108; and centralization as best practice for communications, 87–88; Chief Information Officer Branch (CIOB) (*see* Chief Information Officer Branch [CIOB]); and data standardization, 175; and

experimentation, 216; Federal Identity Program, 59, 64, 75, 89; gap between policies and implementation, 103, 212; Guideline for the External Use of Web 2.0, 74–76, 77, 86, 89, 102, 245n8; and horizontality, 43, 44; InfoBase, 107; and mythbusting, 212; and open data, 114; open data strategies, 18; and open dialogue, 102, 106; Open Government Action Plan and, 200; open government initiative, 97, 128; open government team blog, 208; policies review, 212; *Policy on Acceptable Network and Device Use*, 102, 103; *Policy on Communications and Federal Identity*, 59–60, 212; policy suite, 86, 146; Procedures for Planning and Contracting Public Opinion Research, 59; risk aversion, 146; rules mission creep, 88, 146, 186, 211–12, 214; and rules/reporting requirements, 49; social media guidelines/policies, 84–85, 146, 175, 207–8; Standard on Web Accessibility, 89; *Values and Ethics Code for the Public Sector*, 89

Treusch, Andrew, 93

Trudeau, Justin: and cabinet government, 43–44; commitment to more open communications, 216; and deliverology, 217; and digital government theories, 19; digital skills gap and, 198; early record on digital government, ix–xi; election of, 152, 182; and government advertising, 67; and high-trust government-citizen relationship, 221; inheritance of "fixer upper" bureaucracy, 197; and innovation, 217, 218; leadership style, 30, 152, 222–23; and ministerial mandate letters, 217; and open data, 205; and open government, 36; promotion of cross-government collaboration, 202

TurboTax, 160

Turner, Tony, 224

Twitter, 72; and anonymity, 94; application programming interface (API), 78–79; approval process for tweets, 78–83, 86, 91–92, 94, 129; Canadians' use of, 4; Clement and, 85; and consultations, 120–21; @DMCPI, 142; #GC2020, 138; legislative committees and citizen involvement through, 3; permanent campaigning and, 86; power of, 4; public servant hashtags, 93; public service use of, 78–83, 138–39; time of entry, 84; townhalls, 106, 120, 122, 127, 155, 205; "Tweet Approval Process" (HRSDC), 76–78; #w2p, 136; and Wikipedia edits from anonymous government IP addresses, 219

Uncle Sam's List, 167

United Kingdom: 2012 Civil Service Reform Plan, 149; Advertising Standards Authority, 65–66; Alpha.gov.uk, 176; Behavioural Insights Team, 207, 221; Brexit referendum, 5; data portal, 99; DEG in, 9; DGUs in, 174–75, 175–77; Digital Buyers Guide, 244n13; digital government "revolution" in, 198; Directgov, 168–69; director of digital engagement, 116; focus on open data in, 115–16; Foreign and Commonwealth Office, 126–27, 171, 175; government department websites, 169; Government Digital Service (GDS) (*see* Government Digital Service (GDS)); government-citizen interface in, 117–18; gov.uk, 65, 172; https://data.gov.uk, 116; in-house talent and procurement/partnering strategies, 202; Internet use surveys, 235n2; investment/political attention to digital capacity in, 220; London School of Economics, Government on the Web, 160; Minister for the Cabinet Office, 169; National Trading Standards Board, 65–66; NPM in, 9, 169; and OGP, 113; on online misinformation, 65–66; open data in, 117–18; Oxford Internet Institute, 160; policy making in, 116; reliance on external service providers in, 161

United Nations, E-Government Rankings, 64–65

United States: 18F, 173–74; 18F Agile Purchase Agreement, 244*n*3; Challenge.gov, 115; Code for America, 167–68, 169, 170; data portal, 99; DGUs in, 169, 170; digital government "revolution" in, 198; Digital Service (USDS), 169, 171, 175, 177–78, 194; Executive Order on Streamlining Service Delivery and Improving Customer Service, 149; "fake news" in, 5; Federal Acquisition Training Program, 244*n*3; General Services Administration, 169; GeoQ, 167; healthcare.gov, 169, 194; in-house talent and procurement/partnering strategies, 202; Internet use surveys, 235*n*2; National Security Agency, 26; and OGP, 112, 113; Presidential Innovation Fellows (PIFs), 167–68, 170; Uncle Sam's List, 167; Veterans Employment Center, 167; We the People, 115

Urban Aboriginal Strategy, 44

user-centrism. *See* citizen-/user-centrism

Values and Ethics Code for the Public Sector (TBS), 89

Vancouver Agreement, 44

Vancouver open data initiative, 18

Victoria, University of, 165–66

"Virtual Library," 107

Virtual Policy Challenge, 143–44

"Vision for Canada's Federal Public Service" (Blueprint 2020), 136–37

Voluntary Sector Initiative, 54, 56, 61

Waterloo, University of, Department of Computer Science, 166

Web 1.0, 12, 78, 80, 235*n*4

Web 2.0: about, 235*n*4; Braybrook on, 132; digital government theories and, 8; POR on use of, 70, 195; TBS Guideline for, 74–76, 77, 86, 89, 102, 245*n*8

Web Experience Toolkit, 101

Weber, Max/Weberianism: and accountable governance, 7; and bureaucrat-bureaucrat relationship, 40; and closed government, 28, 127, 178–79; digital open government theories vs, 8; *Economy and Society*, 182; foundational principles of public service, 40; on functional separation of tasks, 44; government-citizen relationship, 63, 68; and impersonal bureaucrat, 126; legacy of, 13, 14, 16, 188; and ministerial responsibility, 45; and PPA, 40; prevention of open government, 185; public servant default identification with silos, 45; relevance of core principles, 30, 183, 189, 196; and silos/hierarchies, 6, 28, 38, 41, 45, 68; traditional public administration principles, 30; wholesale upheaval of, 19

websites: combination into master sites, 65; coordination of control over, 20; guidelines for "look and feel," 64; social media use linked to, 78, 79; in UK, 169; whole of government model, 169

Weibo, 125–26

Wernick, Michael, 197, 198

Westminster system: and accountable governance, 7; anonymity under, 7, 20, 38, 51, 91, 126, 210; decentralized communications and, 210; and digital bargain, 223–25, 229; digital open government theories vs, 8; enduring relevance of values/tenets, 29; government-citizen relationship in, 6–7, 20, 51, 188; legacy of, 14; ministerial accountability under, 7, 41, 51, 95; open data initiative vs public service work historical default, 101; pluralistic government-citizen relationship and, 223; prevention of open government, 185; principles of, 30, 183, 189, 196, 231; and public service neutrality, 95; and Schafferian bargain, 51; and silos/

hierarchies, 41, 68; traditional public administration principles, 30; user-centrism vs accountability within, 228; vertical accountability in, 188; wholesale upheaval of, 19
whole of government: access to social media, 102–3; Blueprint 2020 and, 137; DGUs and, 174–75; as GDS mandate, 169; as hierarchical, 188; and policy development, 103, 105; silos and, 19–20, 42; task forces on, 44. *See also* horizontality; joined-up government

Wiki Government, 9, 12, 14, 36, 185
Wikipedia, 3, 9, 131, 132, 219
wikis: about, 242*n*1; digital government theories and, 9; GCpedia as, 131
Williams, Anthony D., 18–19, 132
Wouters, Wayne, 134, 135, 136

Yes, Minister, 38
YMCA Canada, 144
YouTube, 72
Yukon Environmental and Socio-Economic Assessment Act (2003), 56